Interpreting
the
Prophets

Interpreting the Prophets

Edited by
James Luther Mays
Paul J. Achtemeier

Fortress Press   **Philadelphia**

COPYRIGHT © 1987 BY FORTRESS PRESS

Library of Congress Cataloging-in-Publication Data
Interpreting the prophets.

Appeared originally in Interpretation, 1978–1985.
1. Prophets. I. Mays, James Luther. II. Achtemeier,
Paul J.
BS1505.2.I53   1987   224'.06   86–45223
ISBN 0–8006–1932–3

2528F86   Printed in the United States of America   1–1932

Contents

Contributors

Walter Brueggemann
Professor of Old Testament, Columbia Theological Seminary,
Atlanta, Ga.

Brevard S. Childs
Professor of Old Testament, Yale University Divinity School,
New Haven, Conn.

R. E. Clements
Professor, Fitzwilliams College, Cambridge, England.

John J. Collins
Professor of Old Testament, University of Notre Dame, South Bend, Ind.

James L. Crenshaw
Professor of Old Testament, Vanderbilt University, The Divinity School,
Nashville, Tenn.

Michael Fishbane
Professor of Jewish Religion, History, and Social Ethics, Brandeis
University, Waltham, Mass.

John G. Gammie
Professor of Biblical Literature, The University of Tulsa, Tulsa, Okla.

Moshe Greenberg
Professor of Bible, The Hebrew University of Jerusalem, Jerusalem,
Israel.

William L. Holladay
Professor of Old Testament, Andover Newton Theological School,
Newton Centre, Mass.

Klaus Koch
Professor of Old Testament, University of Hamburg, Hamburg,
Germany.

Werner E. Lemke
Professor of Old Testament Interpretation, Colgate Rochester Divinity
School/Bexley Hall/Crozer Theological Seminary, Rochester, N.Y.

James Limburg
Professor of Old Testament, Luther Northwestern Theological Seminary,
St. Paul, Minn.

Carol A. Newsom
Associate Professor of Old Testament, Candler School of Theology, Emory University, Atlanta, Ga.

Thomas M. Raitt
Professor of Old Testament, The College of Wooster, Wooster, Ohio.

J. J. M. Roberts
Professor of Old Testament, Princeton Theological Seminary, Princeton, N.J.

James A. Sanders
Professor of Intertestamental and Biblical Studies (STC), Professor of Religion (CGS), Claremont Theological School, Claremont, Calif.

David C. Steinmetz
Professor of Church History and Doctrine, The Divinity School, Duke University, Durham, N.C.

W. Sibley Towner
Professor of Biblical Interpretation, Union Theological Seminary, Richmond, Va.

Gene M. Tucker
Professor of Old Testament, Candler School of Theology, Emory University, Atlanta, Ga.

Robert R. Wilson
Professor of Old Testament, Yale University Divinity School, New Haven, Conn.

Hans Walter Wolff
Professor, University of Heidelberg, Heidelberg, West Germany.

Foreword

"Indeed, the Lord GOD does not do anything without revealing his decision to his servants, the prophets."

This claim, found in Amos 3:7, is astonishing. It draws a direct connection between the purpose and plans of the Lord and the mission and message of prophets. It characterizes that connection with the term "reveal." Amos's statement does not refer to prophecy as a religious institution or to prophets in general. Instead, it distinguishes a particular group of prophets from the rest: the ones who are God's "servants" receive the revelation.

The claim expresses an understanding of prophecy which led to the preservation and transmission of the words of certain prophets, to the formation of books bearing their name, and to the status of those books as Scriptures of Judaism and Christianity. The books of the prophets are given different locations in the arrangements of the Hebrew Bible and the Christian Old Testament, but in both they have a structural and indispensable place. Biblical religion would be inconceivable without its prophetic dimension. It becomes less than itself when the influence of its prophetic component is weakened.

The diligent study and interpretation of the prophetic books is the only way the prophets can have their proper and authentic effect. This volume of essays is designed as a contribution to that end.

The contents of this volume appeared originally as five issues of *Interpretation: A Journal of Bible and Theology* (1978–85) which were planned as a coherent series. The purpose of this volume is to offer students and interpreters a resource and companion to the study of the prophets that is somewhat different from the usual historical-critical introduction. Here the concerns of critical research and religious use of the prophets are brought together. Instead of developing one approach to the study of these prophetic books, these studies represent the dynamic variety of approaches pursued in the current study of the prophets. The authors make up a panel of scholars whose contributions to the study of prophecy mark them as the best available.

Knowing some of the other considerations that went into the plan for the series will be a help in assessing and using this volume. The general design will be clear to the reader. There is an introductory set of four studies (chaps. 1–4). The first two cover the historical development of Israelite prophecy in its early and classical periods; together they furnish an overall context into which discussion of particular prophets can be fitted. They make the point that Israelite prophecy is eminently historical in setting and content. The studies on prophetic speech and the shape of the prophetic literature take up two dimensions present in the prophetic books. The books are largely composed of sayings, the oral dimension; but they are at the same time books, the literary dimension. Both dimensions need attention if the full meaning of Old Testament prophecy is to be grasped.

The rest of this volume is composed of sets of essays on the major prophets and on Daniel. The prophets of the Book of the Twelve receive attention only in the introductory essays in order to keep the series within manageable limits of space and time. Daniel appears in the sequence to show the way in which prophecy makes a transition into apocalyptic.

The pattern of the four or five studies devoted to each prophet varies, as a glance at the table of contents will show. The sequence of subjects treated differs from prophet to prophet. Several considerations led to this variety. One is that the prophetic books themselves are quite different in some respects, and the study of them focuses on different major questions. The dominant question in Isaiah studies has been the unity (or disunity) of the book. With Jeremiah the question about the historical Jeremiah, and with which "Jeremiah" one is dealing at particular places in the book, is to the fore. How one sees the relationship of Daniel to the prophetic tradition is crucial for the assessment of Daniel. The pattern of essays for each prophet reflects the shaping of these major questions.

The contemporary study of Israelite prophecy is itself quite varied. A number of different approaches to the literature are being vigorously pursued, and it is important that the essays reflect that variety. In order to do this, the plan allows for the illustration of various ways to look at and question the prophetic books without following one consistent pattern of subjects for each prophet. The reader will find overall attention to the established procedures of traditional literary criticism and of form and redaction criticism. But attention also has been paid to the values of new literary criticism, canonical analysis, and sociological approaches.

Finally, the design would not have been complete without some attention to ways in which the prophets have been interpreted and appropriated as Scripture. So throughout the series there are essays that illustrate various ways and contexts in which that has happened: in the New Testament, in the commentary of theologians, in lectionary selections, in movements of piety. The particular illustrations are meant to raise possibilities for the whole.

The concluding bibliography provides a survey of recent literature on the prophets. It has been prepared with the interests and needs of the general interpreter in mind.

JAMES L. MAYS

Union Theological Seminary
Richmond, Va.

Abbreviations

AB	Anchor Bible
AfO	Archiv für Orientforschung
AnBib	Analecta biblica
ANET	*Ancient Near Eastern Texts*, ed. J. B. Pritchard
ANQ	*Andover Newton Quarterly*
AOAT	Alter Orient und Altes Testament
ASTI	*Annual of the Swedish Theological Institute*
ATANT	Abhandlungen zur Theologie des Alten und Neuen Testaments
AUSS	*Andrews University Seminary Studies*
BETL	Bibliotheca ephemeridum theologicarum lovaniensium
BHS	*Biblia hebraica stuttgartensia*
BHT	Beiträge zur historischen Theologie
BibOr	Biblica et orientalia
BJRL	*Bulletin of the John Rylands University Library of Manchester*
BK	*Bibel und Kirche*
BKAT	Biblischer Kommentar: Altes Testament
BTB	*Biblical Theology Bulletin*
BZAW	Beihefte zur ZAW
CBQ	*Catholic Biblical Quarterly*
CBQMS	Catholic Biblical Quarterly—Monograph Series
DJD	Discoveries in the Judaean Desert
EvTh	*Evangelische Theologie*
FOTL	The Forms of the Old Testament Literature
FRLANT	Forschungen zur Religion und Literatur des Alten und Neuen Testaments
FzB	Forschungen zur Bibel
HAT	Handbuch zum Alten Testament
HKAT	Handkommentar zum Alten Testament
HSM	Harvard Semitic Monographs
HTR	*Harvard Theological Review*
HUCA	*Hebrew Union College Annual*
ICC	International Critical Commentary
IDB	*Interpreter's Dictionary of the Bible*, ed. G. A. Buttrick
Int	*Interpretation*
JAAR	*Journal of the American Academy of Religion*
JAOS	*Journal of the American Oriental Society*
JBL	*Journal of Biblical Literature*

JBLMS	*JBL* Monograph Series
JJS	*Journal of Jewish Studies*
JNES	*Journal of Near Eastern Studies*
JQR	*Jewish Quarterly Review*
JSJ	*Journal for the Study of Judaism in the Persian, Hellinistic and Roman Period*
JSOT	*Journal for the Study of the Old Testament*
JSOTSup	Journal for the Study of the Old Testament—Supplement Series
JTS	*Journal of Theological Studies*
KAT	Kommentar zum A.T.
MT	Massoretic Text
NAWG	Nachrichten (1941-1942 von) der Akademie der Wissenschaften in Göttingen
NTS	*New Testament Studies*
OAB	*Oxford Annotated Bible*
OTL	Old Testament Library
RB	*Revue biblique*
RevExp	*Review and Expositor*
RGG	*Religion in Geschichte und Gegenwart*
RSV	*Revised Standard Version*
SB	Sources bibliques
SBL	Society of Biblical Literature
SBLDS	SBL Dissertation Series
SBLMS	SBL Monograph Series
SBS	Stuttgarter Bibelstudien
SBT	Studies in Biblical Theology
ScrHie	*Scripta Hierosolymitana*
Sem	*Semitica*
SOTS	Society for Old Testament Study
TBl	*Theologische Blätter*
TDOT	*Theological Dictionary of the Old Testament*
ThR	*Theologische Rundschau*
ThLZ	*Theologische Literaturzeitung*
TSK	*Theologische Studien und Kritiken*
TWAT	*Theologisches Wörterbuch zum Alten Testament*, ed. G. J. Botterweck and H. Ringgren (Eng. trans., *TDOT*)
USQR	*Union Seminary Quarterly Review*
VT	*Vetus Testamentum*
VTSup	*Vetus Testamentum*, Supplements
WMANT	Wissenschaftliche Monographien zum Alten und Neuen Testament
ZA	*Zeitschrift für Assyriologie*
ZAW	*Zeitschrift für die alttestamentliche Wissenschaft*
ZTK	*Zeitschrift für Theologie und Kirche*

1

Early Israelite Prophecy

ROBERT R. WILSON

The question about the nature of early Israelite prophecy is a riddle whose solution may well lie in the recognition of different prophetic traditions which have been incorporated into the Old Testament's account of prophecy before Amos.

Prophets have always been surrounded by an aura of mystery. Because they are intermediaries between the human and divine worlds, prophets appear to their hearers as terrifying yet magnetic and fascinating figures. Throughout the history of Western civilization, wherever these divinely inspired individuals have appeared, attempts have been made to penetrate the mystery that surrounds them. The focus of many of these attempts has been the Old Testament prophets, who have traditionally functioned as models for the elucidation of other prophetic phenomena. Yet in spite of a long history of attempts to understand the ancient Israelite prophets, they have retained some of their mystery. There is still no scholarly consensus on the questions of the nature and social functions of Israelite prophecy, and each new generation tends to reinterpret the message of the prophets. This lack of scholarly consensus is particularly noticeable in the case of the early Israelite prophets, those individuals who prophesied before the time of Amos, the first of the writing prophets. If Israelite prophecy in general is still partially a mystery, then it is fair to say that early Israelite prophecy is "a riddle wrapped in a mystery."

The reasons for the persistence of the riddle are not difficult to uncover. While it is possible to place most of the writing prophets in specific historical contexts and to paint a rough picture of their personal backgrounds and professional activities, the early prophets remain shadowy figures. Although they are crucial for understanding the later written prophetic tradition, the Old Testament is surprisingly vague about them. In some cases even their names have not been preserved (Num. 11:24f.; Judg. 6:7-10; 1 Sam. 10:10-13; 19:18-24; 1 Kings 13; 18:4; 2 Kings 17:13; 21:10; 23:2). In other cases, prophets such as Ahijah (1 Kings 11:29-39; 14:4-16), Shemaiah

1

(1 Kings 12:22–24), Jehu (1 Kings 16:1–4), Huldah (2 Kings 22:14–20), Nathan (2 Samuel 7; 12), and Gad (1 Sam. 22:5; 2 Sam. 24:11–14) appear briefly in historical narratives and then disappear entirely. On the other hand, the biblical traditions about some of the early prophets are so complex that the evidence that is available is difficult to interpret. Abraham (Gen. 20:7), Moses (Deut. 18:15–22; 34:10), Miriam (Exod. 15:20), and Deborah (Judg. 4:4) are all called prophets. Yet the traditions about them do not deal primarily with their prophetic activities, and, except in the case of Moses, it is not obvious why these figures were regarded as prophets at all. In contrast, the Old Testament preserves extensive prophetic traditions about Samuel, Elijah, and Elisha (1 Samuel 1—16; 1 Kings 17—2 Kings 9). However, these traditions have gone through a long process of development, with the result that they present a less than fully coherent picture of prophetic activity. Thus the biblical traditions about almost all of these early prophets tend to obscure rather than reveal them, and it is not surprising that scholars who have studied the biblical prophets have been baffled by the riddle of early Israelite prophecy.

EARLY PROPHECY: THE NATURE OF THE RIDDLE

Any attempt to explore early Israelite prophecy must take into account the nature of the available evidence. No writings by the early prophets have been preserved, and only a few of their words have been recorded in the narratives about them. Furthermore, the earliest references to most of these figures appear in what is essentially a single source: the writings coming out of the Deuteronomic tradition. Although this tradition undoubtedly preserves much early material, the Deuteronomic history itself probably received its final editing in the exilic period, and for this reason it may not automatically be assumed that the Deuteronomist's picture of early prophecy is historically accurate. In addition, the historian's apparent interest in prophecy raises the possibility that all of the history's prophetic narratives have been influenced by the Deuteronomist's distinctive religious, political, and social views. Outside of the Deuteronomic traditions, early prophets are mentioned in the Elohistic layer of the Pentateuch and in the work of the Chronicler. The material in Chronicles in particular raises the same sorts of interpretive difficulties raised by the Deuteronomic history. In addition to the biblical evidence, ancient Near Eastern and contemporary anthropological sources provide some data on the nature and functions of prophetic phenomena. This material can provide useful background information for the study of early Israelite prophecy, but the extrabiblical evidence must be used cautiously in order to avoid a biased interpretation of the biblical data.

In the light of the meager sources available for writing a history of early Israelite prophecy, it is not surprising that most scholars have chosen to begin their work with a picture of prophecy drawn from the writing prophets and then have tried to relate this picture to the narrative accounts of earlier prophetic activity. Although most modern scholars recognize some degree of

continuity within the history of Israelite prophecy, there is still a general
tendency to attempt to distinguish the writing prophets from their predecessors. These attempts have usually been based either on the content of the
prophetic message or on the nature and location of prophetic activity.

The most extreme examples of the first approach are found in the work of
early critical scholars who saw the writing prophets as representatives of the
purest form of monotheistic religion and ethics. The work of these prophets
therefore bore little resemblance to the earlier, cruder forms of prophecy
attested in the Deuteronomic history.[1] Although few modern scholars would
subscribe to the evolutionary view of Israelite religion which this approach
implies, there are still attempts to divide the history of Israelite prophecy
into two phases on the basis of the ethical and theological content of the
prophetic message.[2] However, the major difficulty with any such approach is
that it must be based on hypothetical reconstructions of the messages of the
early prophets. The biblical sources provide scant data for making these
reconstructions, and for this reason comparisons based on them are not
always convincing. In addition, where the speeches of the early prophets are
recorded, they frequently contain themes and theological views similar to
those found in the writing prophets. This fact indicates that there was some
continuity in the prophetic message throughout the history of prophecy.

A more common approach to the problem of distinguishing the early
prophets from the writing prophets is based on the analysis of the nature and
location of prophetic activity. Since the work of Hölscher in 1914 and
Mowinckel in 1923, scholars using this approach have focused primarily on
two issues: the existence of prophetic ecstasy in Israel and the participation
of the prophets in the cult.[3] Histories of prophecy concerned with the first
issue normally begin with the biblical descriptions of ecstatic prophetic
groups that seem to have been connected with some of the local sanctuaries
during the period of the Judges (1 Sam. 10:5–6, 9–13). There are indications
that groups apparently composed of ecstatics also existed in later monarchical
times (1 Kings 18:4, 19–40; 22:6, 10–12; 2 Kings 2:3, 5, 7, 15–18), and
important Israelite prophets such as Samuel, Elijah, and Elisha are occasionally portrayed as ecstatics or are said to have been related to ecstatic groups

---

1. Bernhard Duhm, *Die Theologie der Propheten* (Bonn: Adolph Marcus, 1875), pp. 1–34;
Julius Wellhausen, *Prolegomena to the History of Ancient Israel* (Edinburgh: Adam & Charles
Black, 1885), pp. 414–19, 467–77, 484–91; W. Robertson Smith, *The Old Testament in the
Jewish Church* (London: Adam & Charles Black, 1895), pp. 278–308.

2. Johannes Lindblom, *Prophecy in Ancient Israel* (Philadelphia: Muhlenberg Press, 1962),
p. 108; H. H. Rowley, "The Nature of Old Testament Prophecy in the Light of Recent Study," in
his *The Servant of the Lord*, 2d ed. (Oxford: Basil Blackwell, 1965), pp. 128–34.

3. Gustav Hölscher, *Die Propheten* (Leipzig: J. C. Hinrichs, 1914); Sigmund Mowinckel,
Psalmenstudien III: Kultprophetie und prophetische Psalmen (Kristiania: Jacob Dybwad, 1923).
For subsequent discussions of ecstasy and cult see the summaries of Rowley, "Old Testament
Prophecy," pp. 97–118; Otto Eissfeldt, "The Prophetic Literature," in H. H. Rowley, ed., *The
Old Testament and Modern Study* (London: Oxford University Press, 1951), pp. 119–26, 134–
45; and Ronald E. Clements, *One Hundred Years of Old Testament Interpretation* (Philadel-
phia: Westminster Press, 1976), pp. 51–75.

(1 Sam. 10:5f., 9–13; 1 Kings 18:46; 2 Kings 3:15). This sort of evidence has led many scholars to conclude that early Israelite prophecy was characterized by ecstatic behavior. In this respect, the early Israelite prophets resembled the prophets of Canaan (cf. 1 Kings 18:19–40), and some scholars have even suggested that prophecy first arose in Israel because of Canaanite influence during the period of the Judges.[4] Although most modern critics would admit that ecstasy was a feature of early Israelite prophecy, some have argued that the writing prophets never became ecstatic. Other scholars have claimed that the ecstasy of the writing prophets was in some way different from the ecstasy experienced by earlier prophets. In either case, there is an implicit suggestion that a break in the prophetic tradition occurred with the appearance of the writing prophets.

A second line of inquiry has focused on the extent of prophetic involvement in the cult. There is evidence that early Israelite prophets such as Samuel and Elijah were related to the cult (1 Sam. 3; 9:11–14; 13:8–15; 1 Kings 18). On these grounds the claim has been made that most Israelite prophets had some sort of cultic involvement, although few scholars have argued that *all* prophets were so involved. A more common approach has been to suggest that the writing prophets were not normally part of the cult, while earlier Israelite prophets and the "false prophets" mentioned in the prophetic books operated in a cultic context.

However, two serious objections must be raised against scholarly attempts to use the issues of ecstasy and cult to distinguish the early prophets from the writing prophets. First, no single theory is able to encompass all of the available evidence. To be sure, there are indications of ecstasy among some of the early prophets, but the descriptions of others contain no indication of ecstatic behavior. Similarly, some of the writing prophets (particularly Ezekiel) seem to have been ecstatics, while the writings of others show no trace of ecstasy. Ecstasy thus seems to have appeared sporadically throughout the entire history of prophecy in Israel. Theories which trace ecstatic prophecy to Canaanite influence or cultural borrowing may be correct, but they are not necessary to explain the presence of ecstasy in Israel. Prophetic activity, some of which was ecstatic, is well attested in antiquity in Egypt and Mesopotamia, as well as in Canaan, and anthropological studies have shown that ecstasy may appear in any society where the proper psychological and sociological conditions are present.[5] In the same way, it is difficult to argue that only the early Israelite prophets were involved in the cult. Some early prophets, such as Samuel, seem to have had cultic functions, while others did not. Among the writing prophets, both Jeremiah and Ezekiel are said to have come from priestly families, although neither is actually pictured as participating in cultic activities. Thus, if in fact the early Israelite prophets are to be distinguished from the later writing prophets on the basis of the

---

4. For a summary of these theories see Alfred Haldar, *Associations of Cult Prophets Among the Ancient Semites* (Uppsala: Almquist & Wiksell, 1945), pp. 91–110.

5. Cf. Herbert B. Huffmon, "The Origins of Prophecy," in Frank M. Cross et al., eds., *Magnalia Dei: The Mighty Acts of God* (Garden City, N.Y.: Doubleday & Co., 1976), p. 172.

nature of their activities, then that distinction cannot be made on the grounds of ecstatic behavior or participation in the cult.

Second, there is biblical evidence for continuity in prophetic activity throughout Israelite history.[6] This evidence is of two sorts. (1) The Old Testament makes no obvious attempt to distinguish the activities of the early prophets from those of the writing prophets, and in fact the same titles are given in both groups. The primary Hebrew word for "prophet," *nābî'*, is found frequently in the Deuteronomic history and is the title which the Deuteronomist usually uses to describe the early prophets.[7] However, the same title is given to some of the later writing prophets (Jer. 1:5; Ezek. 2:5), and it is doubtful that this would be the case if the activities of the writing prophets were radically different from those of the early prophets.[8] Similarly, the title "seer," *ḥōzeh*, which is used primarily in literature produced in Jerusalemite circles, is applied both to early figures (2 Sam. 24:11) and to later ones (Isa. 30:10). Although these two titles may designate different types of prophetic figures, their continued use throughout the history of prophecy probably indicates a basic continuity in the activities of the figures to which the titles are applied. (2) Form-critical analysis of the prophetic speeches has shown a basic continuity between the speech forms used by the early prophets and those employed by the writing prophets. In fact, it has even been suggested that the "characteristic" forms of prophetic speech originated among the early prophets and then "degenerated" before the time of the writing prophets.[9] Even if this suggestion proves not to be correct, the fact remains that prophets throughout Israel's history shared common forms of speech.

This brief survey of attempts to deal with the beginnings of Israelite prophecy suggests that two major problems remain to be solved. First, the nature of the continuity of the prophetic tradition has yet to be adequately explained. The various attempts to sharply distinguish the early prophets from the writing prophets are not fully convincing. Yet, at the same time there was undoubtedly development within the prophetic tradition, with the result that the later prophets were in some way different from the early ones. Second, the fact that no single approach has thus far been able to characterize accurately the distinctive characteristics of early prophecy suggests that, in fact, prophetic phenomena were more complex than scholars have realized. In order to deal with this complexity, the individuality of each

6. For a discussion of the continuity of the prophetic traditions, see R. E. Clements, *Prophecy and Tradition* (Atlanta: John Knox Press, 1975).

7. The exact meaning of the word *nābî'* is unclear. See the discussion of Rowley, "Old Testament Prophecy," pp. 103–8, 113–15; and Aubrey R. Johnson, *The Cultic Prophet in Ancient Israel* (Cardiff: University of Wales Press, 1962²), pp. 24f.

8. Contrast the title *rō'eh*, "seer," which is given almost exclusively to Samuel (1 Sam. 9:9, 11, 18, 19; 1 Chron. 9:22) and to other figures in the early history of prophecy (2 Chron. 16:7, 10). The functions of the seer were apparently taken over by the prophet *(nābî')*, and the older title ceased to be used (1 Sam. 9:9).

9. Claus Westermann, *Basic Forms of Prophetic Speech* (Philadelphia: Westminster Press, 1967).

prophet must be considered, and generalizations about the nature of prophecy must be made only with great caution.

PROPHECY AND SOCIETY

Important clues about the continuity and diversity of Israelite prophecy can be gleaned from contemporary anthropological studies of prophetic phenomena and from recent studies of prophecy in the ancient Near East. Anthropological studies of prophecy indicate that prophets are essentially intermediaries between the human and divine worlds. Unlike diviners and priests, prophets come into direct contact with the divine, either when they are possessed by the divine or when they supernaturally transcend the human world to enter the divine realm. Prophets are therefore channels through which divine messages reach the ordinary world and through which humans can gain direct access to the divine. Theoretically, these prophetic intermediaries may appear in any society which believes in the existence of divine powers capable of communicating with human beings. However, in reality not all such societies recognize the legitimacy of prophets. Among some groups divination or ritual rather than prophecy is the preferred means of communicating with the divine. In such societies prophets seldom exist, for their existence depends on the society's willingness to tolerate them within the social structure. Without support from the society, or at least from a group within it, prophets can find no permanent place within the social order and are likely to be regarded simply as sick individuals who must be cured or expelled.

Within societies and groups which recognize the legitimacy of prophecy, the behavior of prophets tends to follow traditional, well-defined patterns.[10] This behavior varies from society to society, but within a given society or group prophetic behavior usually conforms to the expected norms. Thus when a prophet receives a divine message, he "translates" it into human terms and communicates it, using traditional speech forms and actions which indicate that he is functioning as a prophet and that the message which he brings comes from the divine realm. The society which he addresses, in turn, recognizes his behavior as prophetic and either accepts or rejects the message which the prophet brings. If a prophet departs radically from the expected speech and behavior patterns which the society recognizes as prophetic, then he runs the risk of being judged insane rather than prophetic, and his message is likely to be rejected. Societies thus exert subtle psychological pressures on prophets to conform to the expected prophetic behavior so that their message will be accepted.

In some societies anyone may become a prophet. All that is necessary is for the individual to be in contact with the divine realm. Thus it is quite possible for a person both to be a prophet and to play other roles in the social

---

10. The behavioral complex that scholars tend to call ecstasy is one type of traditional pattern, but it is not the only pattern.

structure. Being a prophet does not necessarily exclude other activities, and it is possible for a person to be a king, priest, diviner, teacher, or judge and to be a prophet as well. On the other hand, in some societies prophets occupy a well-defined position within the social structure. In these cases it is appropriate to speak of a prophetic "office." In such societies prophets are sometimes professionals who must undergo rigorous training and who have important roles in the maintenance of the social order.

Prophets have numerous social and religious functions, but these functions may be broadly divided into two categories. First, prophets may appear on the periphery of a society and direct their activities toward social and religious change. Peripheral prophets of this sort frequently appear in groups which lack political, social, or religious power within the society and which use the authority of the prophetic message to attempt to rectify their powerless state. Because of the divine authority with which these prophets speak, the society as a whole is usually willing to listen to them and to make social and religious changes which might not otherwise be made. Socially and religiously peripheral individuals who become prophets sometimes join with others who have had the same experience and form a peripheral cult group which is a counterpart to the main cultic organization of the society. This peripheral cult group supports its members and attributes authority to their prophetic utterances, even when the rest of the society will not.

Second, prophets may appear within the established power structure of the society. In this case they usually have the function of maintaining the social order, although this maintenance does not preclude criticism of the society. Prophets of this sort are not usually opposed to social and religious change but are interested in insuring that change takes place in an orderly way so that the social structure as a whole is preserved. Both peripheral and establishment prophets may, of course, appear within the same society.[11]

The ancient Near Eastern evidence on prophecy generally conforms to the picture that emerges from anthropological research. In Egypt prophecy appears to have played a role within the established social order and was probably connected with the priesthood. The Egyptian prophecies which have been preserved seem to have functioned both to authorize the governmental and religious structure at the time they were issued and to advance the political and religious views of particular priestly groups. The behavioral characteristics of Egyptian prophets are unclear but probably did not include features which modern observers would call ecstatic.[12]

In contrast to Egypt, prophets played almost no role in the heartland of Mesopotamia, where divine-human communication took place mainly

---

11. For an introduction to anthropological studies of prophecy, see Jane Belo, *Trance in Bali* (New York: Columbia University Press, 1960); Sheila S. Walker, *Ceremonial Spirit Possession in Africa and Afro-America* (Leiden: E. J. Brill, 1972); John Beatte and John Middleton, eds., *Spirit Mediumship and Society in Africa* (New York: Africana, 1969); and I. M. Lewis, *Ecstatic Religion* (Baltimore: Penguin Books, 1971).

12. For a thorough discussion of Egyptian prophecy, see L. Ramlot, "Prophétisme," in *Dictionaire de la Bible: Supplément* (Paris: Letouzey & Ané, 1972), vol. 8, cols. 812–68.

through omens and dreams. Thus diviners and interpreters of omens had important roles in Mesopotamian society, but prophets did not. Their existence is attested only on the periphery of Mesopotamia, where West-Semitic influence may be present. Thus, tablets from the Mari archives (eighteenth century B.C.) speak of several types of prophetic figures and record some of their words. Some of these figures, such as "the ecstatic" *(muhhū)*, "the answerer" *(āpilu)*, and the *assinnu*, have titles, a fact which may indicate that they had established roles within the religious establishment. Other figures have no titles and were apparently lay persons. The oracles of these prophets concern religious and political matters and are usually directed to the king. Although some of the prophets may have functioned officially within the cult, their general peripheral status is indicated by the fact that the accuracy of their messages is sometimes tested by divination. Several of these prophets, particularly "the ecstatic" and the *assinnu*, seem to have exhibited stereotypical behavior, but it is impossible to reconstruct this in any detail. Prophetic figures appear again in later Mesopotamian history in the time of Esarhaddon and Assurbanipal (ca. 681–630 B.C.), when West-Semitic influences apparently reached the Assyrian royal court.

Canaanite prophecy is mentioned in the Wen-Amun Report from Egypt (eleventh century B.C.) and in a stela of Zakir, king of Hamath and Lu'ash (eighth century B.C.). At least in the first case the stereotypical behavior of the prophet can be called ecstatic, a description that fits the biblical picture of Canaanite prophecy (1 Kings 18:19–40). Some of the Canaanite prophets seem to have been part of the religious establishment, although it is not certain that all of them were.[13]

The extrabiblical evidence thus indicates that prophets may have a number of different functions within a society but that within a given social group there is consistency in the observable characteristics of prophets. These groups support the activities of the prophets, and in return the prophets at least subconsciously make their behavior—although not necessarily the content of their message—conform to the expectations of their support group. Where several prophetically-oriented subgroups exist within the same society, different and sometimes apparently contradictory behavioral characteristics may be observable among the society's prophets. However, these characteristics remain consistent and have continuity within the individual subgroups.

Against this extrabiblical background the early history of Israelite prophecy can be seen in a new light. The scholarly consensus on the early history of Israel suggests that the nation that was finally united politically under the kingship of David was composed of several originally independent, though culturally interrelated, subgroups. The Old Testament itself describes this situation by speaking of Israel as composed of twelve tribes which are "brothers" but which maintain independent identities and characteristics

---

13. For a discussion of Mesopotamian and Canaanite prophecy, see Huffmon, "Origins of Prophecy," pp. 172–76, and the literature cited there.

(Gen. 29—30; 49). Although scholars do not agree on the details of the process that led to the formation of Israel, it is clear that some of the component groups retained their own traditions. These traditions later influenced the overall Israelite tradition and were finally incorporated into it. If the various subgroups which composed Israel contained heterogeneous types of prophetic phenomena which nevertheless had continuity and consistency within the subgroups, then it would explain why the accounts of early Israelite prophecy portray a phenomenon which is both complex and still in continuity with later Israelite prophecy. The solution to the riddle of early Israelite prophecy thus may lie in the recognition of the different prophetic traditions which have been incorporated into our present accounts. Each tradition preserves stories and sayings of the particular kinds of prophets which existed in the group bearing the tradition.

THE NATURE OF EARLY PROPHECY
IN ISRAEL

The earliest biblical source to mention prophecy is the Elohistic layer of the Pentateuch, which in Gen. 20:7 calls Abraham a prophet. This reference cannot be dismissed simply by assuming that it is a retrojection from a much later time.[14] Rather, it must be seen as an indication that the group responsible for the Elohistic material believed that prophecy existed at a very early stage in Israelite history. Furthermore, Abraham is called a prophet because of his ability to intercede with Yahweh for Abimelech, the king of Gerar. This description of Abraham's prophetic activities suggests that within the groups bearing the Elohistic tradition prophets occupied a fixed place in the social structure and their activities included intercession. This picture of prophetic activity is further expanded in the complex story in Numbers 11, which tells of seventy elders being appointed as Moses' aids. As a confirmation of their divine appointment, the Spirit of Yahweh came upon them, and they "acted like prophets." They exhibited characteristic prophetic behavior, although the precise nature of that behavior is uncertain. However, it is clear that prophecy is here functioning as an integral part of the Israelite social structure and that it serves to legitimate political offices.

More light on the Elohist's view of prophecy comes from Numbers 12, where Aaron and Miriam, who is earlier called a prophetess (Exod. 15:20), are said to have disputed Moses' authority. At issue is apparently the question of who is to be the legitimate channel for communication with Yahweh. The argument is thus over prophetic authority, with Aaron and Miriam challenging Moses' claim to be a superior intermediary. The issue is finally resolved by a theophany, which reveals that Yahweh speaks to prophets

---

14. Contrast Frank Moore Cross, *Canaanite Myth and Hebrew Epic* (Cambridge: Harvard University Press, 1973), pp. 223–29, where the claim is made that prophecy appeared in Israel only with the advent of kingship. Cf. William F. Albright, "Samuel and the Beginnings of the Prophetic Movement," in *Interpreting the Prophetic Tradition* (New York: KTAV, 1969), pp. 149–76.

through dreams and visions but speaks to Moses directly (Num. 12:6–8). The other prophets are not illegitimate, but their perception of the divine word is not as clear as is the perception of Moses. Therefore, if their message conflicts with that of Moses, his message is to be considered more accurate. This story suggests that in the group which preserved the Elohistic traditions there was a hierarchy of prophets, with a prophet "like Moses" who was superior to the others. The story ends with Moses interceding for Aaron and Miriam (Num. 12:13), a prophetic function also present in Gen. 20:7.[15]

This fragmentary early material on prophecy reveals an incomplete but consistent view of the phenomenon. The texts suggest that in the group which preserved the Elohistic traditions prophets had social maintenance functions. The prophets had characteristic behavior, which perhaps involved ecstasy and which certainly involved intercession. No references are made to prophetic participation in the cult, although because Moses is involved in one of the prophetic conflicts, priestly connections cannot be ruled out.

A picture somewhat similar to that given by the Elohist is also found in the Deuteronomic traditions. These traditions preserve most of the extant information on early prophecy and present a reasonably coherent account of prophecy as it existed within the Deuteronomic groups.[16] The precise identification of these groups is uncertain, but they were certainly not from Judah and were possibly originally from northern Israel.

A theoretical statement of the nature of the prophetic office is found in Deut. 18:9–22. In the context of a series of laws dealing with the various political and religious offices in Israel, the Deuteronomist considers the problem of prophecy. Israel is specifically prohibited from patronizing various types of diviners and mediums and, as a substitute, Yahweh promises to raise up periodically prophets "like Moses." These prophets will be the *only* legitimate means of communication between Yahweh and the people. Just as Moses interceded with Yahweh for the people and at Horeb protected them from the divine presence, so the Mosaic prophets of the future will be the means by which the people are to approach Yahweh. When they have requests to present to Yahweh, they are to go to the prophets, not to diviners or mediums. Similarly, just as Moses delivered the divine Word, the Law, to the people, so the Mosaic prophets will continue to speak authoritatively for Yahweh and will interpret the people's covenant responsibilities. The prophets will speak only the divine Word and not their own words, with the result that the words which they speak will always prove true. By placing Deut. 18:9–22 in the context of laws organizing the social structure of Israel, the text indicates that among Deuteronomic groups prophets were integral parts of society and had an important role in insuring its well-being.[17]

---

15. In Numbers 22—24 the Elohist has surrounded the old Balaam oracles with a prose framework which seems vaguely to reflect the Elohist's views of prophecy. However, the text never refers to Balaam as a prophet.

16. The continuity and coherence of the Deuteronomist's view of prophecy has been demonstrated by James Muilenburg, "The 'Office' of the Prophet in Ancient Israel," in J. Philip Hyatt, ed., *The Bible and Modern Scholarship* (Nashville: Abingdon Press, 1965), pp. 74–97.

17. However, it is doubtful that this passage can be used to indicate the existence of an office of "covenant mediator." See the analysis of Clements, *Prophecy and Tradition*, pp. 41–57.

This picture of the prophet as part of the established social structure persists in Deuteronomic sources until the division of the kingdom after the death of Solomon. The Deuteronomic accounts of the conquest of Canaan occasionally mention prophets (Judg. 4:4; 6:7–10), although their role in the conquest is unclear. However, because the prophetess Deborah was a leader in one of Israel's holy wars (Judg. 4—5; cf. Exod. 15:20–21), it may be that the prophets, as part of Israel's leadership structure, used prophecy to justify the conquest and to turn the power of Yahweh against the enemy.

A typical Deuteronomic picture of prophetic activity is also found in the Deuteronomic passages dealing with Samuel and the rise of kingship.[18] The Deuteronomist portrays Samuel as a prophet, but also as a judge and as a priest attached to particular sanctuaries. He is thus a central figure in Israel's government during this period, although only one text makes him the leader of a prophetic band (1 Sam. 19:18–24). When the people ask Samuel for a king, he takes their request to Yahweh and then delivers to them Yahweh's stinging reply. The divine response reflects Deuteronomic language and theology, as well as the Deuteronomist's views on the limits and abuses of royal power (1 Sam. 8:4–18; cf. Deut. 17:14–20). Nevertheless, Samuel has the new king chosen by lot and then instructs the people on the rights and duties of kingship (1 Sam. 10:17–27). However, Samuel assures the people that he will continue to exercise his prophetic office by interceding for them (1 Samuel 12) and by granting them access to Yahweh (cf. 1 Samuel 28). Samuel thus plays a crucial role in the establishment of the monarchy. As Yahweh's representative he legitimates the new ruler and fulfills the prophet's obligation to insure that even the king is subject to the divine laws.

This Deuteronomic view of the prophet's role differs markedly from the view found in other accounts of Saul's rise. In the complex narrative preserved in 1 Sam. 9:1—10:16 Samuel is not portrayed as an important religious and political leader but as a seer (rō'eh) who accepts money for his services. When Saul goes to the seer to discover the whereabouts of some lost animals, Samuel unexpectedly informs Saul that Yahweh has chosen him to be king of Israel. Samuel anoints Saul, but confirmation of his election comes directly from Yahweh. Saul meets a group of prophets who are apparently connected with a cultic high place. The Spirit of Yahweh seizes Saul and causes him to join the others in "acting like a prophet." Here the characteristic prophetic behavior is clearly ecstatic and evaluated positively (cf. the more negative evaluation in 1 Sam. 19:18–24). However, the whole story seems to come from a group in which prophecy was somewhat peripheral and did not play the central role that it did among the Deuteronomic groups.

The next Deuteronomic prophet to be mentioned in the Deuteronomic history is Ahijah of Shiloh, who was instrumental in legitimizing the division of the kingdom and in establishing Jeroboam as king of Israel (1 Kings

---

18. For a survey of recent theories on the history of the Israelite monarchy, see Tomoo Ishida, *The Royal Dynasties in Ancient Israel* (Berlin: Walter de Gruyter, 1977).

11:29–39). However, after this event there is a shift in the function of prophecy in the Deuteronomic tradition. No longer do the prophets of the Deuteronomic groups play important roles within the established social order. Rather, they appear as peripheral prophets who deliver divine words of judgment on the king and people for breaking their covenant with Yahweh and for failing to observe the divine Law. The unnamed man of God from Judah (1 Kings 13), Ahijah (1 Kings 14:1–18), Jehu (1 Kings 16:1–4), and Micaiah (1 Kings 22) all function in this way. In the Elijah stories (1 Kings 17—21; 2 Kings 1—2) and to a lesser extent in the Elisha stories (2 Kings 3—9), the Deuteronomist uses older traditional material to portray the prophets fighting a lonely battle against the pervasive Baal worship of the Northern kings. In these sources, too, are references to bands of prophets which seem to be composed of peripheral individuals who have joined together for mutual support in their fight against the people's apostasy. All of these Deuteronomic accounts portray the prophets as having similar characteristics. Form-critical research has shown that their oracles are similar in structure. They all speak from the standpoint of Deuteronomy's covenant theology, and all use stereotypical Deuteronomic language. As Yahweh's messsengers they deliver to the people the pure divine Word, and on occasion they also function as channels through which the people are able to contact Yahweh (1 Kings 13:6; 14:1–3; 18:20–40). Their characteristic behavior sometimes includes ecstasy, although this is not always the case. However, the divine message which the Deuteronomic prophets brought was accepted only by a few kings (2 Kings 9—10; 19—20; 22:11—23:25). During the reigns of these kings the prophets seem to have regained some influence in the royal court. But in general the prophetic message was consistently rejected by both Israel and Judah, so that in the end both the Northern and Southern kingdoms were destroyed because of their failure to heed the prophetic warnings (2 Kings 13f.; 21:10–15; 24:2).

Alongside the picture as it existed in the Deuteronomic groups are traces of a second picture. There is evidence that prophets functioned within the central government in Jerusalem and in Samaria. Both Nathan and God are associated with David (2 Samuel 7ff.; 1 Sam. 22:5), and the latter is specifically called "David's seer" (2 Sam. 24:11) rather than "Yahweh's prophet."[19] Both prophets were instrumental in legitimizing David's political and religious programs (2 Samuel 7; 24), and Nathan played a role in arranging the accession of Solomon (1 Kings 1:8–53). However, this involvement in the government did not prevent the prophets from occasionally criticizing it and delivering judgment oracles (2 Samuel 12). Traditions preserved by the Chronicler speak of other Jerusalemite prophets (2 Chron. 2:15–16). In the North there is also evidence that prophets occupied positions within the central social structure. First Kings 22 speaks of a large group of prophets at

19. The title "seer" (hōzeh) which is given to Gad seems to have been used primarily of Jerusalemite prophets. See Ziony Zevet, "A Misunderstanding at Bethel: Amos VII 12–17," VT 25 (1975) 783–90.

the court of the Israelite king and describes them as giving war oracles (cf. 2 Kings 3:13). The Elijah stories suggest that Baal prophets functioned in court contexts, while Elisha is sometimes portrayed as in the service of the Israelite king (2 Kings 6:8–23). The prophets connected with the Jerusalemite court are never described as ecstatics, although there is little evidence on their characteristic prophetic behavior. They apparently played no role in the cult and did not act as intercessors, but they did have governmental functions.[20] The Northern court prophets may have exhibited ecstatic behavior—certainly the Baal prophets did—but little is known of their characteristic speech patterns.

The early history of Israelite prophecy is thus highly complex. Among the groups which preserved the Elohistic and Deuteronomic traditions, prophets seem originally to have played an important role in maintaining the social structure. Some of these prophets were related to the cult and exhibited ecstatic behavior, but all of them delivered messages based on their understanding of Israel's covenant traditions. They also acted as intercessors and provided the people with a means of contacting Yahweh. After the time of Solomon they played an increasingly peripheral role in the Israelite establishment, which they attempted to reform with their messages. At the same time, court prophets in Jerusalem and Samaria helped maintain the society by delivering their own perceptions of Yahweh's Word. This religiously complex situation and the prophetic conflict which arose from it form the background against which the work of the later writing prophets must be understood.

---

20. Chronicles connects some of these Jerusalemite prophets with temple worship (1 Chron. 25:1–3; 2 Chron. 29:25, 30), but this may be a later development.

2

Prophecy from the Eighth Through the Fifth Century

HANS WALTER WOLFF*

> In the eighth century, prophets began to appear whose words were
> addressed to the nation as a whole, because the mission of these
> prophets was to set the life of the people of God in the light of the
> future God was preparing for them.

The event of classical prophecy will here be set forth in its principal features.
How did it come about? How did it come to be a unique phenomenon within
the history of Israel and within biblical proclamation? What did it bring to
expression? First of all, we must define what we understand by "classical
prophecy."

I. WHAT IS THE MEANING OF "CLASSICAL PROPHECY"?

1. Literary Criteria

The literary source to which we have to turn with our question seems
easily delineated. It is that part of the biblical canon which is transmitted as
"latter prophets." It consists of the Books of Isaiah, Jeremiah, Ezekiel, and
the twelve prophets. It follows that classical prophecy is delimited on two
sides. It is preceded by a series of old, "preclassical" prophets; the canon
tells about them in the "former Prophets," that is, in the Books of Joshua,
Judges, Samuel, and Kings. It is followed by a new type of meditation about
the future which we call apocalyptic and which finds its classical Old Testament expression within the "Writings," in the Book of Daniel. Classical
prophecy is thus to be found only within the "latter prophets," that is, in the
books of Isaiah through Malachi.

To be sure, this does not mean that all texts in these books belong to

---

*Trans. by W. Sibley Towner with Joy E. Heebink.

classical prophecy. Occasionally legendary traditions exactly after the fashion of the preclassical prophetic traditions occur also within the classical prophetic books. The borrowing of the Isaiah narratives from 2 Kings 18—20 in Isaiah 36—39 is the clearest example, but also it is demonstrated in the novelistic form of the Jonah tale (cf. 2 Kings 14:25 with Jonah 1—4). Even more apparent, numerous apocalyptic pieces occur within the classical prophetic books. To the larger literary complexes of this sort belong Isaiah 24—27, Joel, and Zechariah 12—14. Classical prophecy must, therefore, be lifted by literary-critical means out of the part of the canon called "latter prophets." To this end, chronological and, above all, content criteria are most important.

2. Chronological Criteria

The time span within which the classical prophets appeared can roughly be limited to the eighth through fifth centuries B.C. The beginning is doubtless to be seen in the middle and in the second half of the eighth century. In this time of the advance of the neo-Assyrian Empire, Amos and Hosea appeared in the Northern Kingdom of Israel and Isaiah and Micah in the Southern Kingdom of Judah. These prophets of the eighth century are sometimes called "classical" in the strict sense. To the time of transition from the neo-Assyrian to the Babylonian Empire during the second half of the seventh century belong Nahum, Habakkuk, Zephaniah, and above all Jeremiah, who worked up until the collapse of Jerusalem in the year 587. Shortly after this catastrophe, Obadiah appeared in Jerusalem. Before this date, but also long after it, Ezekiel spoke to the deportees in Babylonian exile. In the middle of the sixth century that great unknown whom we call Deutero-Isaiah, whose words are transmitted in Isaiah 40—55, appeared there. To the escape from exile and the fresh start in Jerusalem belongs Zechariah; at the same time as Haggai (521–20), he called for the reconstruction of the temple. Malachi appears in connection with inner crises of the postexilic community in the Persian period of the fifth century. The additions to the Book of Zechariah belong to a time in which prophecy no longer has a legitimate place (Zech. 13:2–6).

3. Content Criteria

Which are the most important features of form and content in classical prophecy?

With regard to the tradition, it is first of all noteworthy that, beginning with Amos, we have purely and simply *collections of sayings* from the classical prophets. Only seldom do narrative elements appear. They have the sole function of making individual sayings understandable (e.g., Amos 7:10–17). In this respect they differ from the purely narrative traditions of preclassical prophecy down to Elijah and Elisha. The boundary with apocalyptic can also be recognized here. Its legacy of narratives and above all of extended vision reports is fundamentally literary in nature; in contrast, the

originally orally proclaimed sayings of the classical prophets were secondarily
assembled in literature (cf. Isa. 8:16; 30:8; Jeremiah 36).

The collections of prophetic sayings differ from other collections of sayings
which we possess in the categories of legal traditions and wisdom in that
they, as a rule, go back to various historical personages whose individual
names are almost always specifically given at the beginning of the collections.
In contrast, the legal sayings from earliest time through Deuteronomy down
to the priestly fragments of the postexilic time were uniformly projected back
to Moses as the original authority; similarly, the collections of wisdom
sayings down to Qoheleth were projected back to Solomon as the prototype
of the wise man. The collections of prophetic sayings, however, differentiate:
"Word of Amos," "Vision of Isaiah," "Word of Yahweh, that came to Hosea."
Often the home place of the prophet and the precise place of his speech are
added, and above all information about time: "two years before the earth-
quake" (Amos 1:1); "in the year that King Uzziah died" (Isa. 6:1). In Jeremiah
and Ezekiel we find exact year designations. The word of Yahweh came to
Jeremiah "in the days of Josiah . . . in the thirteenth year of his reign" (1:2); it
came in "the fifth year of the exile of King Jehoiachin" to Ezekiel (1:2f.). In
Haggai every utterance is exactly dated by month and day: "In the second
year of Darius the king, in the sixth month, on the first day of the month, the
word of the Lord came by Haggai the prophet to Zerubbabel . . ." (1:1). Why
did the various names of the prophets and their exact location in history
seem indispensable? Unlike legal definitions and wisdom sayings with their
generally applicable and mostly individual significance, the prophetic
speeches have a precise historical function. They steer Israel through great
historical changes. In contrast, pseudonymity is characteristic for apocalyptic
and for its comprehensive view, which even incorporates the world beyond.
Classical prophets are, as it were, personally responsible for their proclamation (see below, part V).

As regards those whom they address, the special element in the classical
prophets is to be seen, above all, in the fact that their message generally
touches *Israel as a whole,* and indeed in the contemporary, world-historical
context. Although, like the preclassical prophets, they can also address
individual persons, especially kings or other responsible groups, their
speech nevertheless generally deals with the destiny of all of Israel. Just as
the curses of the law (e.g., Deut. 27:15–26) kept Israel as a whole in
covenant with Yahweh through the extermination of evil individuals, so
the indictments of the prophets give reasons for the end of Israel as a whole
(Amos 8:2) and the dissolution of the covenant of Yahweh with Israel (Hos.
1:9).[1] In looking at Israel's future existence, such world powers as Assyria,
Babylon, and Persia appear without disguise in the horizon of classical
prophecy.

---

1. Cf. the discussion between Walther Zimmerli, *The Law and the Prophets* (Oxford: Basil
Blackwell, 1965), chaps. 7–8, and Gerhard von Rad, *Old Testament Theology* (New York: Harper
& Row, 1965), 1:395–402 (in the fourth German edition, 1965, see pp. 421f.).

Considering the far-reaching meaning of their proclamation, what is the significance of the individual prophetic personalities?

II. CALL AND COMMISSION

The prophets themselves faced the question of what caused their often shocking appearance. They answered unequivocally and uniformly: not personal initiative, not a group, not an institutional responsibility, but Yahweh's call.

1. Call

The reports concerning the impetus for their work are quite varied (Amos 7:14f.; Isaiah 6; Jeremiah 1; Ezekiel 1—3; Isa. 40:1–8; cf. also Amos 7:1–8; 8:1–2; 9:1–4; Hos. 1:2f.; Mic. 3:8). All the more striking is the unanimity of the testimony that Yahweh's call alone had put them into action. He had called them in a way that was direct and unsought. Amos stresses how undesired it was to him: "The lion has roared; who will not fear? The Lord God has spoken; who can but prophesy?" (3:8). As the vision of devouring locusts and destructive fire overcame him, he—in solidarity with the threatened people—immediately objected to Yahweh: "Oh Lord God, forgive. . . . How can Jacob stand? He is so small!" (7:2; cf. v. 5). Even Jeremiah says, as he struggles: "I do not know how to speak, for I am only a youth" (1:6). They all saw an inescapable urgency confronting them. It created entirely new circumstances.

Certainly nothing would be more incorrect than the supposition that being taken over by Yahweh made the prophets ecstatically estranged and that it displaced their own observations, thoughts, and wills. It is refuted by the fact that all call-reports and commissions of the classical prophets are autobiographical in nature. That differentiates them from all ecstatics, for only a third party can report about an ecstatic. The writing prophets experience Yahweh while they are fully conscious; they hear, consider, and answer. Isaiah receives the questioning voice: "Whom shall I send?" In free decision he responds: "Here am I! Send me!" (6:8). However, as he assumes the grim responsibility of "hardening" the people, he does not enter without consciousness, but, as his reluctance wells up, he asks, "How long, O Lord?" (6:11). Jeremiah, like Amos, is called in his visions to observe: "Jeremiah, what do you see?" (1:11, 13; cf. Amos 7:8; 8:2). The prophets themselves have to put into words that which they have discerned. That is a primary proof for the contention that every personal gift of the individual is applied to the discharge of his task of proclamation. Every individual prophet had to see, to test, to decide, and to give shape to the word. None of them is robbed of his selfhood. Each one assumes full responsibility in his own way (cf. further Ezek. 3: 16ff.)

Thus Yahweh's call plunged each prophet into great loneliness, and such loneliness repeated itself many times. Each time Yahweh dealt with each one individually in his own incomparable way. From such isolation they were then released into the public life of Israel. Although call and commissioning belonged to the loneliness, the reports about these were set by the prophets before the public of Israel; for these reports answered the question about the legitimacy of a prophet by which Israel tried to evade the prophetic word. The prophets knew no other answer except that reference to Yahweh's own: new, powerful utterance.

2. Office

In light of this, the problem of whether the classical prophets are associated with an institutional office essentially is settled. It may be that individual writing prophets had a prophetic office in the cult at the Jerusalem sanctuary along with the priests, especially in connection with individual and congregational services of lamentation (e.g., Obadiah and Habakkuk, cf. 2:1). However, in general we see the classical prophets strongly opposed to the official temple prophets and also the priests (Isa. 28:7ff.; Hos. 4:5; Mic. 3:5–8, 11; Jer. 23:11; 26:7f.; Ezek. 7:26; 22:25f.). Amos sharply rejects efforts to associate him with prophetic groups (7:14)[2] and as a free husbandman stresses his independence over against official temple orders. Jeremiah (1:1) and Ezekiel (1:3) come out of priestly families. Isaiah may be identified with early circles of wisdom-influenced teachers in Jerusalem.[3] Micah, like Amos, may have been a free peasant in Moresheth and may have belonged to the elders of his place.[4] It can be said with greater certainty that the classical prophets from the beginning belonged to very different occupational groups and in no way were bound to a homogeneous cultic institution. What distinguished them from the latter and at the same time bound them to each other was the unsought and irresistible tie to a new word of Yahweh affecting all of Israel. They had also to expect it anew from time to time. In other words, their call did not set down a message to be proclaimed for an entire life. In 8:11, Isaiah begins a speech to his disciples, which is to be connected with the commissioning reported in chapter 6: "For the Lord spoke thus to me with his strong hand upon me, and warned me not to walk in the way of this people. . . ." In the absence of a word of Yahweh, Jeremiah, after a few observations of his own (28:6ff.), must abandon the field to his opponent Hananiah (v. 11); the fresh arrival of a speech of Yahweh has to be awaited (vv. 12ff.). Jeremiah 42:7 speaks of a ten-day waiting period. More, therefore, need not be said about the "office" of the classical prophets except that it is always assumed to be and to remain related to Yahweh's word.

3. Public Appearance

It follows that we see them as a rule appearing as detached individuals. This separation is palpably independent from their psychic natures. Micah

---

2. Johannes Lindblom, *Prophecy in Ancient Israel* (Philadelphia: Fortress Press, 1963), pp. 183f.

3. J. W. Whedbee, *Isaiah and Wisdom* (Nashville: Abingdon Press, 1971); cf. also H. W. Wolff, *Amos the Prophet: The Man and His Background* (Philadelphia: Fortress Press, 1973).

4. H. W. Wolff, "Micah the Moreshite: The Prophet and His Background," in J. G. Gammie et al., eds., *Israelite Wisdom* (Samuel Terrien Festschrift) (Missoula, Mont.: Scholars Press, 1978), pp. 77–84.

can hurl himself with defiant force directly against his office-holding hearers (cf. 3:8 with vv. 1–7 and vv. 9–12!), while Jeremiah suffers severely under his isolation (15:17; 20:8–10). Only seldom is there talk about a friend (Jer. 32:12; 36:4ff.; 43:3ff.) or even a circle of disciples (Isa. 8:16; cf. 8:11ff.).[5] Even the linkage of the classical prophets with each other is in essence only to be drawn out of the relationship of their themes, but is hardly of a personal or even organizational kind (cf. Amos 6:1–7 with Isa. 5:11–13; Isa. 5:8–10 with Mic. 2:1–5; Mic. 3:12 with Jer. 26:17–19). Because they are messengers of Yahweh, their own "I" corresponds to the "I" of their God. In their public appearance, the symbolic acts show strikingly how deeply God, with his commission, took hold of their human relationships. Hosea has to marry a harlot (1:2f.); Jeremiah has to renounce wife and children (16:1ff.); Ezekiel must not mourn the death of his wife (24:15ff.); Hosea (1:4, 6, 9) and Isaiah (7:3; 8:3f.) must give their children sensation-provoking names. Isaiah must appear naked for a whole year (20:1ff.) and Jeremiah with an ox-yoke on the back (27:2ff.), both to announce political catastrophes. With the appearance of the prophets, that which has been announced begins to enter into the history of Israel (cf. Isa. 8:1f.).

The prophets are the primary historical instruments of Yahweh, who introduces the unprecedented New into the history of Israel. Through Hosea he says: "Therefore I have hewn them by the prophets, I have slain them by the words of my mouth" (6.5; cf. Amos 3:7).

But what is the New that begins with the appearance of the classical prophets?[6]

III. ANNOUNCEMENT OF THE FUTURE

Although criticism of contemporary circumstances plays an important role in prophecy, even more prominent and characteristic is the prophet's word about the future.[7] Two basic observations support this. First, the decisive content of all call narratives and visions is not contemporary sin, but those coming events brought forth by Yahweh. Second, it is to be observed in the structure of prophetic speech that if both elements are not presented as the word of God, then only the announcement of the future is; the indictment of the hearers is never given alone (cf. Amos 3:9–11; 4:1–3; Isa. 5:8–10; Mic. 2:1–5). But what do the classical prophets announce?

5. The literary-critical and redaction-historical analysis of the prophetic books permits us to go beyond this to postulate circles of disciples of the most influential prophets as transmitters of tradition (tradents). So, for example, the Deuteronomic shaping of the Jeremiah sermons (cf. W. Thiel, *Die deuteronomistische Redaktion von Jeremia 1–25*, WMANT 41 [Neukirchen-Vluyn: Neukirchener Verlag, 1973]); or the "old school of Amos" (cf. H. W. Wolff, *Joel and Amos*, Hermeneia [Philadelphia: Fortress Press, 1977], pp. 108–11).

6. Cf. Georg Fohrer, *Die symbolischen Handlungen der Propheten*, ATANT 54 (Zurich: Zwingli Verlag, 1968²).

7. Cf. W. H. Schmidt, *Zukunftsgewissheit und Gegenwartskritik: Grundzüge prophetischer Verkündigung* (Neukirchen-Vluyn: Neukirchener Verlag, 1973).

1. The End

Amos is the first to express the at once sober and radical word of Yahweh: "The end has come upon my people Israel" (8:2). With variations it reappears in all ensuing prophets. Amos announces nothing less than the death of Israel (5:2), and indeed without limitation and without remnant (9:1–4). Theologically, this means that the former salvation-and-election-history is ended. Those who received from Yahweh the gift of the land will be deported (cf. 2:9 with 7:11, 17), and the elect will be judged (3:2); the people of the Exodus have no more special standing over against the other peoples (9:7). Pentecost appears in the negative. It is precisely against the background of the old salvation-history traditions that the rupture of the former history happens in a total catastrophe such as never before predicted.

Hosea totally negates the old covenant relationship: "You are not my people and I am not your God!" (1:9). Isaiah makes clear that Yahweh has reversed the thrust of the old holy war. Whereas formerly Yahweh struggled for Israel against the nations, now he advances at the head of the foreign nations against Israel (28:21).[8] Jeremiah proclaims Nebuchadnezzar as Yahweh's servant; no politics can preclude submission to Yahweh (27:6). Micah had already announced complete ruin to elect Jerusalem (3:12); Ezekiel warns against the optimism that the city could get by with the moderate conquest of 597. The judgment must be endured up to the point of complete ruin, even including the sanctuary (Ezek. 4f., 24).

So that is the new, hard message of the classical prophets. God's great history of salvation with Israel, which began with the Exodus from Egypt and received a final seal in the election of Jerusalem, will be pushed inexorably to its end.

2. The Turning Point

But this end must not be understood as a concluding point. Even the hopeless, ancient words of Amos were not transmitted without reference to Yahweh's compassion after the expiration of the judgment (9:11ff.; cf. 5:14f.). However, Hosea makes it most clear that Yahweh's harsh measures still are only his corrective by which to lead his beloved people into an enduring and conclusive connection of love with him (2:8f., 16f.; 3:1–5).[9] Israel with its idolatry will be led to the brink of disaster, in order that it might consider repentance (2:9). Isaiah, too, understands Yahweh's punishing treatment of Jerusalem as a judgment of purification (1:21–26). In the midst of the community of the people, hardened and ready for destruction, he assembles a small community of believers who face a new future (7:1–17; 8:11–15; 28:16). Yahweh's instrument of judgment, the mighty Assyria, not only brings Israel and Judah into the greatest affliction (28:1–4; 7:18–20; 8:4), but also, in its arrogance, must itself experience the punishment of Yahweh so that Jerusalem may experience a surprising turnabout in the midst of severe

---

8. Cf. J. A. Soggin, "Der prophetische Gedanke über den heiligen Krieg, als Gericht über Israel," *VT* 10 (1960) 79–83.

9. Cf. Wolff, *Hosea*, Hermeneia (Philadelphia: Fortress Press, 1974), pp. xxviii-xxix.

affliction (10:5–15; 29:1–8). For Jeremiah, too, hope in the turning point lived in the midst of the exigencies of the siege of Jerusalem: "Houses and fields and vineyards shall again be bought in this land" (32:15).

3. The New

The threatened end of the people of God is recognized in the loss of the land, the state, and the sanctuary. The events of 587 thus motivate the collection of the words of the preexilic prophets. Now not only will the end be proclaimed ever more meaningfully than the turning point, but also the New beyond the turning point achieves increasingly clear outlines.

It may be significant that the concept of the New now appears for the first time in classical prophecy. Jer. 31:31–34 will promise "the new covenant," which will be distinguished from the old covenant. The turning point leads, therefore, not to a return to the old history of salvation, even though some of its features will be renewed. The essential novum is anticipated in a threefold form: (1) God's will will "be written on the heart" of Israel; that is, the willingness and capability to obey will be sent along with the instruction (v. 33); (2) mutual teaching is unnecessary, because all live directly before God (v. 34a); (3) above all, however, the blotting out of all sin undergirds the new covenant, so that it becomes unbreakable (v. 34b). Thus the message of a definitive New shines forth here, although it still remains confined to Israel and is not yet extended into the universal dimension as in the New Testament.

The concept of the New rises in a similar context in Ezekiel. After the arrival of the one who announces the fall of Jerusalem, the prophet is able to open his mouth for the message of hope (33:10–22).[10] To that message belongs the proclamation that Yahweh gives a "new" heart and a "new" spirit and will take away the heart of stone (36:26f.; 11:19).

In Deutero-Isaiah simply the "new" actually becomes a theological slogan for the announcement about the future, and he also, for the first time, coins the term "future" for that which is proclaimed (41:22f.). The "new" will be distinguished from the "former" (42:9f.); it was hitherto completely unknown (48:6); over against the New the past can fall completely into oblivion (43:18f.). Accordingly, the new exodus distinguishes itself fundamentally from the old as the onset of the new time of salvation; it takes place in exaltation and peace (52:12; 55:12f.). Now in Deutero-Isaiah the proclaimed new salvation broadens itself into the universal (45:14ff., 20ff.).

In Ezekiel 18 and 33 the new life of every generation of Israel and every individual in every phase is tied (as in Hos. 2:9; 3:5) to repentance. Even Hosea,[11] however, knew that Yahweh in his patient intercourse with Israel through the centuries must, in the end, wait in vain for the repentance of his people—in spite of evidences of love and in spite of punishments. Even the threatened judgment (2:8f.; 3:4f.) would not achieve the goal. So, through

10. Cf. Zimmerli, Ezekiel, Hermeneia (Philadelphia: Fortress Press, 1977), "Introduction," para. 7, 5.
11. Cf. above, n. 9.

Hosea, the unheard of message that Yahweh of his own free will would heal the unrepentant breaks through (2:21f.; 11:8f.; 13:5). In this Hosea is the precursor of the new covenant in Jeremiah (31:31–34), the message of resurrection for the despairing in Ezekiel (37:1–14), and the news of salvation in Deutero-Isaiah (43:22–25). Thus in the word of classical prophetism, with its message of the end of the old salvation-history of God with Israel, with the word about the turning point and about the *New* in the midst of the Old Testament, the way is already prepared for the New Testament gospel. Indeed, the "new heaven and the new earth" were already awaited by the disciples of Deutero-Isaiah in 65:17; 66:22.

Diverse as the details of the future within classical prophecy may be, in one thing absolute unanimity prevails: It is Yahweh who brings in the end, the turning point, and the *New*. For this reason Ezekiel repeatedly brings the goal of all that is coming into conjunction with the formula by which he concludes nearly every one of his speeches: "You shall know that I am Yahweh."[12] All prophetic announcements of the future have to do with the coming God.

IV. INDICTMENT OF
THE CONTEMPORARIES

Certain as it is that the word of the prophets announces that which is coming, it is at the same time obviously aimed at the contemporary hearers.

1. Function

The prophets attest that the threatened judgment is warranted. Israel's own deeds fall back on its head (Hos. 4:9b; 12:3b; Obad. 15b). Yahweh remains righteous; yes, he remains the holy God. But Israel has removed itself far from his holiness (Jer. 2:13). So the most fundamental task of the prophet becomes himself "to declare to Jacob his transgression and to Israel his sin" (Mic. 3:8b). As an appropriate preamble he often places the indictment before the word of God about the future (see Part III and Amos 3:9f. before v. 11; 4:1 before vv. 2f.; Isa. 5:8 before vv. 9f.; Mic. 2:1f. before v. 3). The prophets' criticism of their own time had, therefore, the function of giving the basis for punishment. In contrast, exhortations appear only sporadically, especially in the earlier prophecies of judgment (Amos 5:4; Isa. 1:16f.). Nowhere at all can it be perceived that the prophet expects an alteration of circumstances through repentance of the people on the basis of his indictments. The contrary is the case. The word about repentance usually belongs not in the exhortation but in the indictment itself precisely because it was not accomplished (Amos 4:6–11; Isa. 30:15).

Hosea lamented, "Their deeds do not permit them to return to their God. For the spirit of harlotry is within them" (5:4); "Their deeds encompass them" (7:2). It would be a profound misunderstanding were one to perceive

---

12. Cf. Zimmerli, *Ezekiel*, "Introduction," para. 5c.

these prophets as reformers or even as revolutionaries. Their view of humanity is far removed from the optimism of these people. Jeremiah made drastically clear how little he expected any improvement in humanity: "Can the Ethiopian change his skin or the leopard his spots? Then also you can do good who are accustomed to do evil" (13:23). So, giving a basis for punishment remained the principal function of the criticism of contemporary experience.

2. Themes

Basic anthropological clarifications are seldom found in classical prophecy. Its representatives generally throw very concrete reproaches against their hearers.

From the time of Amos they seize first of all upon the whole breadth of commercial life. Amos summarizes Yahweh's indictment: "For three transgressions of Israel, and for four, I will not revoke the punishment; because they sell the righteous for silver, and the needy for a pair of shoes—they that trample the head of the poor into the dust of the earth and turn aside the way of the afflicted; a man and his father go in to the same maiden" (2:6f.). The rich and the powerful understand how to turn the law to their advantage through false statements and through bribery of the judges (Amos 5:7 plus 10:12; Isa. 5:23; Mic. 3:1ff., 9ff.). At the expense of the poor they get enormous luxury and they throw raucous feasts (Amos 4:1–3; 5:11; 6:1–7). They increase their property so that the real estate is concentrated in the hands of a few (Amos 3:9f.; Isa. 5:8–13; Mic. 2:1f.). An evil style of business defrauds the people through false weights, inferior goods, and inflated prices (Amos 8:4–6). The women of Jerusalem are charged with the most pretentious conceit (Isa. 3:16ff.). The poor and the weak always provide the standard for prophetic judgment.

No less do external political decisions fall under the prophetic indictment. Israel forgets its own way if it entrusts its destiny to clever diplomacy or military might. When under Hoshea ben Elah the Northern Kingdom partially subjected itself to the great king of Assyria, Tiglath-Pileser, the prophet Hosea had to say, "He is not able to cure you or heal your wound" (5:13); in exchange for tribute Israel reaped only "wind"[13] and remained without support (12:2). Even the potential power of great empires is only the product of human hands (Hos. 14:4); the charioteers themselves, as perishable "flesh,"[14] are no match for the absolute power of God (Isa. 31:1, 3). When King Ahaz took political decisions which evaded Isaiah's prophetic word to make them by his own standards (Isa. 7:12), he thereby handed himself over to the judgment of God (v. 17).

Not least does the prophetic reproach apply to cultic praxis. Instead of teaching and learning in it what Yahweh does and wills, the priests enrich themselves with offerings. People seek to produce fertility through op-

---

13. Cf. Schmidt, above, n. 7; for another view see Martin Buber, The Prophetic Faith (New York: Macmillan, 1949).

14. Wolff, Anthropology of the Old Testament (Philadelphia: Fortress Press, 1975²), pp. 31ff.

pressive sexual cults of the Canaanite kind; they seek to get answers through heathen oracle-praxis (Hos. 4:6, 8, 12, 13ff.). People seek self-gratification through pilgrimages instead of submitting to the law of God; they seek to subordinate God to their own wills through pious acts of sacrifice (Amos 4:4f.; 5:21–24; cf. Isa. 1:10–17; Jer. 7:3ff.). Furthermore, Isaiah 58 sharply distinguishes those fasts which Israel practices from those which Yahweh loves. Instead of letting his head hang down like a rush and lying down in sackcloth and ashes, a person should "loose the bonds of wickedness . . . undo the thongs of the yoke . . . let the oppressed go free . . . share bread with the hungry . . . bring the homeless poor in . . . cover the naked . . . and hide not oneself from one's own flesh." Finally, Zechariah (7:4–14) recalls that the hard experience of the exile goes back to judgment against false "fasts" and the failure to recognize the corresponding prophetic words.

The proliferation of the concrete prophetic indictments proves the righteousness of the judgment. However, the abundance of the specifics of contemporary criticism leads one to ask about the essential criteria.

3. Recurring Motifs

Amos recognizes Israel's injustice vis-à-vis the defenseless in the fact that Yahweh has taken his stand on behalf of the weak Israel against the strong (compare 2:9 with vv. 6–8). Hosea also compares Israel to Yahweh's saving deeds: it has forgotten the God who has shown himself to them as the only savior, who brought them through the wilderness and gave them the land (13:4–6; cf. 2:10). Isaiah's indictments are grounded also in the fact that Israel rebels against the God who has raised it, made it great, and has given all good things to it (1:2; cf. 5:1–7). Jeremiah speaks of Yahweh as the living fountain, whom Israel has forsaken (2:13). The ultimate basis of all particular indictments is, therefore, that the God of the history of salvation is forgotten and rejected.

With the knowledge of God, truth and love, justice and righteousness were lost (Hos. 4:2; 6:6). The vital assistance of the traditional legal principles was rejected (cf. Hos. 8:12; Amos 5:24; 6:12; Mic. 3:1, 9; Jer. 22:15). Isaiah's complaint against the perverse politics of his day roots in the remonstrance of the unbelievers against the word of God, which the prophet also makes known: "They do not regard the deed of the LORD" (5:12b; cf. 22:11b; "[they] do not look to the holy one of Israel" (31:1b); "[they] will not hear the instruction of the LORD" (30:9; 28:12) even though "in returning and rest" salvation lies, and strength "in quietness and in trust" (30:15). So all of the sin of Israel, and with it all threatened disaster, too, is rooted in the rejection of Yahweh's offer of salvation (5:24; 30:12).

When later in the midst of dark judgment the entirely new promise of salvation breaks forth, it in no way happens because of a new approach of the people to Yahweh; on the contrary, salvation breaks forth as Yahweh's free gift in spite of the hopelessness and unbelief of the people (compare Ezek. 37:11 with vv. 1–14; and Isa. 40:25ff.; 49:14ff.; see Part III).

V. THE AGONY OF THE PROPHETS

1. Opposition

As far as we can see, no true prophet gets by without great difficulties. Amos can compare his possession by Yahweh only with the terror before the suddenly aroused lion (3:8); it is perilous. Hosea discovers that he is treated like a mad fool (9:7). Isaiah sees himself not only mocked by his hearers (5:19; 28:9f.), but also profoundly disappointed in his God; for the fulfillment of the message announced to him as word of God must always wait upon him. So he must wait and hope on the hidden face of Yahweh (cf. 8:17 and 5:19). He cannot regard the unfulfilled word as settled; therefore, he has it laid up among his disciples (8:16) probably in writing, "that it may be for the time to come as a witness forever" (cf. 30:8). Micah of Moresheth sees his threat of judgment sharply contradicted (2.6f.). Resistance and opposition emanate not least from the bearers of public offices.

2. Confusion

From the time of Micah the main conflict is with other prophets in official position in the temple.[15] Micah unmasks their dependence upon those who pay them: "[They] cry 'peace' when they have something to eat, but declare war against him who puts nothing into their mouths" (3:5). "[The] prophets divine for money" (3:11). Micah brings clarity into the confusion caused in the people by the mutually contradictory prophets in that he asks after their primary allegiance; he presents himself as given authorization by God's just will (3:8).

A hundred years later, Jeremiah finds himself plunged more than any other prophet into the whirl of confusion which emanates from temple prophecy and is also aimed directly at him. Jeremiah, too, points out the dependency of those fellows upon their hearers: "They say continually to those who despise the word of the LORD, 'It shall be well with you'" (23:17). Whoever has stood "in Yahweh's council" cannot do that (23:22). His chief opponent, Hananiah, breaks the yoke which Jeremiah wore as a sign of the subjection to Babylon and proclaims the approaching salvation (28:1ff.; see Part II, 3). Jeremiah initially ventures against him the reminder that among the predecessors, the prophets of doom have as a rule been the true prophets (28:8f.). Elsewhere he also names "adultery and walk[ing] in lies" (23:14; 29:21–23) as identifying marks of the false prophets. It becomes apparent through conduct whether one of these persons subordinates himself to Yahweh's will or more to his own wishes. The self-willed person manipulates. In the last analysis, however, it is only Yahweh's authorization itself, which, with his decree, leads him who takes his place in Yahweh's council out of the confusion (28:11f.; cf. 23:22, 25–28). The hearers, however, can distinguish true and false messages only in the confrontation of the two, in which they can test the dependency relationships: Is the witness free in respect to his

---

15. Cf. Gottfried Quell, *Wahre und falsche Propheten* (Gütersloh: C. Bertelsmann, 1952).

hearers? Does his own desire rule or is he governed by the free will of his God? The truth documents itself especially in suffering, as Jeremiah confesses: "My heart is broken within me, all my bones shake; I am like a drunken man, like a man overcome by wine, because of the LORD and because of his holy words" (23:9).

3. Suffering

For that reason, a coherent story of the sufferings of Jeremiah is transmitted to us (chaps. 37—43). Scene after scene shows how the rejection of the word of God draws after it the rejection of the command of God; in the suffering of the prophet the suffering of the word of God manifests itself.[16]

The real depth of the prophetic suffering breaks out in Jeremiah's exchanges with his God. Here emerges not only the torment resulting from personal assaults of fellow humans (11:18–23), but also his doubt about his commission. If he keeps quiet, the fire of his words burns him in his inner self; if he speaks, scorn and persecution surge around him (20:7–10). He appears as a deceiver. So in wrath he flings his office before the feet of his God: "Wilt thou be to me like a deceitful brook, like waters that fail?" (15:18). The most extreme agony is that which brings him to curse his life right up to the point of the perverse desire that the womb of his mother might have been his grave (20:14–18). Only Yahweh's special, new word can snatch him away from such an ultimate temptation (15:19–21).

A similar and even more far-reaching kind of suffering under the prophetic vocation appears in the Suffering Servant songs of Deutero-Isaiah, in which the unknown prophet himself probably served as model. Isaiah 42:1–4 presents the call of the Servant, whose word shall have to do with the peoples of the world. The second song (49:1–6) shows him ineffectual and oppressed, and yet precisely then he is designated as "a light to the nations." Isaiah 50:4–9 speaks of the further troubles of the obedient disciple who is even physically attacked and whom only his God can rescue. In spite of horrible suffering, this salvation proves to be more powerful than death and grave in 52:13—53:12. Above all, however, the meaning of the suffering of this Servant now emerges: He takes the place of all who have deserved the judgment. So office and person merge entirely together; yes, the message and the messenger become identical. Here the *New* introduces itself in prophecy absolutely prototypically as that which saves.

---

16. Abraham J. Heschel, *The Prophets* (New York: Harper & Row, 1962).

3
Prophetic Speech

GENE M. TUCKER

A new assessment of the way prophets spoke shows that their basic
vocation was to be as speakers who brought a communication from
God announcing future events.

The discussion of Israelite prophetic speech should begin with a note of
caution. After all, none of us has heard an Israelite prophet speak; written
documents are all that remain for us. So one must make certain assumptions
and reach conclusions through a process of critical analysis and reconstruction even to discuss prophetic *speech*. But the literature at hand, the prophetic books and accounts in the books of Kings and elsewhere, contain what
purport to be transcripts of prophetic speeches as well as reports of the
activities of the prophets, especially their oral activities. And even a cursory
examination of that literature justifies the conclusion that oral communication was the essential—if not the only—feature of their vocation and work.
The first body of evidence for that conclusion consists of the numerous
reports, from brief and cryptic to extensive and detailed, of how the prophets
raised their voices in and to Israel and when and where. Then there are the
allusions to the prophetic self-understanding found throughout their words,
for example in vocation reports. Jeremiah resists the prophetic call because
"I do not know how to speak," and Yahweh tells him "whatever I command
you you shall speak" (Jer. 1:6f.). Whatever else it entails, "to prophesy"
means to speak. Furthermore, even if there were no such reports or allusions
but only the prophetic words themselves, it would be clear from the form,
style, and content of those words that the prophets were fundamentally
speakers.

I

Though he was not the first to recognize that the prophets were primarily
speakers rather than men of letters, it was Hermann Gunkel who raised this
observation to the level of methodological consciousness and made it the

27

basis for finding a way through the literature to the speech genres.[1] Since his
time the procedure has been clarified and extended under the heading of the
form-critical method.[2] The aim of this literary-sociological approach is to
analyze the typical features of biblical texts, especially their conventional
forms or structures, in order to relate them to their sociological contexts.

The form-critical analysis of biblical texts, as one step in exegesis, involves
the analysis of the structure (form) of the unit in question, the determination
of its genre, conclusions concerning its sociological setting, and the interpretation of its intention. The first—and at least in the case of the prophetic
literature, the most important—step in the consideration of the structure is
the determination of the appropriate unit for analysis and interpretation.
Gunkel and his successors[3] drew attention to the fact that few if any of the
prophetic books are organized literary compositions, but are rather for the
most part collections of originally distinct materials. An essential step in the
analysis of the literature is the separation of these materials according to
units. In this respect the most useful clues are the introductory and concluding formulas such as the call to hear ("Hear this word . . .") or the prophetic
word formula ("The word of Yahweh came to . . ."), and the typical structures
of the different genres which suggest where they began and ended.

But if our analysis focused only or even primarily on the search for the
"original" units of oral expression we would be reintroducing on a slightly
different level both the ideology and one of the fundamental weaknesses of
the older source-critical approach to the prophets.

Therefore, one should use "unit" as a more or less neutral and descriptive
term applying to all possible levels of the texts at hand, whether viewed
historically or simply in terms of literary organization. A prophetic book itself
is an appropriate unit for such analysis, representing the final stage in the
development of the tradition and a quite distinct genre of literature with
certain typical features.[4] Then there are major sections within the books
which may or may not correspond to the divisions recognized by the source-
critical attribution of literature to different authors and historical circumstances, for example Isaiah 40—55 or 24—27. Further, there may be relatively clear smaller units, many of which reflect an intermediate stage in the

---

1. The major works in English translation are "The Secret Experiences of the Prophets," *Exp,*
ninth series, 2 (1924) 356–66, 427–35, 23–32 (a translation of an essay from *Die Schriften des
Alten Testaments* 2/2, first published in 1915), and "The Israelite Prophecy from the Time of
Amos," in J. Pelikan, ed., *Twentieth Century Theology in the Making* (New York: Harper & Row,
1969), pp. 48–75 (originally published in *RGG,* 1927–32).

2. Cf. Klaus Koch, *The Growth of the Biblical Tradition: The Form Critical Method,* trans. by
S. M. Cupitt (New York: Charles Scribner's Sons, 1969), and Gene M. Tucker, *Form Criticism of
the Old Testament* (Philadelphia: Fortress Press, 1971).

3. Gunkel, "The Israelite Prophecy," pp. 61–66; Sigmund Mowinckel, *Prophecy and Tradition* (Oslo: I Kommisjon Hos Jacob Dybwad, 1946), pp. 34ff.

4. This applies to the characteristic beginnings of the books. Cf. Tucker, "Prophetic Superscriptions and the Growth of a Canon," in George W. Coats and Burke O. Long, eds., *Canon
and Authority: Essays in Old Testament Religion and Theology* (Philadelphia: Fortress Press,
1977), pp. 56–70.

editing of the prophetic tradition. For example, Isa. 1:2–26 (possibly including vv. 27–31) is a distinct composition summarizing the message of the prophet, but composed by his successors of originally discrete sayings of Isaiah.[5] Finally the individual units, for example Isa. 1:2–3, 4–9, 10–17, may be considered. All units of prophetic literature, whether large or small, "original" or late, can be interpreted fruitfully by means of form-critical analysis.

II

Viewing the prophetic books as a whole, virtually all of their genres of literature and discourse fall into one of three general categories: reports, speeches or prayers.[6] The reports may be simple accounts such as the superscriptions to the books (e.g., Amos 1:1; Isa. 1:1) and the notations concerning the time and place of a prophetic speech or experience (e.g., Jer. 21:1; Ezek. 8:1), or they may be stories—narratives which arouse interest by creating and resolving tension—such as accounts of prophetic conflict (Amos 7:10–17), vocation accounts (Isaiah 6; Jer. 1:4–10; Ezekiel 1—3), or reports of symbolic actions (Isa. 8:1–4; Jeremiah 32). Accounts are either in the first person, attributed to the prophet, or in the third person, concerning the prophet. Most of the prayers are either words of praise (Amos 4:13; 5:8f; 9:5f.), complaints (Jer. 11:18—12:6; 15:10–21), or often brief words of intercession (e.g., Amos 7:2, 5; Isa. 6:11). The lines between these general categories should not be drawn rigidly, nor their differences exaggerated, since often they are intertwined. Most accounts include speeches, and prayers will be found in the context of vision reports. Furthermore, many reports served the same functions as the speeches. It was one thing for the prophet to experience a vision; but when that experience was reported publicly, the account became a form of discourse. Furthermore, symbolic action reports ordinarily included an address (by God to the prophet, by the prophet to his audience, or both) presenting the interpretation of the action. Likewise, the report of the action along with the interpretation doubtless was repeated before audiences who had not observed the action itself but nevertheless then received the message it conveyed.

Most of the individual units in the prophetic literature are speeches of various sorts. "Speech" is hardly a precise term, but only a general designation of a spoken address by an individual to an audience. A prophetic speech is simply any address by a prophet speaking as a prophet. These speeches compare with few modern addresses, or even sermons, in terms of either content or form. The longest ones were quite short, if we can judge at all from the written texts. As a rule, the individual addresses of the earlier prophets were very short, while those of the later ones were somewhat

5. Cf. George Fohrer, "Jesaja 1 als Zusammenfassung der Verkündigung Jesajas,"in *Studien zur alttestamentlichen Prophetie*, BZAW 99 (Berlin: Alfred Töpelmann, 1967), pp. 148–66.

6. Cf. Claus Westermann, *Basic Forms of Prophetic Speech*, trans. H. C. White (Philadelphia: Westminster Press, 1967), pp. 90–93.

longer. (Compare Amos, Hosea, and First Isaiah with Ezekiel and Second
Isaiah.)

III

The prophetic speeches, as well as other units of the literature, often have
been called "oracles,"[7] but this classification should not be used indiscriminately. An oracle is a divine communication, usually through an intermediary such as a priest, prophet, seer, or diviner. It may be solicited by the
intermediary on behalf of himself or a third party, or it may come unsolicited. An example of a specific type of solicited oracle is the (priestly?)
salvation oracle (cf. Isa. 41:8ff.; 43:1ff.; 44:1ff.).[8] The solicited oracle could
contain a simple yes or no answer to a specific question, instructions, or any
other revelation. An example of the unsolicited form is the call oracle found
in the vocation reports of the prophets and others (Isa. 6:8ff.; Jer. 1:5; Ezek.
2:1ff.; Exod. 3:7ff.; Judg. 6:14ff.). Without invitation God addresses someone
with the call to a special office or duty. Prophetic speeches, or parts of them,
when they are presented as Yahweh's own words, may be classified broadly as
unsolicited oracles. Often such words will be concluded or introduced by the
oracle formula "says Yahweh" (or "oracle of Yahweh," nĕʾum yhwh). As we
have seen, Gunkel argued that the roots of prophetic discourse as a whole lay
in procedures for soliciting oracles. But this question requires considerably
more attention, especially in the light of ancient Near Eastern parallels to
Israelite prophecy.[9] The issue is by no means simple. On the one hand,
prophetic discourse is not limited to oracles in the sense we have defined
them, but includes many speeches not attributed directly to God. On the
other hand, the oracle-giving function is not limited to or identical with the
role of the prophet. The giving of solicited oracles seems to have been
primarily a cultic activity in the narrow sense.

Similar problems attend the widely accepted classification of prophetic
discourse as messenger speech.[10] The designation is based in large measure
on the frequent appearance of the messenger formula ("thus says Yahweh") in
prophetic literature. The formula seems to have originated in the ancient and
widespread practice of the oral transmission of a message by a third party

---

7. Numerous examples could be adduced. See, e.g., James M. Ward, *Amos and Isaiah:
Prophets of the Word of God* (Nashville: Abingdon Press, 1969), pp. 18, 21, 80, passim; Erling
Hammershaimb, *The Book of Amos: A Commentary,* trans. John Sturdy (Oxford: Basil Black-
well, 1970), pp. 14, 21, passim.

8. Joachim Begrich, "Das priesterliche Heilsorakel," *ZAW* 46 (1934) 81–92, reprinted in
Gesammelte Studien zum Alten Testament, TB 21 (Munich: Chr. Kaiser Verlag, 1964), pp. 217–
31.

9. See esp. Herbert B. Huffmon, "The Origins of Prophecy," in Frank Moore Cross, Werner
E. Lemke, and Patrick D. Miller, Jr., eds., *Magnalia Dei: The Mighty Acts of God* (Garden City,
N.Y.: Doubleday & Co., 1976), pp. 171–86, and the literature cited there.

10. Westermann, *Basic Forms of Prophetic Speech,* pp. 98–128; and James F. Ross, "The
Prophet as Yahweh's Messenger," in Bernhard W. Anderson and Walter Harrelson, eds., *Israel's
Prophetic Heritage* (New York: Harper & Row, 1962), pp. 98–107.

("thus says so or so"). It normally occurs twice in the procedure: (1) it is spoken by the sender when he commissions and instructs his messenger (Gen. 32:5; 45:9), and (2) it is reiterated by the messenger when he delivers the communication (2 Kings 18:29; Num. 22:15ff.). Therefore, many have argued that the prophet was the messenger of Yahweh, and his speeches were messages. But it has been shown that the formula occurs with various kinds of material—not just "messages"—and that messages do not always begin or end with the formula.[11] Furthermore, it turns out that there is such variability in the form of the "message" that it can hardly be called a distinct genre.[12] So when the formula "thus says Yahweh" occurs in the prophetic literature (frequently in Amos, Jeremiah, and Ezekiel; not at all in Hosea, Joel, Habakkuk, and Zechariah), the prophet may be understood in analogy with the practice of commissioning, instructing, and sending a messenger. But to identify prophecy with the message is inadequate, and to argue that prophets were basically the messengers (ambassadors) of Yahweh as a king is to go further than the evidence allows.

IV

It is difficult to conceive of a type of speech or a sphere of Israelite life which is not at least reflected in the words of the prophets. This should not be surprising, since any speaker will tend to draw freely from the language of proverbial wisdom, courtroom process, religious expression, popular songs, or any other well-known traditional expressions in order to make his message understandable and compelling. In the case of the Old Testament prophets, one can add to the original speaker's inclination to employ and adapt diverse genres the work of the tradents and redactors, who will have further modified the material and supplemented it with an even longer list of genres as the prophetic tradition continued to live in Israel.

It would be impossible to catalog here the genres found in the prophetic books; indeed, the list expands as we learn more about the relationship between language and life in ancient Israel. But some examples should be noted. Gunkel, and most who have followed him, attempted to distinguish between the genres which were basically prophetic and those which the prophets had taken over from other spheres of life.[13] Involved in this distinction is the question of the role of the prophet in Israel. If we can determine the specific and distinctive modes of prophetic speech, we will have gained insight into basic questions concerning prophetic activity.

Many of the forms of expression in the prophetic books stem from distinct aspects of Israelite life and institutions. Some are rooted in the cult. In

---

11. Rolf Rendtorff, "Botenformel und Botenspruch," ZAW 74 (1962) 165–77, reprinted in *Gesammelte Studien zum Alten Testament*, TB 57 (Munich: Chr. Kaiser Verlag, 1975), pp. 243–55; and Koch, *The Growth of Biblical Tradition*, pp. 216ff.

12. Rendtorff, "Botenformel und Botenspruch," pp. 247–52.

13. Gunkel, "The Israelite Prophecy," pp. 68ff.

addition to the hymnic units in Amos (4:13; 5:8f.; 9:5f.)[14] there are other examples of cultic songs (e.g., Isaiah 12) which likewise probably were added by later editors. But there are some cultic materials which stem from the earliest traditions of the prophets. For example, Amos 4:4 is a call to worship or a pilgrim song which has been transformed into an ironical indictment of worship. One also finds the prophetic use of the priestly Torah (e.g., Isa. 1:10–17; Amos 5:21–27), originally the priest's instructions, in the form of responses to questions concerning cultic purity, the acceptability of a sacrifice, or the like.[15] Second Isaiah frequently speaks in the form of the priestly oracle of salvation, comparable to a pronouncement of absolution or reassurance (41:8ff.; 43:1–4, 5–7; 44:1–5). It is hardly likely that the use of such expressions proves that the prophets were cultic officials in the narrow sense. In almost every case the language has been made to serve a prophetic perspective.

There are genres similar to those in the wisdom literature, for example, a list of sayings in Amos 3:3–8, a kind of parable in Isa. 5:1–7, and other didactic types such as exhortations and admonitions.[16] Likewise there is frequent use of the language of the legal process (see especially Mic. 6:1ff.; Isa. 41:1ff.; 43:8ff.), where Yahweh through the prophet speaks now as plaintiff, now as judge. Most of this language has been taken over from the ordinary judicial process "in the gate," but some of it may represent a specific covenant lawsuit in which the prophet called Israel to task for violation of the covenant's stipulations.[17] The meaning of such "non-prophetic" genres seldom can be inferred directly from their original setting and purpose, since the prophets hardly used them without modification. Typical is the appearance of a dirge in Amos 5:1–2. The structure, poetic meter, and mood are consistent with songs sung at funerals. But the prophet has introduced a radical content, making the dirge into an announcement of the death of Israel.

Leaving aside for the moment the question of "the basic form of prophetic speech," some of the other distinctively prophetic genres should be noted. We have already alluded to the vocation reports of the prophets and others.[18] This genre took two different forms. One type emphasized the report of a vision of the divine court, similar to other vision reports (Isa. 6:1–13; Ezekiel

---

14. See James L. Crenshaw, *Hymnic Affirmation of Justice: The Doxologies of Amos and Related Texts in the Old Testament*, SBLDS 24 (Missoula, Mont.: Scholars Press, 1975), and the literature cited there.

15. Begrich, "Die priesterliche Tora," BZAW 66 (Berlin: Alfred Töpelmann, 1936), pp. 63–88, reprinted in *Gesammelte Studien*, pp. 232–60. See esp. Haggai 2:10.

16. Hans Walter Wolff, *Amos the Prophet: The Man and His Background*, trans. Foster R. McCurley (Philadelphia: Fortress Press, 1973). For a more balanced view, see Crenshaw, "The Influence of the Wise Upon Amos," ZAW 79 (1967) 41–52.

17. Cf. Huffmon, "The Covenant Lawsuit in the Prophets," *JBL* 78 (1959) 285–95; and Julien Harvey, *Le plaidoyer prophétique contre Israel après la rupture de l'alliance* (Paris: Desclée de Brouwer, 1967).

18. Cf. Norman Habel, "The Form and Significance of the Call Narratives," ZAW 77 (1965) 297–323; Rolf Knierim, "The Vocation of Isaiah," VT 18 (1986) 47–68.

1—3; 1 Kings 22:19–23). The other type concentrated on the coming of the word of God (an audition) to the prophet or other charismatic figure (Jer. 1:4–10; Exodus 3—4; 6; Judg. 6:11–14). None of these reports is biographical or autobiographical in anything like the modern sense. In each case its purpose is the authentication of the prophet's authority and his message: He did not speak on his own but because of a divine commission. The reports were shaped according to traditional structures long after the experiences they report, either by the prophets themselves in situations where their authority was challenged or by later tradents as arguments for the authority of the now departed prophet's words.[19]

Two other reporting genres common to the prophetic literature are the vision report and the symbolic action report. The visions tend to focus on the communication of words in a dialogue or the interpretation by God of what was seen.[20] They range from concise (e.g., Amos 7:1–3, 4–6) to elaborate (e.g., Ezek. 8:1—11:25), but almost invariably emphasize the communication of God's revelation concerning the future. The reports of symbolic actions[21] likewise vary considerably in length, but always contain both an account of the action performed and its interpretation (cf. Isa. 7:10ff.; 8:1–4; 20; Jeremiah 19; 32; Ezekiel 4—5). The actions performed were not simply means of attracting the attention of an audience but were believed to set Yahweh's future into motion (cf. 2 Kings 13:14–19).

One other genre common to prophetic speech is the so-called woe oracle (Amos 5:18–20; 6:1–3, 4–7; Isa. 5:8–12). This speech, easily recognized by its opening cry "Woe," has received considerable attention lately.[22] Does the utterance "Woe" stem from cries of lamentation at the funeral or from didactic exhortations or warnings? This much is clear: Almost without exception the speeches are not given as the words of Yahweh and therefore are not oracles; and the content which immediately follows the woe cry does not convey a revelation concerning the future but rather indicts the hearers in terms of their reprehensible activities.

V

A major problem which confronts us in the consideration of the most typical and distinctively prophetic genres of speech is the diversity in terminology found in the secondary literature. The same genres have been labeled in many different ways. But it is not possible to choose arbitrarily one label or

19. For the latter view see Burke O. Long, "Prophetic Authority as Social Reality," in Coats and Long, eds., *Canon and Authority*, esp. pp. 11–13.

20. Friedrich Horst, "Die Visionsschilderungen der alttestamentlichen Propheten," *EvTh* 20 (1960) 193–205.

21. Fohrer, *Die symbolischen Handlungen der Propheten*, ATANT 25 (Zurich: Zwingli Verlag, 1953); *idem*, "Die Gattung der Berichte über symbolische Handlungen der Propheten," *ZAW* 64 (1952) 101–20.

22. See esp. Erhard Gerstenberger, "The Woe-Oracles of the Prophets," *JBL* 81 (1962) 249–63; and Waldemar Janzen, *Mourning Cry and Woe Oracle*, BZAW 125 (Berlin: Walter de Gruyter, 1972).

another, since each alternative entails certain implications for understanding
Israelite prophecy, for assessing its sociological and ideological background,
and for drawing conclusions concerning the theology of the prophets.

Gunkel took the earliest form of prophetic utterance to be short, oracular
predictions of the future, either in the form of promises or threats.[23] As
prophecy progressed, promises and threats continued to appear, since the
element of prediction was essential to prophecy, but they were expanded and
other genres developed. In particular, first as justification for the threat and
later as an independent genre, reproaches (Scheltreden) were used. Gunkel
introduced the distinction between the threat or promise as the actual words
of Yahweh and the reproach as the result of the prophet's reflection on the
reasons for Yahweh's actions. Such terminology supports an image of the
prophets as preachers of repentance.

Gunkel's categories—if not all of his theories concerning the development
of genres—were widely accepted.[24] But Westermann has argued convinc-
ingly against the terminology,[25] likewise calling into question its implications. Concerning the threatening speech, decisive is the fact that ordinarily
no conditional element appears. "Reproach" is likewise too weak for the
direct address which accuses the hearers of specific sins or crimes, and the
units so described most commonly are linked directly and logically to the
announcement of doom, as the reasons for it.

The two most important recent treatments of prophetic speech in general
are those of Westermann[26] and Koch.[27] What Gunkel had called the threatening speech with a reproach, Westermann identified as the prophetic
judgment speech.[28] He outlined two forms of this speech (against individuals
and against Israel), outlined their typical structures, and drew conclusions
concerning their setting. The "basic structure" of the speech to the nation
consists of the reasons (including accusation and its development), the messenger formula as a transition, and the announcement of judgment (including the intervention of God and the results of the intervention). Westermann
saw this genre as a direct outgrowth of the judgment speech to the individual, which follows patterns and ideas typical of juridical procedure. The
essence of the speech against Israel is that "the judgment of God is announced to the people because of specific failures."[29] The morphological

---

23. "Fundamental Problems of Hebrew Literary History," in What Remains of the Old Testament, trans. A. K. Dallas (New York: Macmillan, 1928), p. 60. For an excellent study of Gunkel
and his early successors, see John H. Hayes, "The History of the Form-Critical Study of Prophecy," in George MacRae, ed., SBL Seminar Papers, 1973 (Society of Biblical Literature, 1973),
1:60–99.

24. See Emil Balla, Die Droh- und Scheltworte des Amos (Leipzig: Alexander Edelmann,
1926), and most recently Ludwig Markert, Struktur und Bezeichnung des Scheltworts: Eine
gattungskirtische Studie anhand des Amosbuches, BZAW 140 (Berlin: Walter de Gruyter, 1977).

25. Westermann, Basic Forms of Prophetic Speech, pp. 64–70.

26. Ibid., esp. pp. 90–188.

27. Koch, The Growth of the Biblical Tradition, esp. pp. 210–20.

28. Concerning the positive counterpart of this genre, see Westermann, "The Way of the
Promise Through the Old Testament," in Bernhard W. Anderson, ed., The Old Testament and
the Christian Faith (New York: Harper & Row, 1963), pp. 200–224.

29. Westermann, Basic Forms of Prophetic Speech, p. 176.

data—the typical structure of the speeches—provided the basis for the conclusions concerning the history and meaning of prophetic speech. Therefore, his terminology—which supports an understanding of the prophets as messengers of Yahweh the judge—can be maintained only so long as his observations concerning what is typical in the structure of the speeches are convincing.

Klaus Koch has attempted to place the interpretation of the prophetic genres on a broader basis. What Westermann had called the prophetic judgment speech, Koch identifies as the prophecy of disaster. With this terminology Koch introduces quite a different understanding of the prophetic language and its background. Koch has rejected the term "judgment speech" because of the theological freight which it carries and because he sees the background of the genres, not in the juridical process, but in the prophet's "private oracle" which preceded the public speech.[30] The genres have been determined by the prophetic institution itself.

These alternative interpretations of prophetic speech plainly are not compatible in important respects, and none is without problems. We can arbitrate among them or be led to other alternatives only on the basis of an assessment of the typicalities in the prophetic speeches themselves.

VI

To be concrete and specific we may use the Book of Amos as a test case, first looking at a typical unit of speech and then moving to the book as a whole. The conclusions will then be tested against other evidence.

The unit is Amos 4:1–3, which we call "a prophecy against rich women," anticipating some of the conclusions which must be argued. The *structure* of the speech may be outlined as follows:

I. Elaborated call to attention (1)
   A. The call itself ("Hear this word")
   B. Addressees ("cows of Bashan")
   C. Designation of addressees
      1. By location ("who are in the mountain of Samaria")
      2. By activity: accusations as reasons for punishment
         a. Their injustice against the poor and needy
         b. Their arrogance, demonstrated by a citation of their words

II. Yahweh speech (2–3)
   A. Introduction: divine oath formula (2aa)
   B. Yahweh speech: an announcement of punishment (2ab–3)
      1. General: the intervention of Yahweh (2ab)
      2. Specific: the results of Yahweh's intervention (2b–3)
   C. Concluding oracle formula

On the basis of introductory and concluding formulas, internal structure,

---

30. Johannes Lindblom called the prophetic literature in general "revelation literature," pointing to an emphasis on what Gunkel had called the secret experiences of the prophets. Cf. *Die literarische Gattung der prophetischen Literatur*, Uppsala Universitets Arsskrift, Teologi 1 (Uppsala: A.-B. Lundequistska Bokhandeln, 1924).

and content these three verses stand as an independent and self-contained unit. Concerning the independence of 4:1–3, virtually all modern commentators are agreed.[31]

The prophet himself speaks first and then quotes the words of Yahweh as a promissory oath which he has sworn. The accusation—or in this context, the reasons for punishment—as a part of a direct address to the accused is distinctive but by no means unique (see Amos 8:4; Mic. 3:9ff.; Isa. 28:14ff.). The first clause in the announcement makes it clear that the word is intended for the future; the following clauses describe the concrete historical doom in store for the accused. Often in such announcements Yahweh describes what he is about to do in first-person style, but passive formulations such as we have here, or statements about the accused, are not exceptional (cf. Amos 7:17; 3:11; 6:7, 11; 8:8, 12; Mic. 3:12).[32]

In terms of *genre*, the unit falls into the general category of speech; that is, it must have arisen as the spoken word and not as pure literature. More specifically, in terms of structure, specific content, and purpose, it is a prophecy of punishment against a particular group in Israel. To call it a threat or a threatening speech[33] is not acceptable; no condition is stated or implied, the punishment is not threatened, but announced. Nor is the unit as a whole an *announcement* of punishment; that is only one of its elements. To characterize the speech as a prophecy of *disaster* (with Koch) does not do justice to the relationship drawn between the crimes and the future suffering or to the fact that this suffering is presented as the word—and hence the will—of Yahweh himself. Likewise one should be cautious about the use of the term "messenger speech"[34] for the reasons stated above as well as the fact that the messenger formula does not appear. And if one introduces the term "oracle," it should be limited to the final part of the unit, the words which Yahweh himself speaks through the prophet.

Specifically, the *setting* of this unit appears to have been a speaking occasion which involved a prophet and his audience. No narrative tells us that, but the language itself—especially the direct address—reveals it. More broadly, the setting of the genre is the Israelite institution of prophecy. To refer to an institution is not necessarily to link prophets with the cult in the narrow sense of formal worship services and official personnel, nor even to assume articulated rules for group membership. An institution is a social structure which has recognizable traditions and practices. There is sufficient continuity of practices, language, and even self-understanding among the prophets over several centuries to speak of prophetic institutions.

One may also consider the setting of the speech among those who collected, preserved, and handed on the words of Amos. Though there is no

31. Wolff, *Dodekapropheton 2- Joel und Amos*, BKAT 14/2 (1969); James L. Mays, *Amos: A Commentary* (1969); Artur Weiser, *Die Prophetie des Amos*, BZAW 53 (Berlin: Alfred Töpelmann, 1929); T. H. Robinson, HAT 14 (1954[2]).
32. Weiser, BZAW 53, p. 159.
33. With Balla, *Die Droh- und Scheltworte des Amos*.
34. Wolff, BKAT 14/2:109ff.

demonstrable modification of this unit by later editors[35] and evidence for the way this particular speech was used later is lacking, the material did, after all, find its way into a particular place in a book which became Scripture.

How typical is this speech, first of the Book of Amos and then of the prophets generally? Answers to these questions must be based on statistical data. There are, according to the principles employed in isolating Amos 4:1–3, forty-seven units in the Book of Amos which can be taken as independent at one level or another.[36] This number includes, for example, the sub-units in 1:3—2:16, which—apart from the later additions—probably existed together from the beginning. Of these forty-seven units, three are hymnic fragments (4:13; 5:8f.; 9:5f.), five are vision reports (7:1–3, 4–6, 7–9; 8:1–3; 9:1–4), one is a story of prophetic conflict (7:10–17), and one is comprised of the superscription and the book's motto (1:1f.). The remainder (thirty-seven) are speeches or fragments of speeches; furthermore, speeches are included in most of the reporting units (1:2; 7:8f., 16f.; 8:2f.; 9:1–4). But the category "speech" is too broad to be very instructive. What kind of speech is characteristic of prophetic activity and literature?

The speech in 4:1–3 focused upon future events. Of the speeches proper, only five (3:3–8; 4:4f.; 5:6f.; 5:10–13; 5:14f.) fail to announce future events; and in five others (4:6–12; 5:1–3, 18–20; 6:1–3, 4–7) the question of the future orientation is debatable, depending upon questions of interpretation (such as the limits of the units). Furthermore, all of the vision reports as well as the other speeches in reporting contexts either describe or announce the future. In only three cases in the book could the future be seen as conditional (5:6f., 14f.; 9:9f.), and in only three other cases is it a positive future (9:7f. in its present form for Judah; 9:11f., 13–15).

Grammatically, this future is most commonly expressed (twenty-eight units) by means of the waw-consecutive perfect, always at the beginning of clauses, and usually opening the announcement proper.[37] In many instances the imperfect tense is used (twenty-two), but usually also with the waw-consecutive perfect and often following the negative lō'. It is tempting to take all of the clauses beginning with the waw-consecutive perfect as result clauses,[38] but we are on safer ground to designate them as consecutive clauses; that is, each is an announcement or description of some future event which follows a (usually stated) prior event or situation. The important point

---

35. Against John D. W. Watts, "A Critical Analysis of Amos 4:1ff.," in Lane C. McGaughy, ed., *SBL Seminar Papers* 2:491.

36. This number assumes the solution to a great many individual questions. On these and related problems see Klaus Koch and Mitarbeiter, *Amos: Untersucht mit den Methoden einer strukturalen Formgeschichte*, 3 parts, AOAT 30 (Neukirchen-Vluyn: Neukirchener Verlag, 1976).

37. Koch's conclusions that the future is usually expressed either "in a brief sentence in the negative with the verb in the imperfect" or "by means of a participial clause, of which Yahweh is the subject and which is usually introduced by 'behold, (I)'" are contradicted by the evidence in Amos (*The Growth of the Biblical Tradition*, p. 211).

38. Cf. T. H. J. Meek, "Result and Purpose Clauses in Hebrew," *JQR* 46 (1955–56) 40–43.

is this: The prophetic announcement of the future is linked logically to the accusation against the addressees.

This interpretation is borne out by the explicit connections which are drawn between the accusation (or reasons) and the announcement when both appear. In most of these two-part units either "because of" (*'al* or *y'n*) stands before the reasons or the announcement is introduced by "therefore" (*'l-kēn* or *lākēn*).

Amos 4:1–3 has two main parts, the accusation or reasons as prophetic address and the announcement of punishment as Yahweh's words. Most of the addresses in the book which speak of a negative future include both main elements, but another ten of these units have only an announcement. In most of the announcements of punishment, Yahweh himself is the subject of the future act; but as 4:1–3 has shown, passive formulations appear as well (3:9–11, 13; 5:3, 10–13; 7:16f.). In many cases both active and passive expressions occur, conforming in general to Westermann's distinction between the announcement of the intervention of Yahweh and of the results of his intervention.

Is there a distinction between the announcement as Yahweh's word and the reasons or accusation as the prophet's? First it should be emphasized that every single announcement of future events in the book is presented as a speech of Yahweh. This applies to announcements of punishment with or without reasons and announcements of salvation. However, it is not only the announcements proper which appear as Yahweh's words, but in most cases the entire speeches. This is clearly the case in fourteen units, virtually all those which include both reasons and announcement. So our speech in 4:1–3, which seems to distinguish between the reasons as the prophet's words and the announcement as Yahweh's, is an exception. The only other text which seems to follow this pattern is 8:4–8.[39] To answer the question which began this paragraph: The view—widely held since Gunkel and perpetuated in another form by Westermann[40]—that the prophets distinguished between the reproach or reasons as their own reflection and the announcement proper as Yahweh's words must be rejected.

VII

The most common and distinctive genre of prophetic speech is the prophecy. The genre is not defined, or even recognized, by a two- or three-part structure as Westermann and Koch have argued. The analysis of the material

39. The distinction might also be claimed for 7:16f., where the announcement is set off by the messenger formula, but here the entire speech (reasons and announcement) is introduced as "the word of Yahweh." We have left out of this particular consideration those few speeches which do not explicitly announce the future, such as 5:1–2, the woe speeches, and parenetic units. In many such cases there is no clear indication of speaker. Some admonitions seem to come from the prophet (5:6–7, 14–15), while others quote Yahweh (5:4–5).

40. Westermann, *Basic Forms of Prophetic Speech*, pp. 132, 179; cf. p. 83. See Wolff, "Die Begründung der prophetischen Heils- und Unheilssprüche," ZAW 52 (1934) 1–22, reprinted in *Gesammelte Studien zum Alten Testament*, TB 22 (Munich: Chr. Kaiser Verlag, 1964), pp. 9–35.

in Amos has shown that the structure is quite variable, and the situation is even more complex when one moves to the literature as a whole. But there are consistent features which allow us to speak of prophecy as the basic form of prophetic speech. The genre is defined by two factors which appear with regularity: The prophet (1) presents a communication from God (2) announcing future events.

Once the general features of the prophecy have been recognized in the Book of Amos, it becomes clear that the genre—and the understanding of the prophetic role which it reflects—is widespread. The prophetic vocation reports presume that the prophets are Yahweh's spokesmen concerning his future. And while other genres abound, the prophecy as we have defined it occurs with regularity from Amos to Second Isaiah.[41] Moreover, the two characteristics of the prophecy frequently shape the use of other genres.

There is corroboration of this understanding of prophecy in texts which reflect on the office. In Deut. 18:15–22 the prophet is the one who will speak Yahweh's words (since Israel cannot hear his voice directly and still live), and he will be recognized as a true prophet (since many will speak in the name of Yahweh) when what he says comes to pass. That is, the text assumes that both true and false prophets claim to announce the future in Yahweh's name. Deut. 13:1–5 imposes a further test, that of orthodoxy, but still views the prophet as one who announces the future in the name of Yahweh. Likewise Second Isaiah frequently identifies Yahweh as the one who announced or proclaimed (through the prophets) the future and it came to pass (cf. 40:21, 27–28; 42:9; 43:9b, 12; 44:26; 45:21).

Those speeches which announce a negative future may be called prophecies of punishment. This is not a new term, but one which has been used frequently—but often loosely—in the literature.[42] It is necessary to employ a term such as "punishment" to do justice to the content and structure of this prophecy. On the one hand, there is the frequent two-part structure which logically binds the accusation to the announcement in terms of cause and effect. On the other hand, the negative future is not just a disaster (Koch), but a disaster set into motion by Yahweh through his word against specific individuals, groups, or nations.

Not much has been said concerning the other form of the basic genre, the prophecy of salvation. While its structural features vary, it shares the basic characteristic of the prophecy: It announces God's word for the future. A fundamental difference between this genre and its negative counterpart is that the reasons for Yahweh's future activities are not spelled out. Examples are Amos 9:11–12 and 13–15, in which Yahweh speaks in the first person, promising to intervene, and also describes the future in passive formulations (cf. also Isa. 2:2–5; 4:2–6; 7:7–9; Jer. 28:2–4; 33:10–13; 34:4; Mic. 4:1–4; 5:7–9; 5:10–15).

---

41. See, e.g., the texts identified in Westermann, *Basic Forms of Prophetic Speech*, pp. 137, 142ff., 171, 174–75, 176, 179. The list expands dramatically when one adds the prophecies of salvation.

42. Cf. Mays, *Amos*, pp. 23, 40, passim. Wilhelm Rudolph, KAT 13/2:168.

If we were to conclude that the prophetic role was identical to the speaking of "prophecies," we would be going too far. Even in Amos we find more than prophecies as such but even prayers of intercession and a few exhortations calling for the addressees to change. When one looks further in the prophetic literature, the range of possibilities expands. Among others there is Ezekiel's understanding of himself as a watchman for his people (3:16–21). But Ezekiel, as all the other prophets, pronounces prophecies; and he is a watchman concerned with what Yahweh has in store for his people. Fundamental to the prophetic role in Israel was the utterance of God's word for the future.

4

The Canonical Shape
of the Prophetic Literature

Brevard S. Childs

A major literary and theological force was at work in shaping the present form of the Hebrew Bible by which prophetic oracles directed to one generation were fashioned in Sacred Scripture by a canonical process to be used by another generation.

THE DEBATE OVER METHODOLOGY

The study of the prophetic literature of the Old Testament has gone through several important phases within the modern period. One thinks of the development of the methods of literary, form, and redactional criticism, as well as the use of comparative materials from the field of history of religions, psychology, and sociology.[1] From this history of modern research a wide consensus has emerged that the present literature is the product of a long history of development, a portion of which can now be successfully reconstructed through critical methodology. It is also generally agreed that the recovery of this prehistory has greatly illumined the study of the biblical literature by bringing into sharp focus the historical milieu of the prophets and by providing criteria for interpreting the peculiar oral and literary forms in which the message was couched.

However, in my opinion, in spite of some impressive gains, the application of historical-critical methodology has resulted in serious weaknesses in the handling of the biblical literature. First of all, the legacy of the literary-critical method in distinguishing between "genuine" and "non-genuine"

---

1. Cf. the most recent survey of the history of research by Ronald E. Clements, *One Hundred Years of Old Testament Interpretation* (Philadelphia: Westminster Press, 1976), pp. 51–75. Walther Zimmerli's *The Law and the Prophets* (Oxford, 1965) also has some pertinent observations on the history of scholarship. Moreover, the specialized treatments of the major figures remain invaluable: E. Sehmsdorf, *Die Prophetenauslegung bei J. G. Eichhorn* (Göttingen, 1971); H. J. Kraus's interesting analysis of G. H. A. Ewald's contribution to the study of the prophets in *Geschichte der historisch-kritischen Erforschung des Alten Testaments* (Neukirchen: Kreis Moers, Verlag der Buchhandlung des Erziehungsvereins, 1956); Werner Klatt, *Hermann Gunkel: Zu seiner Theologie der Religionsgeschichte und zur Entstehung der formgeschichtlichen Methode* (Göttingen: Vandenhoeck und Ruprecht, 1969).

oracles has continued to interject a pejorative category into the discussion. Secondly, the form-critical analysis has increasingly atomized the literature and continued to rest much of its analysis upon fragile and often highly speculative theories of original settings. Thirdly, the redactional and sociological methods have tended to politicize the biblical material and render it into a type of political propaganda.[2] As a result, little success has been achieved in interpreting the prophetic books as Scripture of the church which accords to the Bible an authoritative role in the formation of the Christian life.

The purpose of this essay is to suggest a different approach to the biblical material, which I shall try to illustrate in terms of the prophets. It begins with the recognition that a major literary and theological force was at work in shaping the present form of the Hebrew Bible. This force was exerted during most of the history of the literature's formation, but increasingly in the postexilic period exercised its influence in the collecting, selecting, and ordering of the biblical traditions in such a way as to allow the material to function as authoritative Scripture for the Jewish community. In the transmission process, tradition, which once arose in a particular milieu and addressed various historical situations, was shaped in such a way as to serve as a normative expression of God's will to later generations of Israel who had not shared in those original historical events. In sum, prophetic oracles which were directed to one generation were fashioned into Sacred Scripture by a canonical process to be used by another generation.

The reason for treating the final form of Scripture with such seriousness lies in the peculiar relationship between text and people of God which is constitutive of canon. The shape of the biblical text reflects a history of encounter between God and Israel. Canon serves to describe this unique relationship and to define the scope of this history by establishing an end to the process. It assigns a special quality to this particular segment of history which is deemed normative for all future generations of this community of faith. The significance of the final form of the biblical literature is that it alone bears witness to the full history of revelation. Within the Old Testament neither the process of the formation nor the history of its canonization is assigned an independent integrity. These dimensions have been either lost or purposely blurred. Rather, canon asserts that the witness to Israel's experience with God is testified to in the effect on the biblical text itself. It is only in the final form of the biblical text in which the normative history has reached an end that the full effect of this revelatory history can be perceived.

Certainly earlier stages in the development of the biblical tradition were often regarded as canonical prior to the establishment of the final form. In fact, the final form frequently consists of an earlier, received form of the

---

2. Examples of this approach can be found in the works of Otto Plöger, *Theocracy and Eschatology*, trans. S. Rudman (Richmond: John Knox Press, 1968); Morton Smith, *Palestinian Parties and Politics That Shaped the Old Testament* (New York: Columbia University Press, 1971); P. D. Hanson, *The Dawn of Apocalyptic: The Historical and Sociological Roots of Jewish Apocalyptic Eschatology* (Philadelphia: Fortress Press, 1975).

tradition which has been transmitted unchanged from its original setting. But to take canon seriously is also to take seriously the critical function which it exercises in respect to the earlier stages of the literature's formation. A critical judgment is exercised in the way in which the earlier stages are handled. At times the material is passed on, complete with all of its original historical particularity. At other times the canonical process selects, rearranges, or expands the received traditions. The purpose of insisting on the authority of the final form is to preserve the canon's role of providing this critical norm. To work with the final stage of the text is not to lose the historical dimension, but rather it is to provide a critical theological judgment regarding the process. A reconstructed depth dimension may aid in understanding the interpreted text, but it does not possess an independent integrity for the exegetical task within the context of the canon.

Then again, the final form of the text performs a crucial hermeneutical function in establishing the peculiar profile of a passage. Its shaping establishes an order in highlighting certain features and subordinating others, in drawing elements to the foreground, and in pushing others to the background. To work with the final form is to resist any method which seeks critically to shift the canonical ordering. Such an exegetical move occurs when an overarching category such as *Heilsgeschichte* subordinates the unique canonical profile, or when an historical or rhetorical reconstruction attempts to refocus the picture according to its own standards of historical accuracy or literary aesthetics.

The canonical process was not simply an external valorization of successive stages of literary development, but was an integral part of the literary process. Beginning in the preexilic era, and increasing in significance in the postexilic era, a canonical force was unleashed by Israel's religious use of the traditions which resulted in a collecting, selecting, and ordering process. The motivations behind the canonical process were diverse and seldom discussed in the biblical material itself. However, a major concern was that a tradition from the past be transmitted in such a way that its authoritative claim was laid upon all future generations of Israel.

It is an axiom of many redactional critics that the layering within a biblical book derives from a desire to "update" an original tradition. While this description occasionally applies, the canonical approach to the Old Testament offers a very different model of interpreting the growth of multilayered texts. The major issue turns on how one understands the process by which a biblical text is actualized. It is constitutive of the canonical process that texts have been shaped to provide the community of faith with guidelines for its appropriation. The hermeneutical task of actualizing past traditions for each successive generation lies at the heart of the process. Theological reflection on its actualization has been built into the structure of the canonical text. The modern hermeneutical impasse has arisen in large measure by disregarding the canonical shaping. The usual critical methodology of restoring an original historical setting often involves stripping away the very elements which constitute the canonical shape. Little wonder that once the text has been

anchored in the historical past by "decanonizing" it, the interpreter has
difficulty applying it to a modern religious context!

THE CANONICAL SHAPING
OF THE PROPHETS

The effect of the canonical shaping of the prophetic literature reveals an
enormous variety in the manner by which the traditions were rendered as
Sacred Scripture. A few examples from the canonical process can be sketched
briefly:

1. An original prophetic message was expanded by being placed in a
larger theological context. The Book of Amos provides a classic example of
this frequent canonical move. An important problem within the Book of
Amos turns on how to interpret the sudden shift from a message of total
judgment of Israel to one of promise for Israel in chapter 9. Often the shift in
tone has been understood as an attempt to soften Amos' harsh message by a
later generation who was either offended at the severity or who tried to make
room for the later restoration of Judah. However, the editors of chapter 9 did
not soften Amos' message of total judgment against sinful Israel by allowing a
remnant to escape. The destruction is fully confirmed (9:9–11). Rather, the
tradents effected a canonical shaping by placing Amos' words in a broader,
eschatological framework which transcended the historical perspective of the
prophet. From God's perspective there is hope beyond the destruction seen
by Amos. The effect of chapter 9 is both to confirm the truth of Amos' original
prophecy and to encompass it within the larger theological perspective of
divine will which includes hope and final redemption. To distinguish between genuine and non-genuine oracles is to run in the face of the canon's
intent.

2. The shaping process changed the level on which the original prophecy
functioned in order to afford the witness a new metaphorical role. The
original message of Hosea was directed to the inhabitants of the Northern
Kingdom in the mid-eighth century. The prophet's word constituted a sustained attack on Israel's syncretistic religious worship which had changed the
worship of Yahweh into a fertility cult. Hosea appropriated the language of
his opponents to claim all the areas of fertility, land, and kinship for Yahweh,
Israel's faithful lover. The sign acts of chapter 1 functioned as a history-
creating act of divine judgment which actualized the threat in the giving of
names of judgment. But in its collected form the original material has been
arranged to reflect an important hermeneutical shift on the function of
Hosea's witness. The prophet's realistic language is now understood metaphorically. Regardless of the prehistory behind the sign acts in chapters 1
and 3, the present shape of these chapters has given the material a symbolic
interpretation. It is quite impossible to reconstruct a history of Hosea's
marriage from these two chapters. Rather, the intent that the sign acts be
understood metaphorically is made explicit in both chapters 1 and 3 (cf. 1:2,
4f., 6f., 9; 3:1, 4, 5). Moreover, the placing of chapter 2 as an extended

metaphor in between these two chapters provides the editor's symbolic key for interpreting them.

3. A collection of prophetic material has been detached from its original historical moorings and subordinated to a new theological context. The classic example of this canonical move is so-called "Second Isaiah." Critical scholarship has made out a convincing case for dating chapters 40—55 (some scholars include the remaining chapters of the book as well) to the period of the Babylonian exile. Yet in their present canonical position these chapters have been consciously loosened from their original setting and placed within the context of the eighth-century prophet, Isaiah of Jerusalem. Moreover, the original historical background of the exilic prophet has been drained of its historical particularity—Cyrus has become a theological construct almost indistinguishable from Abraham (cf. Kissane)—and the prophetic message has been rendered suitable for use by later generations by transmitting it as a purely eschatological word.

4. A body of prophetic tradition has been edited in the light of a larger body of canonical literature. From the perspective of literary criticism, the message of Jeremiah has been cloaked in the later prosaic language of the Deuteronomic school. But from a canonical perspective, Jeremiah's words have been preserved in conjunction with a commentary which sought to understand his ministry as part of a chain of divine messengers who were loyal to the law of Moses and who warned of Jerusalem's coming destruction. Thus, the ordering of Jeremiah's message within the tradition of the preachers of the law provides the later community with a prophetic interpretation of how the law properly functions within the divine economy.

Closely allied with this move is the dovetailing of traditions from the oracles of Isaiah and Micah (cf. Isa. 2:1–4 and Mic. 4:1–4). From an historical perspective one could argue for a common circle of tradents who transmitted both sets of tradition. But from a canonical perspective the effect of the process is to provide each prophetic book with a commentary in the light of which a mutual enrichment is to be drawn.

5. By means of a radical theocentric focus in the ordering of a book, the original historical sequence of a prophet's message was subordinated to a new theological function. The Book of Nahum is introduced by a hymn; the Book of Habakkuk concludes with one. But the effect on the material is similar. This shaping process did not require a dehistoricizing of the original oracles. Rather, the material was left virtually untouched; yet a new role was assigned the oracles. They now function as a dramatic illustration of the eschatological triumph of God—whose divine nature is celebrated in a hymn—over his adversaries. In Nahum the destruction of the enemy is explicitly derived from the nature of God—a "jealous God," "avenging and wrathful," "keeping wrath for the enemy"—who claims dominion over the entire world. The threat against Ninevah does not stem from the personal hatred of a Hebrew prophet against Assyria, nor is it evoked by some particular historical event of the seventh century. Rather, the biblical tradents use the initial psalm, even shattering its earlier acrostic form, to establish the true theological

context for understanding the prophecy. Ninevah has become a type of a larger recurring phenomenon in history against which God exercises his eternal power and judgment.

The prophecy of Ezekiel has continued to baffle its readers. The book appears to lack the sharp contours of a definite geographical locality with a concrete group of hearers. The prophet oscillates back and forth between Babylon and Jerusalem. The traditional forms of prophetic oral speech are largely missing; but the book abounds in allegory, sign acts, and visions. Surely the canonical key to understanding this unusual book lies in the radical theocentric perspective of the prophet which has deeply affected its final literary shape. Thus even when his oracles are fixed within a chronological framework, these temporal moorings are immediately transcended when the prophet testifies to the plan of God in terms freed from any such human limitations. Similarly the spatial distinction between Babylon and Jerusalem is completely relativized whenever the people of God are viewed from the divine perspective as one entity.

6. The original prophetic message was placed within a rule-of-faith which provided the material with an interpretative guideline. It is generally recognized by critical scholarship that two appendices have been fixed to the conclusion of the Book of Malachi. To dismiss these verses as a "legalistic corrective" stemming from some disgruntled priestly editor is to misunderstand the canonical process utterly. Rather, the first appendix reminds the whole nation that it still stands under the tradition of Moses. The imperative to "remember the law of my servant Moses" does not weaken Malachi's attack on the nation's sins, but it sets a check against any misuse of the prophet's words which would call into question national solidarity in the name of additional requirements for the pious. The canonical effect of the first appendix to Malachi testifies that the law and the prophets are not to be heard as rivals but as an essential unity within the one divine purpose. The effect of the second appendix (4:5–6) is to balance the memory of the past with the anticipation of the future.

In a similar way, the ending on the Book of Ecclesiastes is another example of a rule-of-faith which would also order a wisdom book from a perspective informed by God's commandments (12:13) and the coming judgment (v. 14).

7. Oracles which originally functioned in a variety of historical settings have been arranged into set patterns which serve a new typological role in relation to the coming rule of God. The clearest examples of a patterning schema are the alternative blocks of oracles of judgment and salvation in the Books of Isaiah (compare 1:1–31; 2:6–22; 3:1–26, with 2:1–5; 4:2–6) and Micah (cf. chaps. 1; 2; 6 with 2:12f.; 4; 5). The effect of this move is that a typological sequence subordinates the original historical one and refocuses the material on the dominant theological purposes undergirding all prophetic proclamation.

8. Prophetic symbolism has been given a radical new eschatological interpretation by shifting the referent within the original oracles. Scholars have long recognized that the visions in Zechariah 1—6 appear once to have

functioned independently of each other and to have been addressed to particular historical situations both preceding and following the return from the exile (cf. Galling). But the tension between the original visions and their present framework points to an intentional theological shaping. The prophetic visions of Zechariah are now set in the second year of Darius, that is to say, some twenty years after the return from Babylon. The deliverance from the exile now lies in the past. Although the traditional language of the second exodus from slavery has been retained, it has been given a new reference. The language of hope now points to a still future event in which Israel's redemption lies. The original focus has been eschatologized and projected once more into the future. The community of faith which lies after the return still anticipates the future in the language of the past. Israel will still "flee from the land of the north," "escape to Zion," and God will dwell in her midst (3:6ff.).

The Book of Joel offers another example of a radical eschatologizing of an original oracle (chaps. 1—2) which had only faintly adumbrated the full dimension of the End in the locust plague, but Israel learned to understand it as the prelude to the Day of Yahweh when God would hold the final assize (chap. 3).

To summarize, these examples of canonical shaping of the prophetic literature in the history of ordering Israel's tradition as Scripture do not begin to exhaust the richness of Old Testament interpretation, but at least they give a hint of the creative dimension involved in the collecting process.

THEOLOGICAL IMPLICATIONS OF THE CANONICAL SHAPING

1. The task of Old Testament exegesis is the interpretation of the canonical text as it has been shaped in the history of Israel's experience with God. The prophetic books show many signs of growth in their composition and different layers are often discernible. But the tradents of the tradition have sought to hide their own footprints in order to focus attention on the canonical text itself and not on the process. The content of the prophets' message is first and foremost a theocentric word. Concern with Israel's own identity is always secondary and derivative from a prior understanding of God.

2. Since the Reformation period there has been a tendency among Protestants, especially from the Reformed wing, to deprecate tradition as a threat to the integrity of the divine word; however, Scripture and tradition belong together. The active participation of the tradents in transmitting and shaping the biblical witness in no way calls into question its divine source. Rather, Israel registered the word of the prophets along with its own reception and saw in both the Spirit of God at work. To speak of the Bible as canon is to emphasize its function as the Word of God in the context of the worshiping community of faith. The canon seeks to preserve the authority of the whole witness and to resist all attempts to assign varying degrees of theological

value to the different layers of Scripture on the basis of literary or historical judgments.

3. To assume that the prophets can be understood only if each oracle is related to a specific event or located in its original cultural milieu is to introduce a major hermeneutical confusion into the discipline and to render an understanding of the canonical Scripture virtually impossible.[3] Rather, the true referent of the biblical witness can only be comprehended from within the biblical literature itself. In the ongoing experience of Israel, as the addressee of God's judgment and redemption, the divine purpose with his creation is revealed. Canon sets the parameters to this unique history which has both a beginning and an end.

4. Biblical texts are made relevant to today's community of faith and to the world, not by first decanonizing them in a claim of establishing an original setting, but by faithfully hearing the intent of the literature which has already been shaped to confront its hearers with the divine imperative. Canon serves as a guarantee that the biblical material has not been collected for antiquarian reasons, but as an eternal Word of God laying claim on each new generation.

5. Any attempt to write a theology of the prophets which disregards the canonical shaping, whether in a search for the prophets' *verba ipsissima* or in a pursuit after prophetic self-understanding, can only end up with a formulation which has little to do with the prophets of the Old Testament. Thus even if it were possible to reconstruct an original Amos, the portrayal would have little in common with the prophetic message which both the synagogue and church heard from his book.

6. Much of the problem of understanding the New Testament's use of the Old Testament prophets lies in the failure to take seriously the canonical perspective held in common by both Jews and Christians of the first century. Thus, the New Testament understands "Second Isaiah's" message eschatologically as the proclamation of the immanent fulfillment of the promised new age. It interprets Joel's vision in the radical eschatological terms of the kingdom. It hears Hosea's promise of a divine reconciliation in which God restores to himself a new people. It is quite impossible to read the Old Testament prophets through the eyes of Duhm and Hölscher and yet understand what the New Testament is hearing in the Old!

7. A final word is in order regarding the effect of canon on the larger exegetical enterprise of interpreting the Old Testament. The approach which I am advocating has been described by others as "canonical criticism."[4] I am not happy with this term because it implies that the concern with canon is viewed as another historical-critical technique which can take its place alongside of source criticism, form criticism, rhetorical criticism, and the

---

3. Hans Frei's critique of a referential reading of the Bible which emerged in the eighteenth century and gained hegemony in the nineteenth marks a major advance in biblical hermeneutics (cf. *The Eclipse of Biblical Narrative* [New Haven: Yale University Press, 1974]).

4. To my knowledge the term first appeared in J. A. Sanders's *Torah and Canon* (Philadelphia: Fortress Press, 1972).

like. I do not envision the approach to canon in this light. Rather, the issue at stake in canon turns on establishing a stance from which the Bible is to be read as Sacred Scripture.

The concern with canon plays both a negative and a positive role in delineating the scope of biblical exegesis. On the one hand, its negative role consists in relativizing the priority claims of the historical-critical method. It strongly resists the assumption that every biblical text must first be filtered through an established historical-critical mesh before one can even start the task of interpretation. On the other hand, its positive role seeks to challenge the interpreter to look closely at the text in its received form, and then critically to discern its function for a community of faith. Attention to canon establishes certain boundaries within which the tradition was placed. The canonical shaping serves not so much to fix a given meaning to a particular passage as to chart the arena in which the exegetical task is to be carried out. Attention to canon is not the end but only the beginning of exegesis. It prepares the stage for the real performance by clearing away unnecessary distractions and directing the audience's attention to the main show which is about to be experienced.

In one sense the canonical approach sets limits to the exegetical task by taking seriously the traditional parameters. In another sense the method seeks aggressively to liberate the interpreter. By insisting on viewing the exegetical task as constructive as well as descriptive, the interpreter is forced to confront the authoritative text of Scripture in an ongoing theological reflection. By placing the canonical text within the context of the community of faith, a variety of different exegetical models, such as the liturgical or dramatic, are freed to engage the text. In sum, the canon establishes a platform from which exegesis is launched rather than a barrier by which creative theological struggle is cut off.

5

The Unity of
the Book of Isaiah

R. E. CLEMENTS

The connection between the prophecies of Isaiah and the subsequent destruction of Jerusalem provides the essential clue to understanding the unity of this prophetic book.

The Book of Isaiah comes to us as a single literary whole, comprising sixty-six chapters, and this given datum of the form of the book must be regarded as a feature requiring explanation. It establishes a basis for the interpretation of the individual sayings and units of which it is made up and provides a literary context which must inevitably affect the interpretation of the several parts of the whole. Furthermore modern critical scholarship has become accustomed to the working principle that the long process of formation of such an ancient literary text reflects a number of levels of interpretation. The examination of features relating to the editorial structure of the book carries with it a number of important considerations and expectations regarding the situations to which its sayings were related and, not least, to the delicate task of establishing some reasonably convincing chronology of the origin of its various component parts. At times we may assume that the literary order of the collection of prophetic sayings points to varying stages in the chronological order of their inclusion in the overall collection. At other times, however, it appears probable that the order has been determined by editorial considerations in which certain literary and theological interests must be postulated in order to account for the positioning of the material. It is several years since Georg Fohrer drew attention to the importance of this factor in accounting for the distinctive structure of Isaiah 1, which has been put together in order to provide a general thematic introduction to the book.[1] It is largely built up from authentic Isaianic sayings, but these must certainly have appeared originally in different parts of the collection where their historical setting would have been more clearly apparent. As it is, their

---

1. Georg Fohrer, "Jesaja 1 als Zusammenfassung der Verkündigung Jesajas," ZAW 74 (1962) 251–80; see *Studien zur alttestamentlichen Prophetie*, BZAW 99 (Berlin: Alfred Töpelmann, 1967), pp. 148–66.

extant form establishes a broad appeal for repentance, rather than pointing to a particular historical epoch of the ministry of the prophet Isaiah.

In an earlier age of scholarship the opening reference (Isa. 1:1) to "Isaiah the son of Amoz" was taken to indicate that all of the prophecies which it contains were given in the eighth century B.C. A few commentators have continued to defend such an assumption, seeking to relate each of them to the ministry and thought of the great prophet of Jerusalem.[2] Yet the development of a historical-critical method of analysis has shown that only by doing violence to a reasoned and meaningful interpretation of many passages can such an assumption be defended. By the time of the publication in 1892 of B. Duhm's classic commentary on the book[3] all the evidence that is reasonably necessary for the task of literary-critical analysis had been assembled to show that the contents of chapters 40—55 must be ascribed almost entirely to the era of the Babylonian exile in the sixth century B.C. and the contents of chapters 56—66 must be later still. As a consequence the ascription of these sections to a Deutero-Isaiah and Trito-Isaiah respectively has been adopted by a number of scholars. Especially in the case of chapters 40—55 their interpretation has been undertaken with little or no consideration for their setting within the book as a whole. More recently some attempts have been advanced to relate chapters 56—66 to the preceding chapters 40—55, with a consequent questioning of the hypothesis of a "Trito-Isaiah,"[4] but little at all to explain their connection with chapters 1—39. For the most part the Book of Isaiah has been interpreted as comprised of two separate parts which bear little real relationship to each other. Frequently it has not even been felt necessary to explain how these two parts came to be linked, and when this has been forthcoming it has taken the form of an argument based on literary convenience. It is argued that a leather scroll would be of a certain length, and it would be an economic necessity to make full use of this. Later prophecies might therefore be added in order to fill up a scroll with little concern for the mutual relationships of the content of the various sayings, save in the broadest possible way.

A second possibility, however, has at times been aired by scholars, based upon an argument put forward by the Norwegian scholar Sigmund Mowinckel.[5] This is that the book as a whole should be regarded as the work of "Isaiah's disciples" (cf. Isa. 8:16), so that the unnamed prophets who stand behind chapters 40—66 should be claimed as, in some sense, the disciples of

2. Cf. O. T. Allis, *The Unity of Isaiah: A Study in Prophecy* (Philadelphia: Presbyterian and Reformed Pub. Co., 1950). Reprinted in 1972, distributed by Baker Book House, Grand Rapids.

3. Bernhard Duhm, *Das Buch Jesaja*, HKAT 3/1 (Göttingen: Vandenhoeck und Ruprecht, 1892, 1902, 1968[5]).

4. Cf. James D. Smart, *History and Theology in Second Isaiah: A Commentary on Isaiah 35; 40—66* (Philadelphia: Westminster Press, 1965). J. L. McKenzie, *Second Isaiah: Introduction, Translation, and Notes* (Garden City, N. Y.: Doubleday & Co., 1968).

5. Sigmund Mowinckel, *Jesaja-disiplene: Profeten fra Jesaja til Jeremia* (Oslo: Forlagt AV. H. Aschhoug & Co. [W. Nygaard], 1925).

the earlier Isaiah of Jerusalem.[6] The argument here is essentially an adaptation of the earlier assumption that the unity of the book is based upon a
certain unity of authorship, with the modification that the author is no longer
a single individual but rather a "school," or body of "disciples." Their
existence over a period of at least two centuries is postulated without any
clear identification of where, or how, such a group maintained itself. The
argument in fact rapidly becomes completely circular in that the existence of
such a group is attested from the book, the structure of which is assumed to
be illuminated by the identification of such disciples. The value of such a
hypothesis, therefore, becomes gravely vitiated in the absence of any clear
indication of what constituted membership of such a body of prophetic
disciples. We have no information to confirm that such a circle actually
existed, and to postulate their existence for such a long period of time after
the original prophet's death renders the concept of a "disciple" virtually
meaningless. What entitled a later figure to claim to be such a disciple, and
how far could such a later figure introduce new prophecies of his own
alongside the task of preserving and interpreting those of the original master? In the end such a hypothesis seems almost exclusively designed to
defend the assumption that the unity of the book can be explained as based
upon a form of community authorship. If the historical evidence is so
overwhelmingly clear that the book cannot be understood as the product of a
single author, then it is assumed that it can nonetheless still be defended as
the work of a single identifiable group of authors. Mowinckel himself, who
did not in his later work develop this suggestion concerning the circle of
Isaiah's disciples, understood the hypothesis in so broad a compass as to
separate it from the composition of the Book of Isaiah. Such "disciples" were
held to have been so central a group in the formation of the Old Testament as
to have composed a significant number of psalms, the Decalogue, and the
Book of Deuteronomy. In other words they were identified by him as a major
circle of Jerusalem scribes and legislators.

In reality, however, it is not the questionable character of the hypothesis
concerning Isaiah's disciples that should concern us, but rather the questionable nature of the assumption that the unity of the Book of Isaiah is to be
explained somehow as a unity based on authorship. When we look at the
Book of Isaiah as it now exists, we can discover a considerable number of
indications that it has been assembled over a long period, but with a very
clear concern to group prophecies in a thematic fashion. This is most noticeable, for example, in the case of the "Babylon" prophecies of Isa. 13:1—
14:23 where we have a whole series of separate prophecies brought together
under the general heading of Israel's encounter with Babylon, dating from
the eighth to the sixth centuries B.C.[7] Whether any of the prophecies derived
from the eighth-century figure of Isaiah of Jerusalem is uncertain, but it is

6. Cf. D. R. Jones, "The Tradition of the Oracles of Isaiah of Jerusalem," ZAW 67 (1975) 226–
46.

7. For more detailed exegesis of the contents of these chapters reference may be made to my
commentary Isaiah 1—39, New Century Bible (Grand Rapids: Wm. B. Eerdmans, 1980).

quite certain that most of them did not. What is clear, however, is that Judah's political involvement with the neo-Babylonian empire began during the period of Isaiah's ministry, as the narrative incident recounted shows (chap. 39). This was eventually to lead to the political submission of Judah to Babylonian power and the destruction of the temple of Jerusalem and the cessation of the rule of the Davidic monarchy from there. The sequence of "Babylon" prophecies (13:1—14:23) is then to be explained as a kind of commentary on Judah's fortunes vis à vis Babylon over a period of two centuries, rather than as the work of a single author. In a not dissimilar fashion we can see that the attempt on the part of editors to build up an extensive group of prophecies concerning foreign nations and cities (13—23) marks a related attempt to establish a measure of editorial unity and connectedness. What we see to be the case in regard to the Babylonian prophecies (13—14) is, in a larger and more complex fashion, true of the book as a whole. Where these two chapters reflect Israel's fortunes at the hands of the neo-Babylonian empire, the book as a whole covers the wider political fortunes of Israel from the eighth to the fifth centuries B.C. Possibly a few prophecies are to be dated later still, but in all essentials the main contents belong to the period of just over two centuries which began with the prophet Isaiah's call in 737 or 736 B.C.

When we look at the literary structure of the sixty-six chapters some considerations stand out with relative clarity. In the first place, chapters 36—39 have evidently been taken from the corresponding sections in 2 Kings 18—20, with the main addition of Hezekiah's psalm (38:9–20).[8] They have been inserted before chapter 40 at a relatively late stage in the compilation of the book and thereby assist the reader in making the transition from the "Assyrian" part of the book (1—35) to the "Babylonian" part (40—66). In fact the report of the visit of the Babylonian emissaries to Hezekiah (chap. 39) makes a very convenient transition to this Babylonian background by introducing the question of what is to be the fate of Jerusalem and its Davidic monarchy in the face of the threat posed by Babylon. Such a conclusion becomes all the more convincing once we recognize that chapter 35, with its theme of the transformation of the wilderness and the appearance of a highway in it for the return of Yahweh's people to Zion, is basically a summarized "digest" of the main content of the prophecies of chapters 40—55.[9] In other words it makes a suitable conclusion for the first half of the book by introducing an abbreviated summary of the message of hope which occupies the second half.

All of these considerations are sufficient to indicate that the overall structure of the book shows signs of editorial planning and that, at some stage in its growth, attempts were made to read and interpret the book as a whole.

---

8. Compare my exegesis of these narratives in *Isaiah and the Deliverance of Jerusalem: A Study of the Interpretation of Prophecy in the Old Testament*, JSOTSup 13 (Sheffield: University of Sheffield, 1980), pp. 52ff.

9. This point was made by Heinrich H. Graetz, "Isaiah xxxiv and xxxv," *JOR* 4 (1891) 1–8; cf. also M. Pope, "Isaiah 34 in Relation to Isaiah 35; 40—66," *JBL* 71 (1952) 235–43.

There are also many indications, however, to show that the contents of the book have passed through a number of stages of ordering and redaction and that what we now have is the result of a process of editing and addition. It would be possible to suppose therefore that the kind of editorial unity which now binds chapters 1—39 with chapters 40—66 belongs to a late, and relatively superficial, stage in the book's compilation. Yet this appears unlikely. There is evidence which suggests that an overall unity is a prominent feature of the book as a whole. In the first place it is not just in chapter 35 that the message of chapters 40—55 is introduced into the earlier part in order to balance out the predominantly threatening note of chapters 1—35. There are earlier, similar summarizing assurances of the return of Yahweh's people to Zion (11:12–16; 19:23; 27:12–13), which are based upon the prophecies from chapter 40 on. Even more strikingly, a promise is made (18:7) that the people of Ethiopia will bring gifts to Yahweh's people in Zion, which must certainly have been taken from the prophetic promise given in Isaiah 45:14. Brief as such sayings are, their location and their character point to a clear and concerted attempt to provide certain interim summaries of the overall message of hope so that the separate parts of the book may be appropriately rounded off.

More important than the existence of these brief summaries, however, is the further fact that the overall structure of chapters 1—35 is an unusually complex one, so far as its chronological growth is concerned. By comparison, chapters 40—55 provide the longest single coherent block of prophecies in the whole book. Any process of literary agglomeration, such as is usually postulated, whereby later material was simply added on at the end of an established literary collection, fails to account for the structure of this material. Whereas chapters 40—55 form a reasonably coherent and unified whole, which are usually dated with confidence in the period of 546–538 B.C., chapters 56—66 are much less clearly to be assigned to so compact a historical period. Nevertheless, even here, it is highly likely that the various sayings are in a rough chronological sequence and that all are to be dated later than chapters 40—55.[10] This is certainly not so with chapters 1—35, however, where not only do we have sayings which are clearly dependent on the contents of chapters 40—66, but other indications show us that it is within these chapters that we have the latest parts of the book. Most notably chapters 24—27, which are often described as the "Isaiah Apocalypse," must belong to the Persian period and are to be understood as a very late section.[11] Moreover, these chapters should certainly not be regarded as forming a self-contained unit which can be read in isolation from the rest of the book. Rather, they can be better interpreted as a late apocalyptic

---

10. The distinctive role of these chapters in relation to Deutero-Isaiah and the development of apocalyptic is examined in Paul D. Hanson, *The Dawn of Apocalyptic* (Philadelphia: Fortress Press, 1975), pp. 32ff. Cf. also J. Vermeylen, *Du Prophete Isaïe à l'apocalyptique: Isaïe i—xxxv, miroir d'un demi-millenaire d'expérience religieuse en Israel* (Paris, 1977), 2:449–517.

11. Cf. Otto Plöger, *Theocracy and Eschatology*, Eng. trans. S. Rudman (Oxford, 1968), pp. 53–78.

recasting and development of earlier prophetic images and themes. This is fully borne out by the large number of references and allusions which are to be found in them, drawn from earlier prophecies.[12] Most prominent in this respect is the New Song of the Vineyard of 27:2–5,[13] which undoubtedly alludes to the earlier Song of the Vineyard (5:1–7). Unfortunately the textual problems and difficulties of Isaiah 27:2–5 prevent a very full and clear comparison between the two songs, the first of which is undoubtedly a complex allegory, or *māshāl*. Noteworthy too is the fact that the allegorical interpretation of the theme "thorns and briars" (27:4) has been taken from 5:6 by way of a whole sequence of intervening interpretations which are to be found elsewhere in the book (Isa. 7:23–25; 10:17; 32:13). However, the indications are sufficiently firm and impressive to show that there is material present in chapters 1—35 which points to a process of adaptation, reinterpretation, and development in the buildup of the book.

Within recent years two major works have been devoted to the study of the redactional history of Isaiah 1—35.[14] At some stage chapters 36—39 were added to this earlier Isaianic collection, but if we follow the indications which we have already noted, it would appear most probable that this step was taken at a time when much of the material of chapters 40 and following had already been joined to this earlier prophetic book. Recent study of chapters 56—66 has tended to reinforce the awareness that these chapters are closely related to chapters 40—55, even though it is highly improbable that they derive from the same prophetic author. Rather, they belong to the period of the late sixth and early fifth centuries B.C. when the restoration of religious and political life was taking place in Judah under Persian imperial supervision. To that extent these chapters highlight the way in which the promises and rich assurances given by the exilic prophet of chapters 40—55 began to take effect. The connection of chapters 56—66 with 40—55 can therefore be regarded as certain and clear, whether the chronological gap which separates these two parts was a very wide one or a narrow one. All of this shows that the major question about the unity of the Book of Isaiah concerns the relationship of chapters 40—55 with 1—35. It could be that this relationship is a relatively late feature which emerged only when the separate collections of material were fairly close to their present shape. On the other hand, since we have already been able to note a number of passages in chapters 1—35 which show a literary dependence upon some of the themes of the subsequent chapters, it may well be that we can discover some clues to suggest that the linking of the prophecies of chapters 40 and following with the tradition of Isaiah's prophecies belongs more fundamentally to the structure of the book.

---

12. Cf. Hans Wildberger, *Jesaja*, BKAT 10/2 (Neukirchen-Vluyn: Neukirchener Verlag des Erziehungsvereins, 1965–72), pp. 910.

13. Cf. Edmond Jacob, "Du premier au deuxième chant de la vigne du prophete Esaïe: Reflexions sur Esaïe 27, 2–5," in *Wort - Gebot - Glaube: Festschrift W. Eichrodt zum 80 Geburtstag*, ATANT 59 (Zurich, 1970) 325–30.

14. Cf. Hermann Barth, *Die Jesaja-Worte in der Josiazeit*, WMANT 48 (Neukirchen-Vluyn: Neukirchener Velag, 1977); also Vermeylen's study, *Du prophete Isaïe à l'apocalyptique*.

Perhaps more important even than this, however, is the recognition that careful examination may be able to show the basis of the connection between the two main parts of the book. That a difference of authorship and of historical setting lies between what we have called rather loosely the "Assyrian" and the "Babylonian" parts of the book is undoubted. Only a very forced and artificial mode of exegesis can associate the prophecies of these chapters directly with the person of Isaiah, whose latest prophecies must be dated very shortly after 701 B.C. The most likely conclusion for us to draw from these facts is that, at some stage in the growth and compilation of the book, the contents of the prophetic message of chapters 40 and following were felt to be an appropriate, and even necessary, complement to the message given earlier in chapters 1—35.

It is not necessary here to reexamine the contentions of those scholars who have sought to trace the collecting, preserving, and editing of the prophetic sayings of Isaiah of Jerusalem whose ministry spanned the years between 737–701 B.C. These were the years of Assyrian imperial expansion and aggression which brought an effective end to the old Northern Kingdom of Ephraim (cf. esp. Isa. 9:8–21; 5:24–25) and which left a much reduced Kingdom of Judah as a small surviving vassal kingdom under Assyrian rule (cf. Isa. 1:8). The central message of Isaiah therefore was concerned with the circumstances and reasons for this political ruination; and it was very rightly addressed, in the first instance, to the sister kingdoms of Israel and Judah. Israel and Judah formed Yahweh's vineyard, which had proved unprofitable and which was now about to be laid waste (Isa. 5:1–7). The Song of the Vineyard therefore quite appropriately serves as an introduction to the prophet's message and must once have formed an introduction to a primary collection of his prophecies which is now included in the unit 5:1—14:27. Undoubtedly, a number of additions have been made to this, but we can detect that it began with a warning of the arrival of the Assyrians (5:26–30) and concluded with an assurance of their eventual demise (14:24–27).

That Isaiah had foretold the eventual overthrow of the Assyrians and the removal of the threat which they posed to Yahweh's people Israel (Isa. 10:5–15) appears certain, even though the elaboration of this prophetic assurance of the overthrow of the Assyrians appears to have been undertaken later, building on the prophet's own language.[15] This is the main thrust of the argument presented by Hermann Barth for recognizing a Josianic anti-Assyrian redaction of a collection of Isaiah's prophecies.[16] Since the thesis proposed by Barth has now been widely described and discussed, it is not necessary to examine its major contentions at this stage. It is sufficient simply to note that it sets out a very strong case for recognizing that a major written collection of Isaiah's prophecies was extant before the death of King Josiah in 609 B.C., and that this prophetic corpus was edited and shaped in such a way as to show how Yahweh's purpose had been fulfilled vis-à-vis

---

15. Cf. my *Isaiah and the Deliverance of Jerusalem*, pp. 41ff.
16. Cf. Barth, *Die Jesaja-Worte*.

Israel and the Assyrians in judgment and eventual deliverance and vindication. All of this renders it perfectly possible and feasible that the great unnamed prophet of Isaiah 40—55, who appeared with a message of hope during the latter years of the Babylonian exile, could have known and made allusion to the earlier prophetic collection now embedded in Isaiah 1—35.

Such a conclusion is argued in a rather brief fashion by J. F. Sawyer.[17] It must certainly be regarded as a possibility, although it is by no means a necessary conclusion. Apart from the rather indecisive arguments put forward by Sawyer, two individual considerations should be noted. The first of these concerns the much discussed question of the identification of the "former things" to which the prophet refers (Isa. 42:9; 48:3). It must be held as possible that by such references the prophet was alluding to earlier prophecies of judgment upon Israel, Judah, and Jerusalem which had been fulfilled.[18] That these were specifically the subject of earlier prophecies of Isaiah is a possible explanation of these claims, although it is difficult to determine whether the prophet himself, or his subsequent editor, made such a conscious connection.

Rather more direct and imposing in their support for the belief that the exilic prophet of Isaiah 40—55 did know and allude to the prophecies of Isaiah are two references to the unresponsiveness of Israel to the divine message (see 42:18–20; 43:8). The explicit declaration of the blindness and deafness of Israel described there echoes very strikingly the words of the prophetic commission of Isaiah (found in Isa. 6:9–10).

The metaphors of blindness and deafness used to describe spiritual insensitivity may appear sufficiently obvious and straightforward so that we could conclude that it has been purely a fortuitous chance which has led to their being adopted by two quite independent prophetic figures. Nevertheless, the very strong and unanticipated way in which they appear in Isa. 42:18–20 and 43:8 suggests that their employment here is due to a conscious allusion to the commissioning speech of the prophet Isaiah. Furthermore, the metaphors of blindness and deafness used to describe the condition of Israel which made it unable to respond to the divine warning through the prophet Isaiah are given a unique emphasis in the call narrative. It would be quite understandable, therefore, that a later prophet, who had come to view the entire period of Israel's subjugation to the Mesopotamian powers of Assyria and Babylon as one of national blindness and deafness, should have deliberately picked up such a theme in stressing the joyousness of his new message.

Nor is this all, since, in a short redactional passage (Isa. 32:1–8) which must derive from the Josianic editors of Isaiah's prophecies, it is the theme of blindness and deafness which is expressly picked up (see Isa. 32:3). If Deutero-Isaiah had access to a written collection of his predecessor's proph-

---

17. J. F. A. Sawyer, *From Moses to Patmos: New Perspectives in Old Testament Study* (London, 1977), pp. 113ff.

18. Brevard S. Childs said, "The 'former things' can now only refer to the prophecies of First Isaiah. The point of Second Isaiah's message is that this prophetic word has been confirmed" (*Introduction to the Old Testament as Scripture* [Philadelphia: Fortress Press, 1979], p. 329).

ecies, it would have been most natural that the theme of Israel's blindness and deafness should have appeared in it as a very striking feature of the prophetic explanation for the catastrophes which had overtaken Israel. Nor is this the end of the matter, since we find that in the hopeful summary of the message of Isaiah 40—55, which is set out in chapter 35, once again it is the theme of Israel's blindness and deafness which is pointedly referred to (35:5).

Looking at it overall we can see that a striking instance of unity in the Book of Isaiah is provided by the idea that the prophetic message from God falls upon deaf ears and is set forth to people who are unable to comprehend what their own eyes see. It marks a theme which was introduced by Isaiah himself in his account of his call. It was thereafter taken up by the later prophet of the Babylonian exile and by at least two groups of editors who used it to shape and interpret the material which they helped to compile. In particular, it is the manner in which that theme reaches across the major division of the book which marks it out.

This brings us back to the leading issue that confronts us in studying the structure of the Book of Isaiah and which has in reality remained a pressing question ever since a technique of literary-historical criticism came to be applied to it. What is the fundamental connection between the predominantly hopeful message of chapters 40—55 and the largely threatening one of chapters 1—39?

Primarily, we must recognize that prophecy was a message about Israel and its destiny, so that the factors which have led to the bringing together of its various sections and sayings were essentially thematic and religious rather than literary or biographical. In this regard it is evident that Isaiah of Jerusalem had delivered a sharply threatening announcement of judgment and disaster upon Jerusalem. Most of all this is to be seen in Isa. 2:6—4:1, although other passages, too, appear with a similar note of threat. I have argued fairly extensively elsewhere for a recognition that these threats came to be linked with the capture and destruction of Jerusalem by the Babylonians in 587 B.C.[19] Although it may at first appear strange to associate the prophecies of Isaiah with an event which took place more than a century after the latest of his sayings had been delivered, it would not have appeared so to ancient scribes and editors. Prophecy was regarded as a "living" word from God which could take effect in more than one way and at more than one time. There are, in any case, a significant number of glosses and additions in the book which show that a significant revision was made in the wake of the destruction of Jerusalem in 587 B.C.

Alongside this phenomenon, we already have in the Book of Jeremiah a most instructive narrative instance showing the way in which a prophecy concerning the fate of Jerusalem (Jer. 26:16–24), given more than a century before, could be cited to help illumine a later event. We can add to this the point already made, namely, that Isaiah 39 was incorporated into the Book of

---

19. Cf. my essay "The Prophecies of Isaiah and the Fall of Jerusalem in 587 B.C.," VT 30 (1980) 421–36.

Isaiah precisely to associate the fate of Jerusalem and the Davidic monarchy at the hands of the Babylonians with the prophecies of Isaiah. Taken together, these factors point to the conclusion that the body of Isaianic prophecies which had taken shape by the time of Josiah's death in 609 B.C. came subsequently to be used in order to obtain some understanding of why the catastrophes of 598 and 587 B.C. had happened.

In broad measure the prophecies of Isaiah had provided a divinely given insight into the reasons for the judgments which had befallen Israel and Judah at the hands of the Assyrians since the beginning of the Syro-Ephraimite crisis in 736 B.C. Out of this series of disasters Judah had at first survived with a Davidic ruler still on the throne and its chief city Jerusalem relatively intact. It is small wonder that the institution of the Jerusalem temple, as well as that of the Davidic monarchy, should have become regarded as especially favored by God (cf. Isa. 37:35). Yet the events of 598 and 587 had overthrown even these convictions, which certainly were not part of the message of Isaiah himself, but which had nonetheless come to be associated with his prophesying and with the events of his prophetic ministry. Once the Jerusalem temple had suffered destruction and the Davidic dynasty had been removed from Judah, a renewed urgency and severity attached to Isaiah's prophecies which had warned of judgment even upon the city of Jerusalem itself. It is entirely understandable in the light of this that a further revision of the written Isaianic collection was made.[20] We have good reason, therefore, for concluding that the prophecies of Isaiah came to be used and interpreted by the survivors of 587 B.C. in order to understand the reasons for what had befallen them. To this extent the Book of Isaiah was set alongside the Books of Jeremiah and Ezekiel, both of which, in the hands of different scribal groups, came to be focused sharply upon the fate that had befallen Judah and Jerusalem.

Once the connection between the prophecies of Isaiah and the destruction of Jerusalem is recognized as a factor in the way the Book of Isaiah came to be developed, we have the single most essential clue towards understanding why the prophecies of chapters 40 and following came to be incorporated into the book. It was a fundamental aspect of the motives and interests which influenced the scribes who have preserved and ordered the various prophetic collections that they have sought to ensure that divine threats be followed and counterbalanced by divine promises. With this in mind, it is not difficult to see why prophecies which had foretold Jerusalem's destruction should have been followed by the much warmer and reassuring note found in Isaiah 40:1–2.

In the absence of any other note concerning the historical background of this exilic prophet, or of the reasons for the punishment which Yahweh had inflicted upon Israel, it would appear intentional that these reasons should have been found in the prophecies and forewarnings of doom which abound in the earlier part of the Book of Isaiah. Far from Deutero-Isaiah having an

---

20. Ibid., pp. 425ff.

entirely independent and self-contained message of his own to declare, his
message can quite properly be understood as a complement to that which
has preceded it in the earlier chapters of the book. Whether the original
prophet of the exile saw this, or whether it was a circle of later editors who
felt the appropriateness of adding his message to that of Isaiah, makes very
little difference to its distinctive meaning. The main point is that the earlier,
and more primary, collection of prophecies in which the fate of Jerusalem
figured prominently was seen to be effectively filled out and complemented
by those from the exilic age. In a similar fashion the threat of the Day of
Yahweh in the "Babylonian" prophecy (13:6–8) must refer to the day in
which the Babylonian armies destroyed Jerusalem. Yet this was subsequently
complemented by a prophecy of the overthrow of Babylon (13:17–22).

Our major contention here, therefore, is that the conjunction of the
prophecies of chapter 40 and those following with those that precede them
was a deliberate step taken by the scribal redactors of the book for a
profoundly religious reason. It had nothing to do with matters of literary
convenience or assumed identity of authorship but was designed to clarify
and fill out the divine message given to Israel, and especially to Jerusalem.
In this regard we find that this thematic connection between the two major
parts of the Book of Isaiah was especially concerned with the fate of Jerusalem and with the Davidic dynasty.

The relationship of chapters 56—66 of the book with its preceding parts is
still a topic requiring fresh investigation and discussion. Nevertheless, it is
reasonably clear that these eleven chapters, with their proto-apocalyptic
character, were intended to be understood, not as a fresh and entirely self-
contained declaration from Yahweh to the postexilic community, but rather
as a carrying forward of the divine word as it had been declared on the eve of
the overthrow of Babylon by the unnamed prophet of chapters 40—55.[21] Its
central concern with Jerusalem, instead of with the wider political entity of
Israel, marks the bringing of the divine message into the changed circumstances of the new era. Even so, in chapter 62 (vv. 6–12), it manages to retain
an effective link with the earlier prophecies of the book in which the fate of
Jerusalem, Zion, and the temple that stood there had occupied a prominent
place.

This passage (62:6–12), declaring in colorful and vivid imagery the glories
of the rebuilt and restored Jerusalem, develops and rounds off fittingly the
promise given earlier (55:11–17). This in turn redresses the note of warning
and threat to Jerusalem which is to be found in a number of earlier passages
in chapters 1—32. It can hardly be satisfactory, therefore, to seek an interpretation of a passage such as this as though its literary context made little
difference to the way in which we are to understand it. It stands at a

21. Cf. Gerhard von Rad, *Old Testament Theology*, trans. D. M. G. Stalker (Edinburgh:
Oliver & Boyd, 1962–65), 2:279ff. For a more detailed examination of the language, reference
should also be made to Walther Zimmerli, "Zur Sprache Tritojesajas," *Festschrift L. Köhler*
(Bern, 1950), pp. 62–74; see *Gottes Offenbarung: Gesammelte Aufsätze, IBI* 19 (Munich: Chr.
Kaiser Verlag, 1963), pp. 217–33.

significant end point in a series of declarations of Yahweh's word concerning Jerusalem. To this extent there is a measure of connectedness and unity imposed upon the Book of Isaiah. This is not in any way to minimize the achievements of those scholars who have shown how varied are the component parts of the book and who have sought to trace the particular historical contexts to which each unit belongs. Nevertheless, such a process has tended to highlight the disunity that abounds and has encouraged a pattern of interpretation which has paid too little attention to the links and interconnections which are also present. Not least it has often led to the treatment of passages in isolation which were never intended to be so understood since, from the outset, they took the form of additional interpretations and applications of more primary units.

To trace the process of literary growth by which the Book of Isaiah came to assume its present shape is a task which cannot yet be regarded as completed. The useful essays into tracing the redactional history of such a large and primary work have not yet achieved anything approaching a consensus regarding the relative dating of each of its component parts and sayings. Nevertheless, it must be claimed that the recognition that such a redactional history was undertaken by ancient scribes and interpreters for profound spiritual and interpretative reasons is an important factor for us to bear in mind. The prophetic word of God is essentially a divine message concerning his actions and intentions towards his people, and it should not be surprising for us to discover that it has been the continuity and connectedness of this divine purpose which provides the proper basis of unity in the four major prophetic collections.

6

Isaiah in
Old Testament Theology

J. J. M. ROBERTS

Isaiah's recurring emphasis on God's plan gave impetus to the conception of an overarching divine plan for history, a conception the New
Testament found useful for interpreting the meaning of Jesus Christ.

It has become traditional to treat the theological message of Isaiah in terms of
the distinct theologies of First Isaiah, Second Isaiah, Third Isaiah, and
"Other" Isaiahs.[1] Outside very conservative circles there has been little
concern to treat the theology of the book as a unified whole, though recently
Brevard Childs has forcefully reminded the scholarly guild that it was as a
single book that Isaiah was received into the Christian canon.[2] Yet it remains
a very serious question whether one can describe "the" theology of the Book
of Isaiah without sacrificing many of the important exegetical and theological
insights of several generations of scholars. A simple return to precritical
scholarship implicitly demands a sacrifice of the intellect that is unacceptable. Nor can this writer agree with Childs's assessment of the degree to
which the "canonical editors" stripped Second Isaiah of its original historical
context.[3]

An adequate treatment of the place of the Book of Isaiah in Old Testament
theology cannot simply ignore the evidence of different historical settings
preserved in the book. Nor can one simply read the book in its present
literary sequence as though there were no evidence for that sequence being
the result of a rather haphazard use of the catchword principle of arrangement. To do so would be to engage in an elaborate pretense that we know far
less about the book than we actually do.

On the other hand, there is a certain inner consistency in the growth of the

---

1. This formulation comes from William L. Holladay, *Isaiah: Scroll of a Prophetic Heritage*
(Grand Rapids: Wm. B. Eerdmans, 1978).
2. Brevard S. Childs, *Introduction to the Old Testament as Scripture* (Philadelphia: Fortress
Press, 1979), pp. 311–38.
3. Ibid., p. 325. See the trenchant critique of Sean E. McEvenue, "The Old Testament:
Scripture or Theology?" *Int* 35:229–42 (1981) 234.

Isaianic tradition—over against the apparently more mechanical expansion of Zechariah, for instance—which together with its canonical form justifies an attempt to sketch a theology of the Book of Isaiah. Even the latest additions to the book owe a great deal to the earlier Isaianic theology. All, or almost all, the components of the Isaianic corpus move in the same stream of tradition. It should be possible, therefore, to delineate the central core of Isaianic theology, while not ignoring the different accents placed on that core in the different stages of the book.

In what follows I will attempt to sketch the main lines of Isaianic theology, trace the shifting accents in the different stages of the material, and then point to the effect of this theology on later biblical thought.

I. THE CENTER OF ISAIANIC THEOLOGY:
THE HOLY ONE OF ISRAEL

If there is any one concept central to the whole Book of Isaiah, it is the vision of Yahweh as the Holy One of Israel. Isaiah's inaugural vision of the awesome majesty of Yahweh with the seraphs' thundering, three-fold proclamation of Yahweh's holiness, left a lasting impression on the eighth-century prophet's whole ministry.[4] His message can be unfolded as a transformation of inherited traditions in the light of that central vision, and the same conception of God underlies the message of Second Isaiah, though the later prophet further elaborates this conception with new themes.[5] Even Third Isaiah and the "Other" Isaiahs, though they make less use of the term *holy*,[6] present a basically similar portrayal of the divine reality.

Holy and *holiness* are difficult terms to define, and to get at Isaiah's meaning perhaps it is best to begin with a closer look at his inaugural vision in Isaiah 6. The whole scene may be seen as an explication of what the seraphs meant when they proclaimed Yahweh as holy. Their cry ends with the affirmation, "his glory fills the whole earth" (author's trans.), and this point was visually impressed on Isaiah by his view of the towering divine figure, the mere hem of whose robe filled the whole temple.[7] Moreover,

---

4. The adjective "holy" (*qados*) is used in reference to Yahweh seventeen times in material normally assigned to First Isaiah (1:4; 5:16, 19, 24; 6:3; 10:17, 20; 12:6; 17:7; 29:19, 23; 30:11–12, 15; 31:1; 37:23), and the *niphal* (5:16) and the *hithpael* (8:13; 29:23) of the verb of the same root are used with God as either the subject or the object of the action. Yahweh himself is called a sanctuary (*miqdas*, 8:14), and his abode is characterized as a mountain of "holiness" (*qodes*, 11:9).

5. Second Isaiah uses the adjective "holy" (*qados*) of God thirteen times (40:25; 41:14, 16, 20; 43:3, 14, 15; 45:11; 47:4; 48:17; 49:7; 55:5). He uses the noun "holiness" (*qodes*) three times, once to characterize Yahweh's arm (52:10) and twice to characterize Yahweh's city (48:2; 52:1).

6. The adjective *qados* is only used of God twice (60:2, 14) and the noun *qodes*, apart from two references to God's spirit (63:10–11), is used only of things that have a close relationship to God such as his abode, mountain, city, courts, house, people, way, or special day (4:3; 35:8; 56:7; 57:13; 58:13; 62:9; 12; 63:15, 18; 64:9–10; 65:11; 66:20).

7. This discussion is heavily dependent on the treatment of this passage by Othmar Keel in *Jahwe-Visionen und Siegelkunst*, SBS 84/85 (Stuttgart: Verlag Katholisches Bibelwerk, 1977), pp. 46–124.

Yahweh reveals himself to Isaiah as king, sitting on a high and exalted throne. Together, the portrayal of Yahweh as king and the affirmation of the world-wide extent of his glory constitute a claim for the sole sovereignty of Yahweh.

This is underscored by yet another feature in the visionary experience. The terrifying six-winged seraphs, at whose voices the very foundations of the temple shake, show a striking deference toward Yahweh. These creatures, who are to be identified with a supercharged variety of the winged uraeus or cobra well known in Egyptian art, behave differently from their Egyptian models. In Egyptian iconography the winged cobra occupies the same position vis-à-vis the deity as Isaiah's seraphs, but he stretches his wings out over the deity in a protective gesture. Isaiah's seraphs, on the contrary, cover their own faces and pudenda from the presence of Yahweh. Yahweh needs no protection. Instead, even so awesome a creature as a six-winged seraph must hide his face from the fearsome glory of Yahweh. Even the seraphs cannot look upon God and live. One could hardly express any more vividly the sole lordship and matchless majesty of Yahweh. Yahweh alone is Lord. He brooks no rival.

But in the presence of such glory, all that is defiled and profane appears in its true ugliness. This vision of the divine reality opens Isaiah's eyes to his own and his people's sin. Thus there is an ethical element in Isaiah's understanding of Yahweh's holiness. Fellowship with the holy God demands that one be purged of one's sins. It is probably no accident that that cleansing takes place in Isaiah's vision by means of a burning coal from the altar. The initiative is taken by God, but the cleansing takes place by fire.

Nevertheless, this divine willingness to enter into relationship with humans is an important aspect of Isaiah's understanding of Yahweh's holiness. Despite Yahweh's awesome majesty, despite his universal rule, despite his devouring righteousness, God is not simply the Holy One, but the Holy One of Israel. This point, repeatedly made by Isaiah, is not clearly articulated in Isaiah's inaugural vision, but it is probably presupposed by the setting of that vision in the temple. Yahweh, though his glory transcends the confines of Jerusalem, its temple, and the Israelite people and fills the whole world, is nonetheless enthroned there in the house, the city, and the people he chose.

II. IMPLICATIONS AND DEVELOPMENT

The implications of this central theological affirmation are spelled out in the Book of Isaiah. The eighth-century prophet further elaborates on each of these aspects of Yahweh's holiness, and that elaboration is continued, expanded, and sometimes altered in the later Isaianic tradition. What results is a remarkably complete theology rooted in a theocentric vision.

Yahweh Alone Is Lord

At the heart of Isaiah's message lies the awesome majesty of Yahweh's holiness. It underscores his claim to exclusive allegiance and unshakeable trust. This vision of the exalted Yahweh certainly lies behind the terrifying oracle in chapter 2, where Isaiah proclaims a day of judgment against all that is high and lifted up. In that day anything or anyone who sets himself up or is extolled by others as a possible rival to God will be abased, and Yahweh alone will be exalted. Yahweh's intolerance of human pride expressed in this passage is basically a rejection of man's attempt to put his trust in anything but God. The idols that the terrified fugitives from God's judgment cast aside are simply paradigmatic for any and all false hopes and bogus sources of security.

Other passages spell out what some of these false hopes were for Isaiah's contemporaries. They ranged from the vain trust in ostentatious wealth and physical beauty on the part of the prancing women of Jerusalem (3:16; 32:9–11) to the confidence in military preparation and political alliances on the part of the royal court (22:8–11; 30:1–5; 31:1–3). Yahweh's threatened response was to strip the women of their beauty and cover them with shame (3:17—4:1), to turn the protection of military allies into a shameful debacle (30:3–5). If Israel refused to look to Yahweh, to trust in the quiet waters of Shiloah, God would send the raging waters of Assyria against them to reveal the vanity of their trust in human power (8:5–8).

For Isaiah, Yahweh's holiness meant that Yahweh alone was to be feared (8:12–13). The true fear of Yahweh would drive out all other fears. Indeed, the reverse side of the fear of Yahweh is implicit trust in Yahweh. Reliance upon his promises—quiet, confident trust in his word—was the key to rest, security, and wellbeing (7:9; 28:12, 16; 30:15). Those who looked to him with this kind of faith would be established and have reason to rejoice.

Second Isaiah continues this emphasis on Yahweh's sole exaltation and gives it new depth by his use of the doctrine of creation. For this later prophet, Yahweh, the Holy One, has no rival in all the world. No power among gods or men can be compared to him, for he alone created all that exists (40:25–26). His power exhibited in creation remains the power which has directed and will continue to direct history, as is demonstrated by his fulfillment of his ancient prophecies (41:21–29). Hence Israel may confidently trust in Yahweh's new promise of salvation.

In Third Isaiah, Yahweh remains the "high and lofty One" (57:15). Heaven is his throne and earth is his footstool. No manmade temple can contain him, for he has created all these things (66:1–2). Moreover, his majesty will be manifested in fearsome judgment against all those who oppose him (59:16–19; 63:1–6; 66:14–16), but those who put their trust in Yahweh will be vindicated for the sake of the Holy One of Israel (57:13; 60:9).

The so-called Isaianic Apocalypse (chapters 24—27), though it makes no use of the term "holy" or "holiness," also speaks of Yahweh's exaltation. The majesty of Yahweh is to be praised from one end of the earth to the other (24:14–16). In the coming judgment he will strike down all his rivals, whether they are in heaven or upon the earth (24:21), and Yahweh alone will be enthroned and manifest his glory on Mount Zion (24:23). On that day a song of trust will be sung in Judah, and a few lines of that song give an

appropriate summary of the message of the whole Book of Isaiah concerning
where one's confidence in life should lie:

> The mind stayed on you, you keep in peace,
> in peace because it trusts in you.
> Trust in Yahweh for ever, for Yahweh
> is an everlasting rock.
>
> (26:3–4; author's trans.)

The Moral Dimension

The ethical or moral dimension reflected in Isaiah's initial experience of
Yahweh's holiness remains a constant ingredient throughout all the stages of
the Isaianic tradition. Isaiah of Jerusalem was a constant critic of his people's
sins. Injustice, oppression, greed, drunkenness, and social irresponsibility
will bring God's judgment. The only escape from such judgment is by a
radical reversal of one's behavior (1:17–19), and Isaiah was not too sanguine
about that taking place on any significant scale (6:9–10). Thus he saw Israel's
salvation as taking place only through a purging judgment. When the refining fire had stripped Jerusalem of its corrupt judges, vain women, and
other sinners, Jerusalem would again be called the righteous city (1:21–26).
Such an ordeal was necessary to jolt the populace out of its moral stupor
(33:10–14).[8]

The ethical demands Isaiah makes of his contemporaries are simply those
demands that were traditional in Israelite society. It is difficult to attribute
them to particular religious traditions, though one can isolate several sources
that probably contributed to this ethical teaching. Isaiah imitates the so-
called Torah entrance liturgy in 33:14–16 and that, together with the role of
the temple cult in his inaugural vision, suggests that for all its corruption in
Isaiah's day the official temple cult remained a source of religious instruction.[9] Many scholars have denied any influence of covenant theology on
Isaiah, but the summary of Isaiah's teaching in Isaiah 1 is heavily dependent
on Deuteronomy 32,[10] and like Deuteronomy 32 it can best be analyzed as a
covenant lawsuit.[11] Whether this Deuteronomistic influence reached Isaiah
through refugees from the north may be debated, but there does seem to
have been a Deuteronomistic element in Hezekiah's religious reform—the

---

8. Chapter 33 is normally assigned to a later writer than Isaiah of Jerusalem, but see J.J.M.
Roberts, "Isaiah 33: An Isaianic Elaboration of the Zion Tradition," in C. L. Meyers and M.
O'Connor, eds., *The Word of the Lord Shall Go Forth* (David Noel Freedman Festschrift),
(Winona Lake, Ind.: Eisenbrauns, 1983), pp. 15–25.

9. That is not to say that Isaiah approved all that was taught by the religious authorities (29:13;
cf. Mic. 3:11).

10. H. L. Ginsberg, "First Isaiah," *Encyclopaedia Judaica* 9 (Jerusalem: Keter Publishing
House, 1971), p. 50.

11. Julien Harvey's work is the most extensive treatment of this passage as a covenant lawsuit,
but my analysis would differ from his at certain points (*Le plaidoyer prophètique contre Israël
après la rupture de l'alliance*, Studia, Travaux de Recherche [Bruges and Paris: Desclée de
Brouwer, 1967]).

composition of the Deuteronomic law book found in the temple by Josiah's men may date to this period of Hezekiah's reform. At any rate, Isaiah does seem to have been influenced to some extent by covenant theology. Finally, one cannot ignore the influence of the wisdom tradition of Isaiah's ethical formulations. He may have been a critic of the professional counselors, but his criticism was in some sense an inside job.[12] His formulation of ethical demands often takes the form of wisdom maxims.[13]

Second Isaiah, who saw himself as living after God's refining judgment on Jerusalem (40:2), does not put as much weight on ethical demands, but this dimension is certainly not absent from his message. Israel's current predicament was due to the sins of her people (42:24–25). Their plight was well deserved, their coming salvation was due simply to Yahweh's graciousness, and the appropriate response was to return to Yahweh in trust and confidence (43:22—44:2). Second Isaiah's major concern appears to be religious, to turn his people away from the temptation to idolatry (chap. 44), but moral admonition is not totally lacking. Indeed, Second Isaiah's material ends with an admonition to the wicked to forsake wickedness and to turn to Yahweh while the deity may still be found (55:6–7).

With Third Isaiah, ethical admonition has returned to the place of prominence it had in First Isaiah, though there is a heightened tendency to divide the community into two camps, the righteous and the wicked. As does First Isaiah, this prophet denounces as vain any attempt to win God's favor based on cultic performances that leave the rest of life unaffected (58:3–5). True cult must issue in relief for the oppressed and downtrodden (58:6–14). Moreover, God's fiery judgment lies not just in the past, but it remains a future possibility (65:11–15; 66:15–17). Along with the promise, that threat stands as an incentive for obedient submission to Yahweh.

The Isaianic Apocalypse, with its vision of world judgment, universalizes this demand for ethical behavior. The whole world shares both in Yahweh's judgment and in his salvation. While Israel still occupies a special place in this vision of the future, God's demand for "righteousness" and covenant faithfulness extends beyond the boundaries of Israel.[14]

---

12. See esp. Johannes Fichtner, "Jesaja unter den Weisen," *ThLZ* 74 (1949) 75–80; Robert Martin-Achard, "Sagesse de dieu et sagesse humaine chez Ésaie," in *Hommage à Wilhelm Vischer* (Montpellier: Castelnau, 1960), pp. 137–44; and Joseph Jensen, *The Use of tôrâ By Isaiah: His Debate with the Wisdom Tradition*, CBQMS 3 (1973). One should also consult J. William Whedbee, though neither his rejection of covenant theology nor his wisdom derivation of the "woe oracles" is convincing (*Isaiah and Wisdom* [Nashville: Abingdon Press, 1971]).

13. Note esp. 3:10–11 and 32:1–8. Over against the tendency to reject such wisdom material as non-Isaianic, see in J.J.M. Roberts, "The Divine King and the Human Community in Isaiah's Vision of the Future," in Alberto Green, Herbert B. Huffmon, and Frank A. Spida, eds., *The Quest for the Kingdom of God: Essays in Honor of George E. Mendenhall* (Winona Lake, Ind.: Eisenbrauns), and in "The Teaching Voice in Isaiah 30:20–21," in Everett Ferguson, ed., *Christian Teaching: Studies in Honor of LeMoine G. Lewis* (Abilene, Tex.: Abilene Christian University, 1981), pp. 130–37.

14. Isa. 24:4–6 apparently presupposes an understanding of the covenant with Noah similar to that in later rabbinic sources according to which the Gentiles were obligated to keep certain minimum commandments.

Of Israel

For Isaiah, Yahweh is the Holy One of Israel, and this implies a special relationship between God and his chosen people. The prophet develops this aspect of his theology by reference to the far older Zion tradition, which appears to have been particularly cultivated by the royal court in Jerusalem and seems to have been a major formative influence on Isaiah's thought.[15] This tradition has two major poles: (1) Yahweh is the great king, suzerain of the whole world, and (2) he chose Zion as his dwelling place.[16] Because Yahweh is the great king, his choice of Jerusalem has implications for Zion's topography, for her security, and for her inhabitants.

The topographical features appear only in Isaiah's visions of the renewed Jerusalem. When the city has been purged of sinners, it will be exalted above the mountains (2:2), and it will be a place of broad streams (33:20–21).[17] Both motifs, of the divine mountain and the river of paradise as features of the topography of Yahweh's abode, are elements taken over from Canaanite mythology. Isaiah picks them up from the Zion tradition where they were already at home, but he does alter the significance of the tradition by projecting this vision into the future. These features are no longer present realities, but future promises. The vision of the future Jerusalem has the effect of devaluing the present city.

Isaiah's condemnation of the present Jerusalem, however, appears to be a conception at which he only slowly arrived. During the time of the Syro-Ephraimitic war, he appears to have stood far closer to the tradition as he had received it. Zion was Yahweh's city, and, therefore, God's people could rely on God to protect it.[18] One did not need to turn to Assyria or any other human helper, because Yahweh who dwelt in Zion (8:18) would be her defender. He would destroy her enemies before morning (17:14).

The royal court's refusal to trust in the divine promises (7:13; 8:6–8), however, joined with the corruption that Isaiah saw grow rampant in government circles (1:22–23; 3:12–15; 10:1–2) and gradually caused the prophet to shift his views. Jerusalem had once been a city of righteousness, but had become a whore (1:21). That could not but alter God's plans for the city. If Zion was to be the city of the great king, her inhabitants must be fit to live in his presence (33:14). Thus Isaiah developed the view that Yahweh would purge Zion. God would still save his city as the tradition had it, but the way to that salvation would be through judgment (1:24–28). Before Yahweh would fight for Zion, he would fight against her (31:4–5). Jerusalem would be

---

15. For Isaiah's dependence on this tradition, see esp. the excellent discussion in Gerhard von Rad's *Old Testament Theology* (New York: Harper & Row, 1965), 2:155–75.

16. For a detailed analysis of the structure of this tradition see my study, "Zion in the Theology of the Davidic-Solomonic Empire," in the forthcoming collection of essays from the International Symposium for Biblical Studies held in Tokyo, 1979, edited by Tomoo Ishida and others.

17. The authenticity of both passages is disputed, but see my discussion in the study referred to in n. 8.

18. Isaiah 7:7–9 and 17:1–6 clearly date from this period, and 2:5–22; 8:9–10; 14:28–32 (emended); and 17:12–14 may also reflect the background of the Syro-Ephraimitic war.

humbled and humiliated, but in the hour of her desperation, when Yahweh had cleansed her in the fiery judgment, God would intervene to save her from her arrogant enemies (29:1–8). Then Jerusalem would be exalted and glorified, and those who survived in her would be devoted to the Lord (33:10–24).

Isaiah refers to this patterned future as Yahweh's plan.[19] The judgment aspect of it, which he refers to as God's strange work, is almost like a reversal of David's victories over the Philistines near Jerusalem (28:21), which were important elements behind the original formation of the Zion tradition.[20] But the ultimate vindication of Zion as Yahweh's city was also a part of God's plan. He planned to destroy the Assyrian on the mountains of Israel (14:24–27). Judah's deliverance would result from a miraculous divine intervention; it would not be saved by human strength (30:29–33; 31:8–9). That deliverance would take place before the walls of Jerusalem.[21]

Such a view implies a history of salvation. It is important to grasp this point in order to understand Isaiah's commission to harden the hearts of his people (6:9–10). As von Rad pointed out, "we must learn to read the saying about hardening of the heart with reference to the saving."[22] Yahweh had decided to purge Israel for her sins, and no premature repentance was going to turn Yahweh aside from the course he had chosen. Yet this judgment was not the last word. Out of this judgment would arise a purged and glorified city of God, a new Jerusalem to which nations would come to have their disputes arbitrated (2:2–4). Thus Isaiah could assert that Israel's disobedience, God's judgment, and his ultimate redemption of Zion were all taken up in Yahweh's plan for his people and the world.

Two participants in this plan need to be discussed. The first is the Davidic monarch. Isaiah's conception of the Davidic monarch owes its basic contours to the royal theology associated with the Zion tradition. From the formative period of the Zion tradition, Yahweh's choice of Jerusalem had been linked to and had presupposed his choice of the Davidic dynasty (Ps. 132:11–14). The two were inseparably joined. Indeed, the later Davidic kings were conceived of as Yahweh's adopted sons whom God had installed in his holy city as his vice-regents on earth (Psalm 2). As Yahweh's regents, these human kings had both an external responsibility to maintain Yahweh's imperial rule and an internal responsibility to maintain ("build") the city of God and keep it free of evildoers.[23] This conception of human kingship underlies the Zion tradi-

---

19. Isaiah often speaks of Yahweh's plan (5:19; 14:24, 26–27; 19:12, 17; 23:8–9; 28:29; 30:1) or his work (5:19; 10:12; 28:21). See J. Fichtner, "Jahwes Plan in der Botschaft des Jesaja," ZAW 63 (1951) 16–33; Gerhard von Rad, "Das Werk Jahwes," Studia Biblica et Semitica Theodoro Christiano Vriezen . . . dedicata (Wageningen: H. Veenman & Zonen, 1966), pp. 290–98. Note also the healthy corrective in Bertil Albrektson, History and the Gods (Lund: C. W. K. Gleerup, 1967), pp. 68–97.

20. See my article "The Davidic Origin of the Zion Tradition," JBL 92 (1973) 329–44.

21. This aspect of the Zion tradition lies behind the Isaianic material preserved in Isaiah 37:21–35 as well as in 29:6–8 and 31:5.

22. G. von Rad, Old Testament Theology 2:155.

23. See my discussion in the work referred to in n. 16.

tion, though in the hymns written to glorify the divine ruler of Jerusalem the human king is understandably ignored or neglected.

As in these hymns, Isaiah very often appears to ignore the human king, but several of his oracles do reflect the basic conception of kingship culti-vated in Jerusalemite royal circles. The prophet's appeal to Ahaz for faith is based on the double promise of God concerning both Jerusalem and the Davidic dynasty (7:7–9). Isaiah's coronation oracle, presumably for Hezekiah (9:1–7; Heb. 8:23—9:6), and his prediction of a new shoot from the stump of Jesse (Isa. 11:1–5) come out of the same conceptual world as this traditional royal theology. It should be noted, however, that the Davidic ruler, in Isaiah's vision, is not so much the agent to bring to fruition God's plan as he is the beneficiary of that plan. The righteous king plays no role in Yahweh's fiery purging of Jerusalem and plays only a passive one in Yahweh's deliverance of his city. Only when Yahweh himself has delivered his city does the king take up his traditional task of maintaining God's just rule. Nevertheless, one should not downplay the importance of that task in Isaiah's vision for the future of Jerusalem. A righteous king and righteous officials are necessary to achieve and maintain the obedient and righteous citizenship required by God's presence in his city.[24]

To a great extent Isaiah's description of the ideal future king, as does his description of the future Jerusalem, represents a devaluation or criticism of the holders of that office; and his disgust with the contemporary house of David may be one reason why the promises to David figure no more prominently in his message than they do. Moreover, as in the case of the Zion hymns, Isaiah was more concerned with glorifying the divine king than with spelling out the role of his human regent.

The situation is rather different with regard to the other major participants in Yahweh's plan—the foreign nations. The Book of Isaiah contains a number of oracles against the foreign nations.[25] In general these oracles are directed against those nations who oppose God's plan, who exalt themselves against Yahweh, or who become a false source of security for Israel. Assyria, how-ever, plays a special role. In the divine plan Assyria functions as Yahweh's agent or tool for purging Israel (10:5–15). In developing this conception of Assyria's role, Isaiah was dependent on earlier prophetic models which he used to modify important features of the Zion tradition. Prior to Isaiah the Zion tradition apparently knew nothing of an attack by Yahweh against Jerusalem. His cultic and moral demands on those who would enter his gates were recited in the temple entrance liturgies, and the king was expected to keep the holy city free of evildoers, but a major divine purging of the city was not expected. The Zion tradition spoke of the nation's assault on Jerusa-lem, but this was understood as the attack of rebellious vassals, not as God's agents for punishing his city. Moreover, the outcome of this battle was the

---

24. See my discussion of Isa. 32:1–8 in the work cited in n. 13.

25. These oracles, not all of which can be attributed to Isaiah, are concentrated in chaps. 13—23, but other oracles, particularly against Assyria or Egypt, are scattered in other sections of First Isaiah.

utter consternation of these enemies and the vindication of Yahweh, his city, and his king. Far from a judgment on Jerusalem, it was merely an occasion for God to reveal his majesty.

Isaiah altered this picture by appealing to older prophetic models of God's use of foreign nations as agents of punishment. The old ark narrative told of God's punishment of Israel through the Philistines,[26] Deuteronomy 32 spoke of judgment through their enemies, and Amos spoke of Yahweh's attempts to discipline through military defeat (4:10). Isaiah adopts this model, perhaps showing particular dependency on Amos, but gives it a new texture by tying it in with the Zion tradition's motif of the nation's assault on Jerusalem. Assyria was God's agent for punishing Jerusalem, but Assyria did not acknowledge her position as a mere tool in the hand of Yahweh and moderate her actions accordingly. Instead of recognizing her appropriate role and sticking to it, Assyria vaunted herself against Yahweh and his city as though her military successes were her own doing. Such hubris could not go unpunished. Thus, after Yahweh had finished his strange work of purging Jerusalem, he would break Assyria on his holy mountain. Here the old motif of the nation's assault on Jerusalem has acquired a double function. It becomes Yahweh's attack upon his own city to purge it of evil before, at the last minute, Yahweh turns to save the city from these foreign tools of his wrath. The motif thereby acquires a new complexity and underlines Isaiah's conception of salvation through judgment.

Second Isaiah also develops his understanding of Yahweh's special relationship to his people through use of the Zion tradition, but he supplements that tradition by appeal to the creation, exodus, and patriarchal traditions. This prophet of the exile follows First Isaiah in attributing the present plight of Jerusalem to Yahweh's purging judgment, brought on by Israel's sins (40:2; 42:24-25; 48:10). Nonetheless, Yahweh has not forsaken his people or deserted his city forever. The great king will return to his city, and Babylon, the agent God used to punish Jerusalem, will in turn feel the fury of God's wrath because she showed no mercy and misunderstood her real role in God's plan (47:1-7). Zion will be glorified, and the nations will stream to her, escorting her children back in honor (49:22; 51:3; 54:11-17).

Here the pilgrimage-of-the-nations motif of the old Zion tradition has been assimilated to the exodus tradition in a new and creative combination. Second Isaiah is a master at such interweaving of traditions. He also weaves together creation, the patriarchal traditions, and the exodus tradition to create an extraordinarily rich portrayal of the new exodus (51:1-11). Like Jacob returning from Mesopotamia, Yahweh, after smashing the powers of chaos and making a way in the wilderness, gently leads his flock home to Zion (40:10-11).

The Davidic king plays hardly any role in Second Isaiah's vision of the future. Though he mentions Yahweh's covenant promises to David, Second

---

26. See Patrick D. Miller, Jr., and J. J. M. Roberts, *The Hand of the Lord* (Baltimore and London: Johns Hopkins University Press, 1977).

Isaiah democratizes this motif so that the people as a whole are the recipients
of these promises (55:3–5). Far more important than the Davidic king as a
positive agent in the execution of Yahweh's plan is the Persian ruler Cyrus
(46:10–11). Second Isaiah can even apply to him titles that were originally
attached to the Davidic monarch. Cyrus, not a future Davidide, is Yahweh's
shepherd, his messiah, or anointed one (44:28; 45:1).

More difficult to identify is the figure the prophet designates as Yahweh's
servant. The use of the same terminology to refer to Israel suggests a
corporate identity for this figure, but the radically contrasting portrayals of
blindly disobedient Israel who suffers justly for its own sins and the humbly
obedient servant who suffers for the sins of others make a simple identification of Israel and the servant highly improbable. The role of the servant
seems to combine elements drawn from both royal and prophetic experience. The prophetic component in this portrayal is unmistakable and therefore generally acknowledged, but the servant's mission to Israel and the
nations also takes up a royal dimension. Just as did the Davidic monarch of
First Isaiah, the servant establishes and maintains justice for Israel and the
other nations, though he achieves this in a strikingly nonroyal way. Any
attempt to identify this figure with a particular individual known to Second
Isaiah is doomed to failure.[27] One should probably regard the servant as an
idealized figure, representative of Israel, but distinct enough to be assigned a
mission to Israel.

Third Isaiah also makes use of the Zion tradition to express Yahweh's
special relationship to Israel in the coming age of salvation. The prophet also
refers to the exodus and patriarchal traditions (63:8–19), but it is the Zion
tradition to which he continually returns for his imagery. He particularly
exploits the pilgrimage motif to indicate Israel's special blessing. Zion will
once more be the center of Yahweh's imperial rule. Foreigners will call her,
"the city of Yahweh, Zion of the Holy One of Israel" (60:14). Any nation that
refuses to serve her will perish (60:12), and the wealth of the nations will flow
into Jerusalem as Yahweh beautifies the place of his sanctuary and glorifies
the place of his feet (60:13). The basic thrust of this material, even when the
prophet speaks of the nations as addressing the Israelites as "priests of
Yahweh, ministers of our God," is to glorify Israel (61:1), not to emphasize
their responsibility toward the nations. Nonetheless, a certain universalism
does come through. The nations do refer to Yahweh as "our God," and the
temple will be called a house of prayer for all peoples (56:7).

For all its suggestive imagery and despite these elements of universalism,
however, Third Isaiah's view of salvation remains basically nationalistic.
Though it would probably be false to call his view materialistic, his portrayal
of salvation uses highly materialistic imagery. At one point, however, he
spiritualizes elements in both the new exodus and Zion traditions in a
striking fashion. Second Isaiah had spoken of preparing a way in the wilderness so that the exiles could return to Palestine. The Zion tradition spoke of

---

27. See the judicious remarks of Childs, *Introduction*, p. 335.

Yahweh living on his exalted mountain, and First Isaiah had emphasized that only the righteous could live on the heights with Yahweh. Third Isaiah, however, speaks of preparing the way in a moral rather than a literal sense; and he claims that the exalted Holy One lives not only on the heights, but also with the contrite heart:

> And it shall be said,
> "Build up, build up, prepare the way,
>   remove every obstruction from my people's way."
> For thus says the high and lofty One
>   who inhabits eternity, whose name is Holy:
> "I dwell in the high and holy place,
>   and also with him who is of a contrite and humble spirit,
> to revive the spirit of the humble;
>   and to revive the heart of the contrite."
>
> (57:14–15)

The Isaianic Apocalypse uses various traditions to picture Yahweh's close relationship to his people. He picks up First Isaiah's parable of the vineyard (27:2–5) and reverses it, turning it into an oracle of salvation. His dominant note, however, is derived from the Zion tradition. He contrasts the wicked city (24:10; 25:2), destroyed according to Yahweh's ancient plans (25:1), with Mount Zion where Yahweh reigns in Jerusalem (24:23). His presence gives Jerusalem security (26:1), and thither Yahweh will gather his scattered people to worship him on the holy mountain (27:13). This gathering recalls the new exodus of Second and Third Isaiah. The apocalypticist also adapts a motif from the first exodus tradition when he speaks of Yahweh revealing his glory before his elders (24:23) and preparing a banquet on Mount Zion (25:6). This is clearly derived from the tradition of Yahweh's covenant meal with the elders of Israel on Mount Sinai (Exod. 24:9–11). In the banquet passage, however, the prophet universalizes this motif to make it a promise to all peoples (25:6).

This prophet hardly speaks of any human agents of Yahweh's developing plan at all. Though specific historical events appear to lie behind many of the references in his prophecies, the author of Isaiah 24—27 has left us too few hints to grasp that historical background with any certainty. For him the human agents of judgment or salvation are irrelevant. The important thing is to recognize Yahweh at work. Characteristic of this outlook is the way he has reinterpreted a passage in First Isaiah, which spoke of the task of the righteous king and his princes (32:1–2), turning it into a description of Yahweh's own behavior (25:4–5).

III. THE LEGACY OF THE BOOK

The prophet Isaiah and the other prophets whose oracles fill out the Book of Isaiah share much in common with the theology of the rest of the Old Testament, but this book also makes its own special contribution to that theology. Isaiah's transformation of the royal ideology and the Zion tradition became the wellspring from which the later messianic expectations and the hopes for a new Jerusalem arose. The later Isaianic corpus' elaboration of the new Jerusalem theme in quasi or overtly mythological colors was a, if not the, major impetus toward the conception of a heavenly Jerusalem and a transhistorical view of salvation that includes even the ultimate victory over death.

Though one could not assert that all these references envisioned one and the same plan, the recurring emphasis on Yahweh's plan in the various parts of Isaiah tended to create the conception that Yahweh had an overarching plan for human history. Isaiah's *heilsgeschichtlich* treatment of Israel's hardening, purging, and eventual salvation through judgment strengthened that tendency and played a big role in Paul's understanding of God's eternal plan of salvation (Rom. 9—11). Finally, the interpretation of that plan of salvation as centered in the vicarious death of Jesus Christ is dependent on Second Isaiah's portrayal of the suffering servant, and the New Testament emphasis on the reception of that salvation through faith picks up and continues the Isaianic demand for faith.

7

Isaiah in Luke

James A. Sanders

Luke, steeped in the Old Testament, makes clear that to understand
what God was doing in Christ, one has to know Scripture; and
especially the Book of Isaiah.

I

Isaiah is cited, alluded to, or otherwise appears in the New Testament
more than any other Old Testament book.[1] Five hundred and ninety references, explicit or otherwise, from sixty-three chapters of Isaiah are found in
twenty-three New Testament books (239 from Isaiah 1—39; 240 from chaps.
40—55; 111 from 56—66).[2]

Isaiah was apparently the most helpful single book of the Old Testament in
assisting the early church to understand the sufferings and crucifixion of the
Christ, but Isaiah also provided help in understanding nearly every phase of
Jesus' life, ministry, death, and resurrection. Isaiah was of service, too, in
helping the early churches to understand who they were and what their role
was as witnesses to the Christ event and as those who prepared for the
eschaton's fulfillment by proclamation of what God had done in and through
Christ. Christology and ecclesiology were formulated in the early churches
with the help of Isaiah.

---

1. Y. H. Songer, "Isaiah and the New Testament," *RevExp* 65 (1968) 459–70; and J. Flam-
ming, "The New Testament Use of Isaiah," *Southwest Journal of Theology* 11 (1968) 89–103.
Using the Scripture index in the 26th edition of the Nestlé-Aland *NT Graece*, one sees that
Isaiah works the hardest in the Book of Revelation with some 155 occurrences, whether citations
or allusions. Next would be Matthew with 87 occurrences, then Luke with 78, Romans with 46,
Acts with 39, John with 37, Mark with 28, and Hebrews with 23. Such statistics have a limited
value, and the student should be cautious in drawing too many conclusions from them. One of
the things that need yet to be done is the compilation of a really significant and useful Scripture
index for the NT. See Henry M. Shires, *Finding the Old Testament in the New* (Philadelphia:
Westminster Press, 1974), and my review of it in *USQR* 30 (1975) 241–46. At the Ancient
Biblical Manuscript Center in Claremont we plan to compile a Scripture index to all the films of
manuscripts we hold. It will be a massive undertaking, but with computer technology and a
clear method of work we hope eventually to be able to provide this further service to
scholarship.

2. Mark Kispert, Ph.D. candidate in biblical studies in the Claremont Graduate School, did
some of the basic research for this article, esp. working through the Nestlé–Aland scripture
index, 26th edition.

While there have been quite a few studies of the Old Testament in the New, and more specifically of Isaiah in the New,[3] the work has really hardly begun.

The Old Testament in general, and Isaiah in particular, are sometimes used in the New as *dicta probantia;* but it is becoming clear that early Christians searched Scripture to try to understand why Christ suffered the fate of a common criminal, a *lēstēs,* why he was so ignominiously treated, why he was crucified. They found help in the prophets, especially in Isaiah, to understand how God could turn tragedy into triumph.

Isaiah was particularly helpful in the attempt to understand why Christ's own people and contemporaries rejected him. The hard words of Isaiah 6:9–10 were specifically illuminating: Sometimes God hardened the heart of a foreign authority like Pharaoh or sent someone like Isaiah whose proclamation had the purpose, or at least the result, of making his own people's eyes blind, ears deaf, and heart dull. Passages such as Isaiah 42, 49, and 53 and Psalms 22 and 118 illuminated for early Christians the heartbreaking tragedy of the crucifixion in such a way that they could perceive its transformation from ignominy and shame to the symbol of salvation for the world.

Just as the old Israel and Judah had died in the assaults upon them by Assyria and Babylonia but were resurrected (Ezekiel 37) as the new Israel, Judaism in the Exile, so God was effecting through the crucified and resurrected Christ a new Israel, the church. Such citing of Scripture is not prooftexting; it is midrash (Scripture searching) at its best.

Early Christian readings of Scripture shaped the thinking of the church about what God had done in Christ and was doing with them—and it shaped the writing they did when they wanted to share that thinking, whether in gospels, letters, or other literary forms. The basic hermeneutic emerging over and over again as the work progresses on how the Old Testament served the New Testament writers is theocentric. They wanted to know what God was doing and saying to them.

II

Luke's knowledge of Scripture was rather remarkable. His RSV, so to speak, was a Greek text of what the Old Testament was to that point. There is abundant evidence in Luke and Acts that Luke knew his ancient RSV very well indeed, especially certain portions.[4] Whatever Semitisms are in Luke's

---

3. See the still excellent, though now somewhat dated, critical bibliography in Merrill P. Miller, "Targum, Midrash, and the Use of the Old Testament in the New Testament," *JSJ* 2 (1971) esp. 43–78. His can now be supplemented by the bibliography in Paul E. Dinter, "The Remnant of Israel and the Stone of Stumbling in Zion According to Paul (Romans 9—11)," (Ph.D. diss. Union Theological Seminary, 1980).

4. Traugott Holtz claims that Luke knew the Minor Prophets, Isaiah, and the Psalter best of all for this was where he stayed closest to a recognizable Septuagint text (*Untersuchungen über die alttestamentlichen Zitate bei Lukas* [Berlin: Akademie, 1968], pp. 37–43 and 166–73). He also states that Luke did not know the Pentateuch at all. I must disagree with these conclusions: in fact, they are simply wrong.

work can be accounted for otherwise. There is nothing in Luke that exceeds the normal bounds of Semitization already widespread in the Hellenistic language and literature of his time. He thought and wrote in the koiné Greek of his world. And here is a major observation about Luke's knowledge of his Scripture: In no case of Luke's reading and understanding of Scripture does one *have* to go to a Pharisaic-rabbinic type Jewish interpretation of an Old Testament passage to see how Luke moved through the ancient text to his modern message. Quite often one must rummage around in the Targumim, midrashim, and Jewish commentaries before one finds the key to how an Old Testament passage functioned for Matthew. He was sometimes dependent on a particular interpretation or understanding of a passage of Scripture: indeed, it would have been that which he had in mind even as he read or cited a text.[5]

Not so Luke. What is remarkable about Luke's knowledge of his Scripture was that apparently it came from his assiduous reading of it, or portions of it. Luke had his canon within the canon just as everyone and, indeed, every denomination has. That is not the point. The point is that whether before conversion Luke had been a Gentile or a reform Jew, he knew certain parts of Scripture in such depth that unless the modern interpreter of Luke also knows the Septuagint or Greek Old Testament very well indeed, he or she will miss major points Luke wanted to score. And those portions were centrally Deuteronomy and the Deuteronomic history, that is, Deuteronomy to 4 Kingdoms (2 Kings).[6] That particular section of Scripture not only helped shape Luke's understanding of what God was doing in Christ (the gospel) and in the early church (Acts) but also helped shape Luke's two-volume report of that activity.

Luke's reputation as the New Testament historian is well deserved *if* one understands by that term what Luke's Scripture already contained as history. While Luke had some acquaintance with Herodotus, and perhaps other historians known in the Hellenistic world, it was Luke's intense acquaintance with the history of the work of God in ancient Israel, as presented in the LXX Deuteronomic history, that shaped the way he wrote his own. Luke's reputation, since 1954, of being also a good theologian is in no way tarnished by re-appreciation of his work as *the* New Testament historian of the work of God in

---

5. One has to do a bit of sociology of ancient knowledge when attempting to interpret any ancient text, especially when attempting to understand how an ancient author used a text or tradition older than that author. In order fully to understand Matthew's parable of the Great Banquet in 22:1–14, one needs to know the Targum pseudo-Jonathan to Zephaniah 1:1–16, as J. D. M. Derrett has shown in *Law in the New Testament* (London: Darton, Longman & Todd, 1970), pp. 126–55. One needs no such thing to understand Luke's form of it in 14:15–24, as I tried to show in J. Crenshaw and J. Willis, eds., *Essays in Old Testament Ethics* (New York: KTAV, 1974), pp. 245–71.

6. For the central or special section of Luke's Gospel, 9:52—18:14, see C. F. Evans, "The Central Section of St. Luke's Gospel," in D. Nineham, ed., *Studies in the Gospels* (Oxford: Basil Blackwell, 1955), pp. 37–53; and my study of Luke 14:15–24, *Essays in OT Ethics*. Full evidence that the work of Luke as a theological historian was shaped by his understanding of the LXX form of the Deuteronomic history must await further publication.

Christ in the gospel, and the work of God in the early church in Acts. Like
his Old Testament predecessors, he was a good theological historian.

Just a few observations will have to suffice. Luke's two annunciations in
chapter 1 follow, in detail, the great annunciations in Genesis 16—18, 1
Samuel 1, and Judges 13, especially the annunciation to Hannah.[7] The fact
that Mary's Magnificat is but a bare reworking of the Song of Hannah (1
Samuel 2) is another signal Luke offers as to what he is doing. The new
kingdom being announced by God in the first century, to be fully understood, has to be seen in the light of the kingdom introduced by God through
Samuel, culminating in David. In many ways Luke presents Christ as the
new David, even to the point of reporting that Christ asked Saul of Tarsus on
his journey to Damascus (Acts 9:4) a question very similar to the one the
young David had asked King Saul at Ziph (1 Samuel 26:18 LXX). King Saul
had not joined the new kingdom under David; on the contrary, he fell on his
sword and died ignominiously (1 Samuel 31:4). Saul of Tarsus, by contrast,
not only joined the new kingdom under the new David; he became its
greatest herald.

And how does Luke conclude his second volume? "And he [Paul] lived
there [Rome] two whole years at his own expense, and welcomed all who
came to him, preaching the kingdom of God and teaching about the Lord
Jesus Christ quite openly and unhindered" (Acts 28:30–31). Compare that to
what we find at the end of Second Kings. "So Jehoiachin put off his prison
garments. And every day of his life he dined regularly at the king's table; and
for his allowance, a regular allowance was given him by the king, every day a
portion, as long as he lived" (25:29–30). The point is not that King Jehoiachin
was a type for the apostle Paul; the point is that Luke leaves his theological
history of what God was doing in his time as open-ended as the Deuteronomic historian had left his. Jehoiachin was freed from prison in Babylon
at the beginning of the Dispersion of Jews throughout the world; Paul,
though awaiting trial, was free to witness in Rome at the beginning of the
dispersion of the church throughout the world. Each was in the capital of the
dominant power of the time; each was on the threshold of something new in
the work of God. This was undoubtedly Luke's theocentric way of suggesting
a solution to why the Parousia had not taken place upon the fall of Jerusalem
in A.D. 70. He searched the Scriptures and found a way to understand what
God was doing. The eschaton was still expected, no question about that. But
an equally important observation is that it is not for us to know the times and
the seasons of God (Luke 12:35–56). The God who made the first annunciations way back then to Abraham and Sarah, and especially to Hannah, has
announced a new kingdom to come in a spectacular way; and it will come in
God's good time. God is continually active, working his purposes.

III

Luke is the most explicit of the evangelists in insisting that to understand
what God was doing in Christ one had to know Scripture. Nowhere is his

7. See the brilliant work on the annunciations in Raymond E. Brown, *The Birth of the Messiah* (Garden City, N.Y.: Doubleday & Co., 1977), pp. 256–329.

conviction in this matter clearer than in his telling the parable of Lazarus and the rich man in 16:19–31. At the point where the rich man in Hades finally understands why he is there and asks Father Abraham to send Lazarus back from paradise, where he had gone at death, to explain to the rich man's five brothers how matters really lay in ultimate truth, Abraham patiently explained that if they would not read Scripture, Moses and the Prophets, using the right hermeneutics, then they would not be convinced by someone rising from the dead (16:27–31)—which is what would have had to happen to Lazarus if he had been sent back to explain. This passage, set near the climax of Luke's central section, when matched with the same kind of emphasis in the last chapter of the Gospel (24:13–49), after another had indeed been resurrected, conveys Luke's deep-seated conviction that a correct reading of Scripture, Moses and the Prophets, gives one the eyes to see what is going on in the real world.

Luke is interested in eyewitnesses in both his volumes, those who can see what God is doing in the midst of current events. Luke makes it clear that it was not just the appearance of the resurrected Christ, on the road to Emmaus and in Jerusalem, that convinced the disciples of what had been going on and what was happening to them; it was the fact that the resurrected Lord gave them exegesis classes that their eyes were opened and the disciples finally became witnesses (24:48). The disciples, who had been dull and uncomprehending throughout the Gospel, became wide-eyed apostles upon being instructed by the risen Christ through the Scriptures as to what was really happening (24:25, 27, 32, 44, 45); they were then ready for Pentecost, as Luke makes clear at the beginning of Acts. Luke further underscores his point by engaging in a solecism in Greek in 24:32 in his use of the Greek word, *dianoigō*. That verb was used in Greek for the opening of eyes. As in the Semitic languages, there was another word for opening a scroll, but Luke used the same word to speak of how it was when Christ opened the Scriptures to Cleopas and his companion on the road to Emmaus: their eyes were opened.

Luke's Scriptures functioned for him in various ways, not only when he cited a passage or alluded to an Old Testament passage or event or figure, but also when he did not do so. That is, his knowledge of his Greek Old Testament was so remarkable that it helped in numerous ways to shape his history of God's work in the first century. When Luke writes in his prologue of those who from the beginning had been eyewitnesses and servants of the word (1:2), he meant from the beginning of God's work as Creator, Judge, and Redeemer as revealed in the Old Testament. Luke constantly weaves phrases and images from his Greek Old Testament into his writing. A beautiful example is Gabriel's word of assurance (and also chiding) to Mary that with God nothing is impossible (1:37). Those are exactly the same words as those spoken by the heavenly visitors in LXX Genesis 18:14. In Genesis they are in the interrogative form while in Luke they are in the declarative. This shows that Luke not only knew the annunciations generally in the Old

Testament but he knew the ones in Genesis explicitly.[8] It is as though
Gabriel answered his Genesis colleagues back across the centuries, "No,
nothing is impossible with God." Again, Luke's basic hermeneutic was
theocentric.

At this point one might ask how Luke came to know the Old Testament so
well, or, supposing him to have been a reform Jew who already knew
Scripture in Greek, how his congregation knew it well enough to appreciate
all the subtle ways in which he used it. The answer is that new converts are
usually enthusiasts. One of the things that the first-century Christians did
upon conversion, apparently, was to become intimately acquainted with the
Old Testament, whether in Hebrew or in Greek, the only Scripture they
had. Reports out of the new China of today give a picture of churches packed
with young people seeking copies of the Bible which they then read avidly
and with great hunger. One can just imagine in what great demand copies of
the Greek Old Testament were in the Hellenistic churches springing up
around the Mediterranean area. And one can imagine what an insistent
teaching elder Luke was in the instructional life of his own congregation.

Part of that program of instruction clearly included reading Isaiah. Only
three times does Luke actually cite Isaiah or use a formula introduction for a
clear citation. But if the Scripture index of Nestlé-Aland is reflective of the
actual situation, even relatively speaking, Luke falls behind only the Book of
Revelation and the Gospel of Matthew in terms of use of Isaiah in the New
Testament. The three quotations of Isaiah with formula are in Luke 3:4–6
(Isa. 40:3–5); 4:18–19 (61:1–2 and 58:6); 22:37 (53:12). Explicitly clear Isaianic phrases also appear at Luke 2:30–32 (Isa. 52:10; 42:6; 49:6); 7:22 (26:19;
29:18; 35:5–6; 61:1); 8:10 (6:9–10); 19:46 (56:7); and 20:9 (5:1–2). Isaiah 49:6,
which is explicitly cited in Acts 13:47 and is reflected in Luke 1:79 and 24:47
as well as in Acts 1:8 and 26:20, apparently influenced the shape of the whole
of Luke's work.

IV

In order to probe seriously and deeply into what Isaiah is doing in such
passages in Luke, one needs to work on each one in terms of text criticism,
comparative midrash, and canonical criticism in relation to form-critical work
and redaction-critical work. Two which have been so treated are the reflection on Isaiah's Song of the Vineyard (5:1–7) in the Luke 20 parable of the
wicked husbandman[9] and the citation of Isaiah 61:1–2 (with a phrase from
58:6) in the Luke 4 account of our Lord's sermon at Nazareth.[10] The following

8. *Pace* T. Holtz. See n. 4 above.
9. Done by Merrill Miller in his dissertation titled "Scripture and Parable: A Study of the Function of the Biblical Features in the Parable of the Wicked Husbandmen and Their Place in the History of the Tradition" (Columbia University, 1973).
10. See James A. Sanders, "From Isaiah 61 to Luke 4," in J. Neusner, ed., *Christianity, Judaism, and Other Greco-Roman Cults: Studies for Morton Smith at Sixty* (Leiden: E. J. Brill, 1975), part 1, 75–106.

remarks will be based on those studies, especially on work done on Luke 4. One can see how much more needs to be done on other passages in Luke, but our work on Luke generally over the past twelve years indicates that what can be learned from the function of Isaiah 61 and Luke 4 .can be generalized to the rest of the Gospel.

Recent work indicates that Isaiah 58 and 61, or portions of them, constituted the *haftarah* lesson attached to the Torah portion on the death of Israel as lectionary readings already in the first century.[11] It hardly matters actually in terms of how Isaiah functions for Luke in Jesus' sermon. The report of this same event in Mark (6:1–6) and in Matthew (13:53–58) actually focuses on Jesus' works rather than on his preaching, as Luke has it. Furthermore, the other two synoptists place it in the middle of Jesus' Galilean ministry whereas Luke puts it at the very beginning. It is only Luke who provides a citation from Isaiah and a sermon based on it. Luke in effect highlights the event as a harbinger of the crucifixion, for in it he clearly states that Jesus' own home congregation, his relatives and friends, reject him because of his interpretation of the Isaiah passage. This is the opposite of what Mark and Matthew report, where it is Jesus who rejects the people for their unbelief. Therefore in this manner Luke stresses that what offended Jesus' contemporaries the most was his hermeneutics, the way he interpreted one of their favorite passages of Scripture.

First, Jesus read the passage from the Isaiah scroll; then he sat down. The whole congregation waited to hear how he would comment on the passage or what homily he would give. He electrified them by saying that on that day the Scripture was fulfilled in their ears. One has to understand how much that particular passage meant to Jews in the first century under Roman oppression and rule. Isaiah in the Septuagint spoke of a herald anointed by the spirit of God to preach good news to the poor, to heal the brokenhearted, to proclaim release to captives and recovery of sight to the blind, and to proclaim the acceptable year of the Lord. Jesus' reading of the passage in Luke stopped at that point. According to Luke, Jesus omitted the phrase about healing the broken-hearted and inserted one from LXX Isa. 58:6 about sending the oppressed away in release, literally, or to set at liberty those who were oppressed. The phrase in Luke 4:18 is verbatim what we have at LXX Isa. 58:6.

Why could Luke, or Jesus, mix Scripture like that, and could he get away with it? It was not at all uncommon as a practice in the first century to pull two or more passages out of their original literary context and read them together. This was most often done by word tallying, that is, each passage would have had in it one word at least that was the same. In this case it was the Greek word *aphesis*, meaning release or forgiveness: to preach *aphesis* to captives (Isa. 61:1) and to send the oppressed in *aphesis* (58:6).

What one has to realize to get the full impact of this word tallying is that

11. See Robert B. Sloan, Jr., *The Favorable Year of the Lord: A Study of Jubilary Theology in the Gospel of Luke* (Austin, Tex.: Schola Press, 1977).

the word *aphesis* is the Greek translation of the Hebrew *shemittah* in Deuteronomy 15 and the Hebrew *deror* in Leviticus 25—the two passages in the Old Testament which provide legislation concerning the Jubilee year. Luke's Jesus, in conjoining the two passages from Isaiah, did so fully in the spirit, and even the letter, of Isaiah 61 which was itself composed out of the Jubilee traditions.[12] The central concept of Jubilee was periodic release or liberty: letting the land periodically lie fallow, releasing of debts, releasing of slaves, and repatriating property. The Lord's Prayer is basically a Jubilee prayer.[13]

The matter of greatest interest to the congregation in Nazareth hearing Jesus reading the Isaiah passage was release from the burden of Roman oppression, though they would supposedly have been interested in any release the Jubilee might afford. Although release of slaves presented problems (Jeremiah 34), release of debts had proved the most problematic aspect of the old legislation. This is already recognized in Deut. 15:7–11. As time wore on, the problem was met in early Judaism in two ways: in Pharisaic circles it was met by a juridical ploy called *prosboul* whereby waivers could be obtained when the Jubilee year was approaching so that the economy would not collapse; but in eschatological denominations in Judaism it was met by a growing belief that the real Jubilee would arrive in the eschaton and be introduced by the messiah. God's kingdom would come and his will be done on earth as it was in heaven precisely at the introduction on earth of the great Jubilee. That is when the divine economy, or superstantial (not daily) bread of the Lord's Prayer, would be manifest on earth. The congregation in Nazareth may well have been thinking at first that Jesus was the herald of Isaiah 61 sent to proclaim the great Jubilee release from slavery to Roman oppression and economy.

In order fully to grasp Luke's point in placing this episode at the very beginning of Jesus' ministry and in providing us with one of the most precious passages in the New Testament whereby to discern the hermeneutics applied to interpretation of Old Testament Scripture, one does well in reading Luke 4 to resist the temptation to which we usually succumb of identifying with Jesus when we read a gospel passage. We should instead identify with the congregation which, recall, was made up of Jesus' family and friends. Isaiah 61 we now know was one of the favorite passages in Judaism in the time of Jesus.[14] If the faithful in the Nazareth synagogue understood the passage in the way other Jews understood it at that time, they would have interpreted it, just sitting there hearing Jesus read it, as beneficial to themselves. They would have identified, in their turn, with the

---

12. As shown by Walther Zimmerli in the Galling Festschrift, *Archäologie und AT* (1970), pp. 321–32.

13. See Sharon Ringe, "A Gospel of Liberation: An Exploration of Jubilee Motifs in the Gospel of Luke" (Ph.D. diss., Union Theological Seminary).

14. See my "From Isaiah 61 . . ." (above, n. 10), pp. 89ff. See also David Tiede's excellent study, *Prophecy and History in Luke-Acts* (Philadelphia: Fortress Press, 1980), including his sound critique of my own work on pp. 47ff.

poor (which they were), with the captives (which they felt themselves to be under Roman rule), with the blind (feeling themselves like dungeon inmates who suffer prison blindness), and the oppressed (which they surely were). They had every right to feel that the blessings of Jubilee would devolve on themselves when the eschaton arrived and when the messiah, or Elijah, the herald of the eschaton, came.

Therefore, when Jesus seemed to bolster their hope by saying that the passage was fulfilled that very day, of course they spoke well of him. Not because he spoke graciously, as some of the translations lead one to think, but because (a) he had read one of their favorite passages about the grace of God and (b) he had apparently said it would be fulfilled immediately. They were very pleased so far with what he had read and said but only because they had applied a hermeneutic for understanding the passage so as to make themselves the recipients of its blessings. They were hearing it by the hermeneutic of the grace of God; they understood it in terms of God as Redeemer of Israel. God's purpose in sending the herald would have been to save his own people, who were in a bad way, enduring a plight comparable to that of the slaves in Egypt when God sent Moses to release them from Pharaoh's bondage. They would have had every right to understand the passage in such a manner.

But then Jesus went on: "Truly, I say to you, no prophet is acceptable in his own country" (4:24). Why? Because he was Joseph's son? Not primarily; on the contrary, all the great prophets of the Old Testament had been home-grown. Amos had gone from Judah to Israel to preach, but they all had the same covenant identity. Being known in the community in which the prophet preached was common. Nay, it was the kind of message those prophets bore to their people which made them unpopular and unacceptable in their time and to their own people. It was the hermeneutics they applied to the people's most precious traditions, turning those traditions into the authority whereby the prophet exposed the secrets of the hearts of his own people and whereby he exposed their corruption of consciousness. Luke's Jesus makes this point abundantly clear in the blessings and woes of Luke 6:20–26.

Note two things now. Luke has Jesus stop his reading of the Isaiah passage after the first phrase of Isa. 61:2, ". . . to proclaim the acceptable year of the Lord." The rest of the passage goes on to speak of a day of vengeance and how God will bring joy and gladness to a Zion that then mourned. Why would Jesus stop short of reading the rest of the passage which supposedly gave such explicit comfort? First, he stopped reading just before Isaiah spoke of vengeance, supposedly against Israel's enemies, and comfort, supposedly for Israel. But second, he made a telling rhetorical or midrashic point by ending his reading on the Greek word, *dektos*. This word means "acceptable." And it speaks of a year acceptable to God. A later Jewish interpretation understood it to mean a year acceptable to Israel! That indeed would be based on a hermeneutic of grace emphasizing God as Israel's own particular redeemer: God only.

But Luke hereby signals for us his and Jesus' hermeneutic in interpreting the Isaiah passage. No prophet is *dektos* to his own people when he applies their precious, authoritative traditions in such a way as to challenge the thinking of the people and their corruption of consciousness. Here is a word tally in the Lukan passage: the Jubilee will come at a time *acceptable to God;* and the prophet who wrests a prophetic challenge to his own people out of their identifying traditions, precisely by the hermeneutic of the freedom of God as Creator of all peoples, is himself *not acceptable to them.* Isaiah had said to his hearers that they were right to think that God was a Holy Warrior who had aided David in his battles against the Philistines (Isa. 28:21; 2 Sam. 5:17–25; and 1 Chron. 14:10–17), but they were wrong to think that that meant God was shackled to them. On the contrary, Isaiah went on, God as Holy Warrior *and* Creator of all peoples would, this time, be at the head of the Assyrian troops fighting Judah. God was not only Israel's redeemer, God was also Creator and Judge of *all* peoples, including his own. Jesus went on to say something similar to what Isaiah had said.

Did they really want Elijah to come? Why did they not look back at what he did when he was here? Back then when he had a blessing to bestow, he was sent not to a widow in Israel but to a foreigner: a Phoenician widow (1 Kings/3 Kingdoms 17—18). And when Elisha had a blessing to bestow, it was bestowed not on an Israelite leper but on a leper from Syria, Israel's worst enemy (2 Kings/4 Kingdoms 5). The freedom of the God of grace is perhaps the most difficult concept for any generation of believers to grasp.[15] Jesus interpreted Scripture (Isaiah 61) by Scripture (3 Kingdoms 17 and 4 Kingdoms 5) using the hermeneutic of the freedom of the God of grace—free even at the eschaton, in the great Jubilee, to bestow the blessings of Isaiah 61 on other than those who felt quite sure they were elect.

Little wonder the congregation wanted to lynch him. They put him out of the city and attempted to stone him, the punishment for blasphemy (to throw an offender down a cliff is preparatory to stoning). If in reading Luke 4 one identifies with the congregation, one can go with them from the feeling of hope and elation, after Jesus had simply read the Isaianic passage, to the feeling of intense anger which they understandably would feel at hearing the favorite passage (something like John 3:16 for Christians) interpreted in such a way as to indicate that at the eschaton, when the curtain of ultimate truth lifted, God might freely bestow his favors and blessings on folk outside the in-group in "true believers."

What was the real prophetic offense in Jesus' sermon? It was theological: in other words, it was serious, it was ultimate. Jesus was saying to the congregation that God was not a Jew. It would be comparable for us to having the preacher say that God is not a Christian. Of course, God is not a Muslim, Buddhist, or Communist either. That is not the point. The point is that when a people or a church or a denomination so emphasizes God's work as

---

15. See James A. Sanders, *God Has a Story Too* (Philadelphia: Fortress Press, 1979), pp. 14–26.

Redeemer that it feels that it has God boxed up and domesticated, then a prophet must appear to expose this corruption of consciousness. Whenever we feel we have a corner on Truth or a commanding grip on Reality, then, if we are fortunate, a prophet will appear to shock us into realizing that God is God. It is not that God is not our Redeemer. Thank God, he is! But God is also the Creator of all peoples. God is both committed in his promises and free to surprise and even re-create us. God is free to bestow his grace where he will. Grace is a form of divine injustice. It was undeserved when God first bestowed it on Israel, and it may well be undeserved when at the last he bestows it on Phoenician widows and Syrian lepers. This passage stresses what is *acceptable* to God, not what is acceptable to the faithful; it disengages any thought that God's agenda has to follow Israel's. It also stresses *release* or *forgiveness* and how God is free and will be free to dispense it to any or all of his creatures.

In the context from which Luke's Jesus drew the phrase, ". . . set at liberty those who are oppressed . . ." (Isa. 58:6), the prophet challenges the people for feeling God owed them something because they were faithful. "Why have we fasted but you have not seen it? Why have we humbled ourselves but you take no knowledge of it?" The faithful seem always tempted to feel that God should honor their efforts on his behalf.

By dynamic analogy Jesus and Luke bring Isaiah to us as a challenge whenever we as Christians feel we have God boxed into *our* ideas of the Incarnation. The temptation for Christians to feel they have God tamed in the Incarnation is perhaps even greater than it was for Jews to feel they had God on a leash as children of Abraham (Luke 3:8). If one takes a cue from Luke and does a theocentric reading of Isaiah as a whole without, like Luke, worrying for the moment about whether it is First Isaiah, Deutero-Isaiah, or Trito but, instead, looking at the Isaiah book canonically, one would have to say that Luke's Jesus has brought Isaiah forward to the first-century believer and to the twentieth-century believer in a dynamic way true to the canonical Isaiah.

8

John Calvin on Isaiah 6: A Problem in the History of Exegesis

DAVID C. STEINMETZ

> Careful attention to precritical exegesis provides a constant stimulus
> to modern interpreters by offering suggestions they would never
> think of and by allowing them to hear, with ears not their own, voices
> too soft for their own ears to detect.

It is no secret that the history of biblical interpretation in the sixteenth
century represents one of the last, great, virtually unexplored, frontiers of
Reformation history. While the hermeneutics and, to a lesser extent, the
biblical exegesis of Martin Luther have been explored (though we still lack a
synthetic study of Luther as an interpreter of Paul), no one has as yet done
for the history of biblical interpretation in the sixteenth century what
Smalley, Spicq, and De Lubac have done for the history of exegesis in the
Middle Ages. Even less has been done in relating the academic study of
the Bible by theologians to the popular use of the Bible in poetry, story,
and song—to say nothing of its use by lawyers, politicians, exorcists, and
physicians.

In a sense, this lacuna is very puzzling. There was no book more important
in the sixteenth century than the Bible. Cicero, Seneca, Aristotle, Plato,
Quintilian, Augustine, Chrysostom, and Jerome were all important authorities whom intellectuals in that century quoted with great regularity. But
there was no book, honored by intellectuals and ordinary people alike, which
received more attention, was better known, influenced more readers, or was
talked about or commented on more frequently than the Bible. That is a
shining and obvious fact. And yet the study of the history of the interpretation of the Bible in the sixteenth century is still an infant science.

While we have no statistics as yet for the frequency with which editions of
new commentaries on Isaiah were published in the sixteenth century—
though we do know that by 1567 Oecolampadius (1525), Zwingli (1529),
Luther (1532), Münster (ca. 1540), Brenz (1550), Castellio (1551), Musculus

(1557), Calvin (1559), and Bullinger (1567) had all published at least one edition of a commentary on Isaiah—we do have preliminary statistics for the Gospel of John.[1] In the period from 1477 to 1515 not a single living author published a commentary on John in spite of the fact that there were numerous reprints of Patristic and medieval commentaries during the same period. From 1516 to 1555, however, around thirty authors published approximately ninety editions of new commentaries on John. The increase is by any measure an astonishing one.

While it is doubtful that the Book of Isaiah was ever as popular a subject for commentators as the Gospel of John, there is still a significant body of commentaries on it.[2] Among the Greek fathers, Origen, Eusebius of Caesarea, Theodore Heracleensis, Cyril of Alexandria, Theodoret of Cyr, John Chrysostom, Hesychius, Didymus the Blind, and Procopius of Gaza either preached homilies or wrote commentaries on Isaiah. Jerome alone among the Latin fathers wrote a commentary on the whole book, a commentary which, as Jerome freely admits, is heavily indebted to the Greek exegetical tradition stemming from Origen. If we discount, however, the partial commentaries of Augustine, Godefrid, Alan of Lille, and Joachim of Fiore, we still have complete commentaries from such medieval expositors as Walafrid Strabo, Haymo of Halberstadt, Rupert of Deutz, Hervaeus, Thomas Aquinas (including his reflections on Isaiah 6 in the preface to his commentary on John), Albert the Great, Hugh of St. Cher, Nicholas of Lyra and Dionysius the Carthusian. If we add the sixteenth-century Roman Catholic commentators Vatable and Forer to the Protestant commentators we have already mentioned, we find that we have a substantial, if somewhat diffuse and unwieldy, body of Christian literature on Isaiah.

In what follows I want to take one of the more famous oracles of First Isaiah, the vision of the prophet in the temple (Isa. 6:1–13), and examine the treatment of this passage in the history of Christian exegesis. In order to give some focus to this discussion, we will concentrate on the exegesis of one of the most influential and widely read of the sixteenth-century commentators, John Calvin, a theologian whose commentaries are still easily accessible in English translation. In our analysis of Calvin's exegesis we shall focus particu-

---

1. These preliminary statistics were compiled by Timothy J. Wengert, candidate for the Ph.D. in religion at Duke University.

2. The critical apparatus for this chapter could be very extensive and complicated. The editors and I agreed that it would be better to restrict the footnotes to an absolute minimum. Scholars who wish to trace my footsteps can easily do so by looking up Isaiah 6 in the commentaries which I cite. Whenever possible, I read in the Corpus Christianorum or Sources chrétiennes editions and, only when they failed, in Migne. For Hugh of St. Cher, I used the Venice 1732 edition. Nicholas of Lyra was available in a fifteenth-century edition from Nuremberg, while Oecolampadius and Brenz were consulted in their original sixteenth-century printings. Luther, Calvin, Zwingli, Thomas Aquinas, and Dionysius the Carthusian were read in nineteenth-century (more or less) critical editions. Albertus Magnus was available in a 1952 printing from his opera omnia. The quotations from Calvin are for the most part taken from the Edinburgh edition of his commentaries, recently reprinted by Baker Book House. I also read, but did not cite, the marvelous Great Commentary of Cornelius a Lapide, S. J., published at Antwerp in 1654.

larly on five interrelated questions: (1) How often did Calvin comment on Isaiah 6 and in what contexts? (2) What exegetical issues interested Calvin and how did he resolve them? (3) Was Calvin's exegesis altogether new or did it fit into a longer history of commenting on the text? (4) What characterizes the precritical tradition of exegesis on Isaiah, especially as that tradition is exemplified in the exegesis of Calvin? and, finally, (5) Is the precritical tradition still valuable to us, whose exegetical starting point is the historical-critical method?

                                              I

In the preface to his commentary on Romans (1540), Calvin discusses his own exegetical method. While he confesses that he has learned an immense amount from reading the commentaries of Melanchthon and Bucer, he finds that he must develop an exegetical method somewhat different from theirs. Bucer, for example, discusses at length all the theological problems which he encounters in the text. The unhappy result of this procedure is that Bucer's comments are frequently much too long and stand between the student of Scripture and the biblical text. Melanchthon, on the other hand, only discusses the important themes or *topoi* in each chapter, omitting the discussion of many lesser—but to Calvin still important—details.

Calvin attempts to resolve the dilemma posed by the exegetical methods of Bucer and Melanchthon by commenting on each verse of a chapter (*contra* Melanchthon) and by making those comments as brief as the nature of the text will allow (*contra* Bucer). All lengthy discussions of theological topics are reserved for the pages of the *Institutes*, where they do not distract the reader from the immediate task of exegesis and where they can serve as a kind of general orientation to the structure and message of Scripture as a whole. Calvin called his exegetical method "lucid brevity" and it is one of his principal contributions to the intellectual heritage of the Reformation.

If we consult the first edition of the *Institutes* (1546), we find that Calvin makes only one allusion to Isaiah 6:5 (I.vi.15) in order to emphasize that prophets preach folly if they proclaim their own word rather than bear the Word of the Lord. In the final Latin edition of the *Institutes* (1559), Calvin repeats this allusion (IV.viii.3) and adds eleven new ones: seven in book 1, one in book 2, two in book 3, and one additional in book 4. Calvin seems much impressed with John's interpretation of Isaiah's vision as a vision of the glory of the Son and uses Isaiah 6 against Servetus and the antitrinitarians (I.xii.11, I.xiii.23). The vision describes the dread and wonder which one experiences in the presence of God (I.i.3) and contains a warning that one cannot see the incomprehensible essence of God (I.xi.3). Calvin finds in this pericope proof not only for the deity of the Son but also—especially in view of Acts 28:25–26—for the deity of the Holy Spirit (I.xiii.15). There is a cluster of allusions dealing with the doctrine of election and its conse-quences. While Calvin believes that Isaiah teaches that those who extinguish the light of nature befuddle themselves (I.iv.2), he denies that the hardening of the reprobate can be explained by appeals to divine foreknowledge or permission (II.iv.3) and even admits that preaching can lead the nonelect to greater hardness of heart (III.xxiv.13). He will not concede, however, that the doctrine of election makes exhortations to godly living pointless (III.xxiii.13). For the rest, Calvin seems primarily concerned with the implications of Isaiah 6 for ecclesiological questions, such as the authority of the prophets over against false Roman notions of teaching authority (IV.viii.3) and the unity of the covenant of God under two different testaments (IV.xvi.6). In short, Calvin finds in Isaiah 6 resources for dealing with such theological topics as the incomprehensibility of God, the doctrine of the Trinity, the nature of the proper worship of God, the mystery of election and reprobation, and the authority of the church in the Old and New Testaments.

When we turn from the *Institutes* to Calvin's sermons, we find that Calvin preached two series of sermons on Isaiah. The first series, begun in 1546, was not taken down by a secretary and so was lost, though Colladon claims that these sermons became the basis of the 1551 commentary on Isaiah. The second series of sermons ran from July 16, 1556, to sometime just before September 4, 1559, when Calvin began to preach on Genesis. While Calvin's sermons were esteemed in Elizabethan England (indeed, Arthur Golding's translation of Calvin's 159 sermons on Job went through five editions in ten years), they have fared less well in more recent history. Although Denis Raguenier had transcribed 2,042 of Calvin's sermons (all of which were delivered extempore), the Genevan Library in 1805 disposed of forty-four of the original forty-eight sermon manuscript volumes, pricing them according to their weight. Later, of course, the officials of the library realized their mistake and attempted to recover the volumes which had been sold, but thirty-five volumes eluded recovery. Some had been purchased by the Bodleian, some by Bern, some by the Bibliothèque Nationale. Of the 2,304 sermons which we know were transcribed by Raguenier or others (including the 780 sermons published while Calvin was still alive), we have the text of 1,460. Over eight hundred sermons have simply disappeared. Unfortunately, the sermons of Calvin on Isaiah 6 were among the sermons which were lost.

The best and most authoritative text of Calvin's interpretation of Isaiah 6 is the Latin commentary of 1559. Behind it lies Calvin's experience with the text in his French sermons of 1546, his Latin and French commentaries of 1551 and 1552, and his French sermons of 1556–59. While Calvin claimed in his dedicatory letter to Queen Elizabeth I (1559) that he had "bestowed so much care and industry" on the final edition of his commentary "that it ought justly to be reckoned a new work," there is reason to believe that Calvin exaggerated and that the changes are less sweeping than he suggests, more matters of style than of substance. Nevertheless, as the final form of Calvin's exegesis of Isaiah 6, the 1559 commentary represents the distillate of his repeated exegetical work on the text.

II

All of the theological issues which Calvin discussed in the *Institutes* when he alluded to Isaiah 6—the incomprehensibility of God, the doctrine of the

Trinity, the nature of worship, the mystery of election, and the authority of the church—are repeated in one form or another in the 1559 commentary, though without lengthy systematic development. In addition to these theological issues, Calvin raises some exegetical problems, issues such as the order and composition of Isaiah, the nature of Isaiah's vision, and the character of the prophetic message which he bears. Since we cannot discuss in a brief essay all of the theological and exegetical issues which Calvin raises, we shall limit ourselves to these last three exegetical issues, indicating their relationship to larger doctrinal questions as Calvin feels it is appropriate to do so.

1. The Order and Composition of Isaiah

Because Isaiah 6 is dated by the prophet himself as a vision which occurred "in the year that King Uzziah died," Calvin feels himself obliged to comment briefly on the historical circumstances surrounding this oracle. There are two historical-critical problems which Calvin finds in the antecedent exegetical tradition and which he attempts to resolve. We know that these are traditional problems because Calvin introduces them with the words "some think."

Calvin shows himself extraordinarily reluctant to name the commentators with which he disagrees. It is, of course, a fairly common medieval convention to refer to theologians with whom one disagrees as "some" commentators and to be much more explicit in listing by name the authorities with whom one agrees. But Calvin seems to carry such anonymity further than medieval custom requires. That this is a conscious policy T. H. L. Parker has shown by quoting a letter of Calvin to Francis Burkhard, secretary of the Elector of Saxony: "If others have gone wrong on something, I reprove it without mentioning names and without violence, and indeed I bury errors in silence unless necessity forces. . . ."[3]

This policy, admirable in itself, makes it exceedingly difficult to locate Calvin's sources and to retrace the series of preliminary steps which led him to an exegetical decision. Fortunately, however, one of the two historical-critical problems discussed by Calvin in Isaiah 6 is relatively easy to run down. Calvin mentions the opinion of "some" that the death of Uzziah means leprosy, which was a kind of civil death. This is the opinion of the Jewish commentator Rashi, based on a Talmudic saying and repeated by the later Jewish commentator Ibn Ezra. While Calvin may have read this exegetical judgment in Jewish sources, it seems far more likely that he came across it in the commentary of the Franciscan expositor, Nicholas of Lyra, who cites Rashi by name.

Calvin, however, accepts death in its literal sense and is convinced that Isaiah prophesied in the interval between the onset of the leprosy of Uzziah and his subsequent death. The blindness of the people about which Isaiah so feelingly speaks in chapter 6 is a blindness which he has already experienced

---

3. Cited by T. H. L. Parker, *Calvin's New Testament Commentaries* (Grand Rapids: Baker Book House, 1971), p. 86.

and the vision is intended to encourage him in the further discharge of an office which he has already accepted and undertaken.

When Calvin accepts a literal reading of "death," he agrees with the vast majority of patristic, medieval, and Reformation commentators. He does not suggest, however, some of the possible exegetical implications of a literal meaning of the text developed in the preceding tradition. Jerome argued that people could not see God in a temple defiled by Uzziah's illicit offering of incense any more than we can see God so long as we are ruled by the leprosy of sin. The death of Uzziah was the precondition for the vision of God. Other fathers, such as Eusebius, Chrysostom, and Cyril, suggest that there was no prophetic oracle during the reign of Uzziah after he was struck down with leprosy and argue that the death of Uzziah marked the resumption of prophecy. Theodore of Moepsuestia in his commentary on Amos rejected the notion that there was an interruption in prophecy during the reign of Uzziah, though he was unable to prove that any of the prophecies were delivered after Uzziah's sacrilege in the temple. Theodoret of Cyr agreed that there was a cessation of prophecy between the sacrilege in the temple and the death of Uzziah but blamed Isaiah for this cessation rather than the king. Had Isaiah denounced the act of the king in the temple, prophecy would not have come to an end. Chrysostom, and to some extent Cyril, disagree with this interpretation. Chrysostom finds no reason to impugn the character of Isaiah or to blame the temporary loss of prophecy on him.

Of this patristic debate or the suggestion that prophecy was interrupted during the reign of Uzziah, Calvin mentions not a word. Calvin's view was that Isaiah prophesied throughout the reign of Uzziah and that, while the death of Uzziah was marked by the "various commotions . . . produced by a change of kings," it did not mark the resumption of prophecy or the lifting of a penalty imposed by God on Judah for the sacrilege of its king or the cowardice of its prophet.

The second historical-critical problem is somewhat more difficult to trace down to its roots. Calvin reports the opinion of "some" commentators that chapter 6 is misplaced and belongs really at the beginning of the Book of Isaiah, prefatory even to chapter 1. Calvin cites three reasons which have been given in support of this judgment on the composition and order of Isaiah: (1) First of all, Isaiah in chapter 6 declines an office which he already appears to exercise in chapters 1—5; (2) furthermore, he talks like a novice and seems to be unacquainted with the demands of his office; and (3) finally, Isaiah claims that this is the first vision of God which he has received and that he was the recipient of no such prior ecstatic experience. Calvin dismisses all of these arguments as "feeble and unsatisfactory." He regards Isaiah in the temple as so "overpowered by the presence of God," so "like one who had lost his senses," that he forgot that he had been a prophet and the recipient of previous oracles. The principal reason, however, why this overwhelming vision of the presence of God was delayed until Isaiah had begun his work as a prophet was in order to confirm him in the discharge of his office. He could have been disheartened by the "hard-hearted obstinacy of the people" and unsettled by the "changes of times and kings." It was only after Isaiah had begun to prophesy that God appeared to him. The new vision was necessary in order to encourage him to persevere. Therefore the order of chapters at the beginning of the Book of Isaiah is the correct one.

It is very difficult to know who the "some" are who argue that Isaiah 6 has been misplaced. Oecolampadius in 1525 also mentions that this is the opinion of "some" commentators, though he gives so much less detail than Calvin does that he cannot be Calvin's primary source. Zwingli, Luther, and Brenz do not mention the problem at all. The suggestion that Isaiah 6 is misplaced is not found in Origen, Eusebius, Theodore, Cyril, Theodoret, Chrysostom, Procopius, Jerome, Walafrid Strabo, Haymo, Rupert, Ibn Ezra, Hervaeus, Thomas Aquinas, Albert the Great, Hugh of St. Cher, Nicholas of Lyra, or Dionysius the Carthusian. Clearly, whoever the "some" commentators are to whom Calvin alludes, they represent an exegetical minority. The majority of expositors seem, like Calvin, to be satisfied with the canonical ordering of chapters 1—6.

2. *The Nature of Isaiah's Vision*

Far more interesting to most patristic and medieval commentators than the order and dating of Isaiah's vision are the theological and epistemological implications of Isaiah's claim, *vidi dominum* ("I saw the Lord"). How is it possible, the commentators wonder, to see a God whose essence is invisible and cannot be seen? Yet Isaiah attributes to this invisible God "a throne, a robe and a bodily appearance." What did Isaiah see and how did he see it?

Both Nicholas of Lyra and Dionysius the Carthusian mention the suggestion of pseudo-Dionysius that what Isaiah saw was an "angel." Nicholas, who is always sympathetic to Jewish readings of Old Testament texts, softens what other commentators regard as the trinitarian setting of this vision by pointing out that the threefold repetition of the *sanctus* ("Holy, holy, holy is the Lord of hosts") was an ancient Hebraic way of giving greater expression to the notion of divine sanctity. None of the Christian interpreters, however, picks up the comment of Ibn Ezra that the heavenly conversation which Isaiah overhears ("Whom shall we send and who will go for us?") is in fact a conversation between God and the seraphim.

The Christian commentators feel themselves bound by John 12:41 to regard the theophany as in some sense a revelation of Christ and by Acts 28:25-26 to regard the voice which speaks to Isaiah as the voice of the Holy Spirit. Coupling these verses with the threefold *sanctus*, the Pauline and Johannine notions that the Son is the image of the Father, and the trinitarian traditions of Christian theology, most Christian commentators—including Calvin—conclude that the vision is a vision of Christ, but a vision which involves in one way or another the whole Trinity. Only Zwingli among the early Protestants keeps his options open by calling it a vision of an image, type, form, or even sacrament of God. Calvin argues that while Isaiah saw the glory of Christ, what he saw cannot be limited to the person of Christ, since the word *Adonai* ("Lord") is applied to God "in an absolute and unrestricted manner." Furthermore, while Calvin accepts the traditional view that the repetition of the *sanctus* points to the doctrine of the Trinity, he regards that proof by itself as weak. The heretics have a point when they object that three denotes the perfection of holiness and may say more about the "unwearied perseverance" of the angels in singing the praise of the holiness of God than it does about the Trinitarian doctrine as such. Still Calvin is willing to agree with the "ancients" that the passage is Trinitarian, however reluctant he may be to use the passage polemically.

The early Christian fathers do not spend time discussing the epistemological implications of Isaiah's vision. Theodoret warns that the fact that God has appeared under many forms to the patriarchs and prophets does not mean that God is polyform. His essence is simple, without parts, invisible, and inaccessible. For the rest Theodoret prefers to talk about the nature of God apophatically and to insist that the Son who knows the nature of the Father has never revealed it.

By the later Middle Ages, however, scholastic commentators show an interest in the psychology and epistemology of prophetic vision. Nicholas of Lyra refers his readers back to his comments on the nature of prophecy at the beginning of his commentary on Psalms, while Albert the Great and Dionysius the Carthusian discuss the nature of Isaiah's vision in some detail. Though not all scholastic commentators agree exactly in their outline of the structure of the problem, there seems to be fairly wide consensus that Isaiah's vision was not corporeal; it was imaginative and intellectual. That is to say, no one standing beside Isaiah would have seen what he saw, as everyone at Belshazzar's feast saw the handwriting on the wall. The images which Isaiah saw were implanted in his imagination by God. The prophet was also given an understanding of the intellectual signification of those images, otherwise it would have been an hallucination rather than a prophetic vision. What Isaiah saw he did not see with his eyes but with his mind. Nevertheless, he was not given intuitive knowledge of the nature of God, only knowledge by abstraction.

Calvin seems to prefer to return to the simpler discussion of this verse which marked patristic exegesis. Rather than engage in extended epistemological discussions he simply invokes one of his most characteristic theological principles: the principle of accommodation. "When God exhibited himself to the view of the Fathers, he never appeared such as he actually is, but such as the capacity of men could receive." The vision of the throne, the robe, and the bodily appearance were adapted to the capacity of Isaiah "to perceive the inconceivable majesty of God." What is true of Isaiah's vision is true of all human knowledge of God from whatever source. No human being knows God as he is but only as he has adapted himself to the limitations and capacities of human nature. All knowledge of God is accommodated knowledge.

3. The Character of the Prophetic Message

In his vision Isaiah was given a troubling message: "Go and say to this people: 'Hear and hear but do not understand; see and see, but do not perceive.' " It appears on the face of it that Isaiah has been commissioned as a messenger of bad news, a herald of an inevitable judgment to come which cannot be avoided. Everything Isaiah says, so the vision seems to imply, will harden the people of Judah in their obstinate defiance of God. Is God the author of the opposition to his message? Has he foreordained the resistance which Isaiah meets? Is there a possibility of free response to Isaiah's message or has divine predestination foreclosed the possibility of repentance? It is not an easy question to answer, and it is clearly a question which troubles the Christian interpreters of Isa. 6:9–10.

Theodoret of Cyr speaks for the overwhelming majority of patristic commentators when he stresses human freedom and responsibility rather than divine foreordination. The infirmities of the congregation to whom Isaiah preaches are not the work of nature; they are the result of deliberate choice. Nature did not blind the eyes of Isaiah's listeners; the listeners themselves have closed them. What is at stake is not the physical weakness of organs but the stubborn refusal to believe. God has predicted the response of Judah; he has not preordained it. Judah will persist in its perversity until destruction is brought down around its ears. Like most of the patristic and medieval commentators, Theodoret feels himself bound by John 12:39–40 to regard the destruction which is foretold as the final destruction by Vespasian and Titus. For the rest, the spirit of torpor which overcomes the Jews was "given" by God only in the sense that God has permitted them to be overwhelmed by the accumulated consequences of their own free decisions. Jerome feels that the point of the passage is that God has concluded Israel in unbelief that he might have mercy on the Gentiles and that the text celebrates the mercy of God rather than his cruelty—especially since repentance is still a possibility for at least a remnant of the Jews. Neither the freedom of the human will (Theodoret) nor the mercy of God (Jerome) is seriously in question.

Dionysius the Carthusian feels that what we have in this oracle is a prophetic denunciation of future evils, not a command or exhortation to commit evil. While people may hear the words of the prophet, they will not understand internally what he is saying. Dionysius is keen to distinguish what happens consecutively from what happens causally. It is true that hardness of heart follows consecutively upon the denunciation which the prophet preaches. It is not true that the proclamation of the prophetic message is itself the cause of that hardness of heart. Judah is blind because it deserves to be, and the attitude of God toward this blinding is permissive rather than active. Walafrid Strabo, Haymo of Halberstadt, Rupert of Deutz, Hervaeus, and Thomas Aquinas all echo to a greater or lesser degree the exegesis of Jerome.

When we come to the Protestant reformers, the stress remains on the responsibility of the congregation to whom Isaiah preaches for their own blindness. Luther, who believes in predestination, nevertheless believes that Isaiah is not invoking predestination at all when he bemoans the voluntary obtuseness of Judah. Johannes Brenz, the Lutheran reformer of Schwäbisch Hall, who gives one of the two or three very allegorical interpretations of

Isaiah 6, is convinced that the blindness of the Jews which concerns Isaiah is blindness concerning the gospel of Christ. Zwingli interprets this verse in the context of sixteenth-century eucharistic controversies and explains the blindness of the Jews as a blindness with respect to Christ's word that he would give them his flesh to eat.

Even Calvin stresses, both in his commentary on Isaiah 6 and in his commentary on John 12:39–40, the responsibility of unbelievers for their predicament. In the commentary on John (1553), Calvin makes an important point not made by other commentators. God wills that Isaiah speak his Word. It is accidental to that Word and not essential to it that it blinds the men and women who hear it. In itself the Word is life-giving. When it meets adamant unbelief, however, it leaves the unbelieving hearers in a far worse state than it found them. The Word of God, in other words, is never ineffectual. It either produces death or life. It never leaves things as they are.

In his commentary on Isaiah, Calvin makes much the same point. God foretells a state of affairs for which unbelievers themselves are responsible. "Such blinding and hardening influence," says Calvin, "does not arise out of the nature of the Word, but is accidental, and must be ascribed exclusively to the depravity of man." On the other hand, Calvin is willing to admit, when pressed for an answer, that ". . . if you inquire into the first cause, we must come to the predestination of God." Still, having said this, Calvin shows no eagerness in his commentary to discuss predestination. What he prefers to stress instead is the function of this oracle as an encouragement to Isaiah.

Only in the *Institutes* does predestination come to the fore. There Calvin attacks the patristic notion that the hardening of unbelievers takes place through foreknowledge or permission (II.iv.3). Indeed, Calvin refers his readers to the chapter in which he attacks the notion of permission as Epicurean (I.xviii), epitomized by his image of "God in a watchtower," a lazy deity who is an idle spectator of a history which he neither can nor will influence. Calvin wishes to talk about the ways in which God carries out his judgments through Satan as a minister of his wrath. God is not merely passive in the process of the hardening of sinners, in spite of the fact that sinners are responsible for their own condition. Something more is involved, even though that "something more" ought not to become the object of curious speculation.

III

While it is dangerous at any time to make generalizations, it is especially dangerous to make generalizations about the whole history of Christian exegesis in the light of the analysis of a small part. Nevertheless, some observations can be made in the light of our analysis of the history of the exegesis of Isaiah 6, so long as it is understood that these observations are only tentative hypotheses which should be tested further in other contexts.

1. Christian interpreters of Isaiah 6 show very little interest in the allegorical interpretation of their text. Hugh of St. Cher suggests an allegorical

interpretation of the seraphim and Luther offers an alternative allegorical interpretation, almost as a theological exercise. Only the Lutheran Brenz is thoroughly committed to an allegorical interpretation of Isaiah 6 as its sole meaning. Most interpreters are concerned with the literal-grammatical interpretation of Isaiah. The fact that they are willing to consider that the vision of Isaiah was a vision of the glory of Christ does not mean that they are any the less interested in the literal sense, but only that the literal sense of the Old Testament must be subordinate to the literal sense of the New. The Old Testament is not attached for Christian interpreters to the Talmud (though they may make use of Jewish insights) but to the New Testament. There are only two possibilities for them: Old Testament plus Talmud or Old Testament plus New. There is no such thing as the Old Testament in itself abstracted from the religious communities in which it lives.

2. On the whole, Christian interpreters seem conservative about the canonical shape of the text as it has been received from the synagogue by the church. Most Christian interpreters think that Isaiah did in fact prophesy before Isaiah 6 and that chapters 1—5 contain early oracles. At the same time most interpreters agree that there was an interruption in the prophetic activity of Isaiah associated with the sacrilege of Uzziah in the temple, a reading which Calvin rejects. Very few authors are impressed with the suggestion of Rashi that the death of Uzziah was the civil death created by his leprosy. Some interpreters think that the vision in Isaiah 6 and the oracles in chapters 1—5 all occur in the same year, the year in which King Uzziah died, an interpretation to which Calvin himself does not subscribe. In short, while commentators do raise historical-critical questions, only a very few interpreters (Calvin calls them vaguely "some" commentators) seem inclined to rearrange the canonical order of the oracles. Calvin even draws a spiritual lesson from an order which places Isaiah 6 after chapters 1—5.

3. While Christian interpreters are reluctant to tamper with the canonical shape of Isaiah, they do not regard the canonical shape itself as theologically determinative. They are not interested in the theology of a redactor of whom they have never heard. The theological context for considering an oracle of Isaiah is not merely the theology of First Isaiah as a whole or even the theology of First Isaiah as reinterpreted in the New Testament but the theology of the Christian church in the whole sweep of its historical development. God did not become a trinity at the Council of Nicaea, though Nicaea clarified what had always been true. The God who created the world, who called Israel out of bondage, who revealed himself in the temple to Isaiah, was and is one God eternally subsisting in three Persons. Therefore it is not anachronistic to detect hints of the Trinitarian nature of God in the vision of Isaiah, though Isaiah himself may have seen more than he explicitly understood. It is simply sound exegesis. The hermeneutical key to the Old Testament is the *regula fidei* (in the broadest sense) of the Christian church.

4. There seems to be a tendency in the history of exegesis, arrested by the Protestants who wish in this instance to return to an earlier form of exegesis as preferable, to use materials and methods drawn from the general cultural

history of Western civilization in the exegesis of a text. Medieval interpreters are fascinated by the epistemology and status of prophetic vision. They do not attempt to explain prophetic ecstasy by appealing solely to other biblical traditions or to the traditions of Christian theology. They unashamedly make use of philosophical traditions which had their origins in Greek antiquity but which have been commented on for centuries by generations of pagan, Islamic, Jewish, and Christian interpreters. Secular learning has its rightful place in the exegesis of Scripture and a question cannot be shunted aside as irrelevant or unanswerable simply because the Bible does not give an answer to it. Universal natural truths concerning prophetic ecstasy are as true of Isaiah in the temple as they are of any other religious ecstatic, whether pagan, Islamic, Jewish, or Christian. The explanations which are offered are, of course, not historical but philosophical. The exegete is not interested in particular but relative "truths," limited in their cultural application. He is interested in universal and unchanging truth, transcending every particular instance of its application.

5. The Christian exegetical tradition appears to be conservative both in its method of procedure and in its exegetical results. All the later commentators seem to know and quote the earlier commentators, at least those commentators whose writings have been widely preserved. While commentators disagree (though disagreement seems to oblige the dissident to offer a reasoned explanation for his opinion) and while at times those disagreements take on a polemical tone, nevertheless the disagreements demonstrate that commenting is not an art which begins *de novo* with each generation. It belongs to the art of commenting to read all the commentators who have gone before. This exegetical tradition serves as a check on the singular opinions of various enthusiastic commentators and acts as a control on the practice of exegesis as such.

Indeed, it appears on occasion that the exegetical tradition may even be more conservative than the traditions of dogmatic theology. Calvin joins the almost universal chorus of previous commentators on Isa. 6:9–10 when he shows himself reluctant to talk about predestination in the context of his commentary on Isaiah. When he talks about predestination in the *Institutes* in the context of dogmatic theology, Calvin is not at all hesitant to quote Isa. 6:9–10 in support of this discussion. The shift of contexts seems to give him greater freedom. In the context of the genre of commentary he seems restrained by the overwhelming weight of the exegetical tradition, not to deny that predestination is suggested by the words of Isaiah (Calvin does not have an uncritical respect for the opinions of the Greek Fathers), but to stress rather (even if on his own terms and in his own way) the importance of human responsibility.

IV

In 1885 Frederic W. Farrar, chaplain to Queen Victoria and later Dean of Canterbury, delivered the Bampton Lectures at Oxford on the subject of the history of interpretation. The book is a triumph of what the late Sir Herbert Butterfield of Cambridge called "Whig" historiography. Farrar admires about the past precisely those elements in it most like the present and regards the present, indeed, as the inevitable culmination of all that was best in the past. The history of exegesis becomes for Farrar the history of "more or less untenable" conceptions of the Bible, "a history of false suppositions slowly and progressively corrected."[4] Not surprisingly, Farrar admires Antioch over Alexandria, Luther over Thomas Aquinas, Calvin over Luther, and the moderns over all. Farrar catalogues with obvious delight every strained allegory, every factual inaccuracy, every philological howler committed by precritical exegetes in the name of biblical interpretation. While he admits that ancient commentaries are full of practical instruction aimed at moral and spiritual edification and that much of this instruction is "of the highest intrinsic value," he nevertheless warns that frequently such material "has but a slender connexion with the text on which it is founded."[5]

It is difficult to recognize the exegesis of Isaiah 6 which we have just examined in the general description of the history of exegesis which Farrar has offered. To be sure, it is true that the older consensus on the historical-critical setting of Isaiah 6 would find few supporters among modern commentators, but the older discussion of these questions does not seem arbitrary or strained, even by modern standards. The judgment of Christian commentators that Isaiah saw the glory of Christ was an exegetical conclusion forced on the commentators by the New Testament itself, though there was a tendency on the part of some commentators—including Calvin—to soften the hard edges of that exegesis. The discussion of free will (Theodoret of Cyr), divine mercy (Jerome), and predestination (Calvin) stimulated by Isa. 6:9–10 may have gone far beyond the intentions of the author of the text; but one could not say that the theological discussion had no intrinsic connection to it. While the precritical exegesis of Isaiah 6 is not an exegesis we can simply adopt, it is still not accurate to regard it as arbitrary and strained, of value only for its homiletical asides.

It is no answer to Farrar to point out that there is a good deal in ancient commentaries which is surprisingly modern, even from an historical-critical or philological viewpoint or to argue that the modern reader can find insight into the "literal" sense of the text in precritical commentaries. That is to admit his principle that precritical exegesis is good in the proportion that it anticipates or agrees with modern exegesis. Nor is it an answer to reply with a *tu quoque* and to list the exegetical atrocities which have been committed from time to time in the name of the historical-critical method, though such a list is disquietingly easy to compile.

The principal value of precritical exegesis is that it is not modern exegesis; it is alien, strange, sometimes even, from our perspective, comic and fan-

---

4. Frederic W. Farrar, *History of Interpretation* (Grand Rapids: Baker Book House, 1979), p. xiv.
5. Ibid., p. vii.

tastical. Precisely because it is strange, it provides a constant stimulus to modern interpreters, offering exegetical suggestions they would never think of themselves or find in any recent book, forcing them again and again to a rereading and reevaluation of the text. Interpreters who immerse themselves, however, not only in the text but in these alien approaches to the text may find in time that they have learned to see, with eyes not their own, sights they could scarcely have imagined and to hear, with ears not their own, voices too soft for their own ears to detect.

9

A Living Tradition:
The Book of Jeremiah in
Current Research

James L. Crenshaw

> Careful study of the Book of Jeremiah helps us remain faithful to the
> prophet's legacy by learning from him to weigh the traditions of the
> past and to use them in the struggle to forge a better world.

The thirty-first meeting of the Biblical Colloquium at Louvain, Belgium on
August 18–20, 1980, was entirely devoted to the Book of Jeremiah. The
twenty papers of this session covered a broad range of topics; seventeen of
them subsequently appeared in volume 54 of *Bibliotheca Ephemeridum
Theologicarum Lovaniensium*.[1] In addition, two surveys of research on the
Book of Jeremiah have recently appeared[2] and another was published in
1983.[3] Naturally, these assessments of the status of research on the biblical
book were prompted by a spate of articles and monographs, and the future
promises more of the same, including four commentaries currently under
way.[4] Since others have provided comprehensive surveys of research, I shall
restrict the present discussion to the issues that seem most problematic at
the moment.

The fundamental issue can be stated forthrightly: How can we recognize

---

1. P. M. Bogaert, ed., *Le Livre de Jérémie* (Leuven: University Press, 1981).
2. Siegfried Herrmann, "Forschung am Jeremiabuch," *ThLZ* 102 (1977) 482–90, and Georg
Fohrer, "Neue Literatur zur alttestamentlichen Prophetie (1961–1970). VII. Jeremia," *ThR* 45
(1980) 109–21. See also T. R. Hobbs, "Some Remarks on the Composition and Structure of the
Book of Jeremiah," *CBQ* 34 (1972) 257–75, esp. 261–67.
3. Leo G. Perdue, "Jeremiah in Modern Research: Approaches and Issues," in Perdue and
Brian W. Kovacs, eds., *A Prophet to the Nations: Essays in Jeremiah Studies* (Winona Lake,
Ind.: Eisenbrauns, 1983). The following topics are discussed at length: (1) the date of Jeremiah's
call, (2) Jeremiah and the Deuteronomic reform, (3) the foe from the north, (4) the text of the
book, (5) the composition of the book, (6) the quest for the historical Jeremiah, and (7) new
directions of research (rhetorical criticism, canonical shaping, and social dimensions).
4. ICC (McKane); OTL (Carroll); New Century Bible (Jones); BKAT (Herrmann). John
Thompson, *The Book of Jeremiah* (Grand Rapids: Wm. B. Eerdmans, 1980), provides a recent
study of Jeremiah from the conservative perspective.

authentic materials of Jeremiah when the book contains distinctive literary styles? The differences in style are so pronounced that they have given rise to a theory of four sources in chapters 1—45 (the remaining chapters 46—52 are usually considered secondary): (A) poetic oracles in 1—25; (B) biographical narrative in 26—45; (C) prose sermons in 1—45; and (D) a book of consolation in 30—31. The issue is further complicated by similarities in style and language between Deuteronomy and the "prose sermons." Five significant questions therefore require attention: (1) What texts really derive from Jeremiah? (2) Did the prophet borrow the language and style of a book toward which he must surely have felt ambiguous? (3) Who speaks in the book, Jeremiah or the later community? (4) Do the so-called confessions reveal anything about the prophet Jeremiah? (5) Did Jeremiah stand alone over against the other prophets of his day? In this essay we shall address these five issues and endeavor to clarify the basic problems that have surfaced thus far.

I. THE INSPIRED POET

Bernhard Duhm's legacy has come to dominate Jeremianic studies in one important respect. This is the assumption that prophets were inspired poets. To be sure, other scholars such as Hermann Gunkel and Hugo Gressmann took for granted the originality of the poetic word. This position has recently been reasserted with reference to Jeremiah by Robert Carroll. He writes: "The difficulties encountered by biblical scholars in determining which elements are primary and which secondary may be modified by attending to the poetic sections as primary, with some poetic additions, and the rest as secondary."[5] The qualifying phrase, "with some poetic additions," suggests that Carroll, like others before him, is unwilling to reckon every poetic saying as an authentic word from Jeremiah. In practice a further distinction has often been made: Inferior poetry is considered secondary. One could point to numerous instances of such reasoning, but it would serve no real purpose.

Now if, first and foremost, prophets were poets, it follows that we should look only to the poetic texts for authentic words from Jeremiah. Such is the conclusion that many critics have reached. But the situation becomes considerably more complex when the problem of the original scroll enters the picture, for our information about that early document comes entirely from the narrative accounts within the book. Both the fact of the scroll and the description of its contents derive from the prose itself.[6] What if the story about King Jehoiakim's destruction of the scroll is tendentious? This pos-

---

5. *From Chaos to Covenant: Prophecy in the Book of Jeremiah* (New York: Crossroad, 1981), p. 11.

6. William L. Holladay observes that there is no reason to doubt the accuracy of the account, in *The Architecture of Jeremiah 1—20* (Lewisburg and London: Bucknell University Press/ Associated University Presses, 1976), p. 174; others are not so sanguine.

sibility has not prevented a search for the original scroll and the expanded version that Jeremiah is said to have dictated to Baruch.

Seizing a clue from the narrative description, scholars look for poetic oracles which pronounce judgment. For example, William Holladay believes that he has succeeded in isolating the contents of the original scroll and the expanded one. To the first scroll belong the call (1:4–14), the harlotry cycle (2:2–3, 5–37; 3:1–5, 12b–14a, 19–25), and the foe cycle (4:1—6:30; 8:4–10a, 13). The second scroll includes these poetic units plus a supplementary foe cycle (8:14—10:25).[7]

The title of Holladay's book calls attention to the architecture of the book. By this he means the rhetorical features that comprise the structure itself. Jack Lundbom's study of the rhetoric in the Book of Jeremiah[8] argued that chapters 1 through 20 comprise a distinct unit, one that is held together by the inclusio in 1:5 and 20:18 ("you came forth from the womb"/"from the womb did I come forth"). Whereas Lundbom restricted his analysis to inclusio and chiasmus, Holladay takes into account a wide range of rhetorical features. While I appreciate the emphasis on stylistic expression, especially by a scholar with the linguistic gifts of Holladay, I have reservations about his basic argument for two reasons. First, I fail to see why one inclusio (that observed by Lundbom) is preferred over several others, the most notable being the verbs about building and planting, tearing down and uprooting in chapters 1 and 24. The second reason is even more weighty. Given the extensive redactional activity that shaped the final form of the book, how do we know that a particular stylistic device indicates the original structure of the book? For instance, if chapter 24 is the result of redaction in Deuteronomistic circles, as most critics assume, then inclusios may derive from a later hand than the original compiler. How does one determine the stage at which such poetic niceties entered the text?[9] In the final analysis the issue is the *extent* of editorial work.

As a matter of fact, the argument from rhetoric cuts two ways. Helga Weippert has launched a concerted effort to demonstrate that a formal prose was widespread in the ancient Near East during Jeremiah's day.[10] Her most recent essay examines the Aramaic texts from Tell Deir 'Alla and neo-Assyrian salvation oracles, concluding that a formal prose similar to Deu-

---

7. In this analysis Holladay differs from Claus Rietzschel, for whom the original scroll extends from 1:4 to 6:30 (*Das Problem der Urrolle: Ein Beitrag zur Redaktionsgeschichte des Jeremiabuches* [Gütersloh: Gerd Mohn, 1966]).

8. *Jeremiah: A Study in Ancient Hebrew Rhetoric,* SBLDS 18 (Missoula, Mont.: Scholars Press, 1975).

9. Carroll raises similar objections: "The way the chiasmus has been fractured by redaction or transmission makes one less impressed by the claims of Lundbom and Holladay for rhetorical criticism. It is an important approach to the text, but the redaction or transmission has been content to destroy the chiastic symmetry in order to incorporate into the statement a number of elements from the tradition" (*From Chaos to Covenant,* p. 294).

10. *Die Prosareden des Jeremiabuches,* BZAW 132 (Berlin and New York: Walter de Gruyter, 1973), and "Der Beitrag ausserbiblischer Prophetentexte zum Verständnis der Prosareden des Jeremiabuches," in *Le Livre de Jérémie,* pp. 83–104.

teronomy was in existence throughout the area. If her thesis can be sustained, it calls into question the assumption about poetic oracles as the original nucleus and the claim that the Book of Jeremiah has been edited by persons who were influenced by Deuteronomy. In Weippert's view the formal prose within the book actually goes back to the prophet.[11] Here she moves one step further than John Bright, according to whom the rhetorical prose arose in the decade following Jerusalem's downfall,[12] and Artur Weiser, who believed that a liturgical prose was widespread in Judah, a type of preaching that occurs both in Jeremiah and in Deuteronomy.[13]

One significant feature of Weippert's argument is that the prose sermons are actually the paraenetic part of Jeremiah's attempt to move the people to repentance.[14] This demetrification of poetry had as its goal the turning of the people to God. The Deuteronomists are therefore dependent upon Jeremiah for the form of their sermons, Weippert contends. Naturally, her thesis collapses if one adopts the view that Jeremiah did not begin his ministry until after Josiah's death. Holladay, for example, believes Jeremiah modeled his prose sermons after Moses' speeches in Deuteronomy just as he used the form of Deuteronomy 32 as a model for his poetic oracles.[15]

II. REDACTIONAL ACTIVITY

The striking affinities between the prose "sermons" in the Book of Jeremiah and Deuteronomy have been explained in yet another way, specifically through the hypothesis of redactional activity by persons under Deuteronomic influence. One of the earliest efforts to clarify the nature of such editing was an article by J. Philip Hyatt[16] in which he significantly altered the predominant source theory proposed by Sigmund Mowinckel and essentially endorsed by Wilhelm Rudolph in his contribution to the *Kommentar zum Alten Testament* series. Mowinckel himself shifted from literary analysis to tradition history in 1946, and Hyatt later worked out his views in the *Interpreters Bible*.

Two scholars have pursued this line of thinking with important results.

---

11. Holladay concurs in her judgment that the prose sermons go back to Jeremiah, but differs from her over Deuteronomic influence, which he thinks is very real. See "A Fresh Look at 'Source B' and 'Source C' in Jeremiah," *VT* 25 (1975) 394–412, esp. 409–12.

12. "The Date of the Prose Sermons of Jeremiah," *JBL* 70 (1951) 15–35. See also *Jeremiah*, AB 2 (Garden City, N.Y.: Doubleday & Co., 1965).

13. "Here it is a matter of phraseology in public worship" (*The Old Testament: Its Formation and Development* [New York: Association Press, 1961], p. 217).

14. A. Vanlier Hunter denies the view that prophets endeavored to call the people to repentance. In his opinion, the exhortations are subsumed under the larger sentence of a judgment that has already been established (*Seek the Lord! A Study of the Meaning and Function of the Exhortations in Amos, Hosea, Isaiah, Micah, and Zephaniah* [Baltimore: St. Mary's Seminary and University, 1982]). The issue is more complex than that in my judgment. I am not prepared to rule out altogether a summons to repentance as an intrinsic function of Israelite prophecy.

15. "'Source B' and 'Source C' in Jeremiah," pp. 410–11.

16. "Jeremiah and Deuteronomy," *JNES* 1 (1942) 156–73. See also "The Deuteronomic Edition of Jeremiah," *Vanderbilt Studies in the Humanities* 1 (1951) 71–95.

Ernest W. Nicholson explained the prose tradition as preaching to the exilic community.[17] This means that the sermons addressed specific concerns of the Jews who resided in Babylon rather than those of Jeremiah's immediate environment. Nicholson thinks the likely place for such preaching and teaching activity was the synagogue.[18] Nevertheless, he regards some of the material in these prose sermons as Jeremianic and insists that the Deuteronomists have altered this authentic nucleus to meet their own needs at a later time. Other materials were, in his opinion, created *ad hoc* by the exilic teachers. In the first of these techniques, the adapting of earlier material to later situations, Jeremiah himself paved the way, according to Nicholson.

A similar emphasis underlies Winfried Thiel's exhaustive studies of the redactional activity behind chapters 1—45.[19] Authentic words of the prophet have been subjected to a thorough Deuteronomistic editing so as to present the people with a choice to accept or reject the divine word. This redactional activity led to the juxtaposing of a word of judgment and a promise of deliverance. The people's response to the two words in the exilic situation determined which one became operative in their own lives. If Thiel is right, the Book of Jeremiah illuminates the exilic community as well as the Judahite, and a mere surface reading of historical narrative in the Book of Jeremiah obscures the richness of the text.

Even this interpretation of the evidence may be less complex than the actual situation warrants, for Gunther Wanke's investigation of the so-called Baruch narrative has arrived at the conclusion that three different tradition complexes lie behind the biographical material in the book.[20] These are (1) 19:1—20:6; 26—29; 36; (2) 37—44; and (3) 45; 51:59—64. If Wanke is correct, we must reject earlier claims that the biographical sections were written by a single scribe[21] who wished to depict Jeremiah as a suffering prophet. Al-

---

17. *Preaching to the Exiles* (Oxford: Basil Blackwell, 1970).

18. Ibid., p. 134. See also E. Janssen, *Juda in der Exilzeit*, FRLANT 69 (Göttingen: Vandenhoeck und Ruprecht, 1956), p. 107.

19. *Die deuteronomistische Redaktion von Jeremia 1—25*, WMANT 41 (Neukirchen-Vluyn: Neukirchener Verlag, 1973), and *Die deuteronomistische Redaktion von Jeremia 26—45*, WMANT 52 (Neukirchen-Vluyn: Neukirchener Verlag, 1981). William McKane has pointed to the various levels on which such statistical analyses as Thiel's and Weippert's function and has demonstrated the complexity of the problem by focusing upon two brief texts ("Relations Between Poetry and Prose in the Book of Jeremiah with Special Reference to Jeremiah III 6–11 and XII 14–17," VTSup, *Congress Volume, Vienna* [Leiden: E. J. Brill, 1981], pp. 220–37). I share McKane's caution with regard to such endeavors as those represented by Thiel and Weippert.

20. *Untersuchungen zur sogenannten Baruchschrift*, BZAW 122 (New York and Berlin: Walter de Gruyter, 1971). See also Karl-Friedrich Pohlmann, who views certain texts, esp. 37—44, as fourth-century apologetic in behalf of the Babylonian exiles at the expense of those Jews who remained in Judah or who subsequently emigrated to Egypt (*Studien zum Jeremiabuch*, FRLANT 118 [Göttingen: Vandenhoeck und Ruprecht, 1978]).

21. James Muilenburg, "It has been our contention that the so-called 'Deuteronomic additions' by no means represent a separate source, but conform to conventional scribal composition and are therefore to be assigned to Baruch" ("Baruch the Scribe," in John I. Durham and J. R. Porter, eds., *Proclamation and Presence* [London: SCM Press, 1970], pp. 215–38; p. 237 cited).

though first articulated by Heinrik Kremers,[22] the popular presentation of the *via dolorosa* by Gerhard von Rad has influenced countless students of the Book of Jeremiah.[23]

The overwhelming evidence for Deuteronomistic editing obviates the need for justifying Jeremiah's use of language and style from a book that promulgates a theology which the prophet seems clearly to have rejected. Whereas Deuteronomy establishes a single holy place, Jeremiah denounces that temple as destined for destruction. The old covenant was a failure, so Jeremiah proposes another one. The resulting picture of the prophet is somewhat disjointed. Although he insists that all genuine prophets proclaimed a message of judgment, hopeful words are attributed to him. How can we explain this apparent inconsistency?

III. THE BOOK OF CONSOLATION

One explanation proceeds from similarities between Hosea and Jeremiah, which lead scholars to argue that chapters 30—31 contain a nucleus of an early message to the survivors of the Northern Kingdom. Even such a skeptic as Carroll concedes that 31:2–6, 15–20 represent Jeremiah's early preaching of hope to Israel.[24] This tiny ray of hope was subsequently transformed into the bright beam that shines forth from chapters 30—31. In a recent treatment of the themes of "gathering and return" in Jeremiah and Ezekiel, J. Lust acknowledges that an authentic nucleus may underlie chapters 30—31, but in his view the materials have been thoroughly edited by an exilic redactor.[25] In particular, the theme of "return" does not appear in the earliest strata of the Book of Jeremiah, but derives from an exilic redactor. Lust thinks this theme was later adapted to the Diaspora and probably compared with the exodus event. He makes the interesting observation that in several instances the theme is muted in the Septuagint. It is noteworthy that a strong case has been made for preferring the Septuagintal text over the Massoretic, which is expansionistic and represents later redactional activity.[26]

Another response to the question about the inconsistency of attributing positive words to Jeremiah focuses on the changed situation after the fall of Jerusalem in 587 B.C. This argument runs as follows: The collapse of the Judean state confirmed the authenticity of Jeremiah's message, demonstrating to one and all that he was indeed a true prophet. The Deuteronomists therefore chose to use him as a means of addressing their own people with an alternative to opt for or against the divine word. The irony is that they chose

---

22. "Leidensgemeinschaft mit Gott im Alten Testament," *EvTh* 13 (1953) 122–40.

23. *Old Testament Theology* (New York: Harper & Row, 1965), 2:206–8.

24. *From Chaos to Covenant*, p. 210.

25. "'Gathering and Return' in Jeremiah and Ezekiel," in *Le Livre de Jérémie*, pp. 119–42.

26. J. Gerald Janzen, *Studies in the Text of Jeremiah*, HSM 6 (Cambridge: Harvard University Press, 1973).

a prophet who failed miserably and attempted to bring about a different response to his message in their own day. Carroll perceived this irony quite clearly: "All the time the prophet Jeremiah strides through the tradition as the true prophet, the central focus of the community's life. This is not only hindsight; it is ideology."[27]

IV. THE QUEST FOR THE
HISTORICAL JEREMIAH

The search for the real Jeremiah has recently been likened to the quest for the historical Jesus,[28] and the difficulty is said to be greater in dealing with the prophet from Anathoth. If the teachers in the exilic community shaped Jeremiah's words so as to address their own people, how can we be sure that the stories themselves are not literary creations without any solid basis in fact? What is to prevent critics from concluding, as Carroll has done, that Baruch was a "construct" invented by the Deuteronomists to carry certain elements of the tradition[29] and that Jeremiah's absence from the stories about the organization and life under Gedaliah gave rise to the account of Jeremiah's royal imprisonment?[30]

Is there a single text that offers irrefutable evidence about the prophet Jeremiah? Until a short time ago most interpreters would have answered this question by pointing to the confessions, for in them one seems to encounter the outpourings of a sensitive individual. That consensus has eroded as a result of several analyses of these unusual poems. The unsettled nature of this question is reflected by the two essays on the so-called confessions in the volume which emerged from the Colloquium at Louvain. The traditional view was largely upheld by Franz D. Hubmann, who had earlier written a thorough study of the redaction of these texts,[31] while an opposing interpretation was offered by J. Vermeylen.[32] According to Vermeylen, it is preferable to call these texts *psalms* and to emphasize their place in the *book* bearing the name of Jeremiah rather than to view them as actually having derived from the prophet. Accordingly, each psalm represents the dramatic episodes during the exilic period, then those events associated with the second temple, and finally the sharp conflict between the postexilic community and the impious.

Of course this debate has engaged scholars for some time, but the contours of the argument have changed greatly from those arising out of Henning Graf Reventlow's claim that these texts are best explained in connection with a

27. *From Chaos to Covenant*, p. 255.

28. Ibid., p. 25.

29. Ibid., p. 151.

30. Ibid., p. 228.

31. "Jer 18, 18–23 im Zusammenhang der Konfessionen," in *Le Livre de Jérémie*, pp. 271–96; and *Untersuchungen zu den Konfessionen Jer 11, 18–12, 2 und Jer 15, 10–21*, FzB 30 (Zurich: Echter Verlag, 1978).

32. "Essai de Redaktionsgeschichte des 'Confessions de Jérémie,'" in *Le Livre de Jérémie*, pp. 239–70.

prophetic office in the cult.[33] Naturally, this thesis met stiff resistance, especially from John Berridge, John Bright, and Sheldon Blank.[34] Blank sought to characterize the poems as paradigms which Jeremiah himself provided for later generations who struggled to maintain faithfulness in the midst of adversity. Gerhard von Rad has proposed a sort of compromise,[35] for he believed the prophet Jeremiah took up his commission and internalized it in a manner that was wholly unprecedented. The result was a struggle within Jeremiah's soul that eventuated in no comforting resolution. Von Rad's remarks about a change in literary style as the result of this inner struggle have now been supplemented by Giorgio Buccellati,[36] whose observations about the lyric style appropriate to theodicy are surely applicable beyond the Mesopotamian texts which occupy the center of his attention.

The lyrical character of these soliloquies in the Book of Jeremiah poses an important question: Did ancient poets adapt their style to accord with the subject matter? Perhaps we need to ask whether certain types of material lend themselves more readily to prose than to poetry, and vice versa. It may be that the radical distinction between poetry and prose is both arbitrary and misleading when applied to the matter of authenticity.

To return to the task of establishing the actual account of Jeremiah's life, we note a growing skepticism with regard to the traditional date of Jeremiah's call. In the face of such questioning of the biblical record, which represents the beginning of his ministry in 627 B.C., alternative dates have been suggested that remove the problems presented by the virtual absence of any oracles from a time prior to the death of Josiah in 609. Although Hyatt argued long and hard for the date 609, his view met stiff resistance. It has been championed recently by Holladay,[37] who believes Jeremiah was born in 627 and called to a prophetic vocation then (so 1:5), while his actual prophetic activity did not begin until the death of Josiah in 609. Holladay thinks the words in 1:4—11:6 were delivered between 609 and 601, and that some of the "confessions" emerged early in 600 in connection with a vocational crisis brought on by opposition prophets. Norbert Lohfink endeavors to combine

---

33. *Liturgie und prophetisches Ich bei Jeremia* (Gütersloh: Gerd Mohn, 1963). Compare Erhard Gerstenberger, "Jeremiah's Complaints: Observations on Jeremiah 15:10–21," where it is argued that an older layer, vv. 10–11, was augmented in the tradition by 15–21, and still later by 13–14 (*JBL* 82 [1963] 393–408).

34. Berridge, *Prophet, People, and the Word of Yahweh* (Zurich: EVZ Verlag, 1970); Bright, "Jeremiah's Complaints: Liturgy, or Expressions of Personal Distress?" in *Proclamation and Presence*, pp. 189–214; idem, "A Prophet's Lament and Its Answer: Jeremiah 15:10–21," *Int* 28 (1974) 59–74 ("His faith was neither serene nor unshakable; on the contrary, there were times when it crumbled beneath him and spilled him into the pit of despair," p. 69); and Blank, "The Prophet as Paradigm," in James L. Crenshaw and John T. Willis, eds., *Essays in Old Testament Ethics* (New York: KTAV, 1974), pp. 111–30. See also Muilenburg, "The Terminology of Adversity in Jeremiah," in Harry Thomas Frank and William L. Reed, eds., *Translating and Understanding the Old Testament* (Nashville: Abingdon Press, 1970), pp. 42–63.

35. "Die Konfessionen Jeremias," *EvTh* 3 (1936) 265–76, published in Eng. trans. in *Theodicy in the Old Testament* (Philadelphia: Fortress Press and London: SPCK, 1983).

36. "Wisdom and Not: The Case of Mesopotamia," *JAOS* 101 (1981) 42–44.

37. "A Coherent Chronology of Jeremiah's Early Career," in *Le Livre de Jérémie*, pp. 58–73.

both views; he thinks Jeremiah worked prior to 609 as a propagandist and poet for Josiah's court, but became a prophet in 605.[38] If the dramatic events of 609 and 605 radically affected the life of Jeremiah, can one conclude the same about the severe drought that devastated the country in 601? The latest examination of the liturgy associated with that drought (14:1—15:9) has yielded an affirmative answer to this question.[39]

By far the most devastating attack on the traditional view that we can discover the real Jeremiah has come from Robert Carroll. He writes: "The prophet behaves as a perfect deuteronomist because to the deuteronomists that is how a prophet working in Josiah's time should behave. Ideology shapes and creates the representation of the prophet, and helps to explain why the deuteronomists produced the Jeremiah tradition. . . ."[40] In Carroll's view, the prophet who pronounced judgment gradually became in the hands of the traditionists a preacher of the community's well being. Similarly, the prophet preached repentance, failed, became more negative, and lost all hope; whereas the tradition then developed the motif of repentance into a dogma of repentance.[41] The deuteronomists also created the image of Jeremiah as intercessor and suffering just one.[42] Still Carroll recognizes the polyvalency of the Jeremianic materials, the wide latitude of interpretation that such texts evoke. Of the soliloquies he writes:

> . . . it [this material] is the outpouring of Jeremiah's own confessions, it is the redactors' shaping of those confessions, it is the community's response to the tragedy, it is the laments of various sixth-century groups, it is a later presentation of the community's responses to grief under the image of the prophet, or it is even a theologization of the divine suffering brought about by the destruction of the people. . . .[43]

While the general tone of Carroll's book is negative, here he approaches an appreciation for the contribution of the traditionists. Perhaps the words of Siegfried Herrmann provide the ablest corrective to the denigration of the activity of the Deuteronomists.

> What has been handed on to us is, in the best sense of the term, "living tradition," reminiscences which are unsimplified, restricted to a few lines, given uniformity by only a few witnesses. The text points to history, and has itself undergone a history. It is not insignificantly shaped for further historic effect.[44]

---

38. "Der junge Jeremia als Propagandist und Poet: Zum Grundstock von Jer 30—31," in *Le Livre de Jérémie*, pp. 351–68.

39. W. A. M. Beuken and H. M. W. van Grol, "Jeremiah 14, 1—15, 9: A Situation of Distress and Its Hermeneutics. Unity and Diversity of Form—Dramatic Development," in *Le Livre de Jérémie*, pp. 297–342. While the emphasis falls on unity of structure and drama, the authors do think the text can derive from Jeremiah or nearly so. Holladay would seem to be even more convinced of the Jeremianic origin of this text, at least in nucleus (14:2–6; 15:5–9; *The Architecture of Jeremiah 1—20*, pp. 147–48).

40. *From Chaos to Covenant*, p. 105.

41. Ibid., p. 77.

42. Ibid., pp. 115, 124.

43. Ibid., p. 261.

44. "Forschung am Jeremiabuch," p. 488.

Herrmann goes on to describe the living tradition as a process by which the Word of God became visible to the community, a point which Nicholson has made most effectively.

V. PROPHETIC CONFLICT

The implications of extensive redactional activity behind the Book of Jeremiah are immense. If the prose sermons and biographical material, together with the soliloquies of the book, reveal a great deal about the exilic and postexilic Jewish community, can we trust the account that represents Jeremiah as a prophet standing alone over against a host of prophets who uttered a different word for the people? Do the stories of confrontation fall into the same category as other Deuteronomistic narratives whose purpose is essentially didactic (for instance, 1 Kings 13),[45] so that the issue of historical veracity was subsumed under an eminently greater purpose? Those scholars who have discussed the problem of prophetic conflict have by and large not addressed this issue, for they take it for granted that the stories are rooted in fact even though they often use stereotypical features.[46] There is one exception to this judgment, the study by Ivo Meyer.[47]

The thesis of this book is that in genuine oracles deriving from Jeremiah, other prophets opposed the people, not Jeremiah. Meyer does grant that prophets occasionally confronted Jeremiah (5:30–31; 6:9–15), and this fact gave the later redactors a polemical stance that they developed for all it was worth. In short, passages like 23:9–32 are comprised of a number of disparate elements. They are literary mosaics rather than historical accounts. In Meyer's view the polemic reflects the Deuteronomistic theology according to which the prophets played a decisive role in accomplishing the divine judgment against Jerusalem.

The disquieting feature of Meyer's monograph derives from its method rather than its conclusions. He makes absolute claims about genuine and spurious texts on the basis of various literary traits: tension within a unit; repetition; doubling of introductory formulae; linguistic affinities; colorless, superfluous, or characteristic vocabulary and the like. To be sure, these are judgments that most of us make to a greater or lesser extent. Yet I think Meyer says far more than can be known about a given text. What is at stake is the precise nature of poetry, the freedom to shock, to startle, to lull the

---

45. For recent discussion of this fascinating text, see Werner E. Lemke, "The Way of Obedience: 1 Kings 13 and the Structure of the Deuteronomistic History," in Frank M. Cross, Werner E. Lemke, and Patrick D. Miller, eds., *Magnalia Dei: The Mighty Acts of God* (Garden City, N.Y.: Doubleday & Co., 1976), pp. 301–26.

46. For works prior to 1971, see my *Prophetic Conflict: Its Effect Upon Israelite Religion*, BZAW 124 (Berlin and New York: Walter de Gruyter, 1971). A more recent discussion of the problem is by James A. Sanders, "Hermeneutics in True and False Prophecy," in George W. Coats and Burke O. Long, eds., *Canon and Authority* (Philadelphia: Fortress Press, 1977), pp. 21–41.

47. *Jeremia und die falschen Propheten, Orbis Biblicus et Orientalis* 13 (Freiburg: Universitätsverlag; Göttingen: Vandenhoeck und Ruprecht, 1977).

audience to sleep by repeating what has already been said, and so on. In my judgment, we must begin to search for ways to recognize a poet's freedom of expression that departs from custom, both syntactic and grammatical.[48]

The essential truth in Meyer's thesis is the recognition that the conflict between Jeremiah and the other prophets functions in the book as a sort of theodicy. The collapse of the Judean state was interpreted as divine punishment for the villainous conduct of the professional leadership in Jerusalem. If Carroll's promised monograph[49] on the struggle among prophets in Jeremiah's day follows up this lead, which he has himself recognized and remarked upon again and again, we shall begin to understand better the texts concerning the prophets in the Book of Jeremiah.

In my analysis of prophetic conflict I characterized the history of prophetic research under three rubrics according to the emphasis of a given period. Those three foci were (1) the prophet, (2) the message, and (3) the audience. As I saw it, a decisive shift occurred from the great individual, the ethical monotheist, to the actual content of the prophetic word, especially its formal characteristics; and then yet another emphasis emerged, specifically the community within which prophets spoke their words. The three foci are integrally related, and our conclusions about one radically affect what we think about the other two.

If my earlier assessment of the situation is accurate, the next step in research requires a thorough examination of rhetoric, for one cannot attend to the audience without taking into account modes of speech that were shared by the prophet and those who heard the prophetic word. The art of persuasion was a point of contact between the two, prophet and people, just as it provides for us a means of access to the worlds of the prophet and the audience. It follows that sociological analysis is essential to this task of understanding the means of persuasion adopted by a given prophet. Although still in its infancy, this sort of approach has received impetus from at least two fronts. Robert R. Wilson has drawn heavily upon the ancient Near Eastern world of prophecy and mediation to clarify the issue of a "support group,"[50] while Thomas W. Overholt has turned to the native American scene in an effort to understand how groups determined authentic words when bogus messages were also falling on their ears in abundance.[51] Perhaps

---

48. I have tried to address this issue in several recent studies, the latest of which is "Wisdom and Authority: Sapiential Rhetoric and Its Warrants," *VTSup, Congress Volume, Vienna* (1980), pp. 10–29. A recent analysis of a text in Jeremiah by Phyllis Trible is especially pertinent here: "The Gift of a Poem: A Rhetorical Study of Jeremiah 31:15–22," *ANQ* 17 (1977) 271–80.

49. *From Chaos to Covenant*, p. 319.

50. He argues that Jeremiah championed older Ephraimite traditions and was supported by certain Levitical groups and kinsmen. If the materials on which Wilson draws have undergone extensive editing, his historical conclusions become problematic (*Prophecy and Society in Ancient Israel* [Philadelphia: Fortress Press, 1980]).

51. "The Ghost Dance of 1980 and the Nature of the Prophetic Process," *Ethnohistory* 21 (1974) 37–63. See also "Jeremiah and the Nature of the Prophetic Process," in *Scripture in History and Theology: Essays in Honor of J. Coert Rylaarsdam* (Pittsburgh: Pickwick Press, 1977), pp. 129–50.

one should also mention in this connection Douglas A. Knight's study of moral consciousness as reflected in the Book of Jeremiah.[52]

CONCLUSION

Thus far we have asked five questions as a means of introducing some important studies about specific problems of interpreting the Book of Jeremiah. The lack of any adequate answers should occasion little surprise for the readers of this essay. The issues are by no means simple ones, for they concern the nature of religious language itself. The divine word cannot be isolated from human speech by resorting to a theory of poetics or syllable counting,[53] and stories do not necessarily connote secondary derivation. In a word, the later traditionist may be no less inspired than the original prophet; and the prose which confronts the exilic and postexilic community with a spiritual choice must surely be on par with enigmatic poetry. What we witness in the history of the text that bears the name "Jeremiah" is a living tradition, one that is absolutely essential to the spiritual health of a community. Indeed, that vital tradition is kept alive by those of us who read the Book of Jeremiah and endeavor to grasp its meaning in an age when the ancient faith stood in jeopardy. The threat to survival of cherished convictions fashioned a crucible from which emerged new words for the people. If in the process clear distinctions between fact and fiction disappeared, who can say that the end result was a mistake? The real error, in my view, is the dogged insistence that the words attributed to Jeremiah and the stories about him are understood correctly only on the "factual" level. What we have lost as the result of recognizing that the text gives us limited and debatable information about Jeremiah is more than compensated for by the emerging insight into the religious concerns of the later community.

Perhaps a final word about this "debatable" information is appropriate. While I think the emphasis on redactional activity in shaping the present form of the Book of Jeremiah is salutary, I do believe a caveat is necessary in the light of extreme conclusions of the sort Carroll advances.[54] Do we know enough about the circumstances of exilic and postexilic life to insist that certain stories and themes belong there rather than in Jeremiah's time? Are the circumstances of the communities so distinct that every line of continuity is severed? Could not some of the stories and theological expressions function in both contexts? This is the decisive issue; if theodicy, for example, was

---

52. Two things dominate the discussion: the conditions of the moral agent (rationality, volition, affectivity, sociality, temporality, and historicality) and the ambiguity of hope. Knight concludes that Jeremiah adopted an equivocal position on the question of moral freedom ("Jeremiah and the Dimensions of the Moral Life," in James L. Crenshaw and Samuel Sandmel, eds., *The Divine Helmsman* [New York: KTAV, 1980], pp. 87–105, esp. pp. 100–101).

53. I have reference here to David Noel Freedman's simplistic solution to the problem of determining authentic prophecy: "Pottery, Poetry, and Prophecy: An Essay on Biblical Poetry," *JBL* 96 (1977) 5–26, esp. 24–26.

54. For an assessment of Carroll's book see Gordon H. Matties's review, *CBQ* 45/2 (1983): 276–80.

a burning question in both communities, in Jerusalem and in Babylonia, there was a line of continuity that later redactors wished to claim for their own time. Since Carroll believes the operative word is discontinuity, he remains consistent when insisting that Jeremiah has no word for us today, but grandly inconsistent as well: "Surely here is word from Jeremiah if any will receive it—yesterday's dogma is today's life" and "To enshrine his tradition in the same way so that we revere it is to have learned nothing from his work."[55]

The point is well taken, but one does not have to enshrine or revere a tradition to appreciate it. Jeremiah's opposition to the dogma of his own day was grounded in an understanding of reality that had been transmitted to him from previous generations; in the same manner we can remain faithful to his legacy by weighing the traditions of the past and by using those which survive critical scrutiny in the struggle to forge a better world. Still, we have no assurance that we shall be any more successful in that endeavor than Jeremiah was; and we may be "torn and shattered by the sense of the apparent absence and neutrality of God."[56]

---

55. *From Chaos to Covenant*, p. 278.
56. Muilenburg, "The Terminology for Adversity in Jeremiah," in *Proclamation and Presence*, p. 62. Jeremiah 20:7 advances beyond an apparent absent or neutral God to one who seduces and overpowers innocent people. I intend to publish a monograph on this perception of God as "enemy" in the near future.

10

The Book of
Jeremiah: Portrait of
the Prophet

WALTER BRUEGGEMANN

The Jeremiah portrayed in the Old Testament book bearing his name
has become the paradigmatic figure of the prophet as he struggles
with his God and with his own vocation of announcing God's Word to
his time.

Our theme does not invite us to a new quest for the historical Jeremiah. The
critical problems concerning the relation of the person of Jeremiah to the
Book of Jeremiah are notoriously difficult, and there seems to be no great
progress on that question in current scholarship. It is fair to say that current
scholarship tends toward a "minimalist view" concerning the historical Jeremiah. Scholars are assigning more and more work to the redactional process,
which leaves less and less material assigned to the "authorship" of Jeremiah
and yields (according to the hypothesis) less reliable historical information
about the prophet.

On the relation of the person to the redactional process, we may identify
two tendencies. On the one hand, there is a scholarly tradition which pays
attention to the person of Jeremiah. This tradition generally regards the
early part of the book as coming from Jeremiah and credits as historically
reliable much of the material in the Baruch section of the book. In English
literature the older book by John Skinner[1] is a powerful statement of this
view, which is also the working assumption of John Bright's commentary.[2] It
is the inclination of William Holladay,[3] who has published a series of important articles, and it is indirectly the basis of Robert R. Wilson's[4] sociological

1. John Skinner, *Prophecy and Religion* (Cambridge: Cambridge University Press, 1922).

2. John Bright, *Jeremiah: Introduction, Translation, and Notes*, AB 21 (Garden City, N.Y.:
Doubleday & Co., 1956).

3. William Holladay, *Jeremiah: Spokesman Out of Time* (Philadelphia: United Church Press,
1974).

4. Robert R. Wilson, *Prophecy and Society in Ancient Israel* (Philadelphia: Fortress Press,
1980), pp. 231–51.

analysis. This view tends to accept (in broad outline) the presentation of Jeremiah offered to us.[5]

The alternative view (which currently is on the increase) pays much more attention to the redactional process and assumes that the person of Jeremiah given to us is largely a reconstruction of the Deuteronomic theologians. That inclination is very much in evidence in the analysis of Ernest Nicholson[6] and is carried to an extreme position in the recent work of Robert Carroll.[7] It is reflected in the title of H. J. Gunneweg's study "Confession or Interpretation,"[8] concerning the confessions of Jeremiah. Gunneweg concludes that what is given to us is an interpretation and not a direct confession of Jeremiah. The confessions are primarily "proclamations and not lyrics." More broadly, Siegfried Herrmann draws a like conclusion:

> In this large perspective, the book of Jeremiah is incomparably more than the record of the man from Anathoth. Under the impact of numerous and different materials, the book is the settlement of the past, the call to repentance, a document of hope for Israel and the future direction of Yahweh for all peoples.[9]

These issues are most complex and cannot be resolved here. They are not irrelevant to our subject of a "portrait," however. It is clear that in the book of Jeremiah we do not have in any simple way a descriptive, biographical report. Indeed this portrait, like every portrait, is passed through the perceptions of the artist. The person of Jeremiah offered to us is in some sense (as is every such piece of literature) a construction of literary imagination.[10] Yet it is also probable that the person, memory, and impact of Jeremiah were so powerful and enduring that that personal reality presided over and shaped the imaginative reconstruction. It is thus plausible to state this premise for our study: We have an imaginative literary construction

5. Discerning studies of the person of Jeremiah from a less critical perspective are offered by Elie Wiesel, *Five Biblical Portraits* (Notre Dame, Ind.: University of Notre Dame Press, 1981), pp. 97–127; and William J. Urboch, "Jeremiah: A Man for Our Seasoning," *Currents in Theology and Mission* 5 (1978) 144–57.

6. Ernest W. Nicholson, *Preaching to the Exiles* (Oxford: Basil Blackwell, 1970).

7. Robert Carroll, *From Chaos to Covenant* (New York: Crossroad, 1981). See also Peter R. Ackroyd, "The Book of Jeremiah—Some Recent Studies," *JSOT* 28 (1984) 47–59.

8. H. J. Gunneweg, "Konfession oder Interpretation im Jeremiabuch," *ZTK* 67 (1970) 395–416.

9. Siegfried Herrmann, "Die Bewaltigung der Krise Israels," in Herbert Donner, Robert Hanhart, and Rudolf Smend, eds., *Beitrage zur Alttestamentlichen Theologie* (Göttingen: Vandenhoeck und Ruprecht, 1977), p. 172.

10. On the "construction" of a person, see Roy Schafer, *Language and Insight* (New Haven: Yale University Press, 1978), esp. pp. 8–18. Two points especially are important. First, that the human person is not given but is constructed, and the particular construction is what interests us. Second, that the construction given us does not concern *the* present or *the* past, but only *a* past and *a* present. A different construction might have been chosen. One must make the move, of course, from Schafer's psychological interest to our concern with this historical literature. Yet the linkage suggests a way around the vexing and interminable critical questions on Jeremiah. Likely the portrayal of David as understood by David M. Gunn, in *The Story of King David*, JSOTSup 6, proceeds on parallel presuppositions. We have there as well a construct of literary imagination.

governed by a powerful person of memory. That reconstruction is not historically precise, but it is not literarily fanciful, undisciplined, or cut loose from its referent. It is not preoccupied with psychological or sociological matters which might interest us. It is theologically intentional, and the theological intent is to articulate[11] this person of Jeremiah as a model or paradigm[12] for what a prophet is, what a believing person is, for what Israel might be. The move from personal history to theological model loses something in historical accuracy (in any case not recoverable by us). Yet this move gains much in generative power that can summon Israel to faith in a profound crisis. The "redactors" are not clerks who play fast and loose or who are indifferent to their subject matter. Rather, as creative theologians they are artists making faith possible in Israel's deepest crisis. We deal with an identifiable man, but with a man now articulated for the sake of God's continuing way with Israel.

JEREMIAH—GOD'S MAN

Jeremiah is presented to us as overwhelmingly God's man. This is the first thing one notices about him in the superscription of 1:1–3. He is a man to whom God's persistent, inescapable, and overriding Word has been delivered. His life consists in coming to terms with that Word, finding ways to articulate it to his contemporaries, and living with the hazardous consequences of that reality.

A person so utterly claimed by and preoccupied with the sovereign Word of God seems an oddity to us, perhaps because we are modern and Jeremiah is ancient. Yet to be so called and identified is an inscrutable oddity in any time, including the time of Jeremiah. This circumstance completely set Jeremiah at odds with his contemporaries. His call and his reference to Yahweh gave him an angle on historical reality which left him at various times anguished, dismayed, depressed, and hopeful. His discernment of his historical moment under the rule of Yahweh caused him to dismiss in judgment much that was valued and to discern in hope possibilities where his contemporaries recognized none.

1. This vocation as God's special agent and messenger is clearest at the outset, in the call narrative of 1:4–10 and in the visions which follow (1:11–16). The call narrative is highly stylized. Perhaps it is intended as a literary statement of authorization rather than a report of an experience.[13] However such a critical issue may be resolved, it is clear that Yahweh holds initiative for Jeremiah's life.

---

11. I use the word in an active, formative way, not unlike Dale Patrick's use of "render" in *The Rendering of God in the Old Testament* (Philadelphia: Fortress Press, 1981).

12. For one discussion of Jeremiah as a paradigm, see Sheldon H. Blank, "The Prophet as Paradigm," in J. L. Crenshaw and J. T. Willis, eds., *Essays in Old Testament Ethics* (New York: KTAV, 1974), pp. 111–30.

13. Carroll, *From Chaos to Covenant*, chap. 2, argues this point vigorously. See his thesis statement on p. 52.

a. He has been "known/consecrated/appointed" by Yahweh (1:5). He has been "made holy" for God's purpose. The narrative account states the point vigorously, but no argument is made or evidence given. It is all prehistorical, prerational. It is "from the womb," which makes it beyond the reach of analysis. There is no "precalled" Jeremiah.

b. He has been "sent/commanded/set" for the sake of a mission (vv. 7, 10). And the mission is to be wrought by words (v. 9). Those words are "mine, not yours" (i.e., from Yahweh, not from Jeremiah). They are words of discontinuity, words which end what was seen to be absolute, words which begin what was seen to be impossible. This man is one who is summoned to shatter and form worlds by his speech.

c. He is a man to whom peculiar promises have been made, promises of safety and defense (vv. 17–19). Indeed, the supreme promise is made to this man: "I will be with you" (vv. 8, 19). The God who authorizes is the one who stands in solidarity. Yet what a strange accompanying presence it is, for Jeremiah often experiences life alone, desolate, and abandoned. One draws the conclusion that often God is present and with Jeremiah only at the "eleventh hour" and not before.

It is worth noting that we have no judgment to make about the historicity of this initial narrative. It is part of the portrait. The Book of Jeremiah here seeks to give a sketch of unchallengeable authority, to provide a basis from which an alternative word can be spoken in the world, a word not grounded in or derived from the official, legitimating apparatus of the day. This person who is utterly claimed by Yahweh is subject to no other authority. His life consists in speaking from this free place of authority precisely to those who do not acknowledge it.

2. It could be that disproportionate attention has been paid to the so-called "lamentations of Jeremiah," the poetry of 11:18–23; 12:1–6; 15:10–21; 17:12–18; 18:18–23; 20:7–13, 14–18.[14] Critical opinion about the character, intention, and function of these poems is divided. No matter how such issues are resolved, it is easy to see how these poems have attracted such attention, both for critical study and for spirituality. What they evidence is that the vocation of the prophet is a conflicted way to live. Jeremiah is completely identified with his call. That much is not in doubt.

Yet Jeremiah's call yields more restlessness. It does not give rest. It renders him "homeless" in the royal world where he is assigned. Jeremiah embodies and acts out the fact that Yahweh's live Word is not easily borne or received. The bearer of that Word—whether of judgment or of hope—may anticipate rejection in the world.

---

14. The most recent discussion known to me is that of Norbert Ittmann, *Die Konfession Jeremias*, WMANT 54 (Neukirchen-Vluyn: Neukirchener Verlag, 1981). See particularly the studies of Reventlow and Gerstenberger cited there. John Bright, "Jeremiah's Complaints— Liturgy or Expressions of Personal Distress?" in J. I. Durham and J. R. Porter, eds., *Proclamation and Presence* (London: SCM Press, 1970), pp. 189–214, has made the best case for regarding these poems as statements of personal experience.

Still the restlessness cuts deeper. Given the conflict in the world, given the sure promise of his call, one might expect that the prophet could withdraw from combat (in the world) for communion (with his God)—but what a strange communion! Jeremiah discovers that his Lord is as inhospitable as his fellows. The neat consignment of combat to earth and communion with heaven does not hold here. Jeremiah experiences in his own spirituality the same rawness from God that he dares to articulate to his contemporaries. One might have expected that this faithful speaker for God would receive from God solace for heeding his call. Jeremiah makes himself desperately vulnerable to the God who has called and sent him (15:17–18; 17:17–18), but Jeremiah's vulnerability is not met by much solace. It is met by toughness and ruthlessness on the part of God (12:5–6; 15:19–21). Jeremiah learns that Yahweh has an overriding and tenacious commitment to his own purposes. The needfulness of Jeremiah will deter Yahweh's relentlessness no more than will the needfulness of Judah. Thus to be overwhelmingly God's person here means to have vulnerability met by ruthlessness.

It is surely the case, as Heschel has seen, that Jeremiah experiences and enters into the pathos of God.[15] He knows about God's suffering love because of the covenant distorted, but that does not mean Jeremiah slides over to God's side of the equation. The combative distance between Yahweh and Israel is and remains a combative distance also for Jeremiah. Even for Jeremiah, as for Judah, this is a God who not only is close at hand but is also at a distance (23:23). Jeremiah's complaints may be a yearning for the closure of the distance,[16] but the cleavage wrought by Yahweh's unaccommodating sovereignty must not be underestimated. This point is important, on the one hand, for understanding the kind of communion Jeremiah finds possible with his God. On the other hand, it helps us see that Jeremiah as a prophet is subjected to and involved in the convenantal crises of his people.

JEREMIAH'S PROPHETIC SPEECH

Jeremiah is a man called and sent as a speaker of words with poetic passion and stunning imagination. Such a point might seem curious in an assessment of the man and the prophetic office, but freshly appreciated among scholars is the fact that the poetic mode of prophetic speech is not accidental or incidental.[17] It is indispensable for what the prophet is about. The sovereign Word of Yahweh is not an absolute word which is everywhere and always the same. It is a particular, concrete word spoken to particular persons in particular contexts, to have an impact on persons, to impinge upon perception and awareness, to intrude upon public policy, and to evoke faithful and

15. Abraham Heschel, *The Prophets* (New York: Harper & Row, 1962), chap. 6 and, more generally, chap. 12.

16. On the theme in Jeremiah see Werner E. Lemke, "The Near and the Distant God: A Study of Jer. 23:23–24," *JBL* 100 (1981) 541–55.

17. On the formal aspects of prophets and poetry, see David Noel Freedman, "Pottery, Poetry, and Prophecy: An Essay on Biblical Poetry," *JBL* 96 (1977) 5–26.

transformed behavior. The prophetic word is not proposition or the announcement of set truths. It is often the playful exploration and processing of insight that it is not known until it is brought to precisely the right shape of expression. It is not that the poet has some content and then finds some words; finding the right words is the way in which the faithful content is determined. The poetic language of Jeremiah is not just a skillful or an occasional cloak for an eternal word. It is part of the strategy for letting the live Word make a difference in historical reality. Words matter—because they limit and permit the reality in which society lives. Prophets therefore attend to words in specific and concrete ways.[18]

We have said that Jeremiah's call is to shatter old worlds (bring them to an end) and to form and evoke new worlds (cause them to be). The shattering and forming of worlds is not done as a potter makes clay bowls or as a factory makes products. It is done as a poet redescribes the world, reshapes public perception, and causes people to relive their experience.[19] To do that requires that speech must not be conventional, reasonable, predictable, or expected. It must shock people's sensitivity, call attention to what is not usually noticed, break the routine, make statements with ambiguity so that people redescribe things that have long since seemed settled, bear surpluses of power before routine assessments.

It is clear that such a linguistic enterprise that redescribes the world is in fact subversive activity. Indeed, such imaginative speech may be the primal act of subversion. On the other hand, such speech functions to discredit and delegitimize the old, conventional modes of perception. When things are seen in new ways, we become aware that the old conventional slogans (e.g., Jer. 7:4) are in fact ideological cover-ups that no longer claim allegiance. On the other hand, such imaginative speech evokes new sensitivities and invites people to hope, to respond to social possibilities which the old administrative language has declared unthinkable, unreasonable, and impossible.[20]

There are several ways of attending to the subversive poetry of Jeremiah which "tears down and builds" (1:10),[21] that is, which shatters and forms:

1. After the manner of Lundbom[22] and Holladay,[23] one can pay attention to the large structural patterns of the poetry. One important gain made by their

---

18. On the creative original quality of poetic speech, see Carl Raschke and Donna Gregory, "Revelation, The Poetic Imagination and the Archaeology of the Feminine," in C. E. Winquist, ed., *The Archaeology of the Imagination*, JAAR Thematic Studies 48/2, pp. 89–104, esp. part 2.

19. On "redescribing" the world, see Paul Ricoeur, "Biblical Hermeneutics," *Semeia 4* (1975) 31 and passim. Raschke and Gregory, "Revelation," 92, quote Wallace Stevens to the point: poetic metaphor "creates a new reality from which the original appears to be unreal."

20. On subversive imagination as a prerequisite to new social possibility, see Paul Ricoeur, "The Language of Faith," in C. E. Reagan and David Steward. eds., *The Philosophy of Paul Ricoeur* (Boston: Beacon Press, 1978), pp. 223–38.

21. On this theme see Carroll, *From Chaos to Covenant*, pp. 55–58.

22. Jack R. Lundbom, *Jeremiah: A Study in Ancient Hebrew Rhetoric* (Missoula, Mont.: Scholars Press, 1975).

23. William Holladay, *The Achitecture of Jeremiah 1—20* (Lewisburg, Pa.: Bucknell University Press, 1976).

work is to observe that 1:4–10 and 20:14–18 form a major *inclusio* which binds the material together in a shrewd and intentional way. There are two major problems with that approach. The first is that such analysis never quite accounts for everything and one may be tempted to force things unduly. Second, one cannot determine what is the work of a redactor rather than the poet. Even with these reservations, such an analysis is sufficient to indicate that the poetic work before us is knowingly crafted. Our insistence is that such an enterprise as this carefully crafted poetry is not simply aesthetically noteworthy but has a dangerous social function, namely to end the presumed world and evoke a new one.

2. One may pay attention to the recurrent and varied uses of poignant metaphors and images around which the poetry clusters. It is clear that the use of words, images, and themes is carefully designed to play upon the imagination of the community. Some of the clearest examples of such a function are offered by Muilenburg.[24] We will mention three of these.

 a. The poetry is graphic concerning war imagery. On the one hand, these imaginative scenarios concern the terror of invading armies (4:13–17, 29; 5:15–17; 6:1–8, 22–25). On the other hand, they describe anguish and alarm in response to the destruction of war (4:19–21, 30–31; 5:26).

 b. Jeremiah articulates the view that all of Judah's life is a lie. There are "constant tensions between the language of *mendacity* and the language of *veracity*, between what is spurious and what is authentic, between truth and falsehood."[25] Thomas Overholt has shown that the motif of falsehood is a primal one for Jeremiah, given Jeremiah's conviction that the entire royal establishment is a house of lies sure to fall.[26]

 c. Jeremiah delights in the language of wounding and healing to characterize Israel's political situation. Remarkably, in a single poem, he is able to speak about both an "incurable wound" (30:12) and a "wound to be healed" (30:17). I do not believe the incongruity can be explained away by reference to a redactor. Rather, I suggest it reflects the constructive, evocative power of this poet.

3. One may identify what seems to be a key theme that recurs at important places in the total literature: "to pluck up and tear down, to plant and build."[27] The theme articulates God's decisive judgment and God's resilient hope. This theme does not function in the same way as the poetic metaphors noted previously. It is not so freely developed as to serve fresh impression-

---

24. James Muilenburg, "The Terminology of Adversity in Jeremiah," in H. T. Frank and W. L. Reed, eds., *Translating and Understanding the Old Testament* (Nashville: Abingdon Press, 1970), pp. 42–63.

25. Ibid., p. 43.

26. Thomas W. Overholt, *The Threat of Falsehood*, SBT² 16 (London: SCM Press, 1970).

27. See the detailed treatment of the theme by Prescott H. Williams, Jr., "Living Toward the Acts of the Saviour-Judge: A Study of Eschatology in the Book of Jeremiah," *Austin Seminary Bulletin* 94 (1978) 13–39.

istic purposes, but it is always carefully placed to function intentionally. The theme appears often in the prose and so functions in a much flatter and more linear form than other metaphors (e.g., 1:10; 18:7–10; 24:4–7; 42:9–12). It may be taken as a repeated main theme of the prophetic perception by which the various metaphors may be organized.[28]

4. Finally, one may pay attention in close detail to one particular poem, to observe the poetic skills of Jeremiah at work. We may consider, for example, the passionate words of 4:19–20, which show the amazing art of the poet. The language of these two verses matches the internal disarray (v. 19) with external disorder (v. 20) to show the close interrelation between the two. In v. 19, we have the double use of "anguish" (or "bowels") and the double use of "heart"; then the "I" is matched in Hebrew with *nephesh*, rendered again "I." The six uses show the total involvement of the person. The transition to public events is made with the word "trumpet." We then have a series of public words—"war," "disaster" (twice), the double use of *shadad* (rendered "laid waste," "destroyed")—five strong, violent words, all of them stating the consequences of the trumpet.

Further, we may note two parallel sounds. The word "I writhe" in v. 19 (*'ohivlah*) seems to be linked to "my tent" (*'ohalay*) in v. 20, and the word "alarm" (*teru'ath*) in v. 19 seems linked to "my curtain" (*yeri'othay*) in v. 20. The tightness of the language shows a profound binding of internal upset and external disarray. The intensity of the scenario of invasion and the help-lessness experienced in the face of the invasion seem evident in the pace of the language. The words seem to rush and tumble in a visceral spree. The purpose of such poetic power is to let the listener experience (at least in imagination) this alternative to a world which still seems peaceful and well ordered. Through such poetry the prophet means to claim that the poetic scenario is closer to reality than conventional discernment, which in fact denies reality, can allow.

My purpose is not to study poetic style nor to celebrate aesthetic qualities. The point, rather, is that Jeremiah the prophet is portrayed as a consummate artist who uses his artistic gifts to overthrow the deathly technique and unexamined ideology of his society. That which finally "plucks up and tears down, plants and builds" is not political strategy or military power. It is the prophet's faithful and authoritative imagination, which cannot be admin-istered by the royal temple establishment. The sovereign formula "Thus saith the Lord" is used as verification for playful, free poetic speech by which God's way is worked against the rulers of this age.

JEREMIAH IN THE PUBLIC SPHERE

Jeremiah's life and ministry are profoundly engaged with public events. There is a great deal of silliness written about Jeremiah, probably because of

---

28. Ronald Clements, "Patterns in the Prophetic Canon," in G. W. Coats and B. O. Long, eds., *Canon and Authority* (Philadelphia: Fortress Press, 1977), pp. 42–55, has shown how this theme governs the present form of prophetic literature.

the so-called confessions. He is frequently portrayed as a man preoccupied with internal spiritual life. He is often said to be a foremost articulator of "individual religion." Either of these judgments requires a highly selective, if not skewed, reading of the evidence. To the contrary, it is clear that Jeremiah is destined (or predestined? cf. Jer. 1:5) to be a public man, preoccupied with public events, responsive to them, and convinced that those public events are the ways in which Yahweh is having his say with his creation and with Israel.

Jeremiah lived at one of the turning points in the public life of the known world of the Near East[29] (as we may be in ours). His long years of ministry covered the span of the rising and falling of empires. He witnessed the fall of Assyria and the destruction of the hated Nineveh. He observed the desperate attempts of Egypt and Assyria to hold on to cruel power, and he saw them fail at Carchemesh. He watched the relentless and haughty rise of Babylon as the new power before whom all would tremble. He brought to speech the terror of an "enemy from the north," conventionally regarded as the Scythians, perhaps reassigned to Babylon. He knew profoundly that everything was loose and being shaken, and he knew that the agent of such rising and falling is none other than Yahweh.

Jeremiah knew with intensity that this world-shattering in the Near East placed the public life of Judah at risk. The redactor of the book of Jeremiah has suggested the public arena of God's Word to Jeremiah (1:1–3) in relation to Josiah, Jehoiachim, and Zedekiah. On other grounds we know also about Jeremiah's involvement with Jehoahaz and Jehoiachin. The purpose of such a summary as is given in 1:1–3 is more than chronology or historical placement. It is also more than spotting the place where God's Word is disclosed. It is a way of drawing God's Word closely and decisively into interaction with a concrete, known world. Thus, to say that God's Word came to Jeremiah in the year of Jehoiachim is not simply to say it came in the years 609–598 B.C. Much more it means that the word borne by Jeremiah came precisely into the "life world" of that king, into a world of conspiracy and self-serving which inevitably was a way to destruction. In that world Jeremiah must say what he must say.

It is difficult for us in our privatized world to appreciate the depth or scope of Judah's public experience of reality. It is not that Jeremiah was a believing man who simply read the newspapers and responded out of faith to the events around him. It is rather that he knew the traffic of public power to be the vehicle and means whereby Yahweh was present to Israel. It is this historical reality which is the mode of revelation and is not to be known in a primary way elsewhere.[30] His conviction of the revelatory character of public events meets us abrasively in our habit of finding God in less public places,

---

29. The standard accounts of Bright, Noth, and Herrmann present the data but perhaps do not always make clear the depth of the upheaval taking place.

30. The point I am making is not the same as the older argument about "God acting in history." Rather, it is the interface of poetic imagination and public events which leads to revelatory disclosure.

in less precarious places, and of thinking of revelation as something exces-
sively "spiritual" and intimate.

Some observations are in order concerning Jeremiah's public discernment
of his prophetic role:

1. It is clear that the word of disclosure given by Jeremiah is aimed at and
impinges upon public leadership. The oracular address of Jeremiah is not as
direct or pointed as is that of Amos or Micah concerning the leaders. Yet it is
clear that the word of Jeremiah is taken seriously by Judah's leaders (especially the kings), those who have authority to set policy and define the world.
We may cite two examples of the way in which the word of Jeremiah is
received. First, in chapter 36 the narrative shows the entire establishment
gathered around, compelled by and resistant to the scroll of Jeremiah. The
scene before the royal fireplace is the dramatic encounter between the
prophetic word, which appears vulnerable but is powerful, and the royal
leadership, which appears powerful but is vulnerable. The narrative shows
how the word of this prophet calls into question the entire world of royal self-
deception.[31]

A very different evidence that Jeremiah's disclosure word is aimed at
public persons and public issues is found in the encounter with Zedekiah
(37:16–21). Whereas the word is foisted upon Jehoiachim and resisted in
chapter 36, it is fervently sought by Zedekiah in chapter 37 and is only
reluctantly given by Jeremiah. Zedekiah seeks a good word and is given an
evil word. In both cases, the word given is a free word which delegitimizes
royal claims to reality and presents an alternative reality that is unwelcome to
the rulers of this age. Jeremiah is confident that Yahweh works his own will
among the nations, without regard to mechanizations of a political kind and
without reference to Israel's special, traditional claims.

2. Jeremiah understands public history as an arena of God's free activity. He
posits an important tension between the realities of public life ruled by God
and the appearances of public life shaped by institutional claims. That
tension is most easily recognized in the famous temple sermon of chapter 7.
The temple is exposed for what it is. The temple claims to be a vehicle for
God's presence in the world, but it is shown to be a fraudulent form of escape
for the special interests which practice social oppression and then claim the
protected status of the temple.[32]

Jeremiah's strictures against the temple provide one of the most radical

---

31. Overholt, *Threat of Falsehood*, has shown that the self-deception is not a deliberate or
specific act of falsehood. Rather, it is foundational and programmatic, a good example of what
Habermas calls "systematically distorted speech."

32. On the function of the temple, see Samuel Terrien, *The Elusive Presence* (New York:
Harper & Row, 1978), chap. 4. Terrien, on the whole, is positive about the temple and does not
explore its temptation in any great depth. For a much more critical comment on the temple, see
John L. McKenzie, "The Presence in the Temple: God as Tenant," in Lawrence E. Frizzell, ed.,
God and His Temple (South Orange, N.J.: Seton Hall University, 1981), pp. 35–38.

and penetrating criticisms of religion as a form of social control. The claim to be a vehicle of God's presence in the world is shown to be a barrier—one that must be destroyed. The same exposé of public religion which blocks God's public history is articulated in 8:8–13, in which the leadership of Judah is indicted for its erosion of the norms of Torah and the inequity of the courts.[33]

Jeremiah's polemical treatment of Judah's public life—especially its religious life—needs to be understood in relation to his conviction of Yahweh's rule of history. Not only are these institutions an inadequate vehicle for Yahweh, but they also provide inadequate resistance against Yahweh. Jeremiah's God does not conform to the workings of public religious institutions. As a result, the historical process is filled with surprises, inversions that are not expected or permitted by these institutional forms.

3. The most striking aspect of Jeremiah's public ministry is that he takes sides on a decisive public question in unambiguous terms. Indeed, the question that Jeremiah addresses is *the* question for Judah's public life: What are we to make of the Babylonian threat? There were many alternative and indeed conflicting political readings of the Babylonian reality. On the one hand, there was the pro-Egyptian party, which always existed in Judah. This party's opinion urged that alliance with and reliance upon Egypt would give security. On the other hand, Jeremiah's contemporaries were close enough in time to Isaiah that they could remember his council to have quiet faith and sure confidence in Yahweh (Isa. 7:9, 30:15).[34] Indeed Hananiah, an alternative prophet (not to say false), is likely in the line of Isaiah (Jeremiah 27–28). His argument has considerable merit, for it asserts that Yahweh governs and Judah can trust him.[35]

Against both such views, Jeremiah takes the harder reading. He concludes that Babylon is the wave of the future and surely will triumph. Judah's best course therefore is to ally early with this very one that appears to be a threat. Jeremiah radically rereads Judah's situation, against all the ready and popular readings, and identifies the perceived threat as the real hope.

It is important to observe that Jeremiah takes this stand on other than political grounds. The "newspapers" did not indicate such a judgment. Rather Jeremiah's decisive political judgment is made on clear theological grounds. He is able to submit his political judgment to his theological discernment that God works in the historical process in free, radical, and surprising ways. The model of Jeremiah does not suggest the necessity of expertise in a secular discipline such as political science, but the prophet knows about the scandalous ways of Yahweh. So he announces not only that

33. On the moral dimension of Jeremiah's words, see the rather theoretical discussion of Douglas A. Knight, "Jeremiah and the Dimensions of the Moral Life," in James L. Crenshaw and Samuel Sandmel, eds., *The Divine Helmsman* (New York: KTAV, 1980), pp. 87–105.

34. On the vitality of the Isaiah tradition in the time of Jeremiah, see Hermann Barth, *Die Jesaja-worte in der Josiazeit* (Neukirchen-Vluyn: Neukirchen Verlag, 1977).

35. Henri Mottu, "Jeremiah vs. Hananiah," in *The Bible and Liberation* (1976), pp. 58–67, has subjected this narrative to a most helpful criticism of its social intent and function. See also Overholt, *Threat of Falsehood*, chap. 2.

Babylon will triumph but that—astonishingly—Yahweh wills the triumph of Babylon. "Pax Babylonia is the plan of Yahweh."[36] The statement rings like a refrain in the prose literature:

> I will give all Judah into the hand of the king of Babylon. (20:4)

> I will deliver . . . the people in this city . . . into the hand of Nebuchadrezzar, king of Babylon. (21:7)

> . . . yet I would tear you off and give you into the hand of those who seek your life, into the hand of those of whom you are afraid, even into the hand of Nebuchadrezzar, king of Babylon. (22:24–25)

> I will send for all the tribes of the north . . . and for Nebuchadrezzar, the king of Babylon. (25:9)

> Now I have given all those lands into the hand of Nebuchadrezzar, king of Babylon. (27:6; cf. vv. 12–13, 16–22)

> Behold, I am giving this city into the hand of the King of Babylon. (34:2)

> You shall be delivered into the hand of the king of Babylon (37:17).

> This city shall surely be given into the hand of the army of the king of Babylon. (38:3; cf. v. 23)

Now to be sure, this shocking judgment is not made in a vacuum, either political, literary, or theological. In the person and tradition of Jeremiah, this statement rests on an acute moral analysis and on a poetic deposit which is poignant in its anger, anguish, and eloquence. The conclusion repeated so often comes at the end of a career urging repentance, exposing falseness, and symbolizing failure. Yet the conclusion is there. It attests Jeremiah's certainty that poetic speech has to do with public reality, and his disclosing word concerns precisely the realities of Judah's life.

4. Perhaps the most staggering statement about his public judgment linking Yahweh's resolute will and the public realities of Judah is the specific speech about Nebuchadrezzar (25:9; 27:6). Much of Jeremiah's dismal anticipation is expressed in quite elusive, impressionistic language. We have seen, however, that it is not elusive but incisive on the judgment made about Babylon. The most concrete affirmation of this judgment for Jeremiah is that Nebuchadrezzar is Yahweh's servant, an alien ruler commissioned for Yahweh's purpose (see also 43:10).[37] In saying this, Jeremiah is of course in the prophetic tradition of Isaiah who speaks so about Assyria, though not specifically about Sennacherib (Isa. 10:5), and of Second Isaiah, who refers to Cyrus as "my shepherd, his anointed" (44:28; 45:1).

The theological import of such a designation for the king is the unspoken

---

36. Norman K. Gottwald, *All the Kingdoms of the Earth* (New York: Harper & Row, 1964), p. 260.

37. Caution should be exercised on this point in light of the critical suggestion of Werner Lemke, "Nebuchadrezzar, My Servant," *CBQ* 28 (1966) 45–50. See also the response of Overholt, "King Nebuchadrezzar in the Jeremiah Tradition," *CBQ* 30 (1968) 39–48.

conclusion that the king in Judah is no longer Yahweh's servant, shepherd, or anointed. The king has forfeited his role. In such forfeiture, the linkage of Yahweh and Judah is jeopardized, if not broken.

5. Finally, we may observe one other exchange recounted about Jeremiah in 44:11–30.[38] Jeremiah is remembered as frequently in conflict with the Egyptian sympathizers, a conflict which stems from his "Babylonian decision." In this concluding episode he summons the Judeans to true faith against the religious practices commensurate with their Egyptian inclinations (vv. 11–14). His opponents present a tight case against him of a quite syllogistic kind (vv. 17–18):

> We served the queen of heaven—and prospered.
> We stopped serving the queen of heaven—and lacked everything.

The argument of the opponents is formidable! Jeremiah's response in vv. 22–23, 24–30 shows that his judgment is theological and not pragmatic or political. He does not seek to refute the syllogism of vv. 17–18. Instead he ignores it. He overrides it in his moral passion. Instead of an answer, he reasserts once more that the sovereign rule of Yahweh has moral implications which are simply unarguable, the evidence to the contrary notwithstanding. Jeremiah is perhaps Israel's supreme embodiment of the ability to subordinate both personal inclination and political reality to the sovereignty of Yahweh. Any attempt to discern the person of Jeremiah must reckon with that reality.

JEREMIAH IN CONFLICT

The portrayal given us in the text shows that Jeremiah is in every way a man of intense conflict. His calling, his passion, his moral political judgments, his poetic and imaginative power all set him on a course of inevitable conflict. Thus he characterizes himself as "a man of strife and contention to the whole land" (15:10). In pondering the prophetic role, we note that the conflict is not accidental or incidental because of wrong strategy or insensitivity, nor is the conflict about marginal matters on which Jeremiah might as well have compromised. As we have it, conflict is definitional of Jeremiah's call. The promise linked to his call is that he will be "against the whole land, against the kings of Judah, its princes, its priests, and the people of the land. They will fight against you . . ." (1:18). The conflict occurs because Jeremiah has been given a vision of reality and a word about reality that is deeply at odds with the vision of reality held by his contemporaries, and these two visions can in no way be accommodated to each other. Jeremiah witnesses to, speaks from, and hopes for an alternative world which his contemporaries

---

38. See the splendid analyses of this text by David Noel Freedman in "The Biblical Idea of History," *Int* 21 (1967) 32–49.

could not understand or accept. It is this reality which governs the entire portrait and brings him into conflict.[39]

1. On the one hand, his conflict is with the public leaders and world definers of his day. Jeremiah insisted that the reality they thought they governed was a lie, and he insisted on articulating over against that reality the world he knew to be true.

a. Clearly Jeremiah stood in conflict with the royal apparatus. This is most dramatically clear in the showdown of Jeremiah 36, in which Jehoiachin finds Jeremiah's words intolerable. That confrontation then leads to the abuse and harassment which follow. That opposition is more poignantly expressed in 22:13–30, which addresses the wickedness of Jehoiachin, soon to be punished, and the hopelessness of Jehoiachin. The end of the poem in v. 30 seems to anticipate an end to the dynastic succession (cf. the inverse theme of kingship in 23:1–8).

b. Jeremiah is in conflict with his prophetic counterparts, who tend to support the political establishment and to speak assurances based on present policy. The most dramatic statement is in the exchange with Hananiah (27—28), in which Jeremiah even has a wistfulness that Hananiah should be right about his good news, even though Jeremiah knows he is not right (28:6). The more poetic articulation of the same issue is in 23:9–22, in which all such established prophets are dismissed as fakers.

c. Though difficult to assess, there is evidence of Jeremiah's conflict with his own family and kinspeople from Anathoth (11:21). It could be that the "Anathoth connection" (cf. 32:6–15) relates Jeremiah to the old priestly tradition of Abiathar.[40] Whether that can be sustained or not, there is a suggestion that Jeremiah is alienated from his own rootage. Indeed the poem of 8:8–13 pictures him in deep conflict with every element of leadership, and he indicts them all.

2. We should not overstate the leadership conflict, however. Many oracles and poems of Jeremiah are not limited to the leadership. Most of them are undifferentiated in having a general aim for the whole people. Jeremiah does not believe that it is a wrong decision by a judge or a wrong policy act by a king that needs to be righted. Rather, it is the whole people in its long history with Yahweh that has been recalcitrant and obstinate (2:13, 20; 18:12). It is for that reason that the lawsuit language of indictment and sentence (even though handled with freedom and imagination) is the dominant mode

---

39. On the counter-perception of reality, see Walter Brueggemann, "The Epistemological Crisis of Israel's Two Histories (Jer. 9:22–23)," in John G. Gammie, ed., *Israelite Wisdom* (Missoula, Mont.: Scholars Press, 1978), pp. 85–105. The disputive character of prophetic word is also expressed in Isa. 6:9–13.

40. See Wilson, *Prophecy and Society*, 233–35.

of speech. Jeremiah is convinced that Judah is against Yahweh and against covenant in its most fundamental claims.[41]

3. The conflict in Jeremiah's life does not end with these two areas. The so-called confessions show that Jeremiah is also in deep conflict with Yahweh. While he publicly proclaims Yahweh's will with passion and authority, these texts show that Jeremiah also resisted the disclosures and in his own life did not find Yahweh to be his "best friend" or special support. We may single out two motifs which disclose this man in his strife with Yahweh. First, he hopes for retaliation and vengeance (11:20; 12:3; 15:15; 17:18; 18:21; 20:11). He keeps a long "enemy list," and he dares to presume that his enemies are the enemies of Yahweh (cf. Ps. 139:21). He yearns to see these enemies done in. He has cast his lot with Yahweh against the others, and he counts on his ally.[42]

Jeremiah's other motif in these texts is that he senses he is betrayed, deceived, and abandoned—if not by Yahweh, then in general. After he has cast his lot with Yahweh, forsaking all others and being rejected, he concludes that the God who promised to be with him (1:19) is not there. From Yahweh's side, this is perhaps a statement that none may draw close to Yahweh in his sovereignty, not even his called prophet. From Jeremiah's side, this is experienced as fickleness, and at no point do we see any clear resolution. This sense of estrangement belongs to Jeremiah's character and perhaps to the prophetic role more generally.

CONCLUSIONS

The four factors articulated here could be nuanced differently, but I think they cannot be resisted:

1. Jeremiah is overwhelmingly God's man.
2. Jeremiah is a speaker with poetic passion and stunning imagination.
3. Jeremiah is profoundly engaged in public events.
4. Jeremiah is a man of indignation and excruciating conflict.

This peculiar configuration of characteristics evokes one concluding judgment. Jeremiah is seen to be a man who speaks the truth into a world of falsehood and self-deception. In drawing this conclusion, I make two points:

---

41. Finally, it is the whole people which is under indictment, not simply the leaders. Thus 2:4–13 is model of the lawsuit form. Cf. Herbert Huffmon, "The Covenant Lawsuit in the Prophets," *JBL* 78 (1959) 287–88. The use of the term *rîv* (lawsuit) in Jeremiah is instructive, for the prophet seeks judgment for himself and against his people (cf. 11:20; 12:1; 18:19; 20:12). In other derivative uses, the worm has turned and the term is used for the sake of Israel against the hostile nations who warrant judgment (25:31; 50:34, 51:36).

42. On vengeance as the other side of compassion, see George Mendenhall, "The 'Vengeance' of Yahweh," in *The Tenth Generation* (Baltimore: Johns Hopkins University Press, 1973), pp. 69–104.

(1) We should not be so fascinated with Jeremiah's person that we minimize his historic role as a bearer of truth into his situation.[43] (2) The four marks listed may be the indispensable basis for one who speaks truth in the public arena. Jeremiah could not have spoken the truth if he were not overwhelmingly God's man, if he were without poetic imagination, if he were not engaged in public events, and if he were not in deep conflict. This is because, as the Jeremiah tradition knows,

> truth is not our autonomous judgment but is only from God (cf. 23:18–22);
> truth is given not in prose but in poetry, which allows for God's freedom;
> truth is not private, apart from public events;
> truth is not without dispute in a world of deception.

Jeremiah's truth is not eternal truth. He did not announce grand principles or abstract meanings. His truth was always as poignant and dangerous and timely as his moment. His truth from God for Judah is about "plucking up and breaking down," about "building and planting" (1:10).

1. Jeremiah's word borne in Israel concerns the end of the known world, the world presided over by the kings and priests of this age, who imagine themselves secure and stable and safe. Jeremiah must assert that that world, organized against God's covenantal faithfulness, will and must end, perhaps by the hand of Babylon. Such a terrible ending is always thought to be "too hard" (impossible) for Yahweh (32:27), but Yahweh can do it. Life is forfeited if it tests Yahweh too long.

2. Jeremiah's word borne among Judah's exiles is about the beginning of a new world wrought only by the mercy and freedom of God. This is a new possibility, judged by hopeless, former rulers to be impossible. They believe that there can be no new thing. Such a new world with a new David (23:5–6), a new convenant (31:31–34), a new healing (30:17), is always thought to be "too hard" (impossible) for Yahweh (32:17); but Yahweh can do it. Life is given again when Yahweh is known to be the giver of newness.[44]

3. Jeremiah, the man and his truth, is time-bound. He belongs to his time and place, deeply in love with his people and deeply in hate with them too. So he spoke his truth to his time, and not more than that. The community around Jeremiah, however, was concerned that his words have futures within them, and so his passionate, painful way in the world continues to spill over

---

43. A close parallel may be drawn to the call of Paul in the New Testament. J. Christiaan Beker, *Paul the Apostle: The Triumph of God in Life and Thought* (Philadelphia: Fortress Press, 1980), esp. chap. 1, has shown that Paul's call to be an apostle is completely subordinated to and derived from the mission of the gospel. The same is clear for Jeremiah. The word rules the person.

44. On the paradoxical act of speaking salvation after judgment, see A. H. J. Gunneweg. "Neil im Gericht," in Bernd Jospert and Rudolf Mohr, eds., *Traditio-Krisis-Renovatio aus theologischer Sicht* (Marburg: Elwert Verlag, 1976), pp. 1–9. See esp. his last sentence, indicating that to speak a word of hope when human possibility is exhausted requires belief that this is indeed the word of God.

into worlds coming after him. On the one hand, the generation of exiles immediately after him found that his words still had authority and power.[45] This is why we have an ongoing Deuteronomic trajectory out of Jeremiah, which continues to present echoes of his words.

On the other hand, Jeremiah, as the person who suffers and hopes most in ancient Israel, continues as a powerful presence into the New Testament. The suffering of Jeremiah and the end of Israel which he embodies, the hope of Judah and the new Israel he articulates, have become modes for understanding Jesus, the one who can be destroyed and raised up (John 2:19). Jeremiah led faithful people to listen for the weeping of death (31:15; Matt. 2:18) and to live in hope of newness (31:31–34; Heb. 8:8–12; 10:16–17). The words linger with power. This speaker in whom they are rooted continues as an agent of hard, hopeful truth.

---

45. This is the main point of the argument of Nicholson and Carroll, but that continuing dynamic must not be regarded as a formal literary and redactional process alone. It is at the same time a vigorous, creative act of theological fidelity. Thus the portrait drawn is both imaginative and faithful.

11

The Years of
Jeremiah's Preaching

WILLIAM L. HOLLADAY

A reconstruction of the chronology expressed and implied within the
Book of Jeremiah helps us glimpse the man behind the biblical book
as he seeks to relate God's word to events in the life of God's people.

In the course of preparing a fresh commentary on the Book of Jeremiah,[1] I
am attempting to discern the settings of the poems and speeches of the book
and thus have been developing a chronology for the prophet, one which in
my own mind at least gains in convincingness as I continue to work at the
texts. Portions of the scheme have been published recently;[2] the complete
reconstruction, with some of the supporting data, may be useful now as a
preliminary report.[3]

Almost every suggestion which I offer here could be challenged, and some
of my suggestions are quite different from anything heretofore proposed. At
the outset I part company with those who assume that Jeremiah began to
prophesy in 627 B.C.[4] and with those who assume that much of the prose
material in the book was shaped by a circle of Deuteronomistic editors.[5] Of
course, modest expansions in the tradition were made during and after the
exile; but I have a different explanation for the so-called "Deuteronomistic
prose" of the book. Scholarly proposals must stand or fall on their merits; this
is the one I hold at present, to be modified by better ones in time to come.

I take it that the "thirteenth year of Josiah" (1:2) is the date of the prophet's

---

1. *Jeremiah*, vol. 1, Hermeneia (Philadelphia: Fortress Press, 1986).
2. "The Identification of the Two Scrolls of Jeremiah," *VT* 30 (1980) 452–67; "A Coherent
Chronology of Jeremiah's Early Career," in *Livre de Jérémie*, BETL 54 (Leuven: University
Press, 1981), pp. 58–73.
3. It is to be noted that I do not deal here with all the possible texts but deal only with a
selection. I also sidestep the bewildering questions of spring vs. autumn New Year and the like,
simply offering my own conclusions.
4. Most scholars, e.g., John Bright, *Jeremiah*, AB 21 (New York: Doubleday & Co., 1965), p.
lxxxvii.
5. On this assumption see, e.g., E. W. Nicholson, *Preaching to the Exiles: A Study of the
Prose Tradition in the Book of Jeremiah* (Oxford: Basil Blackwell, 1970), and Robert P. Carroll,
From Chaos to Covenant: Prophecy in the Book of Jeremiah (New York: Crossroad, 1981).

birth, 627 B.C., not the date of the beginning of his career.[6] The theological burden of the call in 1:5 suggests it—that Yahweh's action through Jeremiah began in the womb—and many other bits of evidence point in the same direction.[7] If 627 is his birthdate, then the puzzle of why we find in the book no clear judgment for or against Josiah's reform in 622 is clear: Jeremiah's proclamations lie years in the future. I propose, then, that the prophet was born when the kingship of Josiah was well along, a time when that king was beginning to feel free of the pressure of Assyria.

Jeremiah would have been a boy of five years at the time of Josiah's reform, a reform (so the consensus of scholars) triggered by the discovery of an early form of Deuteronomy.[8] Since Jeremiah's father, Hilkiah, was a priest in Anathoth (1:1) and since as a consequence of the reform the cult became centralized in Jerusalem, one can imagine the impression made on the boy by the shift of his father's activity from Anathoth to Jerusalem.

Now I assume that the injunction of Deuteronomy 31:9–13 was taken seriously, that the form which Deuteronomy took in those days was recited every seven years at the feast of booths (tabernacles), thus at the end of September or the beginning of October. If the proclamation of Deuteronomy was initially in 622 B.C., then subsequent recitations would have taken place in the autumn of 615, 608, 601, 594, and 587 B.C.. It is my proposal that these occasions offer a chronological structure for the career of Jeremiah and more specifically that several of the parade examples of "Deuteronomistic" prose in the book are Jeremiah's various counterproclamations at those times when Deuteronomy was recited. This proposal, as I shall show, is most convincing for 594 and is plausible for 587; beyond those dates I have suggestions for Jeremiah's proclamations in 608 and 601 (as well as before, after, and between these septennial occasions).

As I have already indicated, Deuteronomy would have been recited again in the autumn of 615; by our reckoning Jeremiah would have been twelve years old. With hesitation I suggest the possibility that this was the occasion for his responding to his call (1:4–10): verses 7 and 9 are similar to Deuteronomy 18:18, the word to Moses about a prophet like him who one day will appear. I have elsewhere proposed that Jeremiah's perception of his call was shaped by this verse;[9] is this not a likely occasion? Jeremiah himself protests that he is "only a youth" (v. 6). We recall that Jesus is recorded as discussing matters with the teachers in the temple when he was twelve years old (Luke 2:41–47). In any event it is clear to me now (against *Spokesman,* pp. 23–24) that during a period of time before Josiah was killed on the

---

6. So also J. Philip Hyatt, "Jeremiah," *IB* 5 (Nashville: Abingdon Press, 1956), pp. 779, 798.

7. See my *Jeremiah: Spokesman Out of Time* [abbrev.: *Spokesman*] (New York: Pilgrim Press, 1974), pp. 17–22; "A Fresh Look at 'Source B' and 'Source C' in Jeremiah," *VT* 25 (1975) 409–10; "A Coherent Chronology."

8. See, e.g., John Bright. *A History of Israel* [abbrev.: *History*] (Philadelphia: Westminster Press, 1981), pp. 317–22.

9. "The Background of Jeremiah's Self-Understanding: Moses, Samuel, and Psalm 22," *JBL* 83 (1964) 153–64; "Jeremiah and Moses: Further Observations," *JBL* 85 (1966) 17–27; *Spokesman,* pp. 26–28.

battlefield of Megiddo in the spring of 609, the youthful Jeremiah acted to
support the king's program of cultic and political reunion between the north
and south (2 Kings 23:15–18).

Some of the evidence for this activity of the young Jeremiah is laid out in a
recent study of Norbert Lohfink.[10] It has long been recognized that some at
least of chapters 30—31 may have been directed to the north (Bright,
Jeremiah, pp. 284–85); Lohfink has subjected these chapters to careful
analysis and isolates 30:5–7, 12–15, 18–21; 31:2–6, and 15–22 as having that
setting.[11] He suggests, then, that the young Jeremiah proclaimed Yahweh's
initiative in Josiah's effort to win the north ("Ephraim") back to political and
religious union with Jerusalem (*History*, p. 322).

I would only add that there are traces of the prophet's words to the north in
chapters 2—3 as well, specifically in 2:4–9 ("families" in v. 4 is really
"tribes," a word which he uses more than once for the northern tribes), and
3:1–2, 4–5, 12, 14–15, and portions of 18 (one notes "north" in v. 12 and
"family" [= tribe] in v. 15), 19, 21a, 22–23, the core of 24–25; and 4:1–2. Of
course the material in chapters 2—3 and 30—31 directed to the north was
incorporated later by the prophet in the context of addresses to the south
(*Spokesman*, pp. 111–14).

In the year 609 events moved quickly. King Josiah was killed at Megiddo in
the spring in a three-cornered fight. Assyria had been defeated by Babylonia
in 612, and Assyria had only the remnant of an army left in the field. Egypt,
recognizing Babylon to be the new enemy, marched north through Palestine
to bolster the fading Assyrian force. Josiah tried to interpose his own army to
prevent the passage of the Egyptians and was killed. His second son,
Jehoahaz, was put on the throne of Judah but ruled for only three months;
the victorious Egyptian army deposed him and took him to Egypt where he
disappeared from history (cf. 22:10–12). His older brother Jehoiakim was
placed on the throne as an Egyptian vassal. By the end of that September,
then, Judah had seen three kings on the throne in the year (*History*, pp. 324–
25), and in the swirl of these events Jeremiah proclaimed the first dated
utterance of his career, the so-called "temple sermon," 7:1–12.[12]

This "sermon" may be dated by the narrative account in chapter 26. It was
uttered in the "beginning" of the reign of Jehoiakim (v. 1), thus evidently
sometime between September 609 and March 608, probably at the Feast of
Booths in September/October 609.[13] By the reckoning adopted here the
prophet would be eighteen.

The sermon is a call to repentance: "amend (improve, literally 'make good')

10. "Der junge Jeremia als Propagandist und Poet, Zum Grundstock von Jer 30–31," *Le
Livre de Jérémie*, pp. 351–68.

11. I agree, only adding 31:1aBb and 9b to this material.

12. The "sermon" is usually reckoned to continue through v. 15, but on stylistic and rhetorical grounds I conclude that vv. 13–15 are a later extension.

13. "Beginning" is evidently a technical term for the "accession year," the partial year of a
reign before the New Year; I assume a spring New Year (see Bright, *Jeremiah*, p. 169). The feast
of booths is a natural occasion during this interval when a large crowd would assemble for
worship (7:2; 26:2).

your ways and your doings" (7:3, 5); if the people do improve, then Yahweh will let them dwell in the land (v. 7). Such a call to repentance is implied in three other verses in the first part of the book (4:4, 14 and 6:8). Of these, 4:14 says it straight out: "O Jerusalem, wash your heart from wickedness, that you may be saved." The other two (4:4; 6:8) say it with "lest" (= "so that . . . not"). If the people repent, Yahweh will stay his hand and not bring destruction upon them.

This is also the purpose of the first scroll which Jeremiah dictated to his scribe Baruch in the course of 605 (36:1–8). The purpose is to preserve Yahweh's words of judgment on Israel and Judah which are to *warn* the people: it is possible they may repent, in which case Yahweh will stay his hand (35:3). We must therefore understand the words of judgment from Yahweh during this period, from 609 at least through 605, to be scenarios of destruction, a proclamation of what Yahweh is capable of doing to his people.

By a variety of paths I have concluded that in the first dictated scroll were included the following: the call of 1:4–10 and an early recension at least of 1:11–16; 2:1–25, 29–37;[14] 3:1–2, 4–5, 12–15, portions of 18, 19, 21–23, the core of 24–25; 4:1–4, 5–8, 13–18, 29–31; 6:1–8; and 7:1–12.[15] Beyond the call, these are words of accusation and scenarios of punishment all of which imply the call to repentance expressed in 4:4, 14; 6:8; and 7:1–12. These passages then, by my proposal, would have been heard in the period 609–605.

I have already indicated that in the autumn of 608 there would have been a recitation of Deuteronomy. The little poem in 2:2–3 carries overtones of the festival of booths; thus both Lev. 23:39 and Deut. 16:13–15, which make provision for that festival, use the term "harvest" ($t^eb\hat{u}'\hat{a}$) which occurs in 2:3. The introductory words, literally "Go call out in the ears of" (2:2), suggest an audience at a festival. The instructions for reciting Deuteronomy use the same phrase (Deut. 31:11). If 2:2–3 was proclaimed by Jeremiah in the autumn of 608, it cannot be all he proclaimed. Perhaps much or all of the material above listed from 2:1 and 4:4 was proclaimed at that time—one notes the likeness of 4:4 to Deut. 10:16.

We cannot ascertain why in 605 Jeremiah was debarred from the temple area (36:5), but events in that year had put a new face on the political map of Judah. In May or June of 605 the Egyptian army was dealt a stunning defeat by the Babylonian army under the command of Nebuchadrezzar, who was still crown prince, at the city of Carchemish in north Syria. Later in the same year the remnant of the Egyptian army was defeated in central Syria. If the leadership of Judah had been convinced after Megiddo (609) that Egypt was invincible, they now thought so no more. Sometime during this period

---

14. I take "Assyria" in vv. 18 and 36 to be the poetic designation of the power in Mesopotamia at the time (Babylon); so also John M. Berridge, *Prophet, People, and the Word of Yahweh: An Examination of Form and Content in the Proclamation of the Prophet Jeremiah* (Zurich: EVZ-Verlag, 1970), p. 81. Compare Zech. 10:10, 11.

15. This list differs slightly from the one in my "The Identification of the Two Scrolls of Jeremiah," pp. 464–65.

Jehoiakim switched sides and became a vassal of Babylon (2 Kings 24:1), probably in 604 (*History*, p. 327).

If Jeremiah's first scroll was dictated in 605, and if, as I believe, it included material about the foe from the north (passages including 4:14 and 6:8), then the most plausible context for such utterances would be in the weeks just after the results of Carchemish became known in Judah.

Eventually the scroll of Jeremiah came to the attention of the king, and he burned it (36:23). There is a chronological difficulty with that event, however, which is crucial to my reconstruction.

The Hebrew text states that the scroll was burned in the ninth month of Jehoiakim's fifth year (so 36:9, RSV), that is November/December 604. The Septuagint, however, gives the date in the ninth month of the *eighth* year,[16] that is November/December 601. Lohfink has pointed out[17] that the historical circumstances of 601 make that date far more plausible than 604 for the burning of the scroll. Thus in November/December 604, the Babylonian army had marched west to the Mediterranean and south along the Palestinian coastal plain, sacking the Philistine city of Ashkelon (*History*, p. 326). This event clearly threatened Judah, and a scroll that included words of warning about Yahweh's sending a foe from the north would hardly have been burned even by so insensitive a king as Jehoiakim. But in November/December 601, the Babylonian army, by then fighting in the Egyptian delta, was dealt a defeat by the Egyptian forces and withdrew to Babylon (*History*, p. 327). If the defeat suggested that Babylon was nothing but a "paper tiger," then one has a plausible motive for the king's contemptuous burning of the scroll.

Text-critically, too, we must choose "eighth" rather than "fifth"; it is the more difficult reading. That is, one could well imagine a scribe consciously or unconsciously changing "eighth" to "fifth" (similar words in Hebrew), assuming a gap of only one year from the "fourth year" mentioned in 36:1, but one cannot imagine a motive for the reverse change.

If the burning of the scroll is to be dated in 601 rather than 604, then the occasion of the fast called by the king (36:9), in the context of which the scroll was burned, was not the threat signaled by the sacking of Ashkelon (against *History*, p. 327; *Jeremiah*, pp. 180–82); it must have been for another reason. I propose with Wilhelm Rudolph[18] that the fast was proclaimed because of a drought, indeed that this is the date for the great drought presupposed by 14:1—15:9; one notes that the passage likewise mentions a fast (14:12). One must imagine, then, perhaps a spring without rain, certainly a hot summer and an autumn without rain, a drought lasting until the "ninth month"; Rudolph cites a passage from the Mishna,[19] "If the first of

16. The passage is 43:9 in the Septuagint.
17. "Die Gattung der 'Historischen Kurzgeschichte' in den letzten Jahren von Juda und in der Zeit des Babylonischen Exils," *ZAW* 90 (1978) 324–28.
18. *Jeremia*, HAT 12 (Tübingen: J. C. B. Mohr, 1968), p. 233.
19. Taanith 1:5.

Chislev [= November/December] was come and no rain had fallen, the court enjoins on the congregation three days of fasting."

Now the autumn of 601 is the next occasion for a recitation of Deuteronomy. If my detective-work to this point is correct, that celebration of the festival of booths already suffered under a drought. Is there a passage of Jeremiah suggestive of both a recitation of Deuteronomy and of a drought? There is; it is 8:4–10a plus 13.[20] In verse 8 the prophet mocks those who assume that "the law of Yahweh is with us," and in verse 13 we hear that "there are no grapes on the vine, nor figs on the fig tree; even the leaves are withered." I submit that this passage was recited on the occasion of the festival of booths in the autumn of 601. Such a dating in turn suggests that the similar 6:9–15 has a setting in the same period. A variety of evidence suggests that 5:20–29 is from the same period (v. 25 indicates a drought), and since the refrain of 5:29 is found also in 5:9 and 9:9 (Hebrew, 8), one may assume the same period as the appropriate setting for 5:1–9 and 8:14—9:9 (does 8:20 have a background in the same drought in the same season?).

The king burned Jeremiah's scroll. The consequence was a word of judgment from Yahweh to the king, a detail of which has not been generally noticed (the word is recorded in 36:29–31). The king is to be without successors on the throne, and his dead body is to be denied burial; but in addition, "I will punish . . . his offspring and his servants for their iniquity; I will bring upon them, and upon the inhabitants of Jerusalem, and upon the men of Judah, all the evil that I have pronounced against them, but they would not hear." That is to say, the king's burning of the scroll was the catalyst which led the prophet to the conviction that Yahweh's words of judgment against the people were no longer simply scenarios for warning but rather plans to be carried out. Repentance was no longer to be expected, and the people stood under irrevocable judgment.

This is a crucial change in Jeremiah's perception, and we can date it to November/December 601. Then and thereafter for many years the prophet insisted that Yahweh's judgment was inevitable. Then, in response to the command from God, he took a second scroll and dictated to Baruch all the words of the first scroll and new words as well (36:28, 32). The new words would be ones he had delivered since 605 and words which came to him in the light of the new situation after the king burned the scroll. But even the old words, those from the period 609–605, would be seen in the light of his new understanding, that Yahweh's punishment is now irrevocable. Was this the occasion when he broke the flask (19:1–15), when he was locked in the stocks overnight (20:1–6)?

I have already cited the long section 14:1—15:9, a passage which has the drought for a background. It is in the form of a liturgy; it is probable indeed that it is the "counter-liturgy" which the prophet delivered in the context of

---

20. Verses 10b–12 are a doublet of 6:13–15 and are lacking in the Septuagint; they are thus secondary here. See Bright, *Jeremiah*, p. 50.

the fast proclaimed by the king (36:9). There it is said that Yahweh will not listen to Jeremiah's intercesssory prayers for the people (15:1–4); nothing is ahead but destruction (15:5–9). The word that Yahweh will not listen to Jeremiah's intercession is found elsewhere as well: 7:16–20 is a striking example.

I have pointed out that Jeremiah felt called to be the prophet like Moses (Deut. 18:18). In contrast, Luis Alonso Schökel in a recent study[21] suggests that Jeremiah was an anti-Moses figure: Moses had been the great intercessor, while Jeremiah is bidden not to intercede (15:1). I propose that it is precisely at this point in his career that Jeremiah shifted in his self-understanding.

The conviction that Yahweh is determined to punish his people is new at this point. We may thus conclude that the call to Jeremiah to abstain from marriage (16:1–4) *cannot* be dated before this time, since it is the sign *par excellence* of the extinguishing of hope for the people. If the prophet was born in 627, he would now be twenty-six years old. (Here is one more argument against the assumption that 627 was the date when he began to prophesy; by that assumption he would be old enough by 601 to make the date implausible for such a declaration.)[22]

Jeremiah declared his celibacy, and he uttered words declaring the extinguishing of hope for the people. The result, as one might expect, was persecution by the optimistic prophets. This is suggested by 14:13–16 and by the collection of material on those prophets in 23:9–32 (one notes the word about the drought in 23:10). The rhetoric of these passages bespeaks a prophet whose credentials are being challenged both by the optimistic prophets and by historical events; if Babylon was a "paper tiger" in the struggle with Egypt, then Jeremiah is a false prophet and must die—so the optimistic prophets would have read Deuteronomy 18:20!

There is another passage that speaks both to the crisis in Jeremiah's vocation and to the drought, and that is 4:9–12. Yahweh is deceiving the people through the optimistic prophets (cf. 4:10 with 14:13), and a desiccating wind (both a physical wind and the metaphorical wind of the Babylonian army) is bearing down on the people (4:11–12).

I conclude that 4:9–12 was an addition in the second scroll, as was also its companion 4:19–28.[23] The terrible vision of cosmic chaos in 4:23–26 is really completed by verses 27–28, and the diction of verse 28a is close to that of 14:2a: that vision finds its origin in the drought.[24] As above, I must confine

---

21. "Jeremias como anti-Moisés," in Maurice Carrez, Joseph Doré, Pierre Grelot, eds. *De la Tôrah au Messie: Études d'exégèse et d'herméneutique bibliques offertes à Henri Cazelles pour ses 25 années d'enseignement à l'Institut Catholique de Paris (Octobre 1979)* (Paris: Desclée, 1981), pp. 245–54.

22. See my "A Coherent Chronology." Rudolph struggles with the same problem; see his *Jeremia*, pp. 111–12.

23. On this matter see in more detail my "The Identification of the Two Scrolls of Jeremiah," pp. 460–61.

24. I revocalize the first word of verse 27b from *kālâ* to *kullāh*; the resultant line reads, "And none of it (i.e., the earth) will I (re)make." This terrible utterance is thus consistent with the rest of the passage. I assume that the negative is secondary in the similar 5:10a to bring it into line with Jeremiah's word in 30:11 which he uttered before Jerusalem fell in 587.

myself to listing other additions in the second scroll—2:26–28; 3:2b–3 and 20; 5:10–17; 6:9–15, 16–26, 27–30—without justifying my decision.[25]

The opposition of the optimistic prophets at the end of 601 and early in 600 gave rise to some of the so-called "confessions" of Jeremiah; one notes in the first occasional sequence (11:18—12:6) a sudden word about the drought (12:4).

The whole set of issues involved in the setting of the "confessions," the laments of Jeremiah to Yahweh and the perceived answers from Yahweh, is too complex for treatment here. I may simply say that I believe a few of these passages emerged during this period, that they were expanded by more confessions in a similar crisis in the prophet's career in the summer of 594, and that it was in that latter crisis that Jeremiah "went public" with the "confessions."

The idea that those persecuting Jeremiah were the optimistic prophets is not a new one,[26] but it has been demonstrated with fresh cogency in the recent dissertation of Franz Hubmann.[27] One notes, to take a single datum, the resemblance between 11:23 and 23:12.

By my analysis the passages which find their setting at this time are 11:18–23 (minus "the men of Anathoth" in v. 21 and "upon the men of Anathoth" in v. 23); 12:1–5; 15:15–19; and 17:5–8 (plus perhaps vv. 9–10), and 18:18–23.[28] In these words Jeremiah pours out to Yahweh his sense of abandonment over against his persecutors. Rather than being destined for slaughter himself (11:19), he affirms that it is his persecutors who should be slaughtered (12:3). He is puzzled why his circumstances turn the norms of Psalm 1 upside-down (12:1b), so that it is the "wicked" (or "guilty") who thrive. His opponents he calls "merrymakers" (15:17), another clue that they are optimistic in their view of the nation's future. He describes Yahweh in terms appropriate to an outer drought as well as an inner one (15:18). Yahweh calls him to repent (15:19), and, by my analysis, he affirms his repentance (17:5–8), again in a variation of Psalm 1, but using words appropriate to a period of drought.

If the Babylonian army paused in its depredations in the year 600, leaving Jeremiah puzzled, the pause did not last long. In December 598 Jehoiakim died (was he assassinated?) (*History*, p. 327) and his son Jehoiachin came to the throne. Neubuchadrezzar besieged Jerusalem, the city fell in March 597, and the young king, members of the royal family, and other leading citizens were led off to exile.

Beyond words from Jeremiah about the fate of Jehoiachin (22:24–30), is there any **material** datable to this siege of the city? Yes, there is 10:17–22.[29]

25. See n. 15.

26. It was suggested by the Jewish commentator Isaac Abrabanel in the fifteenth century and by the Christian commentator Sebastian Schmidt at the end of the seventeenth.

27. *Untersuchungen zu den Konfessionen*, Forschung zur Bible 30 (Würzburg: Echter Verlag, 1978), passim, esp. pp. 136, 279–81.

28. For the judgment that "men of Anathoth" is secondary in 11:21 and 23, and that 12:6 and 15:20–21 are secondary, see ibid., pp. 75–107, 169–75, 290–95; for argumentation in favor of linking 17:5–8 with 15:18–19, see my *Spokesman*, pp. 98–100.

29. So also Bright, *Jeremiah*, p. 73.

There the city is contemptuously addressed by Yahweh as a refugee woman; I would translate verse 17, "Gather up your bundle from the ground, O you enthroned under siege!" Jerusalem is "enthroned (*yōšebet*) geographically above her valleys, but she must get down from her throne to pick up her knapsack like any other refugee. If there is anything like a chronological sequence to many of the passages in this portion of the book (and I now believe there is), then dating 8:14—9:8 to the time of the drought in the latter part of 601 and dating 10:17–22 to the siege of early 597 suggest that 9:17–22 (Heb., 16—21) is to be dated sometime before the siege, perhaps just before it.

The Babylonians put Zedekiah on the throne, and we hear nothing further from Jeremiah for three years. Then a chain of incidents took place which brought Jeremiah into the second crisis in his prophetic vocation.

There was an uprising against Nebuchadrezzar from within his own army in December 595 or January 594. He boasted of killing the ringleader with his own hands.[30] This attempted *coup d'état* must have excited the Jewish exiles into a hope that Nebuchadrezzar could fall, and the news stimulated Zedekiah to call a conference of ambassadors from Edom, Moab, Ammon, Tyre, and Sidon in Jerusalem in the last spring or early summer of 594 (*History*, p. 329). That meeting is presupposed by chapter 27.[31]

Jeremiah was convinced that the optimism of the conference was misplaced. He not only wore a collar of thongs and yoke pegs[32] but gave similar collars to all the ambassadors[33]—everyone must be ready to submit to the yoke of Nebuchadrezzar. Indeed he sent a letter to the exiles instructing them to submit and be prepared for a long stay in Babylon (29:1–23).

Then in late July or early August 594, he was confronted by the optimistic prophet Hananiah in the temple area (28:1–16) (see *Jeremiah*, p. 200). Jeremiah was still wearing his collar. Hananiah proclaimed good news: the exile would be over within two years (28:3). Jeremiah expressed his doubts (28:5–9). Then Hananiah broke the pegs of Jeremiah's collar in a symbolic act, and Jeremiah, dejected, could only go his way (28:10–11). Later Jeremiah heard Yahweh say that the wooden pegs would be replaced by iron ones, since Nebuchadrezzar's yoke would also be one of iron (28:12–14), and Jeremiah's final word to Hananiah was that the latter was an illegitimate prophet and would die within a year. This was not simply Jeremiah's personal curse; the prophet who prophesies falsely was to die (Deut. 18:20).

This opposition from Hananiah was reinforced by opposition from other

30. Cf. Bright, *History of Israel*, p. 329. For Nebuchadrezzar's boast, see D. J. Wiseman, *Chronicles of Chaldean Kings (626–556 B.C.)* (London: The British Museum, 1956), pp. 72–73, lines 21–22.

31. The date in 27:1 is erroneous; on this see Bright, *Jeremiah*, pp. 199, 201–2.

32. The Hebrew *mōtôt*, 27:2, are evidently the pegs fitted into a yoke which rest on either side of the neck of each ox; the pegs are tied with thongs underneath the neck so that the oxen cannot dislodge the yoke. Jeremiah wore the thongs and pegs, not the yoke itself (against the assumptions of most commentators, e.g., Bright, *Jeremiah*, p. 199).

33. The Hebrew reads "send them" in 27:3, i.e., the collars, not "send word," the emended text of the RSV.

quarters which we may discern or surmise. Thus there was opposition from optimistic prophets in Babylon who objected to Jeremiah's word that the exile would be long. These prophets asked the priest in charge of the temple police to lock him up in the stocks (29:24–32) as he had been locked up years before (20:1–6). Though the priest did not accede to the request, it is clear that Jeremiah's word brought enmity.

In this crisis I would find the setting for the rest of the confessions, specifically the addition of "men of Anathoth" in 11:21 and 23, the addition of 12:6, the passage 15:10–12, the addition of 15:20–21, then 17:14–18 and 20:7–12. The warrant for such a setting for these passages is indirect but suggestive. I believe that the addition of "men of Anathoth" in 11:12 and 23 and the addition of 12:6 come from Jeremiah himself.[34] These additions (particularly 12:6) are not likely to have been devised by someone unacquainted with his circumstances. If there was opposition by his fellow villagers and his family, and if it did not take place in the crisis of 601–600, and further if opposition by his family is unlikely when he bought the field at Anathoth (32:1–15), evidently in the summer of 588, then this is the most likely time. Hananiah was from Gibeon (28:1), eight kilometers west of Anathoth. Was there some reason why the folk in these villages thought Jeremiah was too extreme? I have dated the call to abstain from marriage (16:1–4) in the crisis of 601–600. But the command to abstain from attending funerals (16:5–9) is couched as a fresh command. Did that command, more extreme even than the abstention from marriage, come at this period? Would Jeremiah's boycotting of funerals dishonor his family and bring opposition on him from that quarter? These questions are impossible to answer but remain enticing possibilities.

It appears, in any event, that the confessions of 601–600 were useful once more, and those that seem to have been added in 594 have overtones that link them to the encounter with Hananiah. Thus I would now translate the puzzling 15:10–12 as follows:

> (10) Woe is me, my mother, that you bore me, a man of strife and contention to the whole land! I have not lent nor have I borrowed, yet all of them curse me.
> (11) Yahweh said,[35] Surely I have armored you[36] well;[37] surely I have intervened with you[38] in a time of trouble and a time of distress![39] (12) Can he break iron, iron from the north, and bronze? (Author's trans.)

By this understanding the subject of the verb in verse 12 is not the indefinite "one" (RSV) but "he," that is, Hananiah. The three terms are the "iron" of the hypothetical iron yoke pegs, the "iron from the north" of

---

34. Against Hubmann; see n. 27.

35. So the Hebrew, against the Septuagint.

36. Reading the Qere *šĕrîtīkā* as a piel denominative from *širyôn*, "armor," a suggestion of Franz Hubmann in personal consultation.

37. For "well" as a rendering *lᵉṭôb* compare Robert Gordis, "A Note on *ṭôb*," *JTS* 35 (1934) 187.

38. This is the meaning of the verb in 36:25 and Isa. 53:12.

39. I take "the enemy" as a gloss; cf. the same diction in Isa. 7:17 and Mic. 3:8.

Nebuchadrezzar's yoke, and the "bronze" wall into which Yahweh would make Jeremiah (15:20), and the vocabulary of metals is anticipated by the "armored" of v. 11. Jeremiah's complaint in v. 10 is an apostrophe to his mother: Is this evidence of family opposition? Yahweh's answer to Jeremiah's complaint in v. 10 is that the prophet has been satisfactorily armored for the crisis and that Hananiah is bound to fail when he tries to break the iron and bronze.

I thus date 15:20–21 to this period as well, and 20:7–12 likewise, for reasons that will become clear in a moment.

The autumn of 594 is the occasion once more to hear the recitation of Deuteronomy. I propose that 11:1–17 is Jeremiah's counterproclamation on that occasion. The resemblance of "cursed be" in 11:3 and "so be it" (= "amen") in 11:5 to the "curses" and "amens" of Deut. 27:15–26 has long been noted, [40] and Jeremiah has "iron" on his mind (11:4). But most crucially he says (v. 9) that "there is revolt among the men of Judah and inhabitants of Jerusalem." The word "revolt" (or "conspiracy," qešer) does not otherwise appear in Jeremiah (or Deuteronomy). It is typically used of an attempted revolt by a vassal against his overlord (as Hoshea against the king of Assyria, 2 Kings 17:4). And this word precisely fits the situation of 594: a conference to revolt against Nebuchadrezzar. But, says Yahweh, Nebuchadrezzar's yoke is my will, so that the revolt is against me.

So Jeremiah spoke at the festival of booths in late September or early October 594. But something else happened that month, perhaps even during the festival: Hananiah dropped dead (28:17). What a stunning validation of Jeremiah's prophetic word (Deut. 18:20)! The event must have made a great impression on everyone—the month is carefully preserved. I suggest that the event of Hananiah's death explains two puzzles. The first is the meaning of 20:13, a verse otherwise out of the emotional context; I propose that it is Jeremiah's praise to Yahweh that the conspiracy against him has been broken and that in effect his prophetic standing has been validated. The second is why the "confessions" are part of the public record at all. They are after all private transactions between Jeremiah and Yahweh. No one in those days was interested in the "psychology of prophetism." These prayers and answers were made public by Jeremiah to affirm his validity as a true prophet of Yahweh. Yahweh had answered his prayers. Note well; we have 10:17–22 dated 598, then 11:1–17 autumn 594, followed immediately by the whole confessional collection from 11:18 through chapter 20: Hananiah dropped dead. The material was thus collected in chronological order.

If 20:13 marks Jeremiah's response to the death of Hananiah, vv. 14–18 suggest that the prophet's depression continued; and the diction suggests that it was family opposition that continued. One may surmise that the struggle between the optimistic prophets and a pessimistic prophet in Jerusalem meant less to his family in Anathoth than his actions which continued to dishonor them.

---

40. E.g., Rudolph, *Jeremia,* p. 77.

The events of the prophet's career in 588 and 587 are better known (though some details remain obscure), since we have the biographical material of chapters 37—44 (see e.g., *Jeremiah*, pp. 219–66). In January 588 Nebuchadrezzar began a second siege of Jerusalem. During the spring or summer the Egyptian army forced the Babylonian army temporarily to withdraw, but then the siege was renewed and Jeremiah was imprisoned. Two or three times Zedekiah asked Jeremiah to intervene or to give news of any change of heart on Yahweh's part (21:1–10; 37; 38:14–28), but the prophet continued to insist that resistance to Babylon was futile. In July 587 the city fell. Zedekiah tried to escape but was captured near Jericho, taken to Nebuchadrezzar's headquarters, and sentenced (39:1–7). In August of that year the Babylonian general destroyed the walls of the city and burned the palace and temple (*History*, pp. 329–30); Gedaliah was appointed governor, administering from Mizpah a few kilometers north of Jerusalem (40:7–12).

In the midst of these terrible events Jeremiah was bidden to begin to speak optimistically of a new beginning for the people after the exile. This new turn in his message may have begun with the purchase of the field at Anathoth (32:1–15), which perhaps occurred during the respite from the siege in 588 (cf. the puzzling 37:12). Such a gesture by the prophet would at least have helped to heal the breach with his family.

That new beginning was embodied most signally in a new scroll Jeremiah was bidden to prepare (30:2–4) with optimistic words for the future. That scroll evidently contained the old words which in his youth he had directed to the north, plus fresh words more particularly shaped for the south (I believe 30:10–11, 16–17; and 31:7–9a). I further propose that the scroll, in which the last word of poetry was 31:21–22, was rounded off by 31:27–28. This scroll, then, would have been proclaimed between the summer of 588 and the summer of 587.

There still is one more step. In the autumn of 587 it was time to recite Deuteronomy once more. Could one imagine the priests embarking on this ritual at the appointed time, when the temple itself had been burned a scant six weeks before? I submit that they did. I submit that this was the goal of the pilgrims from the north—from Shechem, Shiloh and Samaria—who were coming to present their offerings at the temple "in the seventh month" (41:1–5). The year is not mentioned, but if these pilgrims had remained loyal to Josiah's program of cultic and political reunion between north and south, as their action indicates, then the occasion of the recitation of Deuteronomy was an appropriate one (cf. *Jeremiah*, pp. 253–54). I pass by the assassination of Gedaliah and the massacre of those pilgrims who could not bribe their way to freedom (41:1–10), because I want to deal with the occasion of the recitation of Deuteronomy in the ruined temple area.

Is there an utterance of Jeremiah's which would fit that occasion? I propose that it is the "new covenant" passage, 31:31–34. Note that it is placed after what I take to be the close of the scroll of hope (see above), that its diction is strongly reminiscent of Deuteronomy,[41] and that it states that the old cove-

41. See Hyatt, "Jeremiah," *IB* 5, p. 1038.

nant is obsolete. If this is its setting, then its pure vision of a new initiative by Yahweh is all the more astonishing.

Soon after the assassination of Gedaliah, those loyal to the governor fled to Egypt, taking Jeremiah and Baruch with them (chaps. 42—43). If it was late in the year 587 and if the prophet proclaimed 31:31–34 in the autumn of 587, then that was his last word in Jerusalem. It must have been horrid for Jeremiah to see himself going to Egypt, whence Moses had led the people out (cf. Deut. 17:16). If he were an anti-Moses figure since 601, then this is the crowning deed of an anti-Moses! No wonder his last recorded word to the travelers was, "Behold, I have sworn by my great name, says Yahweh, that my name shall no more be invoked by the mouth of any man of Judah in all the land of Egypt, saying, 'As the Lord Yahweh lives'" (44:26).[42] If Yahweh had taught Moses the divine name and enjoined him to teach the name to his people, then Jeremiah would announce the extinguishing of the divine name in Egypt. The hope for the future of the people lay in Babylon, not in Egypt (29:7). It is the last we hear of the prophet; by my reckoning he would have been forty years old. Perhaps Baruch died first, since we have no notice of the prophet's death.

Here then is a possible reconstruction of Jeremiah's career. If valid, it exposes the shifts of his perception of Yahweh's will through several decades—a prophetic career which we can come to know in unparalleled detail.

Eleven years ago in the pages of *Interpretation*, Stanley B. Frost suggested that the Book of Jeremiah is a memorial to a childless man.[43] It is ironic that some of the wealth of detail which we have of Jeremiah's career is due to Yahweh's command that he not marry and have children. Though a book may be a poor substitute for sons to carry on one's name, Jeremiah's sacrifice is our gain.

---

42. See Schökel, "Jeremías como anti-Moisés," p. 248.
43. "The Memorial of a Childless Man: A Study in Hebrew Thought on Immortality," *Int* 26 (1972) 437–50, esp. 446–47.

12
Jeremiah in the Lectionary

Thomas M. Raitt

When texts from Jeremiah that appear in the lectionary passages are read in conjunction with the accompanying New Testament texts, Jeremiah functions anew as an interpreter of God's Word, providing illumination unavailable to an interpretation of the passages taken by themselves.

A quite different portrait of Jeremiah emerges from the aggregate of the Jeremiah passages in the lectionary than the one in the previous three essays in this book. The historical-literary critical legitimacy of this lectionary portrait is subordinated to the fact that when Christians worship they necessarily act out a Christian identity. That will inevitably lead to reading Jeremiah through the light of Christian experience and New Testament revelation.

When one tries to understand why lectionaries select from Jeremiah what they do, one must come to terms with the anomaly that lectionaries are not much interested in prophetic writings in general. By far the most heavily used prophetic book in the lectionaries is Isaiah, and it sets the tone for the use of other prophetic material. This helps to explain why two of the lectionary selections of the eleven from Jeremiah, which have been almost universally judged as late additions by source critics (23:1–6; 33:14–16), are utilized. They are messianic predictions and thus expand on the Isaianic trend. Another passage, 31:7–9, also doubtful as stemming from Jeremiah himself, puts us in the optimistic era of deliverance after bondage in the Babylonian exile, like the latter parts of Isaiah.

Of the remaining Jeremiah lections, six deal not with his message but with his life. It is with these passages that we come to the heart of the Christian appropriation of Jeremiah into the life of the Christian believer and the early church. The four of these which are autobiographical, Jeremiah's so-called "laments," are, at worst, sub-Christian expressions of vengeance, self-righteousness, and bitterness about the sacrifices involved in filling the prophetic vocation. At their best these four show that being a messenger of God's word is a difficult calling and that often the last thing people want to hear is the

143

truth, even from God, about their specific time and situation (which is precisely why prophets are not without honor except in their own country). There is clearly a significant dialogue between (a) the problems faced in first-century Christian discipleship, (b) the sacrifices involved in Jesus' fulfillment of his own self-understanding of a kind of messiahship leading to the cross, and (c) Jeremiah as the prototype of the faithful but suffering prophet. This is undoubtedly the most verifiable image of Jeremiah which emerges through the lens of lectionary selections: Jeremiah is the prophet par excellence. He is a very human, vulnerable person, vividly portrayed, with whom anyone can sympathize and identify. He is a man of great faith, but acting on the demands of his faith causes him recurrent experiences of persecution and suffering. Nevertheless, in the long run, God sustains Jeremiah in his vocation; and the drama within the book ends in a kind of triumphant resolution (both for Jeremiah and the people of Judah). Of the two biographical passages, one shows Jeremiah thrown into a cistern to starve and die (38:1–13). The other (1:4–10) juxtaposes Jeremiah's call to be a prophet with Jesus' experience of being rejected in his hometown, Nazareth, just after he read and interpreted Isaiah 61:1–2 as a self-realization of his ministry (Luke 4:22–30).

We are down to two remaining passages and yet have encountered nothing to comment upon regarding Jeremiah's own authentic message as he perceived that given to him by God. The Book of Jeremiah is weighted about ninety percent prophetic message to ten percent biography or autobiography. Lectionary selections virtually reverse those proportions. It must be said that the Christian reading of Jeremiah in worship is *highly* selective and one-sided. Christian preaching incorporates Jeremiah's *person* as part of its own faith-understanding far more than it incorporates his God-given message. One of the most important passages in the Old Testament is Jeremiah's new covenant promise in 31:31–34. Lectionaries have traditionally assigned this to a time in the church year and paired it with Gospel and Epistle readings which render it meaningless. I have taken the rather bold step of following a newly unfolding trend of assigning that passage to Maundy Thursday with a Lord's Supper passage in Luke and a pivotally important new-covenant claim in Hebrews which give it the full, maximum, inspiring meaning it deserves. Through these corrected pairings we can claim Jeremiah as a kind of unconscious proto-Christian. The last passage to be mentioned at this point is my favorite lectionary selection from Jeremiah, 7:1–7. This passage is a warning that going to a sanctuary is not an inherently and coercively efficacious act. It calls people to repent so that worship of God will stand in integrity with dealing justly and mercifully with other humans. More than anyone else, Jeremiah is the prophet who calls to repentance. With these verses we are brought toward the center of his message and its dominant role in the book. It can be hoped that lectionary revisers will eventually mature into accepting more challenging words of this sort, because they were also an integral part of Jesus' message.

Having given this introductory overview of the person of Jeremiah that emerges through the lectionary readings, we are now going to consider those readings one at a time in relation to their Gospel pairings and their place in the church year. Lectionary selections make certain important hermeneutical assumptions about the Gospel/Old Testament relationship. For the purpose of this article, we will have to read the Bible both forwards and backwards. Risks are run in reading the Bible backwards, because it is read out of its historical context. In recent years a substantial amount of reflection has been given to assumptions behind lectionary making and the relative success or failure of lectionaries in achieving what they attempt. Lectionaries, even as we have them in recently improved and revised form, are open to many criticisms.[1] Because of that, many denominations have *ongoing* lectionary revision committees. In any case, what is seen is a great deal more interest in lectionary preaching than could be found thirty or more years ago.[2]

A keen interest in the hermeneutical matters at stake is built into my examination of the individual pairings under the heading "logic of the selection" and in reflections which conclude this essay. With each pairing I have also asked whether the Jeremiah selections work as Christian Scripture. That dimension of concern is brought into a particular focus on the implicit Christology of the Jeremiah selections in the first part of the conclusion to this essay.

The dynamics of denominational thinking about lectionary selections is such today that there is no one, perfect way of deciding which Jeremiah passage to consider in a study like this. I have decided to accept as my standard the lections in *Proclamation 2* (Fortress Press). Its most helpful dimension for our purposes is that for each Sunday it gives the specific lectionary selections for five denominational groupings in parallel columns for ease in comparing. I have decided to analyze only those Jeremiah passages which occur in three or more of the five denominational groupings.

Since lectionary selections begin with choosing a Gospel passage and then looking for an Old Testament passage which stands in some kind of discernible relationship with it, one can almost always find some meaningful connection. However, the Epistle selections do not have this acknowledged dependent relationship on the Gospel passages. They are read semi-continuously as valuable in their own right. My experience has been that the Epistle selections usually contribute nothing to understanding the Gospel/Jeremiah dynamics and only infrequently do they add to the meaning of the theme(s) for the particular Sunday, as that is determined by the Gospel selection. Therefore, I will not include a discussion of the Epistle selection unless it

---

1. See Lloyd Bailey, "Lectionary Preaching," *Duke Divinity School Review* 41 (Winter 1976) 26ff. and idem, "The Lectionary in Critical Perspective," *Int* 31 (1977) 139–53; also Gerard S. Sloyan, "The Lectionary as a Context for Interpretation," *Int* 31:131–38.

2. See Roger R. Keller, "The Lectionary: Straightjacket or Coat of Many Colors?" *Duke Divinity School Review* 44 (Winter 1979), and Lewis A. Briner, "Preaching the Lectionary," *Reformed Liturgy and Music* 12/2.

adds something to our understanding of the Gospel/Jeremiah interaction or
clarifies significantly the theme(s) for the particular Sunday.

JER. 33:14–16 AND LUKE 21:25–36
(FIRST SUNDAY OF ADVENT)

1. *Overview:* The Luke lection is a good example of the early Advent
emphasis on "last things"—the eschaton—rather than the coming of the
baby Jesus. With this pair of texts one could discuss the parameters of what
difference Jesus' earthly coming did make and how the "already" is in quite a
different category from the "not yet" of the final apocalypse.

2. *Logic of the Selection:* The tie between the testaments here is not
promise/fulfillment. What we actually have is promise on both levels. It is
hard to understand the heavy apocalypticism of the Luke passage if one does
not first understand the lighter hope and eschatology of the messianic
expectation in Jeremiah. Reading one's Bible backwards, we find that Jesus
Christ's coming (the first time) is promised in Jeremiah and that Jesus
Christ's coming (the second time) is promised in Luke. Neither passage
explains the other, but they show the reader two quite different dimensions
of the same process. It is obvious that apocalypticism presupposes an understanding of eschatology within history.

3. *As Christian Scripture:* If expectations of Jeremiah's disciples and
redactors are counted as valid, then a promise is begun here which is fulfilled
and presupposed in the Lukan apocalyptic promise.

JER. 1:4–10 AND LUKE 4:21–32
(SECOND SUNDAY AFTER EPIPHANY)

1. *Overview:* Having begun as an emphasis on Jesus' baptism, the miracle
at Cana, and the visit of the Magi, the Epiphany season broadens to a time
when the church "stands back and meditates on the identity, attributes, and
divine powers of Jesus Christ."[3] Jeremiah 1:4–10 presents a good Epiphany
theme because it reflects on the beginnings of Jeremiah's ministry. It is the
closest thing to Jeremiah's baptism; it is his call to be a prophet. In the
Gospel selection we find a Jesus who has been reflecting upon his role as that
has gradually unfolded since his recent baptism.

2. *Logic of the Selection:* Both of the passages (Jeremiah and Luke) are
about the vocation of bearing God's word. When Jesus' kinsmen and hometown folk reject him, he says: ". . . no prophet is acceptable in his home
country" (4:24). The two texts *function* in the same way. Jeremiah 1:4–10 is
about the prophet's self-consciousness and self-definition in his vocation.
Luke 4:21–31 treats the same topics in relation to Jesus. It is a splendid
example of responsible and informed Old-New Testament pairing with each
passage throwing light upon the other.

---

3. George M. Bass, *The Renewal of Liturgical Preaching* (Minneapolis: Augsburg Pub.
House, 1967), p. 165.

3. *As Christian Scripture:* God calls all of us. None of us feels worthy to the task. God gives us the power to do that which he calls us to do (see the Epistle, 1 Cor. 12:27f.).

JER. 17:5–10 AND LUKE 6:17–26
(SIXTH SUNDAY AFTER EPIPHANY)

1. *Overview:* Of the three texts given in the lectionary, the Jeremiah passage is in many ways the easiest from which to preach. If the Luke passage is taken as a commentary on the Jeremiah passage, then the Jeremiah lesson almost automatically expands into being Christian Scripture. The fallacies of faith in humans (introduced in Jer. 17:5) are certainly expanded and driven home in Luke 6:24–26. What Luke describes in the four "woe" sayings is a level of life that is subbiblical. Trust in purely human things looks a lot better than it is. It does not look cursed, but it is in the long run. Together these not only turn out to be good texts about faith and doubt; they turn out to be good texts about superficial and deeper levels of living.

2. *Logic of the Selection:* Jeremiah 17:5–8 describes very different kinds of people. They have quite different consequences to face for their action. The prophet is combining his roles of moral teacher and preacher-exhorter here. Luke 6:20–26 also lays out a sharp distinction between two kinds of people. The four "blesseds" are an expansion of the generic kind of person who trusts in God (as in Jer. 15:5f.). They each have their reward. The woes show the opposite kind of person and the opposite reward. Perhaps the strongest Old-New Testament tie is that the Lukan passage is a *midrash* on the Jeremiah passage. As a Jewish rabbi, Jesus certainly was steeped in midrash.

3. *As Christian Scripture:* At many points Christian teaching presupposes prophetic teaching, not least of all in ethics. Jeremiah 17:5f. being used in conjunction with Luke 6:17–26 certifies and validates that Jeremianic teaching at the level of Christian teaching. At least at some points there is full continuity and parity between New Testament teaching and Old Testament teaching.

JER. 7:1–7 AND LUKE 6:39–49
(EIGHTH SUNDAY AFTER EPIPHANY)

1. *Overview:* Both Jeremiah and Jesus are giving sermons, acting out their role of preacher and prophet: saying that the promises of God are not unconditional, giving challenges, threatening and promising, laying out the alternatives, calling to decision. I think that the Gospel text here is not so strong as the Jeremiah text. Other parts of the Gospels revalidate the Jer. 7:1–7 message: (a) Jesus' call to repent because the kingdom of God is coming; (b) Jesus' compassionate concern for the unfortunates in society— tax collectors, harlots, lepers, the poor, children; (c) Jesus' cleansing of the temple.

2. *Logic of the Selection:* The crux of the matter is the interlocking of lessons. A strong conformation of thematic similarities becomes transparent. Here as in the lections for the sixth Sunday after Epiphany we find a midrashic principle at work. The *main statement* of the matter is made in the Old Testament for which there is a shorter and less profound echo in the New.

3. *As Christian Scripture:* I found a number of tightly interwoven themes in Jer. 7:1–7. I think all of them, read backwards through Christian experience and the New Testament, have an important message for Christians today:

(a) The prophet is a reformer and purifier of the cultus. We need continual reform of the church establishment; we need to have a lover's quarrel with the institutional church.

(b) Just as in Amos 5, Isaiah 1, Micah 6, Jeremiah affirms that there are moral prerequisites to worship. We need to articulate what the moral prerequisites to acceptable worship are today. Churches cannot be insulated religious clubs for one race or one economic class.

(c) The election is not unconditional. We cannot assume that Christ is always for us. Christ also judges us and holds us accountable.

(d) Jeremiah is a covenant mediator. Christ is the mediator of the covenant to which we belong. What are the terms of this new covenant? Is it totally permissive?

(e) Jeremiah 7:1–7 includes an example of a major emphasis in Jeremiah's preaching: the call to repentance. Christ calls us to repentance.

(f) God's presence in the house of worship built by human hands is conditional upon God—priests and historical considerations do not affect that. God's presence in worship and Christ's presence in the sacraments are totally up to the divine prerogative and grace; we dare not play "religion" as though it were a game.

(g) Prophetic religion is very humanistic and humanitarian, very horizontal. That is not at the cost of the relation to God, the vertical. But the vertical presupposes, balances, and culminates the horizontal thrust. New Testament Christianity needs the correction of the Old Testament and Judaism to regain its horizontal counterbalance to a dated and mythologized vertical thrust and a phony "spiritualism."

Who can ignore the wealth of sermon topics in Jer. 7:1–7? I think that it is not always true that the light begins in the Old Testament and comes to brightest focus in the New. Here we see rays of light in various parts of the Gospels, but they come to brightest focus here (7:1–7)! We should be prepared for this if we want to read our Bibles backwards honestly and expectantly.

JER. 31:31–34; LUKE 22:7–20; HEB. 10:5–39 (MAUNDY THURSDAY)

1. *Overview:* According to *Proclamation 2*, all five major denominational divisions have traditionally used the pivotally important Jeremiah "new

covenant" passage with John 12:20–33 and some variation of Heb. 5:7–9.[4] I began my work on this accepting those givens. The problem is that the three passages have almost nothing in common, do not fit Lent well, and demonstrate the terrible fallibility of lectionary making rather than its potentially great strength. At length I decided to take the bold step and insist that the normative home for Jer. 31:31–34 is on Maundy Thursday, where two of the groups recently have placed it, having also been joined in very recent days by at least one other group according to the *Index of Readings and Psalms in a Consensus Lectionary* prepared by the North American Committee on Calendar and Lectionary.

Maundy Thursday is certainly one of the most important days in the Christian year, *regularly celebrated* by a wide range of Christian groups and deserving to be considered as the one exception to our otherwise total exclusion of lections for days other than Sunday.

2. *Logic of the Selection:* When Jeremiah announces that the old covenant is over and that God is about to bring a new covenant, he is acting in the traditional role of covenant mediator which began with such towering figures as Moses, Joshua, Samuel, and Elijah. In Hebrews 10 we are so translated into a new era that Jesus Christ is the high priest who mediates the new and eternal covenant. What roles then is Jesus acting out in the last-supper incident depicted in Luke 22:7–20? First of all he is playing the role of father in a Jewish family celebrating the Passover. Then by saying, "This is my body," with the bread and, "This cup . . . is the new covenant in my blood . . . ," he is at once (a) picking up the traditional covenant mediator role, (b) becoming the sacrificed lamb whose shared flesh and blood become the life-seal which mystically binds the members of this new covenant to the benefits of the crucifixion and resurrection, and (c) demonstrating the role which the Hebrews reading makes explicit: Jesus Christ as *the* high priest.

What too few people realize about the Lord's Supper taking place in the context of a Passover meal is that *the gravitational center of Christian worship is carefully placed directly on top of the gravitational center of Jewish worship.*

A beautiful thing about using these three texts together on Maundy Thursday of Holy Week is that the context goes far toward interpreting their meaning without the preacher having to spell that out.

3. *As Christian Scripture:* Read in the context of the Lord's Supper, Jer. 31:31–34 is Christian Scripture. It is my conviction that when there is a conjunction of Old and New Testament readings, then we most assuredly hear ourselves addressed by the Word of God. We who preach must increasingly find that conjunction and proclaim it with clarity and authority.

Those who receive this covenant will know God as humans have never known God before, in a personal, not conceptual, way. The recipients of this covenant are graced with unconditional, eschatological forgiveness. It is

---

4. E. Schüssler Fiorenza and U. T. Jones, *Lent*, Proclamation 2, Series B (Philadelphia: Fortress Press, 1981), p. 53.

important to realize that every time the Lord's Supper is observed the eschatological moment is in the now, the present.

Our remaining six Jeremiah lections fall on the Sundays between Pentecost and Advent. It is the longest season of the church year, but also the least precisely defined. After reading many liturgical authorities' sometimes contradictory and sometimes vague descriptions of the theme of this season, I have come to see the main emphasis as being the human *response* to the great events between Christmas and Pentecost. Half the year we stress key events in Christ's life; the other half we stress response to those events.

JER. 20:7–13 AND MATT. 10:26–33
(FIFTH SUNDAY AFTER PENTECOST)

1. *Overview:* This is for many a favorite biographical section of Jeremiah. In it we see a wide emotional swing from bitter rejection of his appointed role to trust and even praise to God for his help in carrying out the special task. My understanding of this passage and its relationship to the Matthew lection is indebted to a helpful explanation by Reginald H. Fuller:

> Jeremiah was pre-eminently the prophet who suffered persecution because of his prophetic activity. His fate influenced the development of the later Jewish view that rejection, persecution, and martyrdom were inseparable to the prophetic vocation. . . . To be a bearer of the word of God means to suffer because that word inevitably encounters hostility and rejection. It is illuminating . . . that Jesus regarded his own fate as the culmination of the rejection of the prophets and their message.[5]

2. *Logic of the Selection:* Jeremiah's unhappy experience as a prophet is brought forward as an example of what will happen to Jesus' disciples and then more broadly to all who take up Jesus' cause. For the persecuted early church there was an existential interest in the warning and assurance Jesus gave in Matt. 10:26–33. That naturally worked further back into the faith stream to Jeremiah's misery and glory at being chosen to bear God's word.

3. *As Christian Scripture:* What happened to the disciples and to Jeremiah for bearing God's word is a scaled down version of what this ministry cost Christ. It is a call and a challenge to all Christians. Both the Jeremiah example and the Matthew passage help to bridge this paradigm to the average believer. Here, as at so many other points, I believe Gospel and Prophet *together* are more assuredly the Word of God for us than is either alone.

JER. 23:1–6 AND MARK 6:30–44
(NINTH SUNDAY AFTER PENTECOST)

1. *Overview:* The *only* shared theme in the Gospel and Prophet is the sheep/shepherd theme. Israel had plenty of experience with leaders who

---

5. *Preaching the New Lectionary* (Collegeville, Minn.: Liturgical Press, 1971), p. 216.

were the antithesis of shepherds for God's people. As an eschatological act, God himself will intervene in history to play the shepherd role. God also will set shepherds over them. The content of what this kind of religious leader does is more fully spelled out in Jeremiah than in Mark.

2. *Logic of the Selection:* Perhaps some would say that the sheep/shepherd theme in Jeremiah and Mark has a typological relationship. I see the shared images called forth primarily by a similarity of situations addressed.

3. *As Christian Scripture:* The Mark lection in an honest, uncontrived, and legitimate way updates the Jeremiah lection; and with the two conjoined we hear the Word of God. Jesus and the Gospel writers presupposed that their audience knew Jeremiah, the person and the book. Frequently one does not have to force Jeremiah into Christian shape. Its shared themes and imagery often speak, as in this set of lections, almost without any translation or interpretation. The problem of the right kind of religious leadership is timeless.

JER. 38:1–13 AND LUKE 12:49–56
(THIRTEENTH SUNDAY AFTER PENTECOST)

1. *Overview:* Opposite to what I have done with other sets of readings up to this point, I would begin and center my homiletical preparation for this Sunday with the Epistle (Heb. 12:1–13). The unifying theme for all three lections is the need to have faith and courage when one undergoes testing, hardship, and trial. The Hebrews passage says that clearly and relatively simply; the Gospel lesson says that in very complex apocalyptic imagery; and the Jeremiah lection gives us an incident out of Jeremiah's life which illustrates the basic point. My conclusion is reinforced by Fuller: "This is one of the few Sundays when a common theme runs through all the readings, the epistle included."[6]

The Hebrews lesson is preceded by a long and impassioned historical litany (chap. 11) whose point is to show that a whole succession of Old Testament characters are splendid models of what it means to live by faith. In the midst of the Hebrews lection is a quote from Prov. 3:11–12 to prove the point that " . . . the Lord disciplines those whom he loves. . . ." One could move from Hebrews to the Luke lesson and extract the main points for reinforcement. I would use the incident of Jeremiah thrown into the cistern (38:1–13) only as an illustration of faith tested and retained.

2. *Logic of the Selection:* A beautiful thing happens when there is *conjunction* between all three lessons. One discovers that there is a dialogue within Scripture and that *there is revelation in the sum of that dialogue* and not only in its parts. When you hear that dialogue you feel close to the heartbeat and center of Scripture.

In this set of readings I think we find a model of Old/New Testament relations not specifically anticipated in many of the models which denomina-

---

6. Ibid., p. 530.

tions have used. It goes in two stages: (a) main point = Epistle and Gospel; (b) illustration of the main point = Jeremiah. Or, illustration ← interpretation says what we mean. This, I think, is a very creative and responsible way to use the Bible: Let the dialogue within it find full and free expression.

3. *As Christian Scripture:* Here the Old Testament emerges as a fund of resource material from which Christians could draw lived examples as precedents for their teaching and theology.

JER. 15:15–21 AND MATT. 16:21–26
(FIFTEENTH SUNDAY AFTER PENTECOST)

1. *Overview:* Three out of the five denominational groupings use Jer. 20:7–9 with this Gospel lection. That duplicates the Jeremiah lection for the fifth Sunday after Pentecost and gives us a much weaker pairing for Matt. 16:21–26 than Jer. 15:15–21. In this instance I am making an exception to my own standards for selection, going with only two of the groups, but following to the letter the readings given in *Proclamation 2*.

The Gospel passage here is extremely strong and would be the basis for my homily. The Epistle passage (Rom. 12:1–8) is, I think, one of the most powerful from Paul's writings and at least in verses 1–2 deals with the major theme in Jeremiah and Matthew: The cost of discipleship involves suffering for one's faith.

2. *Logic of the Selection:* We have here one of the most typical of Jeremiah's "laments," which, like the laments in the Psalter, goes from initial doubt and self-pity to trust in God's enabling power. The Matthew passage moves from Jesus' question "Who do men say that the Son of man is?" (16:13), to a prediction of Jesus' own passion (16:21–23), to the tremendous statement: "If any man would come after me, let him deny himself and take up his cross . . ." (16:24f.). The Old/New Testament tie is very strong and involves the employment of some unique rationales.

3. *As Christian Scripture:* Questions could be raised, on the basis of the Gospel lection: Well, if I deny myself and take up my cross and follow Christ, what is that going to feel like? Can I actually accomplish that? Jeremiah 15:15–21 is a very human and yet God-centered answer to precisely such a question. The Bible knows our existential situation! With God's help, even our waverings will not undo us.

JER. 11:18–20 AND MARK 9:30–37
(EIGHTEENTH SUNDAY AFTER PENTECOST)

1. *Overview:* It is a subject of considerable scholarly debate whether all or portions of Jer. 12:1–6 should be inserted before or within 11:18–20.[7]

---

7. E.g., Wilhelm Rudolph inserts parts of it within (*Jeremia*, HAT 12 [Tübingen: J.C.B. Mohr, 1958], p. 75) and John Bright inserts all of it before (*Jeremiah*, AB 21 [Garden City, N.Y.: Doubleday & Co., 1965], pp. 83–90).

2. *Logic of the Selection:* All three of the lections are the weakest to be considered in this essay. The assumed parallel between Jeremiah's life and Jesus' life must be the tie between the testaments much more than any congruity between their words.

3. *As Christian Scripture:* The Jeremiah passage is not up to the level of Christian faith, where at least the model is suffering in silence and with acceptance and not complaining and invoking divine wrath on perceived enemies.

JER. 31:7–9 AND MARK 10:46–52
(TWENTY-THIRD SUNDAY AFTER PENTECOST)

1. *Overview:* What we have in Jeremiah is a generic prophecy of deliverance (from exile). In Mark we have a brief description of Jesus' last healing before he goes to Jerusalem.

2. *Logic of the Selection:* Two themes unite Prophet and Gospel: (a) God's unexpected and undeserved grace; (b) God's special compassion toward the blind. However, faith is not an issue in the Prophet; it is a big issue in the Gospel. Identity of the messiah is not an issue in the Prophet; it is a big issue in the Gospel. Primarily what we see here is the reverse of what we found with the pairing of Jer. 38:1–13 and Luke 12:49–53 where the Gospel gave the general teaching and the Prophet gave the example that fleshed it out. Here the Prophet gives the general teaching and the Gospel gives the example.

3. *As Christian Scripture:* The God who saved his elected and faithful remnant from exile saved his son from the tomb. The God of the Old Testament is both a punishing and a redeeming God. The Christ of the New Testament is both a Christ of justice and a Christ of compassion.

THE IMPLICIT CHRISTOLOGY IN THE
JEREMIAH SELECTIONS

After one works through our eleven Jeremiah-Gospel pairings, one can have no question that Jesus Christ saw Jeremiah as a role model for himself. (1) Jeremiah is the quintessential prophet. We know far more about the external events of his life and his internal thoughts and feelings in relation to his fortunes and misfortunes than we know about any other prophet. (2) Jeremiah struggled with the burden of being one whose vocation it was to bear God's word. His moods fluctuated widely from hating to bear that burden to glorying in it. (3) Jeremiah struggled against false prophets and was lonely in his unwavering faithfulness to Yahweh. Far more than is recorded of any other prophet, he was rejected for what he said and did; and he suffered for what he said and did.

Not only did Jesus identify with this, but Jesus' disciples and followers found in the life of Jeremiah a precedent for their own harsh rejection at the hands of most Jews and Romans. That of course includes the Gospel writers and the early lectionary makers.

What we have observed can lead us in three directions. (1) I argue that an independently valid christological model is the faithful and innocent, yet rejected and suffering, prophet. (2) Among candidates for the "suffering servant" role, Jeremiah ranks fairly high amid the plethora of Old Testament models when that servant is interpreted as an individual figure and not as Israel. This interest in Jeremiah could draw upon, without negating the functioning of, what we said about the valid christological model. (3) Another christological model is the "Eschatological Prophet" who will come at the end of days. Jeremiah certainly falls behind the greater interest shown in Elijah and John the Baptist for this role, but he is specifically brought into this context in Matt. 16:14. Again, this could be seen as coordinate and not competitive with the roles of christological model and suffering servant.[8]

We should not assume that early lectionary makers were so unsophisticated as to value less the messianic predictions in our lections Jer. 33:14–16 and 23:1–6 than those in Isaiah. Read in its lectionary context, Jeremiah 31:31–34 is part of a beautiful statement about Jesus Christ as the Pascal Lamb whose sacrifice seals the new covenant and as the high priest who officiates over this covenant. In Jer. 7:1–7 we have an important precedent for a dimension of Jesus' teaching, and in Jer. 31:7–9 we see an example of God's compassion for the blind among the exiles in Babylon which Jesus updates in healing the blind Bartimaeus (Mark 10:46–52). Thus, in all, there are a variety of christological models in our Jeremiah lections, but the important ones were mentioned first.

ON READING JEREMIAH BACKWARDS—
THE HERMENEUTIC ISSUE

We have seen a good employment of the denominational models for relating to Old/New Testament lections, as those were given in the early pages of this essay. Those seem to be useful and valid. To those we have added several other models as a result of our study of Jeremiah lections and paired New Testament texts. The diversity of Old Testament materials requires a multiplicity of models for depicting how Jeremiah relates to the New Testament.

The situation with which we are left is not without problems. For example, the question arises: How would we feel about the Jews reading the Hebrew Bible through the eyes of the Talmud only? In that case we would share no common Scripture with them if we also read the Old Testament through the eyes of the New Testament only. One can readily imagine the following protests: "It is chauvinistic to read the Old Testament backwards; it is

---

8. For more on the "suffering servant" and the "eschatological prophet" see Oscar Cullmann, *The Christology of the New Testament* (Philadelphia: Westminster Press, 1959), and R. H. Fuller, *The Foundations of New Testament Christology* (New York: Charles Scribner's Sons, 1965).

theologically biased; it is historically dishonest; it is a specie of eisegesis and not exegesis"!

Having considered that, I yet admit that when Christians worship they necessarily act out a Christian identity. That will inevitably lead to reading Jeremiah and other portions of the Old Testament backwards through the light of Christian experience and New Testament revelation.

What I personally think is that reading the Book of Jeremiah backwards selectively ought to motivate a Christian to read it forwards in its entirety. All Christians, and not just ministers, ought to read it both ways.

I do not think that you have to drive yourself to schizophrenia between historical exegesis and homiletical exegesis. I have done both kinds of exegesis for this essay, but the reader has seen primarily that portion of my hermeneutical cycle which gives ground for homiletical exegesis. Reading the Old Testament backwards does not create a problem if you know that that is precisely what you are doing and if that activity is informed by a great deal of study of the book in the forwards mode.

One of the most helpful resolutions of this problem comes from Gerhard von Rad: "One must speak of a witness of the Old Testament to Christ, for our knowledge of Christ is incomplete without the witness of the Old Testament. Christ is given to us only through the double witness of the choir of those who await and those who remember."[9] What I understand by this is that the New Testament was written by those who "remember" the historicity of the Christ event and are part of the community which was created in response to it. John Bright calls this "the A.D. perspective."[10]

"Those who await" stand in the stream of an unfolding salvation history which encourages their profound confrontation of the human situation. Our common human nature makes it easy for us to identify with those who know the human dilemma so well. Bright calls this "the B.C. perspective."[11]

In my view, historical analysis (what is usually meant by "exegesis") can never show us the Christian meaning of Old Testament texts. It is only in our faith stance as Christians that we can and must claim for some substantial number of Old Testament texts a meaning for Christians. To take a commonly used distinction, what Old Testament texts "meant" is what they meant for their original audience. The crucial question of what they "mean" depends upon the identity of the religious community which provides the context in which one reads them today. We are stuck with a situation in which Old Testament texts frequently "mean" something different for the contemporary Jewish community than they "mean" for the contemporary Christian community. As historical scholars we can agree about what specific Old Testament texts "meant." If we are honest and consistent about our religious identity, we will often disagree about what they "mean." Today, then, there

9. "Typological Interpretation of the Old Testament," in Claus Westermann, ed., *Essays on Old Testament Hermeneutics*, English trans. and ed. J. L. Mays (Richmond: John Knox Press, 1960), p. 39.

10. *The Authority of the Old Testament* (Nashville: Abingdon Press, 1967), esp. pp. 207–9.

11. Ibid.

are two "choirs." In both cases there is a degree of appropriation which goes on when Old Testament texts are interpreted into terms that address specific and contemporary religious communities. Lectionary pairings of Old Testament texts with New Testament texts are an important factor in the shape of that inescapable act of appropriation. What we have found is that in good pairings the Old Testament passage is not passively appropriated but carries on a lively conversation with the New Testament passage which addresses it.

13
Prophecy in Crisis: The Call of Ezekiel

ROBERT R. WILSON

Great judgment was leavened by yet greater grace when God called a prophet and so continued to reach out to a rebellious Israel suffering under exile, even when Israel refused to accept the prophet's divinely commissioned words.

Even the casual reader of the Book of Ezekiel is immediately struck by the strangeness of the prophet and the literature which he produced. While books such as Hosea and Jeremiah portray prophets that are thoroughly human, Ezekiel describes a remote figure whose personality is almost completely hidden behind his prophetic message. When he does appear fleetingly as an individual, his behavior is often bizarre, and his mental state seems abnormal when judged by modern standards. He describes for his readers extraordinarily elaborate visions (1—3; 8—11; 37; 40—48), during which he is seized by God's spirit and transported from one location to another. In a similar vein, Ezekiel records that immediately after his call to prophesy (1:1—3:21) he was struck dumb and confined to his house until the final destruction of the city of Jerusalem (33:21–22), a period of about seven years according to the book's own chronology. Yet during this time he is said to have delivered a long series of oracles and performed complicated symbolic actions, some of which appear to be physically impossible (4—7).

The strangeness of the prophet's personality also extends to the literary features of the book itself. In contrast to the oracles recorded in other prophetic books, Ezekiel's oracles are extremely long and detailed and are often repetitious (e.g., 16, 17, 18, 20). The characteristic forms of prophetic speech used by other Israelite prophets rarely appear in the book, but much use is made of allegories and accounts of symbolic acts. Equally prominent are the extensive vision reports: the prophet's call vision (1—3), the vision of the departure of God's glory from Jerusalem and the begining of the destruc-

tion of the city (8—11), the vision of Israel's revivification in the valley filled
with dry bones (37), and the complex vision of the restored Jerusalem and
the newly rebuilt temple (40—48). Finally, the book contains several passages that are near duplicates. The most noticeable of these is the account of
Ezekiel's call to be a watchman for the house of Israel (3:17–19), which is
repeated and greatly elaborated in 33:1–9. In addition, the two accounts of
Israel's harlotries are strikingly similar (16 and 23), and the prophet's initial
vision of the divine glory (1:4–28) is clearly reflected in his later visions of the
destruction of Jerusalem (8:2–4; 10:1–17) and of the rebuilding of the city
(43—44).

The unusual characteristics of both the prophet and the book have caused
interpretive problems from the very beginning. The Babylonian Talmud
reports that some ancient rabbis wanted to withdraw Ezekiel from public
circulation because they were afraid that the explicit description of God in
chapter 1 might lead to dangerous mystical speculation. Even more trou-
blesome were the laws dealing with the rebuilding of the temple and the
restoration of worship (40—48), which contradicted the prescriptions of the
Torah and could be harmonized with them only with great difficulty. Thanks
to diligent interpretive efforts on the part of the rabbis, Ezekiel was allowed
to remain in general use; but Jerome reports that some rabbis prohibited the
beginning and end of the book from being read by anyone under thirty. Early
Christian interpreters fared little better than their Jewish counterparts.
Jerome's commentaries contain frequent apologies for his inability to explain
the obscurities of the text, and some patristic writers resorted to numer-
ological interpretations in order to give the book some theological value.[1]

However, in spite of the interpretive difficulties presented by Ezekiel,
most scholars remained convinced that it was to be read as a single literary
unit. This view persisted until the early part of the twentieth century, when a
different approach to the book began to emerge. According to the new
consensus, the bizarre behavior of the prophet was to be explained by
applying some sort of psychological analysis, while literary problems were to
be solved by performing radical surgery on the text in order to remove later
editorial additions. This approach was able to make parts of the book com-
prehensible to modern readers, but it also tended to remove Ezekiel from
the mainstream of biblical prophecy and to ignore the book's overall literary
structure.[2]

In reaction to this extreme form of interpretation, recent Ezekiel studies

1. For a discussion of early Jewish and Christian interpretations of Ezekiel, see Shalom
Spiegel, "Ezekiel or Pseudo-Ezekiel?" HTR 24 (1931) 245–90.
2. For an overview of modern Ezekiel scholarship, see H. H. Rowley, "The Book of Ezekiel
in Modern Study," BJRL 36 (1953–54) 146–90, reprinted in his Men of God (London: Thomas
Nelson & Sons, 1963), pp. 169–210; and Bernhard Lang, Ezechiel: Der Prophet und das Buch
(Darmstadt: Wissenschaftliche Buchgesellschaft, 1981).

have followed the more moderate line pioneered by Walther Zimmerli.[3] By making a careful form-critical and tradition-historical analysis of the book, Zimmerli has clearly demonstrated the links between Ezekiel and earlier Israelite theological and literary traditions. He has also shown how Ezekiel's words were later interpreted by the prophet's followers, the "Ezekiel school," in order to make them speak to a new historical and cultural situation.

Although it is possible to quarrel with some of Zimmerli's detailed analyses of individual passages, his observations on the links between particular historical or social contexts and the peculiar shape and contents of the Ezekiel literature are useful and must be taken seriously by future Ezekiel research. Interpreters must explore the possibility that the aberrant characteristics of the book are not primarily the result of the prophet's "abnormal" personality or of the heavy-handed work of a later editor but are themselves part of the message which the prophet and his disciples sought to deliver to concrete Israelite communities facing specific theological and social problems. The viability of this approach to Ezekiel is supported by the fact that Ezekiel and his disciples seem to have been greatly concerned with setting their oracles and vision reports into definite historical contexts. In contrast to most of the prophetic books, in which oracles are vaguely dated or not dated at all, Ezekiel makes extensive use of highly specific dates (1:1–3; 3:16; 8:1; 20:1; 24:1; 26:1; 29:1; 29:17; 30:20; 31:1; 32:1; 32:17; 33:21; 40:1). Three of these dates seem to mark the book's primary structural units. From Ezekiel's initial call (1:1–3) to the arrival of the first refugees from the destroyed city of Jerusalem in 585 B.C. (33:21), the book for the most part contains words of doom, either against Jerusalem, its inhabitants, and the exiled Israelites (4—24; 33) or against foreign nations (25—32). After the fall of Jerusalem (33:21), the book contains promises of Israel's restoration (34—39). Beginning with the date notice in 40:1, a climactic vision describes in detail a restored Jerusalem (40—48). However, even though some of the dates play a structural role in the book, all of them seem to point to the historical and cultural background against which the prophet's words must be understood. The usefulness of approaching Ezekiel in this way can be illustrated by reexamining one of the most perplexing units in the book, the account of the prophet's call (1—3).

---

3. See particularly his massive commentary *Ezekiel*, Hermeneia, 2 vols. (Philadelphia: Fortress Press, 1979–83). Other useful commentaries, most of which take Zimmerli's work into account, are Walther Eichrodt, *Ezekiel*, OTL (Philadelphia: Westminster Press, 1970); John W. Wevers, *Ezekiel*, Century Bible (London: Thomas Nelson & Sons, 1969); Keith W. Carley, *The Book of the Prophet Ezekiel*, Cambridge Bible Commentary (Cambridge: Cambridge University Press, 1974); Moshe Greenberg, *Ezekiel 1—20*, AB 22 (Garden City, N.Y.: Doubleday & Co., 1983). Among the older commentaries, the work of G. A. Cooke, *A Critical and Exegetical Commentary on the Book of Ezekiel*, ICC (Edinburgh: T. & T. Clark, 1936), is still worthwhile, particularly because of its comments on textual problems.

THE INITIAL CALL VISION
(1:1—3:15)

Scholars have sometimes attempted to divide Ezekiel's initial call vision into two or more literary or tradition-historical layers. However, most modern critics agree that the vision is essentially a single literary unit, although there is some evidence of later additions by the prophet's disciples or even by the prophet himself.

The Superscription (1:1–3)

Ezekiel's initial vision of God is said to have occurred on the fifth day of the fourth month of the "thirtieth year" (1:1), a date that becomes intelligible only when it is equated with the fifth year of the exile of King Jehoiachin of Judah (1:2). The prophet was thus active between July, 593 B.C., and April, 571 B.C. (29:17), although most of his oracles are dated in the relatively brief period between his call and the arrival of the first Jerusalemite exiles in Babylon (January, 585 B.C.), a few months after the city's destruction at the hands of the Babylonians (33:21). Outside of this chronological information, the superscription records that Ezekiel was a priest, presumably one of the Zadokites who served in the Jerusalem temple until they were exiled to Babylon during the First Deportation in 597 B.C. The prophet's call took place by the Chebar Canal near Nippur, where some of the exiles had been settled. There is no evidence in the book to suggest that he ever prophesied outside of Babylon, and he journeyed back to Jerusalem only in his visions (8:3—11:25). It must therefore be assumed that his original audience was his fellow priests and the Jerusalemite officials that had gone into exile with him. His disciples were presumably from the same group.

The period during which Ezekiel prophesied was a time of intense political and religious crisis for Israel. After years of vacillation between acknowledging allegiance to Egypt, Assyria, or Babylon and asserting Israel's independence, King Jehoiakim of Judah finally became a vassal of the Babylonian king, Nebuchadnezzar II, only to rebel against him a short time later (2 Kings 24:1). Nebuchadnezzar retaliated by marching against Jerusalem, which surrendered in March of 597 B.C. Jehoiakim's successor, Jehoiachin, was taken into exile in Babylon, along with many royal and religious officials and the elite of the city. The Babylonians placed Jehoiachin's uncle, Zedekiah, on the throne in Jerusalem but continued to refer to the exiled Jehoiachin as "king of Judah." In the wake of this disaster, the Judaean government seemed to be in a state of permanent chaos, with a number of factions pressing for conflicting political programs. Some people, apparently including Ezekiel, continued to recognize Jehoiachin as the legitimate king, while others acknowledged the legitimacy of Zedekiah. Some counseled cooperation with the Babylonians, while others advocated a league with Egypt or the reassertion of Judaean independence. This instability ultimately led to a final fatal revolt against Babylon, a revolt which Nebuchadnezzar punished by capturing Judah and laying seige to Jerusalem. In July of 586 B.C. the city fell. Shortly thereafter the king was taken into exile, and many of the remaining officials and citizens were executed or deported. Jerusalem was burned, the walls were torn down, and the temple was destroyed.[4]

However, even more significant than the political chaos that existed during the time of Ezekiel's prophetic activity was the religious and theological crisis triggered by the First Deportation and the ever increasing threat of the total destruction of Jerusalem. This crisis had several important dimensions. First, the Jerusalemite royal establishment, including the Zadokite priesthood of which Ezekiel was a part, believed that God had elected the Davidic royal line in perpetuity as Israel's only legitimate rulers (2 Samuel 7) and had chosen Jerusalem as the divine dwelling place forever. Because of God's eternal presence in the temple, both the temple and the city were inviolable.[5] Yet this theological perspective was called into question by the First Deportation, and the threat of the Babylonians actually capturing the city raised the specter of a major theological crisis. Did the exile of Jehoiachin mean that God had withdrawn the promise to David, even though a member of the Davidic house still served as regent in Jerusalem, or was the exile simply a temporary punishment that would soon end when the captives returned from Babylon? If the threat of Jerusalem's fall actually became a reality, what would the implications be for the theology of election and inviolability? Would the fall of the city mean that God had been overpowered by the Babylonian deities, or had God perhaps simply broken the eternal promise to David and rejected both Jerusalem and Israel itself? All of these questions demanded answers, and some of the answers that were being given seemed to spell the end of the cherished theological beliefs of Ezekiel and his fellow exiles.

Second, the First Deportation raised serious questions about the nature of the true Israel. If Judah still occupied its land and the worship of God continued in Jerusalem, then what was the status of the exiles? They appeared to have been separated from God, perhaps as punishment for Israel's sins. Some of those who remained in the land therefore reasoned that they themselves were the true Israel, the heirs to God's promises, while the exiles had no further claim to Israel's promises or to the land itself (cf. 11:14–21). This was a difficult conclusion for Ezekiel's exilic community to accept and may have led many to hope for a speedy return to Jerusalem and the restoration of Jehoiachin as the legitimate king.

Finally, the First Deportation provoked a major crisis with respect to the prophetic office itself. As a result of the chaotic political and religious conditions of the period, prophets began to make conflicting claims about the reasons for the deportation and the length of the exile. A graphic example

---

4. There is still debate over the date of the Babylonian capture of Jerusalem. For a discussion of this issue and a survey of the history of the period, see John Bright, *A History of Israel*, 3d ed. (Philadelphia: Westminster Press, 1981), pp. 324–31.

5. For a discussion of the Jerusalemite royal theology, see Frank M. Cross, *Canaanite Myth and Hebrew Epic* (Cambridge: Harvard University Press, 1973), and John H. Hayes, "The Tradition of Zion's Inviolability," *JBL* 82 (1963) 419–26.

of this sort of prophetic conflict may be found in Jeremiah 27—29, which describes a dispute between Ezekiel's contemporary, Jeremiah, and the prophet Hananiah over the length of the exile. Jeremiah advocated total surrender to the Babylonians and an acceptance of a long exile, while Hananiah prophesied a brief exile and a quick return of the people and goods that Nebuchadnezzar had taken from Jerusalem. Prophecies similar to Hananiah's were being delivered by prophets in Babylon, whom Jeremiah condemned in a letter to the exiles (Jeremiah 29). Other Jerusalemite prophets continued to predict that no harm would come to the city and that Jerusalem would remain inviolable, as God had promised. These prophets too were opposed by Jeremiah, who accused them of creating their own oracles rather than standing in God's council and hearing the divine word clearly and directly (Jer. 23:9–40). These sorts of prophetic conflicts must have caused people to raise questions about the authority of all prophets and to doubt the usefulness of the institution of prophecy itself.

The Throne Vision (1:4–28)

Most modern scholars agree that Ezekiel's account of his initial vision has been secondarily elaborated, either by the prophet himself or by his disciples. At points the Hebrew text is repetitious and contains what appear to be dislocated phrases, while the Greek text is shorter and more intelligible. Various attempts have been made to reconstruct the original vision report, either by assuming the superiority of the Greek text or by eliminating material that seems redundant or out of place, but to date no single reconstruction has proven to be totally convincing. For this reason, and also because of the convoluted and repetitious literary style of Ezekiel's oracles, it is prudent to depart from the Hebrew text as little as possible.[6]

In spite of occasional problems with the Hebrew text, the general outline of Ezekiel's vision is clear. At the outset the prophet saw a radiant storm cloud approaching from the north, and as the cloud drew nearer, details of its shape began to emerge with increasing clarity. Initially the outlines of four gleaming humanoid creatures appeared, each of them having four wings and four distinct faces. These beings were arranged in a square, with the tips of their wings touching. They faced all four of the cardinal points at the same time and as a result were able to move together wherever they wished without turning. Their movement was aided by a complicated system of wheels, each of which was composed of two wheels intersecting at right angles so as to permit motion in all directions (1:4–21). In the midst of the creatures was a flashing form, and as they came nearer Ezekiel saw that they were bearing a brilliant expanse. When they came to a halt on the ground and the noise of their wings ceased, the prophet saw a sapphire throne above the expanse. On the throne was an awesome radiance, in the center of which Ezekiel perceived "the appearance of the likeness of the glory of God."

---

6. For a discussion of the various attempts to reconstruct the original vision, see Zimmerli, *Ezekiel*, pp. 100–106.

When the prophet realized what he had seen, he was overcome and fell on his face to the earth (1:22–28).

Generations of scholars have attempted to cut through the mystical language of Ezekiel's vision in order to describe in concrete terms the objects being portrayed. Some writers have claimed that the prophet saw nothing more than an electrical storm and then imaginatively supplied the remaining details. Others have cited the chariots upon which ancient Near Eastern deities rode, while still others have argued that Ezekiel had in mind the ark flanked by its attendant cherubim upon which God was enthroned in the Jerusalem temple (cf. 2 Sam. 6:2; Pss. 80:1; 99:1). Recently people have even seen in the vision an early reference to spaceships, the "chariots of the gods."[7]

To be sure, most of the elements in the vision can be found in earlier Israelite tradition. In particular, Ezekiel's priestly background suggests that the ark and the cherubim played an important role in shaping his description of his visionary experience. However, to concentrate on the concrete objects lying behind the vision is to misunderstand the realities which the prophet seeks to express. Like his Jerusalemite predecessor, Isaiah, whose call vision in Isaiah 6 most closely resembles the one described by Ezekiel, he sees natural objects that have taken on supernatural dimensions. Just as Isaiah sees temple cherubim that have been transformed into flaming, vaguely human seraphim, so also Ezekiel does not see the cherubim (and does not even use the term in chap. 1) but rather sees composite "living beings" whose features are difficult to describe or even to imagine. Seen from this perspective, some of the so-called inconsistencies in Ezekiel's description actually underline the supernatural aspects of the vision. By using extraordinary images, the prophet seeks to describe the divine world, which is ultimately indescribable. As is frequently the case in dreams and visions, objects begin to blur and events no longer conform to logic or to the laws of common experience.

The supernatural and divine dimensions of the vision are further emphasized by the evocative words that are used in the description, particularly words having to do with brightness and fire. These words are employed frequently throughout the chapter and, far from being redundant, have a cumulative effect that stresses the awesome and incorporeal character of the vision. The chapter thus incorporates both definite, though otherworldly, images and vague, evocative language. This vagueness becomes ever more apparent as the prophet's eye moves closer to the radiance enthroned on the expanse borne by the creatures, a radiance which represents for the prophet the visible aura of God's glory. Even though Ezekiel can see the details of the vision more clearly, his descriptions become more vague; and he begins to

---

7. For suggestions about the ancient Near Eastern and Israelite background of the vision, see Siegfried Sprank, *Ezechielstudien* (Stuttgart: W. Kohlhammer, 1926), pp. 26–73; and Hans Schmidt, "Keruben-Thron und Lade," in Hans Schmidt, ed., *Eucharisterion* (Göttingen: Vandenhoeck und Ruprecht, 1923), pp. 120–44.

employ the terms "appearance" and "likeness" more frequently in order to emphasize that what he describes only approximates what he actually saw. As he approaches the divine presence, his powers of description fail completely, and he says only that he saw "an appearance of the likeness of the glory of the Lord."

The full theological implications of the prophet's vision become clear only as the book progresses, but even at this early point Ezekiel 1 carries several important messages for the prophet's exilic community. First, although there is much in the call vision that is not precise, there is no doubt about what the prophet saw. The Jerusalemite exiles would have immediately recognized the description of the living beings and would have been familiar with the theophanic language drawn from earlier Israelite tradition. The vision makes clear that Ezekiel came as close as any Israelite since Moses to seeing the face of God, and the prophet's message must therefore have divine authority. In a chaotic age, when prophets were making conflicting claims, Ezekiel met all of Jeremiah's criteria for a true prophet. Ezekiel has stood in the divine presence and has been overwhelmed by his experience, but he has seen God clearly.

Second, the call vision assures the exiles that God has not rejected them. Ezekiel actually saw the divine throne come to rest on Babylonian soil, and the divine presence there suggests that the deportees remain part of the true Israel. However, the significance of God's dwelling among the exiles is not yet clear, for up to this point there has been no verbal communication between God and the prophet. God's presence may mean reassurance for the exilic community, but it may also mean judgment.

Finally, the appearance of the divine glory in Babylon has ominous overtones. Seeing God present in Babylon, Ezekiel and his fellow exiles would have immediately wondered how God came to be in Babylon rather than in the Jerusalem temple, the place which God had chosen as an eternal dwelling. Had God perhaps rejected Israel's traditional sanctuary, and if so, what were the consequences of this rejection? The answers to these questions are provided in two complex visions which, along with chapters 1—3, provide the book with another unifying theme. In chapters 8—11 the prophet describes in horrifying detail a visionary trip to Jerusalem, during which he witnessed the abominations being committed there by those who had been left in the city after the Babylonian deportation. As he watched, the glory of God and the attendant cherubim departed from the inner sanctuary of the temple and came to rest on the threshold of the house (9:3; 10:1–5). God then ordered divine executioners to slay everyone in the temple and the city who had not grieved over the abominations that existed there. As a final act of judgment, one of the throne-bearing cherubim provided burning coals which were cast over the city to begin the conflagration that would destroy it (10:6–22). The cherubim then bore the divine throne out of the temple and took it to a mountain on the east of the city (10:18–19; 11:22–23). God had in fact deserted the temple and left the city to the mercy of the Babylonians. The appearance of the divine glory in Babylon in chapter 1 does indeed mean that God has taken up residence temporarily with the exiles (cf. 11:14–21); but it also means that the fate of Jerusalem has been sealed, a point that Ezekiel makes repeatedly in chapters 4—33. By leaving the city God has in fact destroyed it, and there can be no word of hope for it until the judgment has taken place. Only after the fall of the city (chap. 33) does Ezekiel's final vision describe in detail the return of God's glory to Jerusalem and the rebuilding of the temple (chaps. 40—48).

The Prophet's Commission (2:1—3:15)

In contrast to the vagueness of the throne vision, the account of the prophet's commission is clear and specific. The text appears to be a cohesive literary unit without later editorial additions, although it is marked by Ezekiel's characteristically repetitive style.

Immediately after the prophet's stunned reaction to the appearance of the divine glory, he hears God's voice for the first time in the vision (1:28). God commands the prophet to stand, but he is apparently able to do so only after the spirit energizes him and sets him on his feet (2:1–2). This unusual incident marks the first appearance of a motif that recurs periodically elsewhere in the book. Unlike other Israelite prophets, Ezekiel seems to be totally devoid of free will while he is carrying out his prophetic tasks. He does not act unless God through the spirit causes him to act. The prophet speaks only the divine word that is put into his mouth (cf. 3:27) and does not elaborate the message in any way. In contrast to his contemporary, Jeremiah, Ezekiel does not engage in conversations or arguments with God and in fact rarely responds verbally at all to divine commands. The overall effect is to portray Ezekiel as an automaton, an individual who has no human personality but is totally under the control of the divine will.

However, like many other features of the book, this curious portrait seems to be designed to make a theological point. If Ezekiel is completely dominated by God, then there can be no suspicion that the prophet's reason or emotions have in any way interfered with the divine word. Unlike the illegitimate prophets of whom Jeremiah speaks (Jer. 23:30), there can be no charge that Ezekiel has "stolen" oracles from other prophets or delivered genuine oracles that he has reinterpreted. Rather, the prophet is simply the conduit through which the unaltered divine word comes, and it is impossible to accuse him of speaking falsely. Whoever hears Ezekiel hears God's word directly.

This theological point is made graphically immediately after God's initial charge to the prophet (2:3–7). Ezekiel is told to eat a scroll that is inscribed on both sides with "words of lamentation, mourning, and woe." The prophet does so and reports that the scroll tasted sweet. He then is commanded to speak God's words to the house of Israel (2:8—3:4). This striking episode seems to be a concretization of a statement made by Jeremiah in one of his complaints: "Your words were found, and I ate them, and your words became to me a joy and the delight of my heart" (Jer. 15:16). In its original context this remark apparently refers to the joy that Jeremiah receives from hearing the divine word, a joy that makes him willing to suffer the pain and isolation that befall him because of his prophetic status (Jer. 15:15, 17–18). However, by taking Jeremiah's literary image literally, Ezekiel has changed its meaning entirely. For Ezekiel, the eating of the scroll indicates that God has supplied the prophet with oracles in a fixed form that cannot be changed. All of the words which Ezekiel speaks are precisely the same words which God literally put inside the prophet. There can therefore be no doubt about the prophet's authority. Furthermore, by speaking of the divine origin of a completely filled scroll, Ezekiel in fact claims that his entire book was given directly by God. Both the oracles and the context in which they are set are divinely given. Just as Jeremiah delivered a scroll of his oracles to the king of Judah to see whether God's word would be accepted or rejected (Jeremiah 36), so also Ezekiel delivers to the exilic community and to later Israelite communities a prophetic book to which they must respond.

The remainder of the account of Ezekiel's commissioning is unusual in that it reveals almost nothing about the contents of the message that he is to deliver. On the basis of the description of the scroll, it is possible to guess that the prophet was to speak primarily words of judgment or threat that might warn the exiles to repent, but little beyond this can be said. Instead, most of the commissioning account focuses on the prophet himself and on the reaction of the people to his prophetic activity.

At the beginning of the charge to Ezekiel, God states clearly the reason for sending a prophet to Israel. The people are rebels who must be condemned for their crimes. This point is made sharply by the frequent repetition of words having to do with rebellion, and the phrase "for they are a rebellious house" runs like a refrain throughout the commission (2:5, 7; 3:9). At first the text does not make clear whether Ezekiel is to address all of the people of Israel or only his fellow exiles, and in fact the book includes oracles dealing with both groups. However, the general context of the call narrative and the specific command at the end of the commissioning to prophesy to the exiles (3:11) indicates that the rebels are Ezekiel's fellow deportees.

Given the harsh and uncompromising words that Ezekiel is to bring to the exiles, it is not difficult to understand why they would have ignored or even actively opposed him. With some justification the exiles may have thought that they were already being punished for the crimes of earlier generations and that God's next act ought to be one of forgiveness and redemption (cf. 18:1–32). They may well have reacted violently to Ezekiel's charge that they were a "rebellious house" that needed to repent to avoid even stronger punishment. From the beginning of the commissioning God warns Ezekiel of this popular opposition and exhorts him to continue to prophesy even though the people ignore him. God further promises to strengthen the prophet so that he can withstand the attacks of the exiles (2:4–8; 3:8–9).

Ezekiel's call vision closes on a somber note. He is told that the people will not listen to him, for they have already rejected the divine message that he brings (3:5–7). His attempts to save the exiles by exhorting them to repent will fail. It is thus clear from the beginning of the book that the long delayed judgment is inevitable. The prophet's work is to be an exercise in futility. Seen from this perspective, the most remarkable thing about Ezekiel's call vision is that it is there at all. It stands as eloquent testimony to God's unwillingness to allow Israel to be destroyed. Even though it is clear from the beginning that the people will not respond, God continues to call them through the prophet in the hope that at least a few individuals will repent and save their own lives (cf. chap. 18).

THE WATCHMAN'S CALL AND
DUMBNESS (3:16–27)

Many scholars feel that the accounts of Ezekiel's second call and his strange dumbness are late editorial additions that have been constructed out of material found in chapters 18 and 33. The watchman's call (3:16–21) seems unnecessary after the initial call vision (1:1—3:15) and is also repeated in a clearer and more elaborate form in Ezekiel 33:1–9, where it seems to mark a new phase in Ezekiel's career following the fall of Jerusalem. The onset of the prophet's dumbness (3:22–27) appears to be in tension with the sort of prophetic activity described in chapters 4—33 and strikes most scholars as highly improbable. They therefore suggest that the dumbness should be interpreted as a symbolic act or that the account should be relocated to 24:27 or 33:21–22, where there are references to the removal of the dumbness after the fall of Jerusalem. However, the arguments for interpreting these verses as secondary additions are not without critical flaws.[8] In addition, no matter what conclusions are reached on the text's editorial history, it is still necessary to try to understand why the passages were set in their present location.

A week after his initial call, Ezekiel was appointed a watchman for the house of Israel in order to warn the people of impending danger (cf. Jer. 6:16–21). The nature of the danger becomes apparent when God gives the prophet a series of examples of a watchman fulfilling his responsibilities. These examples, which are couched in the legal language of Ezekiel's priestly tradition, describe the events that occur when God issues a death sentence against two types of people: the wicked person who does not repent on hearing the prophetic watchman's warning, and the righteous person who turns from righteousness but who repents after hearing the prophet's words. An illustration of the wicked person who does repent does not appear. However, the emphasis in these legal cases is not on the reactions of the person being addressed but on the prophet's faithfulness to the watchman's office. If the prophet does not warn the people when he hears the divine death sentence, then he is responsible for their deaths and will lose his life. If

---

8. It is not possible to treat all of the critical issues here. For a discussion of the various approaches to Ezek. 3:16–27 and an evaluation of them, see Zimmerli, *Ezekiel*, pp. 143–61; Greenberg, *Ezekiel*, pp. 82–97, 101–21; and Robert R. Wilson, "An Interpretation of Ezekiel's Dumbness," *VT* 22 (1972) 91–104.

he does warn the people, then he preserves his life no matter what the reactions of the people to his warning.

When seen in its present context, Ezek. 13:16–21 reinforces or modifies four themes that appear in the initial call vision. First, there is no doubt about the identity of the enemy against whom Ezekiel is to warn the people. God is personally responsible for giving the death sentence and is therefore directly responsible for the destruction of Jerusalem and the punishment of the exiles. Second, the prophet is to exercise his office faithfully, no matter what the reaction of the people. Third, even though there is little hope that the wicked will repent, God still appoints the prophet to warn them of the approaching divine wrath. God will not desert the people even though judgment is inevitable. Finally, in contrast to the situation in the initial call, not everyone ignores the prophetic warning. The "righteous," perhaps the disciples of Ezekiel, do repent and remain righteous, thus saving themselves from the coming judgment.

Immediately after his call to be a watchman, Ezekiel reports that he was struck dumb by God, shut up in the house, and prevented from mingling with the people (3:22–27). This dumbness lasts until the destruction of Jerusalem, when the prophet's mouth is again opened, an event that takes place directly after a repetition of the watchman's call (33:21–22; cf. 24:26–27). Reports of the prophet's behavior during this period show that he was indeed confined to his house (8:1; 14:1; 20:1), but the fact that he continued to deliver oracles indicates that the dumbness should not be taken literally to refer to a physiological condition. Rather, the juxtaposition of the dumbness motif with the watchman's call in chapters 3 and 33 suggests that the dumbness represents a limitation that was placed on Ezekiel's prophetic activities from the date of his call to the fall of the city. It is difficult to be too specific about the nature of this limitation, but it may have involved the isolation of Ezekiel from his fellow exiles or his inability to intercede with God on their behalf in order to modify the threatened judgment.

PROPHECY IN CRISIS

As Ezekiel, his disciples, and later members of his "school" attempted to make sense of the traumatic events of the exile, they were forced to reexamine their traditional priestly theology and to modify it to take into account Israel's new political, social, and religious situation. The results of this process eventually left their mark on the Book of Ezekiel. At the very beginning of the book, the account of the events surrounding the prophet's call seems to have been shaped so as to speak to the exilic religious crisis and to address a crisis in the authority of the prophetic office itself. The striking call vision and the picture of Ezekiel that it contains are designed to undergird his authority so that his fellow exiles would heed his oracles. Such support was especially needed in Ezekiel's case, for his message cut deeply into the strongly held religious beliefs of his audience. According to the prophet and his disciples, God was indeed punishing the exiles for their rebellion and would continue to do so until they repented. Even individual repentance, however, could not save Jerusalem, which was destined to be destroyed.

Still, the picture was not totally dark. The same God who had deserted the city would ultimately return to it, and those exiles who remained righteous could again worship there. In the crisis of the exile, God did not finally reject the people of Israel but continued to reach out to them through the prophet, even when they refused to listen.

14

Sin and Judgment in
the Prophecies of Ezekiel

Michael Fishbane

Ezekiel's prophecies reveal with sharp clarity what is also the ironic
rhetorical strategy of all Israelite prophets: to bring a faithless and
unknowing people to covenant allegiance and consciousness of God's
Lordship.

A discernible organizational pattern found throughout the prophetic corpus
is the tripartite division of doom oracles against Israel, doom oracles against
foreign nations, and consolation oracles on behalf of Israel. This division also
characterizes the Book of Ezekiel which, after the opening commission scene
(chaps. 1—3), comprises oracles of sin and judgment against Israel (chaps.
4—24), doom oracles against the nations (chaps. 25—32), and prophecies of
hope and restoration (chaps. 33—37; 40—48). Admittedly, this scheme is not
without its apparent exceptions. One may readily observe that the Gog and
Magog prophecies in Ezekiel 38—39 are doom prophecies addressed to non-
Israelites, though found within an anthology of consolation oracles; and one
may also observe that a number of judgment speeches conclude with statements of national restoration (cf. 16:60–62; 12:22–24; 20:33–44). But these
exceptions only prove the rule: first, because they constitute a minor portion
of the content within any subdivision; and second, because they can be
readily integrated into their surrounding theological context. Thus, like the
surrounding restoration oracles, the Gog and Magog prophecies focus attention on Israel's renewal to her homeland (38:16), while the consolation codas
found in Ezekiel 4—24 reinforce the sense of a continuous divine providence
so prevalent in these chapters and of Israel's covenantal destiny. These
considerations anticipate, however, a review of the structure, content, and
theology of Ezekiel 4—24, and it is to this that we now turn.

STRUCTURE

It is commonly accepted that the sin and judgment passages begin at
chapter 4 and end with chapter 24: after the commission scenario and before

170

the oracles against the nations. This view is true enough, but one will also observe that the ensemble of chapters 4—24 is structurally and verbally linked to this earlier and later material. First, as regards the connection between Ezekiel 1—3 and 4—24, it is notable that the sin-judgment theme is sounded right after the theophany of Ezekiel 1. Immediately after his vision, the prophet was told that he was being sent "to the Israelites, to a rebellious people who have rebelled against me" (2:3); subsequently, this people is also called a brood of "scorpions" and a "rebellious house" (2:5–8). Moreover, after this brief prologue the prophet was given a scroll written front and back with "laments, and woes, and wailings" (2:10), which is surely a reference to the collection of doom oracles found in chapters 4—24. It was presumably in consideration of this scroll and the "instruction of the (future) temple" found in chapters 40—42 that Josephus remarked that Ezekiel "left behind him in writing two books" (*Ant.* 10.5.1): a book of doom and a book of consolation.[1]

In addition to these general thematic anticipations, the commission scenario and the sin-judgment anthology are linked by more specific features. Thus, at the conclusion of the commission in 3:22–7, the prophet was told to remain secluded in his house (3:22–3), to bind himself with "cords" (*'abôtîm*, v. 25), and to remain "dumb" (*weneʿelamtā*, v. 26) until the Lord "will open your mouth" (*'eptah 'et pîkā*, v. 27); while in the sequel each of these features is developed. (1) Throughout chapters 4—24 Ezekiel is repeatedly found at his home, where he performs symbolic actions and receives visitors requesting divine oracles (cf. 8:1; 14:1; 20:1); (2) he does in fact bind himself with "cords" (*'abôtîm*) in order to symbolize the fate of the nation (4:4–8); and (3) he apparently remains dumb, as well, since the Lord later reiterates his promise that when the news of Jerusalem's fall would reach Ezekiel in Babylon the prophet would "no longer" be "dumb" (*welōʾ tēʾālēm ʿôd*, 24:26f.). Evidently—despite the difficulties faced by interpreters who must reconcile the references to Ezekiel's dumbness with his many verbal tirades (beginning at chap. 6)[2]—the present textual arrangement was designed (1) to provide a prologue of sorts (3:22–7) to chapters 4—24 in general, and chapter 4 in particular, and (2) to provide an envelope-framework for the whole anthology of doom prophecies: the motif of 3:22–7 is not only repeated in 24:26–7 but also in 33:21–2 (following vv. 1–20, which reprise 3:17–21)— *after* the doom oracles against the nations and *before* the prophecies of consolation. The topos in 3:22–7 thus provides a thematic and structural link between several subsections of the Book of Ezekiel: between the commission scenario and the sin-judgment, and between the latter and the oracles of hope.

---

1. Ezek. 43:12 serves as the colophon to this distinct "temple scroll." See S. Talmon and M. Fishbane, "The Structuring of Biblical Books," *ASTI* 10 (1976) esp. 138–53. Alternatively, Josephus simply meant chaps. 25—48 as his second book.

2. Cf. Moshe Greenberg, *Ezekiel 1—20*, AB 22 (Garden City, N.Y.: Doubleday & Co., 1983), p. 103. Greenberg reconciles the issue by understanding Ezekiel's dumbness as the prophet's state *between* prophecies.

CONTENT

The first major unit dealing with sin-judgment in the Book of Ezekiel comprises 3:22—5:17. Hereby, the prophet is not only confined to his home and told to remain dumb (3:24, 26) but is furthermore instructed to perform several symbolic acts. These include his incising an image of Jerusalem on a brick and constructing miniature bulwarks and battering rams in order to dramatize the siege to come (4:1–3); his lying on his left and right sides for 390 and 40 days, respectively, in order to symbolize the sin of the people (4:4–8); his eating meager rations in order to express the oppressive conditions of the siege (4:9–17); and his cutting his hair into thirds in order to signal the threefold fate—death by siege, death by flight, and exile (after which only a remnant will be saved)—that would soon befall the people (5:1–17). The reasons for this judgment are presented at two points in the course of the haircutting praxis, at v. 6 and at v. 11, where the sins are generally described as rebellion against the laws and defilement of the sanctuary, the two topics which recur with similar generality or greater specificity throughout Ezekiel's oracles. Significantly, the various symbolic actions of chapters 4—5 simply announce the range of dooms to befall the people and are not accompanied by any call to repentance. Given the further fact that the remainder of the sin-judgment ensemble is also characterized by merciless doomsayings with no consideration of the possibility of repentance to avert the severe divine decree (chap. 18 being no exception, as we shall see), one may say that chapters 4—5 sound those dark chords of fatality which echo consistently from shortly after the commission theophany in July 593 (1:2f.) until the commencement of the siege of Jerusalem in January 588 (24:1).

We shall have occasion to return to this fatalistic characterization of Israelite history; it is enough at this point simply to stress the inherently bleak nature of Ezekiel's doomsayings and to pose the problem unavoidably raised by the occurrence of the doom omens of chapters 4—5 (and the subsequent doom visions and oracles) *after* the divine speech to Ezekiel in 3:17–21, which describes the prophet's special obligation to forewarn the people of their sins in order that they may repent and save themselves from doom. Indeed, the interpretative problem is formally the same whether 3:17–21 is to be considered an original feature of Ezekiel's prophetic commission or a redactional component of his school (and so a later ideological feature), since by either alternative the series of divinely sponsored oracles proclaiming imminent doom with no hint of reprieve is radically relativized by this prior announcement about Ezekiel's role as a "warner" and YHWH's concern for the people's repentance. Indeed, with 3:17–21 as a prologue, the doom images of chapters 4ff. no longer prefigure a necessary future but a possible one only; divine judgment is contingent upon whether or not the people repent. Admittedly, Ezekiel may have been ambivalent on the question of Israel's religious freedom or may have changed his mind at a specific point. This latter possibility cannot be excluded, given Ezekiel's strong advocacy of repentance found in chapter 18, whose authenticity is not in question.

However, given the fact that Ezekiel 18 is spoken to the exiles and does not advocate repentance in order that Jerusalem be saved, and given the further consideration that the entire corpus of chapters 4—24 speak of Jerusalem's inescapable doom, it is entirely possible that 3:17–21 is a secondary redactional component (and so comparable with other postexilic ideologies of repentance, such as found in the final Deuteronomistic stratum of Jeremiah and the prophetic speeches of the Chronicler). From this perspective, it may be supposed that later Ezekelian tradents wished to emphasize that divine concern for Israel's repentance was a theological feature of Ezekiel's prophetic message from the beginning. The modern reader, however, cannot easily resolve this text-historical question and must hold both ends of the rope.

Following the ominous symbolism of Ezekiel 4—5, a series of judgments are announced because of the people's civil and cultic sins. In chapter 6 the prophet announces that the altars and the "despicable things" of the people will be destroyed (vv. 3–4, 6) and the people themselves killed (vv. 4–5, 7, 12–13), because of their wayward behavior and "abominations" (vv. 9, 11). As in 5:6, 11 the sins mentioned in chapter 6 are presented in highly general terms. Similarly, the strong forecast of an imminent judgment found in Ezek. 7:2–3, 6 only slightly goes beyond the general reference to the people's "abominations" in vv. 4 and 8 when it specifies the "images of abomination" and acts of "violence" as evidence for cultic and civil malfeasance respectively. The modern reader, who is deprived by this generalized rhetoric of a specific list of particulars concerning religious malpractice in sixth-century Judea, is only apparently treated to a sideshow of cultic "abominations" in chapter 8.

On the face of it, Ezekiel's ecstatic visionary tour of Jerusalem, while he was sitting at home in Babylon, provides a full catalogue of sins. He sees people performing "horrendous abominations" near the "symbol of jealousy" (8:5–6), a secret ritual being performed in the temple courts by an officiant bearing incense amidst seventy celebrants (vv. 9–11), women at the temple gate wailing for Tammuz (v. 14), and "abominations still worse than these" in the inner court of the temple, where twenty-five persons are found prostrating themselves to the sun with their backsides facing the shrine (vv. 15–16). But how must this panoply of flaunted cultic "violence" be evaluated?[3] Certainly one difficulty with the series of "abominations" found in chapter 8 is that they are presented as a series of concurrent practices whose grim picture of paganizing activities in the temple of Jerusalem recalls the period of Manasseh (2 Kings 21) but is hardly reflected in any of the sources depicting post-Josianic worship there—not the Book of Kings, not the prophecies of Jeremiah, and not even the scroll of lamentations. If, then, one may infer that royally sponsored paganizing rituals were stamped out by Josiah, one would be led to conclude that practices known from Manasseh's time

---

3. I do not read v. 17 as another "ritual" but, with the context, as a statement of the people's haughty disregard of the temple's sanctity.

served as the model for Ezekiel 8, the purpose of which would then be to portray the sins of Jerusalem in such a way that the eruption of punitive divine wrath would appear both just and necessary.[4] All of this is not to say, of course, that the stimulus for this catalogue of sins was not rooted in reality, since both Jer. 7:17–18, 31 and Jeremiah 44 clearly show that paganizing practices continued in popular worship. The point is rather to suggest that the sin-judgment nexus found in chapters 8—9 may teach us more about the struggle to produce a viable theodicy in early sixth-century Babylon than about the actual practices in and around the temple of Jerusalem at that time. From this perspective, chapters 8—9 presumably served as a propaganda document whose chief concern was to justify the inevitability of the divine doom to the exiles. It is significant that at other points Ezekiel mentions that sin-filled survivors would arrive in Babylon and, through their abominable behavior, justify the divine destruction (cf. 14:22–3). One may imagine that Ezekiel hoped to foster a similar reaction when he reported his clairvoyant journey to the Judean captivity in Babylon (11:25).

One may further suppose that another function of the envisaged sin-judgment of Jerusalem found in chapters 8—11 would have been to dash any hope among the exiles that the divine judgment was tentative or could be reprieved. From this perspective, the gruesome report of divine destruction given to the captivity in Babylon and the pathetic prophetic appeal for divine mercy would have been designed to have much the same impact as the letter which Jeremiah had earlier sent to the exiles (in Jeremiah 29) in order to squelch premature local hopes of a speedy national restoration. Other oracles in the Book of Ezekiel seem to bear out this interpretation; in fact, it would appear that the series of prophecies that follow the visions were also concerned to rebut any hope among the exiles that Jerusalem's survival was likely or justified. Thus Ezek. 12:1–16 condemns those who have ignored the divine word of doom and, according to Moshe Greenberg, was plausibly addressed to the exiles who were hopeful of "Jerusalem's survival and their speedy return to it."[5] The polemical tone of this rebuke is carried further in vv. 17–20, where the prophet roundly announces the doom of Jerusalem, and in vv. 21–8, where Ezekiel trenchantly rebuts the popular contention that his doomsday oracles would not come to pass. Indeed, in order to underscore his claims, the prophet then presents a divinely sponsored revision of the original timetable of doom. This piece is then followed by an uncompromising negation of all other contemporary prophecies (13:1–23), a rejection of oracular requests from his "idolatrous" compatriots, and a stern broadside against any prophet who would respond to such requests from such citizens (14:1–10). From the range and pathos of these diatribes, it may be inferred that the anxiety of the times produced cadres of prophetic spokesmen, each group vying for a popular following, and each group claim-

---

4. See the important review and evaluation of Moshe Greenberg in his prolegomenon to C. C. Torrey, *Pseudo-Ezekiel and the Original Prophecy and Critical Articles by C. C. Torrey and S. Speigel* (New York: KTAV, 1970), pp. xiv–xxvii.

5. Greenberg, *Ezekiel*, p. 209.

ing to represent YHWH's authentic word. Like his contemporary Jeremiah (cf. 14:13–18), Ezekiel felt that the most dangerous of these prophets were those who spoke deluded and premature oracles of consolation to the citizens of Jerusalem and the exiles in Babylon. Accordingly, also like Jeremiah, Ezekiel was concerned to rebut any notion that the doom of Jerusalem would not come and any hope that a speedy restoration of the exiles to their homeland was possible.

The theme of sin-judgment continues in 14:12–20 with an oracle that further underscores the fate of Jerusalem's population by stressing that there is no vicarious salvation; a righteous person will save himself alone, no matter how righteous he be.[6] Thus, with one sharp stroke, the theological presupposition of Genesis 19, in which YHWH himself acknowledges the theoretical possibility that a minimum number (ten) of righteous men could save a sin-filled city by virtue of their merits, is thoroughly rejected. Indeed, not only can the merits of one person not benefit another, but a righteous father will even be powerless to save his son or daughter (cf. vv. 16, 20). With this oracle the powerful theme of individual responsibility is first sounded in Ezekiel's prophecies and anticipates the treatment found in chapter 18, where the inverse perspective (i.e., no vicarious punishment) is at issue. It is furthermore significant that there is no call to repentance in Ezekiel 14, so that the prophetic speech in vv. 12–20 seems more designed to provide theological doctrine to the exiles than a teaching of hope to the citizens of Jerusalem. One may therefore suppose that 14:12–20 is another prophetic piece attempting to quash false confidence in Jerusalem's salvation among the exiles. This supposition is contextually reinforced by vv. 21–23, which proclaim that when the exiles behold the sins of some of the survivors of Jerusalem's destruction they will be comforted in the justice of divine judgment. Remarkably, this coda is an outright contradiction of the principles enunciated in vv. 12–20, for the sin-filled survivors are saved despite their sins: as an object lesson for the exiles and not because of their own righteousness. For contextual reasons, this chink in the calculus of sin-judgment and individual responsibility is more arresting here than in 6:9 and 7:16–21, where too the survivors of Jerusalem are not saved for their righteousness' sake.

In the oracle that follows, the prophet presents an allegory of a charred vinestock that represents the citizens of Jerusalem—already half burned (exiled) by the deportation of 597 (in the reign of Jehoichin) and soon to be completely consumed (exiled-destroyed). In this piece there is also no call to repentance, and so it fits in with the fatalistic aura of Jerusalem's condition which pervades Ezekiel's oracles to this point. The sins which justify this doom are again portrayed in a general way (15:8); presumably, it was not always necessary to say more.

An arraignment for specific sins does follow, however, in chapter 16, where symbolism and allegory again function as part of an oracle of judgment. In

---

6. The various paragraphs in chap. 14 are linked by the verb *karet* (vv. 8, 14, 17, 21).

the piece, Jerusalem and her population is figured as a foundling-become-wife of YHWH and the prophet is told to "inform Jerusalem of her abominations" (v. 2). The allegory begins with a brief retrospective of divine grace, which provides a foil for the nation's perversity and the divine justice that follows. YHWH finds a female infant exposed to certain death by her parents and rescues her, bringing her up, subsequently pledging his troth to her in marriage (covenant; vv. 3–8) and all the while lavishing upon her great riches (vv. 9–14). The initially favorable imagery of feminine beauty and nubile sexuality that pervades the opening sections is then brusquely inverted and provides the setting for the negative motif of sexual promiscuity that follows: Beautiful Jerusalem squanders her dowry on fornication and forms alliances with other nations (vv. 15–19, 23–29), thus proving worse than "other harlots" (vv. 30–34). Moreover, the initial image of attempted infanticide re-echoes in vv. 20–22, where mother Jerusalem sacrifices her own children. Thus the (attempted) filicide is balanced by the ritual filicides as the mother reenacts her childhood trauma upon her offspring. For these sins, the Lord sentences Jerusalem to a bloody death—at once a measured retribution for her bloody crimes and a poetic reprise of her bloody origins. She will be stripped naked before her lovers (thus reversing the robing motif of her youth) and will then be stoned, hacked with swords, and finally burned (vv. 35–43). By means of this cluster of punishments for murder and adultery, YHWH will judge Jerusalem for her sins and vent his fury against her (vv. 38–42).

The ensuing paragraphs of the chapter provide analogical support for this punishment: Jerusalem is deemed sinful like her mother (v. 45, a Hittite, v. 2) and more depraved than her sisters Samaria and Sodom (vv. 44–47). Indeed, Jerusalem's iniquity makes her sisters appear righteous by comparison (vv. 48–52). And so, to shame Jerusalem further, YHWH promises the restoration of her sinful sisters, in whose apostasy Jerusalem once gloated (vv. 53–58). But then, with unexpected grace, the post-punishment restoration of Jerusalem is foretold: YHWH will remember her "youth," though she has not (v. 43), and he will reestablish her hegemony over her sisters, although "not because of (Jerusalem's) covenant" with YHWH, but because of his own faithfulness and grace. In fact, it is through such unexpected divine grace that Jerusalem will again "know" the Lord; for shamed at the fact of her undeserved restoration, and contrite before YHWH's unrequited absolution of her sins, she shall return to her covenant Lord (vv. 59–63). It must be added that such a promise of restoration does not undermine the stark judgments which precede it. The divine judgments will still come in all their severity, so that if the promises of hope have any anticipatory significance it may be as a sign of the abiding character of Israel's covenant with YHWH and a pledge that the destruction will have positive divine-human consequences.

The movement of Ezekiel's prophecy is thus from sin to judgment to restoration: from marriage to adultery (false alliances) to punishment to remarriage (covenant renewal). This sequence recalls Hosea 2, which also utilizes the allegorical pattern of marriage-adultery-remarriage in order to condemn the nation for covenantal unfaithfulnesss; and it similarly recalls the reflex of that pattern found in Jeremiah 2—3. From a comparative point of view, it is also notable that Jeremiah refers to two sisters, Israel and Judea, while Ezekiel mentions three sisters in his version of the topos and discretely avoids any reference to multiple marriages and divorces, so that there is no implication that YHWH established a covenant with Sodom. A further comparative dimension is introduced by Ezekiel 23, where the motif of wicked sisters is again found, though now only two sisters are mentioned, Ohalah and Ohaliba, who represent the cities of Samaria and Jerusalem (vv. 1–4). Among other contrasts, we may note that in Ezekiel 23 the exposure-foundling motif of chapter 16 is disregarded, and we are also told that the nation's apostasy was first manifest in Egypt (23:2). Moreover, while the fornication motif of chapter 16 is reiterated in Ezekiel 23, the marriage motif is not explicitly mentioned. Nevertheless, one will observe that Ezekiel 23 refers to a "judgment of adultery," as does 16:38; that 23:28–47 list punishments for adultery exactly similar to those found in 16:39–41; and that 23:31–33 portray the sisters as drinking from a cup of wrath which, while conceivably a neutral topos of wrath, is also reminiscent of the draught ordeal required of the suspected adultress in Num. 5:11–31.[7] Accordingly, while Ezekiel 23 discretely avoids all reference to a marriage topos and is thus more cautious in handling a potentially dangerous mythic-anthopomorphic imagery than Hosea and Jeremiah, the images used for sin and judgment do show a direct relationship to the starker version of the marriage motif in chapter 16.

One final contrast may conclude these comparative comments. As against the situation in 16:59–63, the blistering judgments of YHWH in Ezekiel 23 are not relieved by a forecast of physical-spiritual restoration. This lack has led some scholars to conclude that the historical horizon of chapter 23 is pre-fall, whereas that of chapter 16 is sometime after the destruction of Jerusalem. But such a conclusion is suppositious and prescinds the possibility of different theological-psychological emphases from one and the same prophet. On this line of argument, the prophet was concerned in 16:59–63 to emphasize that the punished nation will only come to know YHWH as a result of his gratuitous restoration of them after their judgment. By contrast, his concern in 23:49 was rather to suggest that the people will be brought to know their convenantal Lord (again) *in and through* the judgments. Admittedly, this latter motivation is the more common in the pre-fall prophecies. But the fact that 16:59–63 does not mention national restoration for the sake of YHWH's self-pride, which is the common motif of the post-fall prophecies, is a telling point, demanding due caution before any blanket assertion that 16:59–63 is secondary.

Ezekiel 17 continues the cluster of prophetic similes and allegories found

---

7. Cf. my "Accusations of Adultery: A Study of Law and Scribal Practice in Numbers 5:11–31," *HUCA* 45 (1974) 25–45, esp. 40 ff.

in chapters 15—16 with a fable about two eagles and Jerusalem's decimation. In fact, Ezekiel 16 and 17 are linked by the themes of covenantal faithlessness (expressed in exactly similar terms; cf. 16:59 and 17:19) and Israel's attraction to the surrounding nations. By contrast, Ezekiel 16 depicts Judea as drawn to Assyria and Egypt, while in Ezekiel 17 Judea is drawn to Egypt alone (the allusion presumably being the mission sent by Zedekiah to Egypt to appeal for aid after the Babylonian invasion of 597). In addition, the fable in chapter 17 focuses on the malfeasance of the king of Judea (against the divine covenant and the diplomatic treaty with Babylon), whereas chapter 16 only highlights national sin. And yet, despite its individual and national focus, chapter 17 does cross over to a national perspective insofar as the personal violations of the king are requited upon him (vv. 16, 19) and upon the nation he leads to perdition (v. 21). Perhaps this muted indication of vicarious punishment—the people are punished for the king's transgressions—is the thematic link connecting Ezekiel 17 and 18, where that doctrine is explicitly rejected.

In Ezekiel 18 YHWH, through his prophet Ezekiel, rebuts a proverb which reflects popular belief in the idea of vicarious (or deferred) punishment and stresses that "all persons are mine: the person of the father like the person of the son, [accordingly], the [particular] person who sins shall die" (v. 4). The reason for this salvo is not explicit at the outset, nor even in the intermediate sections of the piece. Only gradually is the prophet's theological strategy and logic made clear. Accordingly, some clarification of this important chapter is in order.

After his rejection of the popular proverb of "sour grapes" (in v. 2 by citing Deut. 24:16), the prophet constructs a theological legal argument in support of the principle of individual responsibility by means of a three-generational model: the first generation is typified by a righteous person, scrupulous in observing the law (vv. 5–9); the second by his son, a renegade, who disregards the law and rejects its obligations (vv. 10–13); and the third by the sinner's son, who sees and rejects his own father's ways (vv. 14–17). This arrangement allows the prophet to develop his case neatly. The first righteous man, who is not related to any previous generation, serves as an absolute beginning: he obeys the law, and so lives. His son, however, is a sinner who "will surely die; his blood being upon *him*": for his father's righteousness will be of no avail to him (cf. 14:18, 20). Theoretically with this dramatization of the separate responsibility of two generations before the law—the father and his son—the argument could have stopped. The reason that it does not is obvious enough: in order to counter the people's proverb (of a sinful father whose punishment was extended—or deferred—to his sons) the prophet had to extend the rhetoric to include one more generation and include a blameless son who has rejected his parent's evil ways. Such a person shall live, says the prophet, and shall not bear the guilt of his father. The prophet then concludes his argument by turning explicitly to the question of individual responsibility and reiterating the Deuteronomic citation found in v. 4.

At this point, the argument—apparently abruptly—turns to the principle of repentance and YHWH's readiness to receive true penitents (vv. 21–32). Once again a series of examples follow: the first case is that of a sinner who repents and is saved (vv. 21–23), the second of a righteous person who sins and is condemned (vv. 24–26). It would appear that the symmetry of this section is disturbed by the rhetorical critique found at v. 25, where the people say that such divine justice (where a righteous person who backslides is punished) is unfair, since it disregards the merits of a righteous person after he sins. No such parallel critique occurs in vv. 21–23 concerning the sinner who repents, and this asymmetry may explain the reiteration of the theme of the sinner who repents together with the critique of divine justice (like v. 25) in vv. 26–29. In any event, both critiques are rejected. The prophet emphasizes that it is not God's ways but the people's that are unjust, and that this fact should be the sole focus of their concern. In the conclusion, Ezekiel emphasizes that YHWH will punish each person according to his deeds, and urges the nation to repent from their evil ways and live (vv. 30–32). This final appeal is the climax of the second section and is apparently the motivation for Ezekiel's entire argument to the exiles.

The two parts of Ezekiel's argument can presumably be accounted for in the following way. In order to reject the notion of vicarious punishment and assert the principle of individual responsibility—a theological necessity if the people in exile were to assume religious responsibility for their lives— the prophet had first to stress the uniqueness of each person (and so each generation) before the law, and this he did via the apodictic legal formulation in v. 4 (and v. 20) and the casuistic legal formulations found in vv. 5–18. He was still left with a religious problem, however, for while the first argument emphasized that there was no transfer of guilt from one generation (person) to another, nothing was said about the sinner and his own lifetime. Was a (repentant) person to be considered guilty in later years for sins committed earlier, and vice versa? Surely not, says the prophet: The Lord wants repentance and so the life of the sinner. Thus, implies the prophet, those in exile are there for their own sins and not those of their parents, and since their relationship with God is not an intractable or inherited fate, they can take responsibility for it and return to YHWH. In presenting this teaching, the prophet Ezekiel wished to rebut any notion of religious fatalism or self-satisfied piety; more positively, he wished to generate a new spiritual realism in the nation and enliven the religiously passive and self-satisfied with the ever-renewed challenge of righteousness. Almost as the counter to chapter 14, where the prophet said that each person in Jerusalem (and Judea) was responsible for his or her own salvation and could benefit no one else, Ezekiel now stresses that the people in exile are also responsible for their religious destiny and are not the victimized recipients of the demerits of anyone else. However, it must be stressed that the repentance advocated in chapter 18 will not save the city of Jerusalem or its inhabitants; the speech is addressed to the generation in exile and to them alone. There is conse-

quently no contradiction between this speech and the hopeless predictions
of Jerusalem's fate found elsewhere in chapters 4—24.

However, the unequivocal emphases on individual responsibility and repentance in Ezekiel 18 *are* in explicit contradiction to what is found in
chapter 20. For in this chapter—surely unique in Scripture—the themes of
repentance and individual responsibility are not so much ignored as radically
flouted. In the context of an oracular inquiry whose purpose is unstated (but
which *may* have concerned the possibility of sacrificial worship in the exile),[8]
Ezekiel launches into a long retrospective on Israelite sins. Four periods are
isolated and presented in a sequential and essentially symmetrical manner:
(1) The first period describes Israel's sinful rejection of YHWH *in* Egypt
when it refused to heed the divine command to abandon idol worship.
Though Israel deserved to be destroyed, YHWH refrained from so doing for
his name's sake and delivered the nation from Egypt in fury (vv. 5–10).
(2) The second period describes the first generation in the wilderness which
received good commandments but refused to heed them. Again, though
Israel deserved punishment, YHWH refrained for his name's sake and
destroyed only the sinners, not their children (vv. 11–17; thus far *pace* chap.
18). (3) The third period describes the second generation in the wilderness,
which also rejected the Lord's command to accept him; and, though Israel
again deserved punishment, YHWH once more restrained himself for his
name's sake but did swear to exile the people as a future punishment (*contra*
chap. 18), a punishment insured by the giving of new (bad) laws that would
bring to Israel sin and ultimate judgment (vv. 18–26). This past situation is
reflected upon in verses 27–29, where Israel's contemporary cultic abominations in her land are underscored and the exile (announced in the past) is
anticipated. (4) The chapter then concludes by focusing on yet a fourth
period, the period of the exile (vv. 30–44). Like their forebears, the exiles
performed cultic abominations in Babylon and expressed the hope that they
might be like all the nations (v. 34). But this was not to be. Though the people
of Israel deserved punishment for their sins, YHWH (as in the past) refrained from due judgment and brought them back to their homeland in
great fury. First cleansed and rededicated to the ancestral covenant in the
desert (vv. 37–38), the nation, it is envisaged, would thereupon receive the
full blessings of the land promised to the patriarchs of old (vv. 39–44).

Various theological motifs are found in this chapter, some of which contrast
quite sharply with earlier Ezekielian notions. Most notable is the way the
doctrine of individual responsibility is treated. On the one hand, this issue is
ignored in the first and fourth periods—the original and new exodus events.
In both cases YHWH recalls his promise to the patriarchs (vv. 5–6, 42) and,
on that basis (the ancestors' merits), delivers the people *despite* their sins,
precisely the theological situation rejected in principle in 14:12–20. On the

8. I am still inclined to the inference of M. Friedmann (1888) and the earlier opinion of
Greenberg, referred to in *Ezekiel*, p. 387. That Ezekiel rejected the inquiry because of the
people's sins follows in 14:1–10.

other hand, it would appear that the principle of individual responsibility is respected in the second and third periods, since only the fathers (not their sons) were killed for the first apostasy in the desert, and the punishment of the sons in the second desert apostasy occurred because they did not reject the sins of their fathers (i.e., they sinned like their fathers and so were punished on their own account). On this basis one could argue that, since all the succeeding generations from the second desert apostasy to Ezekiel's own had sinned, they were justly punished for their *own* demerits. But so to argue would be to ignore the actual flagrant violation of the principle of individual responsibility found in chapter 20. For even if all the generations after the revelation of the "bad" laws sinned on their own account, and so were *formally* culpable individually, the fact remains that YHWH himself determined that the sins of the fathers (the second desert generation) were to be deferred to a later generation. And so, even if all subsequent generations sinned, the generation of the fathers was not punished in its own right and the succeeding generations lived under the onus of a law that led them undeservedly into sin. Since, then, the sons (the generations subsequent to the second desert generation) suffered vicariously for the sins of their fathers by inheriting a law which was an inherent punishment, *the theological core of Ezekiel 20 is diametrically opposed to the teaching of chapter 18.* In short, the people do not live in religious freedom—free from their father's sins and with a chance for repentance—but rather live out the consequences of earlier sins. And, as we noted earlier, the first and fourth periods also flout the principle of individual responsibility, though from a different angle, since both generations reap the merits of their fathers (the patriarchs) even though they themselves do not deserve this beneficence (*contra* chap. 14). Dark, indeed, must have been the mood of a prophet who produced, and a nation which accepted, such a theodicy, deprived as it is of all hope, and filled altogether with the despair of fate and divine doom. So viewed, the final prophecy of an unrequited redemption is nothing more than the hope of hopelessness. To say that Ezekiel's divine prophecies are riven with intense contradictions is an understatement.

The contradictions between chapters 18 and 20 are separated by a double dirge for the kings of Israel (19:1–14). The first section (vv. 1–9) uses the imagery of a mother lion among her cubs and describes the loss of two of them (presumably the loss of Jehoahaz and Jehoiachin to Egypt and Babylon, respectively; cf. 2 Kings 23:30–34; 24:8ff); while the second section (vv. 10–14) uses the imagery of a haughty vine, subsequently uprooted and re-planted in the desert for final ruin, quite possibly the exile of King Zedekiah to Babylon, but this identification is moot. Admittedly, it is hard to understand the logic of the present textual arrangement, which puts the imagery of chapter 19 after chapter 18 and before chapter 20. In search of a solution one may recall the vine imagery in chapter 17 and the royal focus there and wonder whether the compiler intentionally framed chapter 18 with images of blasted trees and royal malfeasance. There is no ready answer to this query, but it should be noted that such a structural explanation is not as farfetched as would appear on first view, since there is an intriguing alternation throughout the Book of Ezekiel of oracles focusing on historical generations and oracles which utilize tree symbolism. Thus chapter 14, dealing with the issue of individual responsibility across the generations, is followed by the vinestock imagery of 15:1–8; this letter is followed by the historical review of sinning generations in chapter 16, which is followed by the eagle fable and the dominant tree-vine imagery of 17:1–24. Further, the oracle of chapter 18, which focuses on individual responsibility across the generations, is followed by the vine imagery of 19:10–14; and the historical review of intergenerational responsibility in chapter 20, which follows this imagery, is succeeded by the oracles in chapter 21, which begin with a prophecy that utilizes the imagery of trees and fire-blasting (vv. 1–4).

After the opening prophecy of 21:1–4, a succession of oracles follows in which the leitmotif is that of a destructive sword which will bring divine doom to Jerusalem for her sins (vv. 10, 22, 32, 36). As commonly in chapters 4—24, the sins for which Jerusalem will be destroyed are not specifically indicated (vv. 28–30). But insofar as these loosely integrated judgments are coordinated by a religious motif, the generalization of sins found in vv. 28–30 serves the purpose. However, punishment for sins is no simple matter even here. For, as if further to complicate the discussion of individual responsibility presented earlier, Ezekiel speaks the following remarkable oracle to the land of Israel in 21:8: "Behold! I [YHWH] am against you, and I shall unsheath my sword and destroy both the righteous and evil [person] from [among] you." The point of this astonishing tirade, of course, is that personal merits count for nothing: not only can one's righteousness not save another person, it cannot even save oneself. Had anything been left to salvage from the sharp contradictions between Ezekiel 14, 18, and 20, one might have supposed that at least the inviolability of the righteous person was an irreducible datum. With the oracle of 21:8, however, this too is utterly demolished. Ezekiel now proclaims that before the terrible swift sword of YHWH's wrath, righteousness earns no more merit than sin—surely a bleak and violent teaching, enough to set fathers' and sons' teeth on edge.

The remarkable inconsistencies in Ezekiel's oracles raise in an unavoidable way the question of historical authenticity: Could one person have spoken such contradictories? Who, we may ask, is the true Ezekiel? Is he the champion of repentance and individual responsibility, or is he the theologian of historical fate and indiscriminate doom? Or is he all of these things and perhaps more, speaking the divine word as it came to him at different times and with different emphases? Admittedly, before this theological tangle our modern sensibilities bristle and beg for some consistency—or at least enough factual information to allow for a resolution of the inconsistencies on the basis of social-historical diversity. To some, of course, this need for consistency may seem an unfair criterion by which to judge divine oracles. But if this is so, one must either take the evidence as it stands—together with the radical (and somewhat anarchic) theological implications which are hidden in such a position—or acknowledge that we cannot identify a clear continuity in the thought and ideology of the prophet Ezekiel. What is the alternative? Surely the evidence of the text surgery performed by commentators on the Book of Ezekiel during the last century evokes the unhappy prospect that one cannot easily determine the "authentic" Ezekiel free of great subjectivism and hypothetical assertions.[9] But raging at the excesses of this type of solution will not conjure away the problem, and even the increasingly cautious text-critical positions of Walther Zimmerli and now Moshe Greenberg (much more so) do not resolve the complexity of the theological problems just raised; they only defer them to another level of analysis. Moreover, if one adds to all this the further possibility that either the Ezekiel corpus was revamped by tradents over several generations or that even the "authentic" Ezekiel does not accurately reflect his own historical period (as was suggested earlier concerning the Manasseh-like sins described in chapters 8—11), then the hope of resolving the historical-theological questions of Ezekiel's prophecies becomes far more complicated and well-nigh utopian. It is enough for us here to confront the issues squarely and acknowledge that most solutions must remain tentative or arbitrary.

On the heels of these reflections, we may conclude this section with another dimension of the historical and theological problems posed by the sin-judgment chapters found in the Book of Ezekiel. As noted earlier, the survey of sins found in chapters 8—11 may tell us more about typical sins in the time of Manasseh than about the actual religious scene in sixth-century Judea. A focus on the list of sins found in chapters 18 and 22 poses a comparable issue, for it would appear that the sins described there are more in the nature of "typical" lists of behaviors deriving from a common literary pattern than "historically accurate" indices of exactly what was or was not done in Ezekiel's day. Indeed, recent examinations of these lists against a broader inner-biblical and comparative framework strongly suggest that the two lists in Ezekiel served a pedagogical and hortatory function.[10] If correct, the implications of such a form-critical evaluation would be effectively to turn the discussion of the sins listed in Ezekiel 18 and 22 away from any social-historical use of them as specific evidence of the times and towards an understanding of them as typifying instances of covenantal disobedience. From such lists, moreover, we would learn much more about the prophet's concern to establish a legal-theological nexus between sin and judgment, and the legal resources upon which he might draw (e.g., Ezek. 22:10–11 is dependent upon Lev. 20:10–18, while the typical crimes in chapter 18 are derived from Deuteronomy 24, precisely the chapter which contains the rule of individual responsibility which he cites), than about anything the people

---

9. For a concise review, consult Walther Zimmerli, *Ezekiel 1*, Hermeneia (Philadelphia: Fortress Press, 1979), pp. 3–8.

10. For the overall form-critical argument, with comprehensive comparative example (also including Ezekiel 18), see Moshe Weinfeld, "Instructions for Temple Visitors in the Bible and in Ancient Egypt," *ScrHie* 28 (Jerusalem: Magnes Press, 1982), pp. 224–50; for Greenberg's concurrence and evaluation of Ezekiel 18 and 22 (and the term "pedagogical") see his *Ezekiel*, pp. 312–47.

did or **did not do**. Moreover, this line of argument would widen the gap between the modern reader and the world of Ezekiel. It is also a warning to contemporary historians to be cautious in using prophet critiques as evidence for popular practices. Other cautions are in order as well.

The collection of Ezekiel's doom proclamations closes with the oracles in chapter 24 (January 588), a bit less than five years after the prophet begins, by rebutting a popular adage (24:3–5) and continues by announcing the destruction of Jerusalem. The collection concludes with the divine oracle to Ezekiel that when the news of Jerusalem's doom will reach him in Babylon, the prophet will open his mouth and no longer be dumb (v. 27). All this had been foretold in 3:27, and was fulfilled in 33:21–22, after which prophecies of consolation and restoration dominate Ezekiel's addresses to the nation.

THEOLOGY

Our review of the chapters dealing with sin and judgment in the Book of Ezekiel has led, in the nature of things, to a consideration of some theological and rhetorical features of the prophecies. A full exposition of these topics cannot be undertaken in this context, which must rather restrict itself to some more general issues.

As we have mentioned, a dominant feature of Ezekiel 4—24 is that YHWH will vent his wrath against Israel for her sins. Repeatedly such terms as "my anger" (*'appî*), "my fury" (*ḥᵃmātî*), and "my zeal" (*qinā'tî*), recur through the sin-judgment chapters (cf. 5:13; 8:18; 14:19; 16:38; 20:33; 22:21–22), together with a panoply of stereotyped dooms (like "sword," "pestilence," and "famine") drawn from the curses for covenant malfeasance found in Leviticus 26 and Deuteronomy 28. The bleak mood of divine violence and destruction which pervades chapters 4—24 is further underscored both by the absence of calls to repentance—that the people may find some reprieve—and by the staccato-like emphasis upon the fact that the avenging Lord will not be merciful in any way (cf. 5:11; 7:4, 8; 8:18; 9:8). Thus, all evildoers will be utterly destroyed, says the prophet in YHWH's name, and survivors shall be saved either for their righteousness' sake (14:12–20) or because they shall serve as a *de facto* justification—an exemplum—to the exiles of the abominable practices in pre-fall Jerusalem (14:21–23).

One is driven to conclude that the foregoing theological element is the mighty theme pressing upon Ezekiel's religious consciousness. So viewed, his primary concern was not to call the people of Jerusalem to repentance but to expound in various ways upon the justice of YHWH *to the exiles*. For it is manifestly for *their* sake that almost all the actions and visions in chapters 4—24 are unfolded. Over and over again, the exiles are confronted with symbolic actions conveying the imminence of the doom to come and visions portraying the sinful treacheries which justify it. As we remarked earlier, the exiles (like the Jerusalemites) must have been denying the reality of the doom forecast, taking comfort in the fact that it had not yet occurred and secretly assuming that they would be speedily restored to their home-land. All this Ezekiel trenchantly denied while emphasizing, in one rhetorical form or another, the necessity and justice of YHWH's ways. Indeed, twice the point is explicitly made that once the exiles would behold the evidence of sin and doom they would know that YHWH had not spoken "in vain" (6:10; 14:22), and many more times the exiles are told that through the havoc of destruction they would "know" the Lord YHWH (and his power to bring judgment for sins). In effect, then, Ezekiel was unconcerned with Zion. To him its fate was sealed—foreseen, prejudged, and even pre-enacted. What concerned him essentially, however, was the religious psychology of the Judeans in exile. It was their false confidence, their sense of divine justice, and their sense of religious freedom that concerned him most.

The persistent theme of divine judgment of Jerusalem (and Judea) for her sins makes it clear that the punishment to come is the personal justice of Israel's convenantal God, not simply the working out of some impersonal principle of natural balance or retribution.[11] Indeed, this quality of a person-alized divine justice is emphasized both by the repeated theme of YHWH withholding his mercy in order to punish sinners and by the attempt, through such transitional terms as "because" and "therefore" (ya 'an; lākēn; 'al kēn), to create a legal nexus between the sins and the divine decision to punish them. At the same time, it bears mention that, despite the frequent indictment—conclusion ("therefore")—judgment sequence in Ezekiel's rhetoric, the relationship between sins and judgments is often quite variable in nature.[12] Thus, whether the sins are lumped together in some generaliza-tion or listed separately (be these accurate depictions of behaviors or "typ-ical" faults), the fact is that there is no focused attempt in the Book of Ezekiel to correlate specific sins with specific judgments. Indeed, where a more precise relationship can be found, as in Ezekiel 16 and 23, the reason usually has more to do with metaphorical consistency than anything else (i.e., the punishment for ritual murder is stoning and for adultery, public shaming and eviction, but these were hardly meant to convey the "historical" dooms to befall the city). Similarly, even where we have the use of such talionic expression as "I shall recompense their ways upon them" (cf. 7:3–4; 9:8; 11:21; 16:43), which would appear to convey the attempt to establish some precise correlation between sins and judgments, the rhetorical strategy appears designed to demonstrate *the reality of divine providence* and *the logic of sin-judgment* more than any strict principle of legal retribution or equivalence. This latter point is most concretely demonstrated by the fact that the apparent "talionic" judgments commonly establish the nexus be-tween sin and judgment in poetic and highly generalized ways. Thus, we find

---

11. This last is the well-known view of such matters of Klaus Koch, "Gibt es ein Ver-geltungsdogma im Alten Testament?" *ZTK* 52 (1955) 1–42. (He speaks of a *Tun-Ergehen Zusam-menhang*.) The most recent and thoughtful reevaluation of the issue is by P. D. Miller, Jr., *Sin and Judgment in the Prophets*, SBLMS 27 (Chico, Calif.: Scholars Press, 1982). See esp. pp. 134–37. Miller's work does not deal extensively with Ezekiel.

12. For some patterns of correspondence elsewhere, see ibid., chap. 4.

such constructions as these: Since the people have acted evilly *(rāʿāh)*, the Lord will do evil *(rāʿāh)* to them (cf. 6:7); or, since the people have rejected the divine statutes *(mišpāṭîm)*, the Lord will judge *(šāpāt)* them in turn (cf. 5:7–8; 11:11–12).

The theme of "knowing YHWH," conveyed repeatedly at the close of virtually every oracle of doom in the Book of Ezekiel, brings us to a final consideration and bears on our contention that the punishments predicted in chapters 4—24 are those of a personal divine judge. What, we may ask, is the meaning and function of the expression "that you will know that I am YHWH"? Several interrelated aspects suggest themselves. Insofar as the predictions of doom are addressed to the Judean exiles in Babylon, the announcement that the people "will know . . . YHWH" through the destruction has a contemporary hortatory intent: It means to exhort the exiles to a consciousness of the fact that they will, in the future, have the knowledge, *which is now lacking*, that YHWH is a god of power who fulfills his doom predictions *as announced*. The people in exile will, moreover, know—as will all later readers of Ezekiel's visions and oracles—that the destruction of Jerusalem is not because an impotent god has "abandoned the land," but rather because a providential and powerful Judge has left his shrine and land in revulsion of the abominations performed there. Relatedly, since the dooms are described in advance, the addressees have *in the present* a proleptic intimation of this future knowledge. Presumably, then, and paradoxically, the previews of doom in chapters 4—24 could bring the people—if they believed the prophet's words—to the same state of knowledge to which the unbelievers would eventually be brought against their will.

The latter reflections bring us to another side of the theme of "knowing YHWH"—and here we shift from the hortatory aspect of the phrase to its pathetic dimension. By pathos I mean here not only YHWH's intense response to Israel's sins but, especially, his desperate desire to be known and acknowledged by Israel. Whether by repeated warnings and predictions or ultimately by wrathful dooms or acts of grace (cf. 16:59–63; 20:33–44), YHWH's concern is to be "known" by his disregarding people. In this sense Ezekiel's prophecies reveal with sharp clarity what is also the ironic rhetorical strategy of all Israelite prophets: to bring a faithless and unknowing people to covenant allegiance and consciousness of YHWH's lordship. The irony is intensified by virtue of the fact that the whole being of the prophet is suffused by this awareness or knowing, while the addressees are partially or wholly lacking it. So viewed, the whole thrust of Ezekiel's visions and predictions is to challenge the people with divine intentions, so that, at the least, they will know this god as the author of their doom.[13] For Israel, then, Ezekiel's ultimate lesson is that there is no escaping the covenantal judgment and providence of YHWH, who will be made known to them even against their will.

---

13. Cf. Zimmerli, p. 192, who notes that the "recognition formula" conveys to the people the idea that their God "lies hidden in [the] judgment."

As a final point we may note the striking fact—of intriguing comparative interest—that the Book of Exodus is also marked by this theme of divine recognition and knowing.[14] The exodus narrative, in fact, begins with the theme of a lack of such knowing (by the Israelites and the Egyptians) and proceeds to show (by mighty divine "judgments") how this recognition is brought about in the mind of Pharaoh and in the believing hearts of all Israel. Moreover, not only the actions themselves but also the *record* of the acts of YHWH in Egypt will serve as the basis for future generations to know and acknowledge the mighty deeds and power of YHWH (cf. Exod. 10:1–2). And so, to some extent, there is an echo in the Book of Ezekiel of the ancient redemption theme. But the chord is discordant and inverted. The exodus account is a celebration of the *magnalia dei*, an account of the providential and promise-fulfilling power of the redeeming Lord YHWH, while Ezekiel 4—24 is a shrill and hysterical forecast of new *magnalia dei*, an anthology of the dark power of the Lord YHWH, whose will to be known and acknowledged by his covenantal people leads him to merciless measures. That these dooms are also ultimately for the sake of the covenant, and that they are no less historical manifestations of Israel's covenanting god, is the dreadful theological paradox that pervades the sin-judgment prophecies of Ezekiel ben Buzi.

---

14. Cf. Exod. 5:2; 6:7; 7:5; 10:2; 14:4, 8.

15

A Maker of
Metaphors: Ezekiel's Oracles
Against Tyre

CAROL A. NEWSOM

A recognition of Ezekiel's skill in manipulating the power of metaphor
to illumine reality helps us to grasp the subtlety, meaning, and
prophetic force of his oracles against Tyre.

After having been charged by God to deliver an oracle in highly figurative
language, Ezekiel protested that he was developing something of a reputation. "Oh, Lord God, people are saying of me, 'He's just a maker of metaphors!' "* (hᵃlō' mᵉmaśśēl mᵉsalîm hu'; Ezek. 21:5; Eng., 20:49). In truth
Ezekiel deserved the reputation, though not the criticism that is implied, for
one finds in Ezekiel a greater number of elaborately worked out metaphors,
allegories, and symbolic speech than in any other prophet. In the oracles
against the nations (Ezekiel 25—32), Ezekiel entrusts a particularly large
part of his argument to metaphorical language. Here Ezekiel does not
merely use striking metaphors to announce judgments. He often begins,
rather, with an image by which a nation might represent itself or one which
Ezekiel's exilic audience might have applied to that nation. Then Ezekiel
subjects the metaphor to scrutiny. Does it mean what it first appears to
mean? Or does it reveal something about the subject rather different from
what the audience first thought? How does it stand up to rival metaphors?
Finally, Ezekiel uses the metaphor to demonstrate the appropriateness and
the inevitability of Yahweh's judgment on the nation in question.

While Ezekiel's original audience may have lacked appreciation of his
metaphorical style, the prophet stands a good chance of getting a sympathetic hearing (for his rhetorical technique at least) from modern readers.
During the past generation there has been a new perception of metaphor as
more than elegant decoration of information that could otherwise be commu-

---

*All translations are those of the author.

nicated in a straightforward manner.[1] It is now generally understood that far from being merely decorative, metaphors have real cognitive content. If one tries to paraphrase a metaphor, what is lost is more than just a certain effect. What is lost is part of the meaning itself, the insight which the metaphor alone can give.

One of the best explanations of how metaphor works to produce meaning is given by Max Black.[2] Black takes a simple metaphorical statement as an example: "Man is a wolf." Here there are two subjects, a principal one ("Man") and a subsidiary one ("wolf"), the word which is used meta-phorically. The reader of the metaphor has at hand a body of common knowledge and attitudes concerning wolves—associated commonplaces, Black calls them—which may or may not be literally true but which are readily brought to mind when one hears the word "wolf" (e.g., fierce, predatory, treacherous). In the statement "Man is a wolf" the reader super-imposes the wolf-system of associated commonplaces onto the rather differ-ent system of commonplaces generally associated with human beings. The metaphor, acting as a filter, brings into prominence human characteristics that are wolf-like and suppresses those that are not. What the metaphor accomplishes, Black says, is to *organize* our view of human nature. Still, no literal paraphrase of wolf-like traits has the power to give insight the way the wolf metaphor does. This is partly because a metaphor is always indetermi-nate. It is the reader who must actively, even if subliminally, decide which implications are relevant, and how much relative weight each bears in producing the new perception of human nature.

Nelson Goodman describes the way metaphor works in a similar manner.[3] He suggests that we have schemata by which we organize certain parts of experience (e.g., plant life) and that we use various labels or words by which we sort out this experience and make distinctions within it. If one takes one of these labels from its home realm and applies it as a metaphor to an alien realm of experience (e.g., emotions), which one normally sorts out with a different set of labels, then one transfers not only a label, but the whole schematic system, a whole configuration of experience. One's perception of the realm of the emotions is then reorganized in a very different manner (as, e.g., in Andrew Marvell's lines, "My vegetable love should grow/ vaster than empires, and more slow"). This transference and reorganization is the means

---

1. Critic Wayne Booth, commenting on the explosion of studies on metaphor in recent years, wryly calculated that by the year 2039 there would be more students of metaphor than people ("Metaphor as Rhetoric: The Problem of Evaluation," in S. Sacks, ed., *On Metaphor* [Chicago: University of Chicago Press, 1978], p. 47). The following are some of the most significant recent works: I. A. Richards, *The Philosophy of Rhetoric* (Oxford: Oxford University Press, 1936; re-printed 1965); Monroe Beardsley, *Aesthetics* (New York: Harcourt, Brace & Co., 1958; Indi-anapolis: Hackett, 1981); Philip Wheelwright, *Metaphor and Reality* (Bloomington: Indiana University Press, 1962); Max Black, *Models and Metaphors* (Ithaca, N.Y.: Cornell University Press, 1962); Nelson Goodman, *Languages of Art* (Indianapolis: Bobbs-Merrill, 1968); Paul Ricoeur, *The Rule of Metaphor* (Toronto: University of Toronto Press, 1977).

2. Black, *Models and Metaphors*, pp. 38–44.

3. Goodman, *Languages of Art*, pp. 71–80.

by which metaphor creates new meaning which is not merely decorative but is a new perception of the relationships within one's world. Metaphor, says Paul Ricoeur, "is the rhetorical process by which discourse unleashes the power that certain fictions have to redescribe reality."[4]

As the recent philosophers of language have described it, to be a maker of metaphors is no insignificant thing. But because of the power which metaphors exercise over our sense of what is real, possible, or true, they have to be subjected to constant critique. The insight which metaphor gives into truth is properly tentative and hypothetical. It has what Ricoeur calls an is-and-is-not character.[5] Often, however, metaphors are absolutized, as though they provided literal descriptions of reality rather than suggestive glimpses. Metaphor derives much of its convincing power from the fact that it does not allow its hearers to be passive but requires them to participate in the construction of the metaphorical meaning. In this process, though, there is a sense of "virtual experience" (Ricoeur's phrase) which can be mistaken for literal truth. Perhaps more dangerous even than the brilliant metaphor is the dead one whose constructed character, whose is-and-is-not nature, has been forgotten. As Goodman provocatively says, "What was novel becomes commonplace, its past is forgotten, and metaphor fades to mere truth."[6] This may often be an innocent process, and one which is necessary to the development of everyday language; but where the metaphors in question guide our knowledge of fundamental human experience, they can be misleading and oppressive.[7] Consequently, the critique of metaphors is a business of equal importance to the making of them.

In his oracles against the nations, particularly in the collections of oracles against Tyre (chaps. 26—28) and Egypt (chaps. 29—32), Ezekiel both creates and criticizes metaphors that purport to give insight into the relationship between the power possessed by human nations and the sovereignty of Yahweh. Date formulae introducing the oracles indicate that with one exception (29:17–21, which comes from 571 B.C.), all the oracles were produced in the three years immediately before and after the fall of Jerusalem (26:1; 29:1; 30:20; 31:1; 32:1, 17). Except in 26:2, however, the oracles against Tyre and Egypt virtually ignore the political events of the fall of Jerusalem and its consequences. In fact these oracles are addressed, not to the political opponents of Judah, but to those of Babylon. The emphasis is easily understood, however. Since Ezekiel, like Jeremiah, was convinced that it was Yahweh's will to give political dominion to Nebuchadnezzar and to Babylon, opposi-

---

4. Ricoeur, *Rule of Metaphor*, p. 7. There is an inherently critical function in metaphor. As Ricoeur notes, "The strategy of language at work in metaphor consists in obliterating the logical and established frontiers of language, in order to bring to light new resemblances the previous classification kept us from seeing" (p. 197).

5. Ibid., p. 7.

6. Goodman, *Languages of Art*, p. 80.

7. See, e.g., Sallie McFague's *Metaphorical Theology: Models of God in Religious Language* (Philadelphia: Fortress Press, 1982), in which she employs recent research into the nature of metaphor in a searching critique of certain fundamental models and metaphors in Christian thought.

tion to Babylon was an implicit rejection of Yahweh's sovereignty. In the oracles against Tyre and Egypt Ezekiel scrutinizes metaphors which express the implicit self-understanding of these nations that underlies their defiant behavior.

Since it is not possible to look at all the oracles against the nations here, the relatively small and self-contained collection concerning Tyre provides an opportunity for examining in a limited way some of the techniques which Ezekiel uses in working with metaphor. This collection consists of four distinct oracles grouped by the use of a concluding refrain into three units, 26:1–21; 27:1–36; and 28:1–19, which pairs two separate oracles, vv. 1–10 and vv. 11–19.[8] There is general agreement about the structure of the chapter 26 (vv. 2–6, 7–14, 15–18, 19–21), though disagreement about the relationship of the various parts.[9] What we are to focus on, however, is the figurative way in which judgment on Tyre is expressed in vv. 3–5:

> See, I am against you, Tyre. And I will bring up many nations against you as the sea brings up its waves. And they will destroy the wall of Tyre and break down its towers; and I will scrape [wᵉsiḥêtî] its soil from it, and I will make it a bare rock; (ṣᵉḥîaḥ sālaʿ). A place for spreading nets shall it become in the midst of the sea.

To appreciate what Ezekiel is doing with this image of judgment, one has to keep in mind that the single most distinctive feature of the ancient city of Tyre was its physical location on a rocky island just off the Phoenician coast. The island site with its natural and artificial harbors provided Tyre not only with economic advantages but with an easily defended position. Nebuchadnezzar's ultimately inconclusive siege of Tyre is said by Josephus (Ant. X.11.1) to have lasted for thirteen years. The island city's defenses were not in fact decisively breached until 332 B.C. when Alexander the Great constructed an enormous mole from the mainland to the island. The significance of this physical location of Tyre seems to have captured the imagination of the ancient world, and in Egyptian, Assyrian, biblical, and classical writings references are repeatedly made to Tyre as the city "in the midst of the sea."[10] In the Egyptian Papyrus Anastasi I, Tyre is described as follows: "They say another town is in the sea, named Tyre-the-Port. Water is taken to it by the boats, and it is richer in fish than in sand."[11]

There was reflection on the significance of Tyre's location in Phoenician lore, too, where it was said that Tyre had been founded on two floating rocks

---

8. Walther Zimmerli, *Ezekiel 2*, Hermeneia (Philadelphia: Fortress Press, 1983): German ed., BKAT 13/2 (Neukirchen-Vluyn: Neukirchener Verlag, 1969), p. 22.

9. Zimmerli, *Ezekiel 2*, p. 33, is correct, I think, in seeing vv. 7–14 as an interpretive commentary on the figuratively expressed judgment in 2–6. Contrast J. W. Wevers, *Ezekiel*, New Century Bible (Grand Rapids: Wm. B. Eerdmans, 1969), p. 200, who thinks vv. 2–6 are secondary and based on 7–14. Verses 15–18 present a lament similar to the one in chap. 27. In vv. 19–21 the description of Tyre's descent to the netherworld recalls the more elaborate description of Egypt's descent in chap. 32.

10. H. J. Katzenstein, *The History of Tyre* (Jerusalem: Shocken Books, 1973), p. 9.

11. Adolf Erman, *Die Literatur der Aegypter* (Leipzig: Hinrichs, 1923), p. 288. *ANET*, p. 477: "richer in fish than the sands."

anchored to the bed of the sea.[12] In fact, the very name Tyre is simply the common noun "rock" (ṣōr). To call the physical location "rock" would be to make a fairly literal description. But to call the city "rock" is to speak metaphorically, to claim for the identity of the city the qualities of the ground on which it was built. To use Max Black's terms, "rock" forms the filter through which the city's existence and character are perceived. A contemporary and rather mundane example illustrates the same process. The use of the emblem of the Rock of Gibraltar by the Prudential Life Insurance Company and their slogan, "Get a piece of the rock," associate with the company the qualities of enduring strength, soundness, dependability, and protection. One might object that the name Tyre is a frozen metaphor and should not be pushed for such connotations. But frozen metaphors can thaw rather quickly in the heat of an appropriate context, and Tyre, by its actions as well as by its name and symbols, represented itself as something of a Gibraltar in the early sixth century. It is this implicit metaphorical claim that Ezekiel attempts to refute by means of the metaphor he chooses to announce Tyre's judgment.

Tyre had relied on its situation "in the midst of the sea" to give it a kind of protection from besieging armies that mainland cities could not hope for. So Ezekiel frames a metaphor for destruction taken from Tyre's image of its own security when he speaks of the "enmity" of sea and land. The significant connotation of the phrase "as the sea brings up its waves" is not difficult to define. It is the utter relentlessness of the ocean. No one wave may bring full destruction, but it does not matter. It is the unending succession of waves that destroys even the strongest rock. The initial comparison is taken up again in the verbs where the two third-person forms describe literally the destruction of the armies, and the final verb in the first person ("I will scrape bare") reverts to the metaphor of erosion. Though Ezekiel makes no explicit word play, one can scarcely avoid the sense of ironic transformation in which Tyre, the protecting rock, becomes the bare, eroded rock.[13] After Ezekiel's efforts to undermine the image of Tyre's island security, the concluding phrase "in the midst of the seas" in verse 5 has a strongly mocking character. The effect of the metaphor in the oracle is to reorganize one's sense of power. The apparent solidity and security of the island is revealed as an illusion of perspective, not a contradiction of Yahweh's power. Equally, the Babylonian opponents of Tyre, included as the "many nations," are imaged in such a way that they appear not as independent powers, but merely as episodes in Yahweh's patient, powerful sovereignty.

The second oracle against Tyre in Ezekiel 27 involves the use of a much more elaborately developed metaphor than the one in 26:1–6,[14] but it too explores the significance of Tyre's physical location and the special status

12. Nonnus Dionysiaca XL. 429–534.
13. In light of Tyre's reputation as a fishing capital there may be further irony in the assertion that when Tyre is worn down by erosion it will become ideally suited for drying fishing nets.
14. See the article of E. M. Good, "Ezekiel's Ship: Some Extended Metaphors in the Old Testament," Sem 1 (1970) 79–103.

which Tyre seems to claim from it. In this oracle Tyre is imaged as a ship. The first lines are somewhat corrupt but are probably to be read as follows: "O Tyre, you are a ship, perfect in beauty. In the midst of the seas are your borders; your builders brought your beauty to perfection" (vv. 3b–4).[15] The basis for the metaphor is obvious—a ship, like an island, is surrounded by water, as the initial words of verse 4 underscore. One wonders if Tyrian poets and artists used this metaphor for their city. Certainly the reader gives immediate assent to the appropriateness of the metaphor.

Though the metaphor is obvious, it is not trite. The reader is invited to consider various connotations also associated with ships that can illumine what Tyre is. Ships are instruments of trade. Since Tyre's wealth and status— in short, its identity among the nations—derived from trade, there is a special rightness in saying that Tyre *is* a ship. Ezekiel develops these con- notations in vv. 5–7, where the construction of the ship from precious materials is described. It is not simply the luxuriousness of the materials that is at issue. They are, rather, examples of the products of Tyrian trade, as the careful enumeration of their places of origin suggests. The metaphor draws the reader to conclude that trade indeed built Tyre.

Playing out the metaphor further, in vv. 8ff.,[16] Ezekiel names the leaders of the surrounding cities as those who row, navigate, and repair the caulking of the ship. Very economically the metaphor suggests the political superi- ority that follows dominance in trade. Each detail enhances one's sense of the aptness of the metaphor as an instrument for exploring the situation of Tyre until the initial vision of the physical similarity of the island Tyre with a ship seems weighted with significance. One is prepared to concede that in a certain sense geography is destiny. Tyre's fortune seems almost to be written into creation—literally and symbolically.

Ezekiel, though, was not a public relations agent hired by the Tyrian chamber of commerce. He has played out the metaphor so that the reader is deeply committed to its power to give insight into the reality of Tyre's situation. But Ezekiel has done that with the intention of undermining the implications which first emerge from that metaphor. He draws on other connotations of the metaphor, what Monroe Beardsley would call "lurking connotations,"[17] which are not among the features one would immediately associate with a ship but which one recognizes as true when they are brought forward. After the long, slow description of the construction of the ship and its staffing, Ezekiel simply takes the ship to sea and sinks it in a single,

15. Reading, in v. 3, '*att 'onî* for MT '*at 'amart* '*ᵃnî*. See the remarks of Zimmerli, *Ezekiel 2*, p. 42. Similar emendations are made by Georg Fohrer, *Ezechiel*, HAT 13 (Tübingen: J.C.B. Mohr, 1955), p. 153; and H. J. van Dijk, *Ezekiel's Prophecy on Tyre*, BibOr 29 (Rome: Pontifical Biblical Institute, 1968), pp. 56–57. Good, "Ezekiel's Ship," p. 82, defends the MT, remarking on the assonance of '*ᵒniyyāh* '*ᵃnî*. The metaphor of Tyre the ship is clear whether or not one accepts the emendation.

16. There is general agreement that the prosaic list of those who traded with Tyre in vv. 12– 25 is secondary. Opinion is sharply divided as to the originality of vv. 9–11. The occurrence of "Tyre" in 8b is probably an error. See the commentaries.

17. "The Metaphorical Twist," in *On Metaphor*, p. 113.

sudden verse (v. 26). Immediately the sense of the fragility of the ship dominates the connotations present to the reader. The metaphoric schema through which the readers have been organizing their ideas of Tyre's wealth and power is itself reordered, so that Tyre is seen to be vulnerable to sudden destruction even at the height of its power. Ezekiel's rather risky rhetorical strategy seems worthwhile, since the more one has become committed to the metaphor initially, the more powerful is the reordering of its connotations.

Here, too, as in chapter 26, there is an ironic note in the way references are made to the phrase so closely associated with Tyre, "in the heart of the seas." It is first mentioned in describing the situation of Tyre in v. 4 and recurs again in v. 26 when the destruction of the ship takes place, when "the east wind broke you in the heart of the seas." In the lament of the onlookers which concludes the oracle, the mourners ask, "Who was like Tyre in the midst of the sea?" (v. 32),[18] but say that "now she has been destroyed from the [high] seas in the depths of the waters" (v. 34). Through their related imagery the oracles in chapters 26 and 27 form a sort of diptych. The sea, the element from which Tyre drew its power and protection, is made the metaphor of Yahweh's judgment, slow but inevitable in the image of eroding waves, sudden and unexpected in the storm at sea.

As the first two oracles form a pair through their related imagery, so the latter two, 28:1–10 and 11–19, are connected by a common redactional conclusion, by being addressed to the ruler of Tyre, and by sharing similar mythological allusions. The third oracle (28:1–10), however, forms a bridge between the two pairs in that it too develops its metaphorical imagery from a reflection on Tyre's island location. The oracle begins with Ezekiel attributing an assertion of divinity to the prince of Tyre: "Your heart has grown proud and you have said, " '*ēl*'*a*nî.'" The translation of that boast has been debated for some time: Should one understand "I am a god" or "I am El"? In Hebrew, of course, the word is ambiguous, and it is quite possible that Ezekiel is using the implications of both meanings in the oracle. Most of the oracle is concerned with a somewhat sarcastic argument about the divinity or mortality of the king of Tyre, suggesting the general appellative meaning. But since Ezekiel never uses the word '*ēl* outside of this oracle, the reader naturally thinks of the proper name El as well. The critical statement is in the following phrase, however, when the king's reason for claiming divinity is apparently given. "I am a god/El; I live in a divine dwelling [*môšab* '*e*lōhîm] in the heart of the seas." Marvin Pope has argued, correctly I think, that the geographical location of Tyre "in the heart of the seas" is being implicitly likened to El's dwelling place "at the springs of the [two] rivers, midst the channels of the [two] deeps."[19] Drawing attention to the physical similarity of

18. Reading *nidmāh*, "to be like," instead of MT *k*e*dumāh*, "like silence."
19. *El in the Ugaritic Texts*, VT Sup 2 (Leiden: E. J. Brill, 1955), pp. 61, 98. It is not necessary to accept Pope's further suggestion of a deposed El in order to recognize here the rhetorical exploitation of a certain descriptive similarity on which to ground a metaphor. The reference to the pit and to being "slain in the heart of the seas" in v. 8 do not refer to El but are part of the contrast between the prince's pretension to divinity and his real mortality. On the other hand those who would deny all allusion to El's abode in v. 2 are left with no basis for the reference to Tyre as a divine dwelling.

the human city and the god's dwelling, the metaphor crystallizes an inchoate sense that there were ways in which Tyre's island location did give it and its ruler at times an almost superhuman exemption from the vicissitudes of ordinary political life as well as provide the conditions for its legendary wealth. Although vv. 3–6 are probably secondary,[20] their concession that the king of Tyre is extraordinary in wealth, power, and splendor may give insight, I think, into the anxiety of the Judean exiles that Tyre and the power on which it drew might be qualitatively different from and greater than their own.

Ezekiel's purpose, of course, is not to create a perception of Tyre as superhuman but to argue against it. Consequently, he adopts a very particular rhetorical strategy with respect to the metaphor he has devised. The metaphorical identification of Tyre with El's dwelling says something true about Tyre's situation only as long as one remembers the tension between the "is and is not" of metaphor. Ezekiel reduces the metaphor to false absurdity by having the prince of Tyre announce as an apparently literal truth, "I am a god/El; I live in a divine dwelling in the heart of the seas." Ezekiel makes short work of the assertion by emphasizing in verse 7 the "is not" side of the underlying metaphor—that the prince is not literally divine (as Tyre is not literally the dwelling of El).

Ezekiel is not finished with the metaphor yet, however, but indulges in a play on words between *ḥll* ("to pierce, slay") and *ḥll* ("to profane, pollute").

> See, I am bringing against you violent men,
> the most ruthless of the nations.
> And they will draw their swords against
>   the splendor of your wisdom
> and *profane* your beauty. (v. 7)

> They will send you down to the pit
> and you will die the death of the *slain*
>   in the heart of the seas. (v. 8)

> Will you then say, "I am a god"
>   before those who kill you?
> You are a mortal and not a god/El
>   in the hands of those who *profane* you. (v. 9)

Commentators often note that after "draw their swords" in v. 7 and "those who kill you" in v. 9 one expects the parallel forms to be from *ḥll* ("slay"), not *ḥll* ("profane"), and many emend the text accordingly.[21] But it is precisely the frustration of the reader's expectation of a form of the word *ḥll*, "to slay," that makes one attend to the implications of the unexpected reference to pollution. Just as the prince claimed to be a god because of his divine dwelling "in the heart of the seas," so Ezekiel promises him that he will be one who is "slain in the heart of the seas." Since the presence of a corpse in a holy place

---

20. So Zimmerli, *Ezekiel 2*, p. 75, and Wevers, *Ezekiel*, p. 213, though one could take the verses as an "aside."

21. E.g., Zimmerli, *Ezekiel 2*, p. 75, and Forher, *Ezechiel*, p. 161, on the authority of the versions.

profanes it and makes it unsuitable for the indwelling presence of deity,[22] Ezekiel is wryly telling the pretentious king of Tyre that once he is killed there, Tyre will be defiled and no longer a suitable residence for a god. One could almost say that Ezekiel undermines the claims of the metaphor first by demythologizing it and then by exorcising it. Though his rhetoric may not seem exactly "fair," it is certainly effective.

Ezekiel 28:11–19, the fourth oracle in the collection and the second against the king of Tyre, is the most intriguing. Textual difficulties, obscurities, and elusive allusions make it equally the most frustrating. Though I cannot pretend to solve all of its enigmas, close attention to the use of metaphor in the passage does clarify some features and illumines the function of the piece. Each of the other three oracles has featured some metaphorical play with the island location of Tyre, but there does not seem to be any such reference in the fourth oracle. Its connection with the other three depends more on its very close relationship with the oracle immediately preceding, 28:1–10. In addition to the connecting features mentioned above, there are a number of significant words and phrases that occur in both oracles: *gābāh lēb* (to be proud of heart, vv. 2, 17), *hokmāh* (wisdom, vv. 4, 12), *yōpî* (beauty, vv. 7, 12), and *rᵉkulāh* (trade, vv. 5, 16). Finally, there are related but contrasting images that form the basis for each oracle—the abode of El and the holy mountain of Yahweh. In the former oracle the extravagant claims of the prince of Tyre are reduced to nonsense and dismissed. In the latter a special status legitimately belonging to the king of Tyre is tragically lost.

What has attracted the most attention in the critical study of the fourth oracle against Tyre are the mythological materials used there, and various attempts have been made to show that Ezekiel presents here an ancient alternative version of the narrative of Genesis 2—3.[23] While there are undoubtedly mythological *allusions* in these verses, one cannot assume that Ezekiel is simply telling a well-defined ancient myth. It seems more likely that Ezekiel is using such allusions, as he uses other materials, to create his own fictive situations for his own rhetorical purposes.

There seems to be no doubt that Ezekiel has chosen to represent the king of Tyre as an "Adamic" figure. Not only the explicit reference to "Eden, the garden of God" in v. 13 makes one think this, but also the references to "the day you were created" (v. 13), the appearance of the guardian cherub (vv. 14, 16), and the motif of sin and expulsion (vv. 15–17). Before one tries to account for the details in which Ezek. 28:11–19 differs from Genesis 2—3, it is worth inquiring how presenting the king of Tyre metaphorically as a figure like Adam affects Ezekiel's analysis of the situation of Tyre. How does it reorganize the reader's perceptions?

Perhaps the most obvious difference from the effect of the metaphors used

---

22. See Ezek. 6:4–5; 2 Kings 23:15–20.
23. The literature is conveniently reviewed in A. J. Williams, "The Mythological Background of Ezekiel 28:12–19?" *BTB* 6 (1976) 49–61.

in the preceding oracles is that another relationship between Yahweh and the king of Tyre is suggested besides that of simple enmity. In the previous oracles Ezekiel had countered the notion of Tyre's strength and invulnerability by undermining various ways in which Tyre's power might be imaged. Precisely by their argumentative quality, however, these oracles imply that Tyre's strength was theologically problematic. The imagery of the present oracle, however, goes beyond a claim of Yahweh's ability to break Tyre's power to assert that in some way Yahweh is the creator of all the advantages which Tyre possesses. It is not the sea that gives Tyre its access to wealth and magnificence and its special protection from foreign attack. Its paradisiacal situation is rather Yahweh's gift, imaged through the jeweled garment (v. 13) and the protecting cherub (v. 14). In this way the inescapable reality of Tyre's wealth and strength could be fully acknowledged and yet incorporated into a perception of the world which made that acknowledgement nonthreatening. The second advantage of the Adamic myth is that its plot provides for the guilt and punishment of the one who was once so favored. In this way the Adamic metaphor supplies a constellation of relationships very suggestive for what Ezekiel wishes to imply about Tyre's past and present situation and its coming fate.

There are a number of details in the oracle which do not seem dependent on a narrative of the first human beings as we have it from Genesis 2—3. Rather than postulate some variant form of the myth of which this oracle is the only surviving evidence, it seems better to suggest that Ezekiel, in his creative freedom, is exploiting a second, independent set of associations derived from the holy mountain/garden of God which have no direct relation to the Adamic myth. In Ezekiel, as in Israelite tradition in general, the mythic language of the mountain of God and the paradise garden is frequently used to describe Mount Zion and the temple.[24] The identification of Zion as Yahweh's cosmic mountain is particularly clear in Ps. 48:1–3: "Great is Yahweh and greatly to be praised, In the city of our God, His holy mountain. Beautiful in height, joy of all the earth, Mount Zion, the far reaches of Zaphon, city of the great king." Moreover, in the call vision of Isaiah the temple is assimilated to the place of the divine assembly on the cosmic mountain. In Ezekiel, too, Zion is alluded to as "my holy mountain" (20:40) and Jerusalem is called "the navel of the earth" (38:12). Like the garden of God, the temple is a place of paradisiacal abundance and the source of life-giving waters (Ps. 36:9–10; Gen. 2:6–10). The association of the river which rose in Eden with a river whose source is in the temple (cf. Ps. 46:5–6; Zech. 14:8; Joel 4:18) is particularly prominent in Ezekiel's vision of the restored temple (47:1–12). There the river which rises in the temple turns the waters of the Dead Sea fresh, supporting huge numbers of different kinds of fish and nurturing on its banks miraculous fruit trees, "whose leaves

---

24. See the lengthy discussion by J. Levenson in "The Mountain of Ezekiel's Vision as Mount Zion," pp. 7–24, and "The Mountain of Ezekiel's Vision as the Garden of Eden," pp. 25–36, in his *Theology of the Program of Restoration of Ezekiel 40—48*. See also Kalman Yaron, "The Dirge over the King of Tyre," *ASTI* 3 (1964) 40–45.

shall not wither nor shall their fruit fail. Every month they shall bear first-fruits, because the water for them flows from the sanctuary" (v. 12).

If the mountain/garden of God can suggest the temple, then there is another set of associations which can be applied to the figure in the oracle. He may be seen as a priest of the sanctuary. In suggesting this, one does not have to assume that there was a myth in which the first human being was a priest. Nor is it necessary to look for evidence that the kings of Tyre had priestly responsibilities. One need assume nothing more than that Ezekiel chose to exploit two parallel lines of imagery suggested by the mountain/garden of God: Eden/Adam and temple/priest. There is abundant evidence that Ezekiel did intend to present the figure in the garden as a priest. The statement in 28:13 that "of every precious stone was your *garment*"[25] evokes the image of the high priestly ephod with its rows of precious stones (Exodus 28). The list of gems which follows is without question drawn from the list of gems in Exodus 28. Even if the list is secondary, as many scholars think,[26] it at least indicates that an early audience identified the allusion as priestly. The end of verse 13 is difficult, but there appear to be references to gold work and to technical terms drawn from the jeweler's vocabulary which recall the gold filigree and engraving mentioned in Exodus 28.[27]

The mention of the cherub in Ezek. 28:14 and 16 provides a point of connection between the imagery of Eden and of the temple. Here again there are textual difficulties,[28] but the cherub's function is evidently to protect the garden and its occupant and later to expel him, much as the cherub functions in Gen. 3:24. One of the words describing the cherub, however, *hassōkēk*, "shielding, covering, protecting," is a form of the word regularly used to describe the wings of the cherubim which cover the ark in the tabernacle and the temple (Exod. 25:20; 37:9; 1 Kings 8:7; 1 Chron. 28:18). Such allusive and double-functioning language aids Ezekiel in keeping both frames of reference, Eden and temple, before the reader.

Finally, the use of the language of pollution in connection with the sin of the king suggests a priestly context. The accusation, "you profaned your sanctuary" (v. 18), can scarcely be a comment on the literal level. It could not be a matter of concern whether the pagan temples of Tyre were defiled or not. This statement, rather, belongs to the metaphorical conceit of the holy mountain/divine sanctuary and the king of Tyre as its priest. The punishment of the king is similarly expressed in the language of pollution, literally, "I defiled you from the mountain of God" (v. 16), undoubtedly elliptical for "I expelled you as a defiled thing from the mountain of God."

---

25. Heb. *mᵉsukāh*. The most thorough recent discussion of the problematic words in this passage is to be found in Zimmerli's commentary.

26. Zimmerli, *Ezekiel 2*, p. 82; Fohrer, *Ezechiel*, p. 161; Wevers, *Ezekiel*, p. 216.

27. See Zimmerli, *Ezekiel 2*, p. 85.

28. Two widely accepted emendations are to repoint the MT in agreement with the versions, reading *'et-kᵉrûb*, "with a cherub," rather than *'at-kᵉrûb*, "you were a cherub," and to delete the conjunction before the verb, reading "with the . . . guardian cherub I placed you." One word, *mimšaḥ*, remains without convincing explanation.

One has to keep a strong hold on the metaphorical quality of the language. The image is a shocking one and perhaps intentionally provocative. Tyre was not, of course, literally the holy mountain/garden of Yahweh, nor was the king of Tyre in any literal sense a priest of Yahweh; but Ezekiel includes sufficient allusions to priestly vocabulary to make one see the king *as* a priest in this fictive scene. The question, then, is how one's perception of Tyre and its king are subtly reoriented by means of the metaphor. One result is that the sense of Tyre's privileged position is emphasized and seen as a blessedness which comes from the special intimacy with God which a priest experiences. But this much is accomplished by the "Adamic" metaphor. The priestly overtones of the oracle are more important, I think, in reorienting one's understanding of the nature of Tyre's sin. What the metaphor accomplishes is to take the political order and to reorganize it according to the schema of the sacral order. A political action (whether the opposition of Tyre to Babylon or its corruption through trade) is seen as a defilement of what is holy. The significance of this reorientation can only be appreciated if one keeps in mind how central the concept of Yahweh's holiness is to Ezekiel.[29] There is one other way in which the sanctuary metaphor in chapter 28 may function, namely, to underscore the certainty of Tyre's destruction. In the long vision report in chapters 8—11, Ezekiel had detailed the way in which the profanation of the temple in Jerusalem had provoked Yahweh to leave the temple and to destroy both temple and city. If, as seems likely, the oracle against Tyre in 28:11–19 was announced after the destruction of Jerusalem, the exilic audience would have known from their own tragic experience that judgment against those who profaned Yahweh's holiness was not an empty word.

As this study of Ezekiel's oracles against Tyre has attempted to show, the analysis of the rhetoric of metaphor is an essential part of critical exegetical method. While it certainly does not replace traditional historical-critical investigations, the study of literary technique and its effect on meaning can both challenge the results of those investigations and produce new insights into the material.[30] Reflecting closely on Ezekiel's metaphors suggests something even more important, however. No less than the Tyrians and the Israelites, modern peoples perceive the realities of national power through metaphors, explicit and implicit. Ezekiel reminds one that it is a prophetic activity to define what these metaphors are, to subject them to critique, and to make new ones which can redescribe reality in a liberating manner.

---

29. It dominates, e.g., Ezekiel's recounting of the history of Israel in chap. 20.

30. See the important articles by Luis Alonso Schökel, "Die stilistiche Analyse bei den Propheten," VTSup *Congress Volume* (Leiden: E. J. Brill, 1960), pp. 154–64; and J. Cheryl Exum, "Of Broken Pots, Fluttering Birds, and Visions in the Night: Extended Simile and Poetic Technique in Isaiah," *CBQ* 43 (1981) 331–52.

16

Life in the Present
and Hope for the Future

WERNER E. LEMKE

By radically undercutting all facile claims on God's mercy and all false
confidence in human merit, Ezekiel laid the sure foundation for the
future hope of his people: God's sovereign freedom to cleanse and
restore them as he saw fit.

On the fifth day of the month of January in the year 585 B.C., a survivor of the
final siege of Jerusalem came to the prophet Ezekiel in Babylon and brought
him the news of the fall of the holy city six months earlier at the hands of
King Nebuchadnezzar's victorious army. This was a momentous event in the
life of the prophet, for it marked an important turning point, not only in the
life of his people, but in his own prophetic career as well. Already on the eve
of the survivor's arrival, Ezekiel had intimations that something big and
significant was afoot, for that night the hand of the Lord had been upon him,
just as it had been on previous occasions, placing him in a heightened state of
prophetic consciousness.[1] Ezekiel's mouth was opened by the Lord for the
last time and the dumbness which had afflicted him until then was lifted for
good, never to return again. Henceforth he was able to move about and
converse freely with his fellow exiles, whereas until then he had been
confined to his house and permitted to speak only on those occasions when
the Lord gave him a special message for his people (cf. 3:22–27).[2] The fall and

---

1. Anthropomorphic references to the hand of the Lord occur over two hundred times in the
Old Testament with variable meanings. First, the expression may refer to Yahweh's irresistible
power, whether manifested in historical acts of deliverance or evidenced in the creation and
maintenance of the world (see, for instance, Exod. 13:9; Deut. 32:39; Isa. 45:12; Ps. 8:7). Second, the expression may refer to divine visitations of judgment, such as illness or calamity (see,
e.g., Ps. 32:4 or 1 Sam. 5:6). And third, the expression describes the agent which induces
prophetic states of inspiration, as for instance in 1 Kings 18:46 or 2 Kings 3:15. In this latter
sense, the idiom occurs seven times in the Book of Ezekiel: in 1:3; 3:14, 22; 8:1; 33:22; 37:1; and
40:1. That such ecstatic states of prophetic inspiration could also be painful and disquieting to
the recipient is suggested by such passages as Ezek. 3:14 and Jer. 15:17.

2. The nature and duration of Ezekiel's affliction have been the subject of much discussion.
The problem consists in reconciling the allusions to the prophet's dumbness (see Ezek. 3:22–27;
24:25–27; and 33:21–22) with the obvious fact that he must have made some utterances during
this period, as recorded for us in chaps. 1—24. It may be that these references are purely

destruction of Jerusalem in 586 B.C. brought final and incontrovertible confirmation to Ezekiel's message of doom. Because of the many sins and idolatries of his people, God himself had forsaken his holy city and abandoned it to the destructive fury of the Babylonian army. Yahweh did precisely what his prophet for seven and a half years had said he would do. The sovereign power and holiness of Yahweh God, the reliability of his word, and the veracity of his prophet had all been vindicated by the destruction of the holy city and the nation.

If Ezekiel only for a moment entertained the hope that he might now retire as a prophet and return to a more normal and tranquil life among his fellow exiles, he was quickly disappointed, for God reaffirmed his call of the prophet and continued to speak through him for at least another fourteen years or so (the latest oracle in 29:17 is dated to the year 571 B.C.). But there was a noticeable shift in the content and thrust of his message. Prior to the fall of Jerusalem Ezekiel had predominantly uttered oracles of judgment and doom, in order to destroy all false hopes and an erroneous sense of security among his people; now that the judgment had come, his message increasingly turned to the future hope and restoration of his people. He thereby sought to counteract the growing sense of despair, frustration, and cynicism which gripped the surviving exiles in the wake of the annihilation of the nation. At the same time he also sought to provide aid, comfort, and direction for carrying on life during the difficult interim period. Such a division of Ezekiel's ministry into two phases, the one before and the other after the destruction of Jerusalem, is suggested not only by the radical change in historical circumstances brought about by the events of 586 B.C. but also by the way the prophet's message is arranged editorially in the book itself.[3] The bulk, though by no means all, of the oracles of hope and

---

literary in character, i.e., they were supplied by an editor to underscore the divine origin and authority of Ezekiel's call and message. If, on the other hand, they do reflect actual historical experiences by the prophet, then one is forced to conclude either that Ezekiel's dumbness lasted the entire seven-and-a-half-year period, but was intermittent, or that it was total, but of considerably shorter duration. A strong case for the latter view has been made recently by Ernst Vogt, *Untersuchungen zum Buch Ezechiel*, AnBib 95 (Rome, 1981), pp. 92–106. Vogt argues that Ezekiel's paralysis and dumbness began on the day of the fall of Jerusalem and lasted for about half a year, or until the news of the fall of the city reached him. In the present author's judgment, however, the biblical data are best accounted for by assuming that Ezekiel's affliction was intermittent, but for the entire duration of the period before the fall of Jerusalem. On this problem, see now also Moshe Greenberg, *Ezekiel 1—20*, AB (Garden City, N.Y.: Doubleday & Co., 1983), pp. 102–3, 120–21.

3. This position, however, must not be pressed to extremes as some have done by assuming that Ezekiel could not utter anything of a more hopeful nature until after the fall of Jerusalem or that he no longer needed to warn or chastise anyone thereafter. In the present arrangement of the Book of Ezekiel, some passages of a more hopeful nature are found in the midst of oracles of judgment (cf. 11:14–21; 16:53–63; 17:22–24; 18:30–32; 20:33–44; 28:25–26; and 29:21). Conversely, in chaps. 34—48, which are predominantly hopeful in nature, elements of judgment are also to be found (cf. 34:1–6, 17–24; 35:1–9; and 38—39). It should also be remembered that the present arrangement of prophetic books is largely editorial in nature and that the major prophets, Isaiah, Jeremiah (LXX), and Ezekiel, exhibit the same tripartite schema: (1) oracles of judgment against Judah and Jerusalem, followed by (2) oracles against foreign nations, followed

restoration are presently found in chapters 33—48. Since chapters 38—39 and 40—48 are dealt with elsewhere in this book, chapters 33—37 will provide the focus for this essay, along with certain related passages in chapters 3 and 18.

Chapter 33 is transitional in nature, connecting as it does the oracles against foreign nations (chaps. 25—32) with the oracles of hope and restoration (chaps. 34—48). The chapter deals with a number of themes, most of which have already been mentioned in the first part of Ezekiel (chaps. 1—24), thus establishing a close link with that section after the intervening oracles against foreign nations. Chapter 33 falls naturally into five sections of unequal length.

THE PROPHET AS WATCHMAN (33:1-9)

The watchman was a well-known figure in ancient Israel. Taking his position on high elevation, such as a tower, rooftop, or hill, he was to look out for signs of the danger posed by the approach of a hostile army or a roving band of marauders, so that the population could take refuge behind city walls or otherwise make adequate preparations for their defense (see, for instance, 2 Sam. 18:24ff.; 2 Kings 9:17ff.). Clearly the watchman's position entailed great responsibility, for the life and death of many people depended on his diligence in exercising his task. On the other hand, however, the watchman's responsibility was limited or circumscribed. He only had to issue the warning. It was the people's own responsibility to decide how to respond to it. In similar fashion the Lord had appointed Ezekiel to act as watchman over Israel, just as he had appointed other watchmen over his people in the past (cf. Jer. 6:17).[4] It was Ezekiel's task to warn his nation of the imminent judgment which Yahweh was bringing against them. The RSV rendering of v. 7 (". . . you shall give them warning from me") somewhat obscures the fact that Yahweh himself is the source of the danger. The underlying Hebrew (*hizmîr min*) may more accurately be rendered: ". . . you shall warn them of me." That is, the people are to be warned against the Lord and against what

---

by (3) oracles of hope and restoration. Bernhard Lang, *Ezechiel*, Erträge der Forschung 153 (Darmstadt: Wissenschaftliche Buchgesellschaft, 1981), rightly cautions against uncritically drawing historical-chronological conclusions from the present redactional arrangement of the Book of Ezekiel.

4. We do not know exactly when Ezekiel received his call as watchman. A shorter parallel to our passage is found in 3:17-21, suggesting that it may have been in conjunction with his initial call in 593 B.C. Many commentators, however, consider 3:17-21 a secondary interpolation based on chap. 33 (see, e.g., the commentaries by Zimmerli, Eichrodt, and Cook). Others, however, argue with equal cogency that 3:16-21 and 33:1-9 are sufficiently different so as to reflect two separate incidents. So, M. A. Schmidt, "Zur Komposition des Buches Ezekiel," *ThLZ* 6 (1950) 81–98; and most recently, Moshe Greenberg, *Ezekiel 1—20*, pp. 90–97. While certainty cannot be had in this matter, it should be pointed out that Ezekiel clearly functioned in the capacity of a prophetic watchman since the inception of his call in 593. We see, therefore, no compelling reason for assuming that 33:1-9 describes a novel shift in the conception of his office, following the destruction of Jerusalem, rather than a reaffirmation of previous task and vocation, albeit under changed conditions and circumstances.

he intends to do to them if they persist in their ways. Interestingly enough, however, the Lord provides an avenue of escape from danger by appointing a prophetic watchman and providing him with advance knowledge of what he intends to do. Consequently there is a sense in which God's judgment is contingent upon human response, both that of the watchman as well as that of the people. To put it another way, the biblical God does not take pleasure in capriciously zapping people like a bolt out of the blue; he would much rather give them plenty of forewarning in the hope that they repent, thereby obviating the necessity of his having to take punitive action. That God prefers to see sinners turn to repentance and live, rather than imposing a sentence of death upon them, is stated explicitly in the next section of our chapter.

GOD TAKES NO PLEASURE IN THE DEATH
OF THE WICKED (33:10–20)

In the wake of the final destruction of the nation in 586 B.C., many of the survivors came to a recognition of their sin which has brought about this state of affairs. For some this was a recognition unto death and despair: "Our transgressions and our sins are upon us, and we melt away because of them; how then can we possibly live?" (33:10). They felt overtaken by the curses of the ancient covenant (cf. Lev. 26:39, which employs the same idiom of "melting away in one's iniquities"). To these Ezekiel responded by saying that the Lord did not take pleasure in their misery and death, but that he would much rather see them repent and turn to a new life of righteousness. God is more than willing and eager to forgive and forget previous transgressions and to grant pardon to any penitent sinner. Conversely, the righteous should not be misled into thinking that they could rest on their past good deeds and turn with impunity to deeds of unrighteousness, as if that did not matter. By holding before them the possibility of repentance, Ezekiel meant to pull his fellow exiles out of the pit of their despair and cynicism and impress upon them the importance of making right decisions in the here and now, each moment of their lives. Just because they were living in exile in Babylon did not mean that all was lost or that they were simply the hapless victims of an impersonal and unalterable fate. God has given human beings a will and the capacity to make decisions each moment of their lives, which have consequences for good or ill, life or death. The life and death of which Ezekiel speaks refer not simply to physical life and death, though that may also be involved, but to life lived qualitatively in the presence of God and as a faithful member of his people.[5]

Before we leave this passage to move on to the next, a look at chapter 18 is in order, for it deals with themes closely related to 33:10–20. Chapter 18 falls naturally into two major subdivisions: verses 1–20, which deal with the problem of intergenerational guilt and retribution; and v. 21–32, which deal

5. For an extensive analysis of the theme of "life" and "death" in the Book of Ezekiel, see Walther Zimmerli's essay, " 'Leben' und 'Tod' im Buche des Propheten Ezechiel," *ThLZ* 13 (1957) 404–8, reprinted in *Gottes Offenbarung* (Munich: Chr. Kaiser Verlag, 1963), pp. 178–91.

with the theme of God's readiness to forgive sinners who repent. The latter is also the subject of chapter 33:10–20, though in a slightly different context.[6] Since we have already dealt with the subject matter of the second part of chapter 18 in our analysis of 33:10–20, it will suffice to look briefly at the material in chapter 18:1–20.

EACH GENERATION HAS A SHARE IN SHAPING ITS OWN DESTINY
(18:1–20)

In this chapter, Ezekiel addresses the issue of intergenerational retribution in response to a saying which apparently had wide currency among the generation of the exile. (It is also found in the Book of Jeremiah; see 31:27–30.) "The fathers have eaten sour grapes and the children's teeth are set on edge" was a saying which summed up the attitude of many exiles who apparently thought themselves to be the innocent victims of the sins of previous generations. Unlike those exiles of 33:10, who were acutely conscious of their own sin and guilt to the point of despair, the folk who repeated this saying denied any personal guilt in the punishment of exile which they were undergoing. Instead they blamed it all on previous generations and in the process accused God of unfairness (cf. 18:25–30 and 33:17–20). Their sentiments were akin to those expressed in Lam. 5:7: "Our fathers sinned and are no more, but we bear their iniquities."

Now there is a certain measure of truth in that saying. Both Scripture and human experience teach us that the consequences of actions taken by some individuals are not necessarily confined to their own lives but may affect the lives of others as well, extending even to generations yet unborn. In the decalogue this was stated as an article of faith (cf. Exod. 20:5 and Deut. 5:9), an article with which all Israelites were well acquainted. It was also part of their historical experience, as when Achan and his entire household were put to death because of his violation of the sacred rules of holy war (cf. Joshua 7). From the realm of ancient Near Eastern politics and warfare we know also that the families and dependents of rebellious vassals were held accountable and punished for the acts of the rebellious vassal. King Jehoiachin, for instance, was taken into captivity by Nebuchadnezzar because of the rebellion of King Jehoiakim, as well as the sins of King Manasseh (cf. 2 Kings 4:1–17); and Hezekiah's sons were killed by the Babylonians because of their father's insurrection (cf. 2 Kings 25:1–9).[7]

---

6. Did Ezekiel address himself to the same issue twice in differing contexts, or did he or one of his disciples apply one of his utterances to another context and situation? The issue is debated among scholars and cannot be settled decisively on the basis of the available evidence. This much is clear, that there is no direct literary dependence between 33:10–20 and 18:21–32, only an affinity of theme and subject matter.

7. A treaty of the Hittite King Mursilis II is interesting in this regard. Not only does it confirm the fact that this was standard procedure among ancient Near Eastern rulers, but it also demonstrates that an ancient ruler was free not to follow that custom, by pardoning the son of a rebellious vassal. For an interesting analysis of this treaty and its implications for our understanding of Ezekiel 18, see John B. Geyer, "Ezekiel 18 and a Hittite Treaty of Mursilis II," *JSOT* 12 (1979) 31–46.

On the other hand, countervailing notions and practices are also attested in the Bible. The Deuteronomic code, for instance, contained this provision: "The fathers shall not be put to death for the children, nor shall the children be put to death for the fathers; every man shall be put to death for his own sin" (Deut. 24:16). That this provision was also obeyed is illustrated by King Amaziah's action, who, when he came to power in Judah, did not put to death the children of the murderers of his father (2 Kings 14:1–6). Ezekiel in chapter 18:1–20 pursues this line of thought and applies it to his generation of the exile.

These conflicting biblical views and practices may seem to the casual reader to be mutually contradictory. But they are not necessarily so. Each, when seen in its own context, embodies an element of truth. Ezekiel, for instance, is not so much attacking the notion of the interconnectedness and shared destiny of human groups as he is attacking the one-sided and fatalistic perversion of such a notion. Contrary to the way chapter 18 has often been understood by modern readers, Ezekiel was not a champion for human individualism against notions of corporate solidarity and responsibility. Rather, what Ezekiel in effect was saying to the generation of the exile was that they were neither wholly blameless for their present predicament nor simply the hapless victims of circumstances beyond their control. Each day was a new day with fresh possibilities and opportunities for decision; the outcome of their destiny lay very much within their power to affect. God did not enjoy bearing grudges or inflicting punishment on his people. God was more than willing and able to forgive if they but gave him the slightest pretext to do so. The past did not have to enslave them forever unless they willed and permitted it to do so.

The second part of the chapter (vv. 21–32) underscores the fact that this biblical truth is operative not only intergenerationally, but even within the life span of one human being or generation. Chapter 18 closes with a powerful appeal to repent and to take an active hand in the transformation of one's own future, confident that God's intentions for his people are fundamentally salvific and not judgmental in nature.

NEWS OF JERUSALEM'S FALL
(33:21–22)

This brief historical reference is a sequel to events related in 24:25–27 and 3:25–27. It records how Ezekiel received the news of Jerusalem's fall on January 5, 585 B.C. That previous night he had been relieved of his affliction of dumbness, the nature and problems of which were discussed more fully in note 2. This event provided confirmation for his oracles of doom and marked the end of an important phase in his prophetic ministry, as well as the beginning of a new one.

AGAINST THE FALSELY CONFIDENT
IN THE LAND (33:23–29)

As a result of the two deportations of 597 and 586 B.C., the Jewish people were split into two communities: one in Babylon, made up chiefly of the royal house and upper classes of Jerusalem, and one composed mostly of the poorer people of Judah who remained behind in the land. There was a certain amount of rivalry and tension between these two communities.[8] Some of those who remained in the land of Judah assumed that, since they had not been carried off into captivity, they were the favored remnant of God with whom the future of Israel lay. Both Jeremiah and Ezekiel attacked this self-serving notion, affirming instead that the future of Israel lay with those who had been exiled to Babylon (see Jer. 24:1–10; 29:1–14; Ezek. 11:14–21; 33:23–29). Here in this passage Ezekiel denounces the impenitent self-assurance of those survivors in Judah who appealed to God's promises to Abraham in support of their arrogant claims to the land. What they forgot, and what Ezekiel had to remind them of with uncompromising candor, was that possession of the promised land was not simply or automatically a function of Abrahamic descent, sheer numbers, or squatters' rights, but, more imporant, was a function of obedience to God's will and of humble trust in his sovereign promises. In the meantime, the land and those remaining in it would be ravaged and remain a desolate horror for years to come. The threefold scourge of sword, pestilence, and wild animals is traditional language drawn from ancient Near Eastern treaty curses. By this the prophet meant to suggest to his hearers that the curses of the broken covenant would have to run their full course (cf. Deut. 28:15–26 and Lev. 26:21–33). Through these acts of judgment they would have to acknowledge that God was true to his word and brought about what had been foretold through his prophets.

AGAINST THE HEARERS OF THE WORD
WHO DO NOT ACT ON IT
(33:30–33)

As if to warn them not to take too much delight in the threats against others, Ezekiel turns in the final segment of chapter 33 to point up some of the shortcomings of his fellow exiles. Apparently many enjoyed coming to Ezekiel and listening to the strange words which he claimed to speak in the name of their God. Some even derived aesthetic pleasure from such activity, reveling in the exquisite artistry of the prophet's semantic and poetic powers. These Ezekiel reminded that neither he nor God's word which he spoke were sent for their entertainment or superficial edification. The function of a prophet is to announce God's purposes in history and, if possible, to induce people to take action which is commensurate with God's announced purpose and intention. Unfortunately, people too often recognize that only in historical retrospect! More often than not, true prophets are recognized and

---

8. In fairness to the community of survivors who remained behind in the land of Judah and who may not have been as uniformly wicked and impenitent as this passage might lead us to believe, it should be pointed out that this passage, like many of the other Old Testament passages which speak about the tensions between these two communities, was edited from the standpoint of the Babylonian exiles. The characterization of the Judean community, therefore, may be a bit one-sided or partisan.

heeded only posthumously. But whether they are or not, God's purposes must ultimately come to fruition, and what God announced through his faithful heralds shall come to pass.

I MYSELF WILL BE THE SHEPHERD
OF MY SHEEP (34:1–31)

The destiny of any nation or people is to a large degree determined by the quality and dedication of its leaders. Ezekiel was aware of this, and consequently it is not surprising that in dealing with the future of his people he should also address the issue of leadership, which he does in this chapter under the imagery of the shepherd and the sheep.[9] Characteristic for Ezekiel, the promise is preceded by an indictment of the bad shepherds of Israel. Instead of properly pasturing their flock, they had been more concerned about feeding themselves. Instead of leading their flock gently and with care, as good shepherds do, the kings of Israel had ruled their people harshly and oppressively.[10] As a result of the shepherds' misrule, the people wandered astray across the mountains and were dispersed across the face of the earth. This may be an allusion to their syncretistic worship on the high places of Israel, as well as to their resultant captivity and exile. But their dispersion was not to be their ultimate end and destiny. Having gotten rid of the bad shepherds, God himself would some day gather his lost sheep, who had been scattered among the nations on that day of judgment.[11] God himself would be their shepherd and bring them back to their own mountain, their own land of Israel. There God would lead them aright, doing everything which the bad shepherds had failed to do (v. 16).

In vv. 17–24 the imagery shifts from the shepherds to the sheep. Not all the blame for the troubles of the flock can be laid at the feet of the shepherds. In times of crisis and lack of adequate leadership, there are

9. The shepherd metaphor was used widely throughout the ancient Near East as a designation for both divine and human rulers. So, for instance, in an ancient Sumerian hymn, the god Enlil is addressed as the "faithful shepherd" of all living creatures; and in the prologue to his famous law code, the Babylonian king Hammurabi describes himself as a shepherd appointed by Enlil for his people. Cf. J. B. Pritchard, *ANET*, 3d ed. (Princeton, 1969), pp. 164, 574f. In the Old Testament, likewise, the shepherd metaphor is applied to both Yahweh-God (cf. Gen. 49:24; Pss. 23; 77:20; 78:52; 80:1; Isa. 40:11; and Jer. 31:10) and to human rulers (cf. Num. 27:17; Jer. 2:8; 3:15; 10:21; 23:1–4; and Ps. 78:70–72).

10. The Hebrew expression *rādāh bepārek*, "to rule with harshness" (v. 4), occurs in only two other passages of the Old Testament. In Exod. 1:13–14 it refers to the manner in which the Egyptians treated their Hebrew slaves, and in the Holiness Code (Leviticus 17—26) the law forbids treating a fellow Israelite in such a manner (cf. Lev. 25:43, 46). Ezekiel's polemic is thus quite pointed: he accuses Israel's rulers of doing what their own history should have taught them to abhor and what the law of Moses expressly forbade!

11. The day of "clouds and thick darkness" (v. 12) in the Old Testament may refer to Yahweh's appearance on Mt. Horeb (cf. Deut. 4:11 and 5:22), which was also commemorated and represented liturgically in the cult of Jerusalem (cf. Ps. 97:2). Here, however, it more likely refers to the concept of the "day of the Lord," a day on which the Lord came in judgment (cf. Zeph. 1:15 and Joel 2:2).

always those who exploit that confusion to their own advantage, making life needlessly difficult and miserable for others. Consequently God would not only judge the bad shepherds but the bad and pushy sheep as well.

Verses 23–24 may appear to be in conflict with some of the assertions of the preceding section. Whereas there God was said to be the shepherd of his people, here a human agent, a new David, receives that designation. To an Israelite, however, these two notions were not necessarily contradictory, for in the theology of Jerusalem the Davidic kings were an extension of Yahweh's kingship. Just as in one and the same ancient Sumerian hymn the designation "shepherd" was ascribed both to the heavenly deity and to the earthly king, so in Israel the same term was applied both to the Lord and to his earthly servant or vice-regent.[12] Another designation which David receives in this passage is the title "prince" (Hebrew, nāsî'), which literally means "exalted one." It originated in the ancient tribal league tradition, where it referred to tribal chieftains or leaders of Israel. Ezekiel seems to have preferred this term to the more common word for king (Hebrew, melek), which in his day may have had misleading or even negative connotations. For Ezekiel the nāsî' was the person who in the coming age of salvation would be the successor of the former Davidic kings and who would exercise limited cultic and rulership functions as a subordinate of Yahweh God.

The concluding section of this chapter (vv. 25–33) moves beyond the shepherd or rulership metaphor to the imagery of peace and blessing which the restored people of Israel would enjoy in the future. As surely as God once unleashed the curses of the covenant which brought desolation upon the land, so in that future day God would activate the blessing and restore paradise-like conditions to the land. No longer would the people have to live in fear and trembling or as the object of derision of their enemies.[13] Thus the coming age of peace and harmonious well-being would embrace the realm of nature as well as the arena of history.

---

12. That this was so is proved by Psalm 78, which is a product of Jerusalemite theology. In this psalm the shepherd metaphor is first applied to Yahweh, who, at the exodus, "led forth his people like sheep and guided them in the wilderness like a flock" (Ps. 78:52). At the end of the psalm, the shepherd title is transferred to David, God's chosen servant: "He chose David his servant and took him from the sheepfolds; from tending the ewes that had young he brought him to be the shepherd of Jacob his people, of Israel his inheritance. With upright heart he tended them, and guided them with skilled hand" (Ps. 78:70–71). Both in Psalm 78 and in Ezekiel 34 David is viewed as an extension of Yahweh's shepherding activity, except that whereas Psalm 78 looked to the past, Ezekiel 34 looks to the future. In the Bible God's future action is often described in terms which are analogous to, though not necessarily identical with, his actions in the past.

13. The expression "and none shall make them afraid" (Hebrew wᵉ 'ên mahrîd) used in v. 28 has an interesting bipolar application in both treaty curses and blessings in the Old Testament. For instance, in Deut. 28:26 and in Jer. 7:33 it describes the curse, in the sense that the bodies of the slain in Israel shall be "food for the birds of the air and for the beasts of the earth, and none will frighten them away (wᵉ 'ên mahrîd)." But in Ezek. 34:28, as in other Old Testament passages like Lev. 26:6; Jer. 30:10; Micah 4:4; and Ezek. 39:26, the same phrase describes the blessing of undisturbed and fearless tranquillity on the part of the restored inhabitants of the land. God is Lord of both the blessing and the curse; it is within his power to undo the latter by the former, or to replace the one by the other.

THE MOUNTAINS OF ISRAEL SHALL
AGAIN BE INHABITED
(33:1—36:15)

On first sight, chapter 35, which contains threats of judgment against Mount Seir, appears to be out of place in a section devoted to oracles of promise and salvation. Upon closer examination, however, it appears that it is only the opening section of a larger literary and thematic unit which extends through 36:15. Mount Seir was the name of the chief mountain range of the kingdom of Edom, situated to the southeast of Judah, between the southern tip of the Dead Sea and Gulf of Agaba. Israel and Edom had been bitter enemies throughout most of their history. That animosity was already prefigured in the rivalry of their respective ancestors Jacob and Esau (see Genesis 27—33). During the period of the conquest, Edom barred the Israelite tribes from moving through its territory and harassed them in other ways (Num. 20:14–21). After David had conquered and subdued Edom (2 Sam. 8:13–14), that country periodically rebelled against Judah and from time to time succeeded in reasserting its political independence. Following the destruction of Jerusalem, in which they had joined forces with the Babylonians, the Edomites exploited Israel's weakness during the exile by appropriating large sections of Judean territory. Small wonder that the writers of the Old Testament had some very harsh things to say about Edom (see, for instance, the Book of Obadiah, Ps. 137:1, and Lam. 4:21–22).

In the pericope under discussion, Edom is promised a fate similar to that which Israel had to suffer. Because Edom had ruthlessly exploited Israel's weakness and taken possession of the Lord's inheritance, the Lord in turn would punish Edom and lay it waste. As the Edomites wished and had done unto others, so it would be done unto them (35:10–15). This, however, was only the necessary prelude to the major concern of this section, which is the restoration of the hill country of Israel. Just as Ezekiel once had to pronounce judgment upon the mountains of Israel (see chap. 6), so now he announces their restoration and blessing. As surely as God had laid them waste because of their inhabitants' transgressions, so surely would he someday resettle them with the remnant of his people, bestowing blessing and fertility upon them.

I WILL RESTORE YOU FOR MY
NAME'S SAKE (36:16–38)

To anyone who was wondering whether, or on what grounds, God would affect the future restoration of his people in their land, Ezekiel provides a clear and unequivocal answer which is recorded for us in the second part of chapter 36. Characteristically he begins with a concise survey of the past which led to the people's present predicament. Because the Israelites had defiled the land through their evil deeds, God removed them from the land

and scattered them among the nations.[14] But this now had created a problem for God! Israel's dispersal among the nations was a "defilement," as it were, of God's own holy name and honor. In the perspective of the ancient world in which Israel lived, the status and effective power of a deity was intimately associated with the land and the people where that deity was worshipped. Given Israel's present exile, the nations might be tempted to make fun of Yahweh-God and to question his existence and power.[15] Mindful of his own honor, therefore, and not necessarily for Israel's sake, God had decided to restore his people to their own land. By this act his name, which had been defiled among the nations, would again be made holy in their sight. By doing the seemingly impossible, the nations would have to acknowledge that Yahweh is a powerful and living God.

Such a motivation for God's future intervention on behalf of Israel may strike the reader as perhaps a bit cold and unfeeling. If only Ezekiel had spoken a little more of God's tender mercy and compassion for his poor suffering people! We would find that much more attractive and praiseworthy in a deity. But it should be remembered that the emphasis on the austere sovereignty of God by Ezekiel not only may have been the result of his priestly upbringing, but perhaps even more so may have been dictated by the particularities of the national crisis during which he had to prophesy. In Ezekiel's prophecies God appears more like an outraged and exasperated lover than a tender and forgiving parent (see, for instance, chaps. 16 and 23). All the rot and vileness of the nation had to be exposed mercilessly; all the false confidence in human merit, all the facile claims on God's mercy had to be undercut radically once and for all. But in so doing, Ezekiel also laid the sure foundations for the future hope of his people. For with human merit and capabilities found so radically wanting, and with Israel's historical existence in exile so abysmally bleak, nothing short of God's own character and overarching purposes in history could become the basis for renewed hope among God's people. Whatever future Israel had would come from God and be the result of God's sovereign freedom to act as God saw fit.

One of the things which God would do for his restored people would be to cleanse them from all their sins and to effect within them a change of heart which would enable them to walk in God's statutes and ordinances. Ezekiel

---

14. Ezekiel likens Israel's defilement to the impurity incurred by a menstruating woman, thereby betraying his priestly origin, for priests were particularly concerned about matters of ritual purity (cf. also Ezek. 7:19; 18:6; 22:10; and 36:17). Modern Bible readers should not interpret this as male chauvinism. The distinction between clean and unclean is rooted in ancient primitive taboos, the precise origin and meaning of which in most instances are no longer apparent to us. According to priestly perspectives, ritual impurity was induced not only by menstrual blood but by any kind of regular or unusual bodily flow, such as the secretion of semen in a male or the festering of a bodily sore (cf. Lev. 15:1–33). Furthermore, the priestly terminology of ritual purity or impurity could also be applied in a transferred sense to moral and religious matters, as Ezekiel does in this passage, for among the things which defiled the land, he singles out the sins of bloodshed and idolatry (v. 18).

15. We may recall that Moses pursued a similar line of reasoning when he pleaded with God not to destroy his own people in the wilderness (cf. Exod. 32:11–14 and Num. 14:13–19).

uses the metaphor of the new heart and spirit, or the heart of flesh which would replace the heart of stone. The heart and spirit in Hebrew psychology were the seat of human volition, thinking, feeling, and aspiration. Thus what Ezekiel in effect is promising is that God will affect a profound renewal and reorientation in the hearts and minds of his people, so that they will want to, and be empowered to, walk in God's ways. Ezekiel's thought here moves along lines which are close to those found in the prophet Jeremiah (see 31:31–34), who spoke in terms of a new covenant which God would make with his people some day and of a Torah which would be inscribed upon the human heart. Similar sentiments are also expressed by the author of Psalm 51, who prayed that God would create in him a clean heart and put a new and right (or willing) spirit within him (51:10). Elsewhere in the book of Ezekiel the same motif, but in slightly differing language, occurs in two other passages. In 18:31, Israel is enjoined by God to repent and to "get yourselves a new heart and a new spirit"; but in 37:14, God promises to place his spirit within the people. Here, as in 36:26–27, the emphasis is more on God's initiative and action. Perhaps Ezekiel became more disillusioned with human capabilities to affect significant inward change as the years went by. On the other hand, it is also true that the Bible knows of an intimate dialectic between divine and human action. Perhaps these passages in Ezekiel also want to remind us that God's people must always earnestly desire and strive in the here and now for that which in the final analysis only the Holy One is able to grant fully in the age to come. To the extent that human beings do this, they may even discover that the gulf between the ages is diminished, that that which is to come may already be here in some incipient way, that God's sanctuary is already among us, at least in some small measure, and that God's sovereign rule has begun to replace the kingdoms of this world.

CAN THESE BONES LIVE? (37:1–14)

This is perhaps the best known passage of the entire Book of Ezekiel. The graphic imagery of the vision has inspired countless artists through the ages, from the painters of the ancient synagogue of Dura-Europos in Babylon to the composers of Negro spirituals in modern America. We do not know when Ezekiel had this vision, but on the basis of its content a date some time after the final destruction of Jerusalem in 586 B.C. seems most likely. At any rate, one day Ezekiel had another one of his visions in which the Spirit of the Lord transported him into the midst of one of the alluvial plains of Babylon. Perhaps it was the same plain as the one in which he had received his initial call (note the definite article in v. 1 and compare with 3:22). Once there, he was made to walk back and forth across the plain, which was full of very dry bones, as if to allow this picture of utter death and desolation to sink in deeply. Suddenly, the eerie silence was broken by a question directed to the prophet by the Lord: "Son of man, can these bones live?" Ezekiel, perhaps a bit startled and not knowing what to make of God's question, replies somewhat noncommittally: "O my Lord Yahweh, *you* [yourself] know!" His answer is ambiguous and admits of several nuances of meaning. It could have been drawn from the traditional language of prayer as a sign of humble submission and trust.[16] In essence Ezekiel would be saying something like this: "Lord, I may not know the answer to this question, but I trust that you do." On the other hand, the same expression may also be used to indicate that something is a well-known fact beyond question or dispute.[17] Ezekiel in this case might be saying something like this: "Lord, you know very well whether they can or not [so why ask me?]!" One may legitimately doubt, however, whether the answer was obvious to Ezekiel. Nor is it likely in this context that he was making some abstract theological statement regarding the Lord's omniscience. There is yet a third way of understanding Ezekiel's answer, and that is to view it as an evasive reply.[18] Ezekiel probably knew, as any normal human being would, that dry bones do not ever come to life again. But he did not want to come right out and say so to the Lord, with whom, after all, all things were said to be possible. If that is the case, one could chide the prophet for having such little faith or for being so evasive. On the other hand, one might prefer to commend Ezekiel for not pretending to know more than he did or for not making facile confessions of faith and trust, when his heart was still gripped by feelings of doubt and disbelief. Be that as it may, the Lord accepted Ezekiel's answer and went on to give him a command to prophesy to the bones to the effect that, contrary to all human expectations, they would live again. Obediently the prophet carried out the Lord's command, ridiculous as it must have seemed to him. But lo and behold, the bones did come alive! In order to remove any ambiguities in the meaning of this vision, the Lord then provided Ezekiel with an authoritative interpretation (vv. 11–14). The vision was an answer to the feeling of despondency and despair current among the exiles. Like the anonymous poet of Psalm 88, they felt like dead bones in a grave, cut off from all life, from the Lord, and from all hope. But even where humanly speaking there is no longer any hope, God can create new hope. God can make a way out of no way! The Lord can bring forth new life, even where we can see only death (cf. 1 Sam. 2:6). The day would come when God would open the tombs of their exile and, by the power of his spirit, bring the people back to full life in their own homeland.

Before we leave this marvelous passage, we should note the central role which the Hebrew word *rûaḥ* plays in this text. It occurs no fewer than ten

---

16. The second person perfect of the verb "to know" with the independent form of the second person pronoun along with various objects occurs for instance in Pss. 139:2; 142:3; 1 Kings 8:39; and 2 Sam. 7:20. Sometimes the idiom is also used in declarations of innocence, such as in Pss. 40:9; 69:5; Jer. 12:3; and Jer. 15:15—which nuance however would not make much sense in our Ezekiel passage, since Ezekiel does not have to affirm his innocence about anything.

17. Examples of this use of the formula, though between two human partners, may be found in Gen. 30:26, 29; 31:6; 44:27; Exod. 32:22; Num. 20:14; Josh. 14:6; 2 Sam. 17:8; and 1 Kings 2:5.

18. That the formula admits of such a possibility is suggested by 2 Kings 9:11, where Jehu uses it in order to avoid giving a direct and truthful answer to a question posed by his fellow soldiers.

times in these fourteen verses, with varying nuances which embrace virtually the whole gamut of meanings which the term has in the Hebrew Bible. In verse 1, *rûaḥ* refers to the spirit of the Lord as the source of visionary rapture and prophetic inspiration. The term *rûaḥ* may also denote the life-giving breath or spirit coming from God, which creates living beings out of inanimate matter (cf. vv. 5, 6, 8, 9, 10 and cf. Gen. 2:4b–7 or Ps. 104:29–30). In v. 9, the term *rûaḥ* occurs in the plural and refers to the four winds of heaven. Finally, in verse 11 a suffixed form of *rûaḥ* clearly refers to Yahweh's spirit as the ultimate source of life in the full range of both its physical as well as its spiritual connotations. That these dimensions should never be separated too far, as religious people are sometimes tempted to do, is perhaps another lesson of which Ezekiel's vision would remind us.

THE TWO NATIONS SHALL BECOME ONE (37:15–28)

The vision of the dry bones in the preceding section had spoken of the restoration of the people of Israel in their own land. The last part of chapter 37 elaborates on this promise by providing some further details, most of which had already been alluded to in one way or another in previous chapters, especially chapters 34 and 36. What is new in this section, however, is the prophetic symbolic act signifying the reunification of the nation. Ezekiel took two pieces of wood, inscribed respectively with the names of the tribes of Judah and Ephraim, and grasped them with his hand in such a manner that the two pieces appeared to be one. This was to represent symbolically that the ancient political divisions of the people of Israel into a southern and a northern kingdom, with separate ruling houses, would not be resurrected in the coming restoration. There is a good deal of evidence in the Old Testament to suggest that the political division of the kingdom of David, following the death of Solomon in 922 B.C., was never accorded binding religious validity by many Israelites. The prophets in particular moved freely across the borders of the two kingdoms and continued to address the inhabitants of both as one people under God. Ezekiel himself reserved the use of the name Israel for the entire people of God, never designating the former Northern Kingdom by that name. Consequently it is not surprising that part of God's future work of restoration will entail the healing and overcoming of ancient animosities and divisions among his people. Various elements are utilized in this passage to underscore this reunification. Brought back home to one land, the people of God will serve one God, around one sanctuary, as one nation, under one shepherd or ruler, just as it had been in the days of David their king. It should be noted that while a messianic motif is present in this passage, it is a rather muted one. Ezekiel and his disciples were not necessarily looking forward to the restoration of the Davidic monarchy. David in this passage is more an ideal symbol of Israelite unity than a specific past or future historical figure. The final goal of God's future activity was his tabernacling presence among his restored people. God's sanctuary, which

God himself once had to destroy and remove from Jerusalem (chaps. 8—11), and which for a season had taken up temporary abode in Babylon (see 11:16), would again be permanently located among God's people as a symbol of the restored covenant between God and people.

The theme of the restoration of God's tabernacling presence in Israel, which is briefly alluded to in vv. 26–28, is more fully developed in chapters 40—48 which, however, fall outside of the limits of this essay. For a discussion of the meaning and significance of these final chapters of the Book of Ezekiel the reader is referred to the essay by Moshe Greenberg which follows.[19]

---

19. It is quite possible that chaps. 40—48 once followed immediately upon chap. 37, before this arrangement was altered by the insertion of chaps. 38—39. In support of such an arrangement, one could cite the fact that 37:26–28 forms a more natural transition to chaps. 40—48 than to chaps. 38—39, and that at least one ancient MS (Papyrus Codex 967) exhibits in fact such an arrangement. Cf. Floyd V. Filson, "The Omission of Ezekiel 12:26–28 and 36:23b–38 in Codex 967," *JBL* 62 (1943) 27–32.

17

The Design and Themes of Ezekiel's Program of Restoration

MOSHE GREENBERG

Although Ezekiel's vision of the return and resettlement of Israel in postexilic times had no effect on subsequent events, his prescriptions for those events display his lofty conception of a prophet's responsibility in an age of ruin.

This essay argues two propositions: (1) The last division of the Book of Ezekiel (chaps. 40—48) is arranged according to a design which, while not *schulgerecht* ("rule-bound" in the sense of nineteenth-century German preaching[1]), follows principles of composition familiar from other biblical and ancient Near Eastern literature; (2) its topics cohere and serve a single overriding purpose. The inference from these propositions is that it is the product of a single mind (and hand) and that, as carrying forward ideas and values found in the preceding prophecies, it may reasonably be attributed to their author, the priest-prophet Ezekiel. My arguments do not depend on this or that solution to the considerable textual and philological difficulties of these chapters; they rest on clear passages or on what may be (and has been) gathered from unclear ones. (Chapter and verse numbers refer to the Book of Ezekiel unless otherwise attributed.)

THE SETTING IN LIFE AND IN EZEKIEL'S PROPHECY

Two passages foreshadow the major themes of Ezekiel's program of restoration and show it to be consequential upon his previous oracles:

For in my holy mountain, in the high mountain of Israel . . . there shall all the

---

1. On this concept see Alexander Altmann, "The New Style of Preaching in Nineteenth-Century German Jewry," in Alexander Altmann, ed., *Studies in Nineteenth-Century Jewish Intellectual History* (Cambridge: Harvard University Press, 1964), pp. 65–116, esp. pp. 65–68.

house of Israel worship me, all of them, in the land; there I will accept them, and
there I will require your contributions and your choice offerings, with all your
holy things. (20:40)

In an angry conclusion of a doom oracle, God rejects the plan of the exiles
to renew sacrificial worship in Babylonia by announcing the conditions of
such a renewal: only in the land of Israel, only on his holy mountain, and
only when the entire nation is reconstituted on its soil. Then he will not only
accept his people (that is, their tenders of worship), but also he will require of
them the holy offerings that signify his reconciliation with them.[2]

They shall follow my rules and carefully obey my laws, and [so] dwell in the land
that I gave to my servant Jacob. . . . They shall dwell in it . . . forever, with my
servant David their chief forever. I will make for them a covenant of well-being;
it shall be a covenant forever with them . . . and I will set my sanctuary in their
midst forever. My tabernacle shall be over them; I will be their God and they
shall be my people. And the nations shall know that I, YHWH, sanctify Israel,
when my sanctuary is in their midst forever. (37:24b–28)

Thus the prophet sums up his prophecies of restoration in chapters 34—37:
The hearts of the people will be bent to observe God's laws; as a result they
will possess their patrimony forever under God's pious chief. The five-fold
repetition of "forever" stresses the irreversibility of the new dispensation.
Unlike God's past experiment with Israel, the future restoration will have a
guarantee of success; its capstone will be God's sanctifying presence dwelling
forever in his sanctuary amidst his people. The vision of the restored temple
(and God's return to it) in chapters 40—48 follows as a proleptic corroboration of these promises.

As when dooming Israel, Ezekiel used the language of the covenant curses
found at the end of the Book of Leviticus (chap. 26), so when describing their
future happiness he uses the idiom of the blessings found there. According to
the priestly view, the climax of the Sinai event was the provision made for
God's residence among the Israelites in the tabernacle. "Let them make me
a sanctuary," says God to Moses before showing him the design of the
tabernacle, "that I may dwell in their midst" (Exod. 25:8; 30:45). Agreeably,
the culmination of the series of blessings promised Israel for its keeping the
terms of the covenant reads: "I will set my tabernacle in your midst . . . I will
walk about in your midst, and I will be your God and you shall be my
people" (Lev. 26:11–12). In terms unmistakably related to this priestly ideal,
Ezekiel first proclaims God's resolve to reestablish his presence again in
Israel and then sets out his blueprint for so doing.

Biblical tradition regards Moses as the mediator of Israel's divine constitu-

---

2. I argue for the integrity of this chapter in my *Ezekiel 1—20*, AB (Garden City, N.Y.:
Doubleday & Co., 1983), pp. 376ff. Walther Eichrodt contends that all the ritual-legal detail of
Ezekiel 40—48 is alien to the prophet's vision of restoration and is inauthentic (*Ezekiel*, OTL
[Philadelphia: Westminster Press, 1970], pp. 555f., 563f., 579f.); but this passage, which looks
forward to the renewal of the sacrificial cult and which Eichrodt allows to be authentic, contra-
dicts his contention.

tion, the Torah; it recognizes no other legislator—excepting Ezekiel. How are we to account for this exception? The position of the Babylonian exiles was analogous to that of the "exiled" (alien and homeless) Israelites in Egypt and the wilderness. Impotent, Israel's only hope was its God whose will (so the prophet declared) was to demonstrate his power in the sight of all mankind by redeeming Israel and settling it in its land. On its part Israel was called to devotion to its God. Thus the first redemption, the Exodus, was accompanied by the stipulations of the covenant that described the righteous behavior required from Israel in order to be a holy nation, worthy of having God as its covenant partner. Centuries later these requirements stood unchanged. Israel's flouting of them had led to a catastrophe, but it could be remedied if Israel obeyed them in the future. God's resolve to replace Israel's "heart of stone" with a "heart of flesh" (36:26) assured that that condition would be met. But the vehicles and guardians of God's indwelling presence—the temple, its rites, and its personnel—had proved inadequate. The terrible vision of Ezekiel 8—11 showed the temple precincts and gatehouses invaded by idolatry; and the most sacred part of the court, the space between the altar and the porch of the temple, occupied by laymen worshiping the sun. The priests had failed utterly to keep guard over the sacred ordinances (22:26). Therefore, God had good grounds for deliberately polluting the already desecrated temple (9:7) and abandoning it (10:18–19; 11:22–23). The lesson of the failed experiment must be put into effect by revision of these sacred institutions. As Moses spelled out the meaning of "a holy nation" to an unformed people just liberated from Egypt, so Ezekiel specified the needful changes in the vessels and symbols of God's presence in the future commonwealth of those near redemption from the Babylonian exile. Analogy of situation produced similar prophetic roles.

THE STYLE OF CHAPTERS 40—48

Like the instructions of the Torah, those of Ezekiel are formulated as utterances of God to the prophet and through him to Israel; hence the recurrent messenger-formula "Thus said Lord YHWH" in 43:18; 44:6, 9; 45:9, 18; 46:1, 16; 47:13 (a commonplace opening formula in the prophetic literature, absent from the instructions of the Torah). The singular temple vision of chapters 40—42 has a framework like that of the vision in chapters 8—11, in which the prophet is "brought" from place to place to see certain things. After being firmly established in chapter 40, this framework fades in the next two chapters (41:1; 42:1, 15), to reappear in 43:1, 5; 44:1, 4; 46:19, 21; 47:1, 2. The style varies in accord with the variety of topics: the vision of the temple and prescriptions of rites, of sacred offices, of boundaries, and of land allotments. But the author of Ezekiel 40—48 did not invent these styles; he lived after centuries of Israelite literary creativity and disposed of models for most of these topics. Examples are found in Hebrew Scriptures, and some familiarity with them is necessary to avoid error in judging Ezekiel's work.

Instructions for making the desert tabernacle are found in Exodus 25—30;

the narrative describing its building is in Exodus 35—40; the narrative description of the building of Solomon's temple is in 1 Kings 6; 7:13–51. None are exactly similar in style to Ezekiel 40—42, which is neither instruction for nor narrative of building, but a vision of an already built complex. Yet useful observations can be made from the first three for appreciating the last.

1. In itemizing, there is no preferred order. The prescription for building the tabernacle proceeds outward from the furniture of the holy place (starting with the most holy object, the ark), to the tent that houses it, to the outer altar, to the court—in descending order of sanctity. Next come items whose description includes the priests and their activity, in no obvious order. The narrative of building the tabernacle reorganizes the items so that the tent comes first, then the furniture it houses, then the outer equipment, and the court. The narrative of Solomon's temple itemizes in several clusters: the basic dimensions and divisions of the structure (1 Kings 6:2–10); its decor, highlighting its splendor (1 Kings 6:15–35); its copperwork, supervised by Hiram from Tyre (1 Kings 7:13–47); and lastly, a bare list of gold or gilded furnishings (1 Kings 7:48–50).

Critics diverge in their assessment of these phenomena. Some systematically rearrange the text according to some logical principle; others explain the disorder by assuming that later glosses or editorial accretions disturbed an originally simple and orderly text. Yet others acknowledge we know too little about the practice of ancient scribes to be dogmatic: "ancient specifications need not have been as orderly as modern."[3]

2. The style and contents of such catalogues are not uniform. Homogeneity or consistency was not characteristic (apparently not an aim) of biblical writing. The narrative describing the building of the tabernacle is the most monotonous of the three—a sequence of bare sentences formulated as "he made this" or "did that."[4] Yet in Exod. 38:8 notice is given of the origin of the copper for the laver. And in Exod. 39:1–10 the number of the verbs vacillates between singular and plural with little pattern (but with good reason, since Bezalel and his helpers are the subjects). In the instructions for making the tabernacle there is variety. Although the prevailing pattern presents God as "I" and Moses as the commanded "thou," scarcely a section fails to show a shift in the commanded: "they" (25:10; 27:8 end; 28:4–6); "you" [plural] (25:19; 30:37); passive formulation (25:31; 27:7); "he" (25:37, 39; 26:31). In several cases ancient translations and medieval manuscripts show harmonization of these "irregular" forms to the prevailing norm. As a rule, the instruction confines itself to a command to produce a given item; occasionally, however, a qualifying clause (25:16, 21) or the purpose or use of the item is added (25:14, 15, 22, 28, 30, 37). This becomes fairly regular in the instructions from 27:20 onward and is a principle of composition of all the items in chapter 30, which combine instruction for making and prescription of use or

---

3. J. A. Montgomery, *The Books of Kings*, ICC (Edinburgh: T. & T. Clark, 1951), p. 143.

4. Aside from such an apparent slip as Exod. 36:39f., in which the tenses of Exod. 28:24f. have not been converted, or 36:38, in which the tense of 26:37 has been converted, but not to imperfect consecutive.

purpose. Another shift is from verbal to nominal sentences or even bare listings, as in the description of the lamp (25:32–35) or the court (27:10–19—which taken by itself could not be identified as prescriptive).

Critics have used such vacillations in style as criteria not only for literary analysis—that is, for distinguishing material of differing origins—but, even more questionably, for deriving conclusions about the process of composition: divergent styles, shifts in grammatical construction, for example, cannot (it is asserted) have arisen from a single author. The complexity of the issue (which such criticism radically simplifies) can now be demonstrated from the Qumran Temple Scroll. This prescriptive document, in all likelihood composed by a single person or at any rate reflecting a single ideology, combines citations and harmonies of biblical passages with editorial and original matter in biblical styles. The author insouciantly juxtaposes passages of divergent styles and sometimes produces new matter showing the same kind of internal vacillations. That tensions in a text may arise out of the combining of different sources is proven by the evidence of the Temple Scroll; but the same evidence undermines the assumption that such combination indicates several stages of development, involving several hands. Moreover, since similar tensions appear in original parts of the Temple Scroll, clearly this late author did not perceive biblical style to be *schulgerecht* in the modern critics' sense. How can we be sure the ancient biblical writers perceived it any differently? Perhaps the most important conclusion to be drawn for critical methodology from the Temple Scroll is the sobering realization that if the Bible was not extant we should hardly have been able to disentangle the various strands of the Temple Scroll's fabric. S.A. Kaufmann concludes his study "The Temple Scroll and Higher Criticism" thus:

> It is a legitimate and worthwhile enterprise to point out inconsistencies, duplications and other irregularities in a biblical text and to compare texts in terms of their language, forms, literary structures and contents. But, except where there are many substantial coincident reasons to suspect that all is not whole, the reconstruction of redaction history on the basis of such ... [phenomena] promises to be nothing more than so much wasted effort.[5]

Legislation makes up the bulk of the Torah; in style and content Ezekiel 43—48 is particularly close to the priestly materials in Leviticus. Critics have long used the criterion of tensions for literary-historical analyses of such material. For example, M. Noth is of the opinion that Lev. 22:27ff. consists of a "medley" of singular and plural, second and third person sentences, "extremely disconnected fragmentary sentences, strung together"—despite his observation of "key words" such as "without blemish" and "well pleasing."[6] Indeed this passage is not as form-bound as others, but can such features as Noth mentions in themselves provide a basis for concluding plural

---

5. *HUCA* 53 (1982) 29–43; citation on p. 43.
6. *Leviticus*, OTL (Philadelphia: Westminster Press, 1965), p. 163.

authorship and temporal diversity? A look at comparable extrabiblical ancient Near East compositions is enlightening.

A shift from "I" to the speaker's name (e.g., YHWH) is often regarded as a sign of editing—namely, the later attribution of an originally anonymous passage to "I."[7] But such a shift is common in ancient treaties[8] and instructions, where it has rightly aroused no suspicion. Even in so finely drafted a document as the bilingual treaty of Ramses II and Hattusilis such shifts occur; in the Hittite version the scribe did not avoid it even where (for us!) it sows confusion:

> If an enemy from abroad comes against the land of Egypt and Rea-mashesha mai Amana, the king of the land of Egypt, your brother, sends to Hattusilis, the king of the Hatti land, his brother, saying: "Come here to help me against him"—lo! Hattusilis, the king of the Hatti land, shall send his foot soldiers . . . and shall slay my enemies.[9]

In the Aramaic Sefire treaties an unpredictable vacillation occurs between second person singular and plural in III, lines 4, 16, 23 (*šqrtm*, plural) and in lines 9, 14, 19, 20, and 27 (*šqrt*, singular). As in scriptural cases, the cause is ambiguity respecting the addressee—in this case a king and his descendants.[10]

The closest similarities to the style of biblical legislative texts are found in the Hittite "Instructions for Temple Officials" and "Instructions for the Commander of the Border Guards."[11] The temple officials are instructed either in third person commands ("let those who prepare the daily loaves be clean") or in direct address ("You who are temple officials, if you do not . . ."). In paragraphs 2 and 3 a meditation on collective punishment interrupts the instructions in order to prepare the reader for punishment clauses beginning in paragraph 4 (though collective punishment first appears in paragraph 6; cf. 9, 13, 18, 19). Obviously such a meditation belongs to another "life context," yet the author appropriated it and inserted it amidst heterogeneous matter for its explanation of the punishment of errant temple officials. Markedly biblical in style is the "medley" in paragraph 5: "Or if you . . . (followed by several coordinate "if yous") you will be held responsible. . . . Do not divide it! He who divides it shall be killed; there shall be no recourse for him" (cf. also in paragraph 10). A notable shift of persons occurs between paragraphs

7. M. Smith, "Pseudepigraphy in the Israelite Literary Tradition," in *Pseudepigrapha I*, Entretiens sur l'antiquité classique 18 (Vandoeuvres-Genève: Fondation Hardt, 1972), 201ff.

8. J. B. Pritchard, ed., *ANET*, 3d ed. with sup. (Princeton: Princeton University Press, 1969), p. 533 (Ashurnirari-Mati'ilu, col. v); p. 533f. (Esarhaddon-Baal, col. iii). D. J. McCarthy, *Treaty and Covenant*, AnBib 21 (Rome: Pontifical Biblical Institute, 1963), p. 181 (Zidanta-Pilliya [Sun-I]); p. 182 (Mursilis II-Niqmepa, line 10 [king-I]); p. 184 (Tudhaliyas IV-Ulmi-Teshub, rev. 5, lines 15ff.).

9. *ANET*, p. 202.

10. J. A. Fitzmyer, *The Aramaic Inscriptions of Sefire*, BibOr 19 (Rome: Pontifical Biblical Institute, 1967), pp. 96–100.

11. *ANET*, pp. 207–11. For the latter composition I have also consulted E. von Schuler, *Hethitische Dienstanweisungen für Hof-und Staatsbeamte*, AfOSup 10 (Graz, 1957), pp. 41ff. Dr. Aharon Kempinski kindly instructed me on many points of Hittite grammar and style.

18 and 19. The former addresses "You who are the gods' cowherds" and retains this address throughout. The latter starts with "you" (the cowherds) but within the sentence switches to "they" (expressly identified with the cowherds); "they" continues to the end.

The "Instructions for the Commander of the Border Guards" illustrates ancient concepts of order. A wide variety of duties is listed in them, including construction work for which measurements and specifications are given. Although the discourse is predominantly in third person, often enough direct address breaks in (quite unexpectedly). In the excerpt translated in *ANET* (p. 210f.) we note the following: the draftsmanship is (to our taste) very loose; it is repetitive with little concern for consolidation. Thus the topics of the first two paragraphs ("In the town," "Furthermore") are alike (responsibility for keeping temples in repair). At the end of the third paragraph (p. 211) the duty of appointing cult officials is repeated (from the first paragraph)—now in the third person plural ("they shall"). Column *iii* continues the third person formulation, though in the first sentence a plural imperative appears ("Provide for them now!"—for which von Schuler adduces a variant: "they shall provide"). The second paragraph of column *iii* ("The rites") shows tiresome repetition, typical of Hittite rituals. The next paragraph ("Furthermore") deals with dispensing justice. It is followed, however, by a paragraph combining admonitions to respect festivals, clerics, and the gods, reverting to the topic of justice only at its end.[12] The last paragraph, still about justice, from the temporal viewpoint precedes all the paragraphs that have dealt with the subject, since its setting is the moment of the officer's arrival at a town. Clearly official Hittite instructions were not formulated according to our notions of good topical order or consistency of viewpoint.[13]

The study of the legal taxonomy (German, *Systematik*) of Mesopotamian law collections has undergone a significant change over time, a change that invites emulation by biblical scholarship. Fifty years ago it was considered enough to say of the greatest of these collections (the Laws of Hammurabi):

> For us at this time the *Systematik* of the Laws is impenetrable. The legal material seems to be organized merely in accord with practical exigencies and from a superficial viewpoint; the use and reworking of older complexes of written laws also patently influenced the arrangement. All attempts made heretofore to find a basis for the arrangement in strict logic or dogmatic principles must be judged as failures.[14]

A generation later, after patient observation of the native contours of Mesopotamian legal draftsmanship, H. Petschow offered a more constructive, nuanced interpretation of the facts. The main basis for classification is not juristic principle but subject—matters dealing, for example, with a given

---

12. Kempinski surmises that the principle of respect for various authorities accounts for the association of the varied subjects of this paragraph.

13. To be sure, one could argue that the lack of order indicates later additions, but how can one support that argument?

14. M. San Nicolò, *Beitrage zur Rechtsgeschichte im Bereiche der Keilschriftlichen Rechtsquellen* (Oslo: H. Aschehoug & Co., 1931), pp. 71f.

life-situation or object are grouped (crownlands, fields, obligations, merchants, family, etc.). Within a group, other guides to arrangement can be discerned: "chronology," that is, a real or potential sequence of events, the social standing of persons or the worth of the subject, frequency, contrast. As a feature alien to the modern critic Petschow underlines "disturbances of structural clarity" by "insertions" caused by association of ideas, or attraction through catchwords (Noth's "key-words"), or the endeavor to "round off" the treatment of a subject.[15]

Modern judgment of Ezekiel 40—48 has been strongly influenced by the thorough, disintegrating (though in its way "conservative") analysis of H. Gese.[16] Gese regarded all the stylistic features listed above, so offensive to modern standards of order and consistency yet common to all of ancient Near Eastern literature, as nothing but criteria for identifying glosses, accretions, strata ("Zadokite stratum," "nāśī' stratum") in these chapters. Exhibiting an isolationism all too prevalent in European biblical scholarship, Gese took no account of ancient scribal practice so abundantly documented outside the Bible.[17] In the following pages a survey of Ezekiel 40—48 is attempted, keeping that practice firmly in view. One result may be stated here: Viewed alongside comparable writings of the ancient Near East, biblical prescriptive and descriptive texts, including those of Ezekiel, show a comparable level of rationalization and organization. Such lapses as occasionally appear are not outside—indeed are quite inside—the bounds of contemporary and cognate standards of practice known to us from native sources.

THE DIVISIONS OF EZEKIEL 40—48

Ezekiel 40—48 has three main divisions:
(1) 40:1—43:12, the vision of the future temple;
(2) 44:1—46:24, "enterings and exitings"—rules governing access to the temple and activity in it;
(3) 47:13—48:35, the apportionment of the land among the people.

Two passages serve as transitions: 43:13–27, on the altar; formally attached to what precedes, it links the static vision of (1) with the activity prescribed in (2); 47:1–11, the vivifying water issuing from the temple; formally attached to what follows, it links the temple (1) and (2) to the land (3).

1. The Vision of the Future Temple (40:1—43:12)

Mention of the destruction of the city (Jerusalem) in the opening date formula (40:1) presages the antithesis between the following vision and the

---

15. H. Petschow, "Zur Systematik und Gesetztechnik im Codex Hammurabi," ZA 57 (1965) 146–72; idem, "Zur 'Systematik' in den Gesetzen von Eschnunna," in J. A. Ankum et al., eds., *Symbolae . . . M. David dedicatae* (Leiden: E. J. Brill, 1968), 2:131–43.

16. Hartmut Gese, *Der Verfassungsentwurf des Ezechiel (Kap. 40—48)*, BHT 25 (Tübingen: J. C. B. Mohr, 1957).

17. This is equally true of the important commentaries of Eichrodt, *Ezekiel;* J. W. Wevers, *Ezekiel* (London: Thomas Nelson & Sons, 1969); and Walther Zimmerli, *Ezechiel*, BKAT 13/1–2 (Neukirchen-Vluyn: Neukirchener Verlag, 1969), esp. pp. 1240–49.

awful event it was meant to remedy. Was the date significant? We know of no event in the year 25 of the exile (571 B.C.E.) with which to connect this vision; but 25 years is half a jubilee ("the year of release," 46:17), and the number and its double, 50, and multiples thereof (100, 500, 5,000, 10,000, 25,000) recur ahead in measurements of the temple and the land. As for "(year) 14 (after the city had been smitten)"—the number is 2×7, and 7 is a key number in the cultic realm (cf. 43:26; 44:26; 45:23). The month called "the beginning of the year" might be either Nisan (spring) or Tishri (fall); the tenth day of each resounds: of Nisan—with the start of the watch over the passover lamb (Exod. 12:2f.), an anticipation of liberation; of Tishri—with the Day of Atonement (Lev. 16:29), when the year of release was proclaimed (Lev. 25:9; but note that neither appears in Ezekiel's cultic calendar). The numbers beg to be interpreted symbolically; perhaps the conjunction of them stimulated this vision of renewal and reconciliation.

An account of the second visionary transportation of the prophet to Jerusalem follows (40:2f.)—the first being in order to witness its abominations and its destruction (chaps. 8—11). Past disaster and future restoration are again counterpoised. The site to which Ezekiel is taken is the temple mount, raised to extraordinary height (as in Isa. 2:2; cf. Zech. 14:10)—a physical token of its supreme value. There he sees "what looked like a city"— evidently an allusion to the walled complex of temple buildings (cf. the prophet's gradual perception of the "chariot" vision, 1:4ff.). A celestial being "who shone like copper" greets the prophet with a command to observe in order to tell Israel the measurements he is about to show him. This "man" will serve as the prophet's guide till the appearance of the divine Majesty (cf. 43:6, in which the "man" is supplanted).

The tour of the temple area follows, moving, generally speaking, from outside inward and returning to its starting point.[18] Beginning with the perimeter wall around the entire complex, the guide takes its height and thickness, then gives in great detail the measurements of the east gatehouse in the wall leading to the outer temple court. It is a "fortified" gate[19] with guardrooms flanking the passageway on each side. Similar gatehouses are measured on the north and south stretches of the wall; all are attained by a seven-step staircase. The space of the outer court, onto which the gatehouses give, is measured by the distance between each of them and an inner set of gatehouses opposite them that give upon the inner court.

The prophet is then taken to each of the gatehouses of the inner court; they are of the same dimensions, but are eight steps higher than the outer court. Installations for slaughtering sacrifice are located in one of the inner gatehouses, and priestly chambers are located in the inner court alongside two of them. The dimensions of the inner court are given (a square of 100

---

18. The architectural details of the temple buildings and the extrabiblical data illuminating them are set forth in T. A. Busink, *Der Temple von Jerusalem, II: von Ezechiel bis Middot* (Leiden: E. J. Brill, 1980), pp. 709–75.

19. André Parrot, *The Temple of Jerusalem* (London: SCM Press, 1957), p. 63. See also C. G. Howie, *The Date and Composition of Ezekiel*, JBLMS 4 (Philadelphia: Society of Biblical Literature, 1950), pp. 44ff.

cubits), and the great altar within it is mentioned, but its description is left for later (40:5–47).

Next comes the temple proper, attained by a stairway of ten steps. Like Solomon's temple, it has three parts on an east-west axis: the porch, the sanctuary (RSV, "the nave"), and the holy of holies. The entrances to each part are successively narrower. Various additional buildings are described: the sidechambers attached to the temple on the three sides, the vacant space at the back (west) of the temple, and the large building behind it. The outer dimensions of all these structures are then given (2 x 100 cubits square; see 40:48—41:15a).

The decorations and woodwork of the temple are next taken up. It is unclear whether the "wooden altar," which the "man" calls "the altar that is before YHWH" (41:22) represents the table that is of showbread or the small inner altar of incense (41:15b–26).

The prophet is led back to the outer court in the vicinity of the building and space behind the temple, where two sets of "holy chambers" to the north and south of the building are located. The description of these chambers is extremely obscure (42:2–12). Only their purpose is clear: to provide a place for the priests to eat sacrificial meat and to deposit such meat, and for the priests to remove their holy vestments before going into the outer (laity's) court (42:13–14). From the apparent contradiction between the location of the "holy chambers" in the outer court and the arrival of priests in that court only on leaving these chambers, it may be inferred that they bordered on the inner court and extended into the immediately adjacent area in the outer court, thus serving as a transit zone between the two.[20]

Then the prophet is led back outside the perimeter wall and is shown its external measurements, enclosing the entire temple complex and "separating the sacred from the profane," a square of 500 cubits (42:15–20).

The temple having been "finished," as it were, it is ready to receive God's presence. The prophet is brought to the east gate (from which he exited to see the measurements of the wall) to behold the awesome apparition of the divine Majesty roaring into view, entering through the gate and filling the temple. The prophet identifies the apparition with the Majesty that he had seen in the vision of Jerusalem's destruction (chaps. 8—11), once again indicating the correspondence between the two (it was precisely through the east gate that the Majesty had left the Solomonic temple in 10:19). From within, the Majesty addresses the prophet: "This is the place of my throne and this is the place of the soles of my feet where I will dwell amidst the Israelites forever" (43:7).[21] A severe rebuke of the people of Israel follows for having "polluted my holy name" (the temple in which God's name "abode;" cf. Ps. 74:6b) by their harloting (a metaphor for idolatry, 6:9) and by the corpses of their kings, since only a wall separated the royal grounds (in which

---

20. Menahem Haran, *miqdāš yeḥezqel* ("Ezekiel's temple"), *Enṣiqlopedia Miqra'it* (Jerusalem: Bialik Institute, 1968), 5:col. 351.

21. On the two symbols of God's throne and footstool, see Menahem Haran, *Temples and Temple Service in Ancient Israel* (Oxford: Clarendon Press, 1978), pp. 251–59.

kings were at times buried: 2 Kings 21:18) from the Solomonic temple precinct. (Pollution of the sanctuary is the concern underlying most of the ordinances of the next division of the program, while the issue of juxtaposition of royal and sacred land will be resolved in the last division.) Perorating, God commands the prophet to tell the people of Israel the plan of the temple that they may be ashamed (when they learn from it how faulty was their past conduct in the sanctuary) and carefully execute it.[22] The repetitious peroration includes some terms that look backward ("plan, design") and some that look forward to the coming "laws" of the temple and "its exitings and its enterings" (43:1–9).

The conclusion of the division imitates a common closing (and opening) formula of priestly writings (Lev. 14:32, 57). Its wording echoes parts of 42:20 ("roundabout, holy") and 40:2 ("on top of the mountain").[23]

The summary declaration at the conclusion of the temple vision, "the entire area of its enclosure shall be holy of holies" (43:12), epitomizes the main themes: separation and gradation.[24] The perimeter wall separates the holy from the profane (42:20). The gatehouses and courts are described in profuse detail; almost half the text of this division is given over to them. The massive size of the gatehouses verges on caricature: their dimensions (25 x 50 cubits) exceed those of the main hall of the temple (20 x 40 cubits); their length is half that of the inner court (100 cubits)! Such disproportion emphasizes the idea of controlled entry, in Ezekiel's phrase, "keeping guard over the temple" (*šmr mšmrt hbyt*, 40:45). What is being guarded is its sanctity— expressed by the rising stages of the courts and the temple platform (the sequence of stairways of seven, eight and ten steps). The temple proper expresses gradation of holiness by the successively narrowing entrances to its inner parts. Along the border between the two courts rooms and zones are appointed for activities which if not properly contained might violate the grades of holiness.

There are some notable omissions. With very few exceptions, measurements are of length and breadth only; in other words, the visionary has effectively conveyed only a ground plan, bounding and describing areas in accord with his basic concern over separation and gradation. Many furnishings of the Solomonic temple and the desert tabernacle are missing: the ark and its cherubs and the lamp; the only interior furniture mentioned is an ambiguous "altar of wood." Very strange is the absence of a wall around the inner court, to which its three massive gates might stand in relation. No equivalent to the lavers or to the bronze sea appears in the outer court. Are

---

22. Is this a hint of an assumption that the future temple would be built by Israelites?

23. On the structure of this division see further Shmarjahu Talmon and Michael Fishbane, "The Structuring of Biblical Books: Studies in the Book of Ezekiel," *ASTI* 10 (1975–76) 29–53.

24. John Skinner, *The Book of Ezekiel* (London: Hodder & Stoughton, 1895), p. 413: "separation, gradation, and symmetry." Skinner confines his remarks on symmetry to a footnote on p. 419. I confess I have not managed to elicit much meaning from this feature, which is surely present to a marked extent. Skinner's exposition of the leading ideas and values of chaps. 40—48 surpasses in lucidity, sympathy, and comprehensiveness anything to be found in more recent commentators.

these omissions haphazard, or is the house emptied purposely of all objects contributing to a mythological conception of God? The latter alternative is contradicted by the presence of the wooden altar called "the table that is before YHWH," nor would it account for the absence of the lavers. (Where were priests to wash? The notion that the water issuing from the temple might serve is unlikely, for until it leaves the temple it is too thin a stream for body washing.)[25] The implications of these omissions must remain obscure. In subsequent divisions of Ezekiel's program, as we shall see, omissions cannot serve as a warrant for negative conclusions—unmentioned, therefore absent.

Transition—The Altar of Burnt Offering (43:13–27)

The temple having been measured, described, and occupied by the divine Majesty, attention turns to the dynamics of worship performed in it. A transition to the new topic is effected by the passage on the altar of burnt offering (mentioned only in 40:47b), consisting of its measurements (looking backward to division [1]) and the ritual of its consecration (looking forward to division [2]). The altar is a large structure, at least ten cubits high, consisting of three blocks, each smaller than the one below it. Its hearth bears the mysterious name 'ărî'ēl, apparently punned on in 43:15—har'ēl, "mountain of God."

The consecration ceremonies of the desert tabernacle as prescribed in Exodus 29:1–37 consisted of the investiture and anointing of the priests and the separate consecration of the altar, each lasting seven days; purgation sacrifices (ḥaṭṭā't) figure prominently in them. The priesthood of the future temple exists; occupation of the temple by the Majesty is the equivalent of its consecration (cf. the story of the consecration of the Solomonic temple, 1 Kings 8:4–11), leaving only the altar, as an object of independent dignity, to be consecrated. This is done by purgation and whole offerings (ḥaṭṭā't, 'ōlāh) whose function is to kippēr, "purge," ḥiṭṭē', "decontaminate," and ṭihher, "purify" the altar so as to make it fit for the regular worship (43:20, 22, 26).[26] These rites have nothing to do with a supposed heightened consciousness of sin in and after the exile, as some critics have thought, but with the very ancient idea that all pollutions—natural (severe genital fluxes, corpse, "leprosy"), inadvertent, as well as culpable-moral—occurring anywhere in Israel contaminated the sanctuary (e.g., Lev. 15:31; 20:3).[27] Before the altar can

---

25. The notion is Haran's, miqdaš, cols. 355f. Here and in Temples, p. 287f., Haran grounds the omission of furniture in Ezekiel's temple on historical accidents that befell the Solomonic temple (e.g., looting). This requires him to supply a couple of alternatives for the "survival" of the wooden altar in Ezekiel. What remains to be explained is why the prophet's vision of the restored temple should have been constrained by such accidents.

26. On these three verbs of purgation see Jacob Milgrom, "Atonement in the OT," IDBSup (Nashville: Abingdon Press, 1976), pp. 78ff.

27. Milgrom, "Sacrifices and Offering, OT," in ibid., pp. 763ff., esp. pp. 766ff. on the ḥaṭṭā't. He maintains his position against that of B. A. Levine, In the Presence of the Lord (Leiden: E. J. Brill, 1974), in "Israel's Sanctuary: The Priestly 'Picture of Dorian Gray,'" RB 83:390–99, reprinted in his Studies in Cultic Theology and Terminology (Leiden: E. J. Brill, 1983), pp. 75–84. For a critical survey of recent theories on atonement see B. Lang's article "kipper," in G. J. Botterweck and Helmer Ringgren, eds., TWAT 4 (Stuttgart: Kohlhammer, 1983), cols. 303ff.

acquire the sanctity that fits it for regular service, it must be "decontaminated" by the *ḥaṭṭāʾt*.

2. *"Enterings and Exitings"—Rules Governing Access to the Temple and Activity in It (44:1—46:24)*

Chapters 44—46 regulate access to the sanctuary; but this division has attracted, by natural association of ideas, paragraphs on the temple personnel, on the chief, and on the cultic calendar.

A short passage precedes the formal opening of the division in 44:4. The prophet is led again to the outer east gatehouse where he hears God's command that the gatehouse should forever be locked, inasmuch as the Majesty entered through it; however, the chief may use its vestibule for his sacrificial meals. As an extreme constraint on access—a total ban on passing through one of the gatehouses—this regulation takes precedence over the other rules of access (44:1–3).

These are formally introduced in 44:4–5: Brought before the temple by way of the north gate, the prophet falls prostrate in the presence of the Majesty. He is admonished to attend to all the laws and instructions concerning the temple, "to the entering [*mbwʾ*] of the temple with all the exitings [*mwṣʾy*] from the sanctuary." The verbs *bwʾ*, "enter," and *yṣʾ*, "exit," constantly recur in the sequel; they are key terms and indicate that the main concern of this division is to prescribe who may enter where and do what in the temple precinct.

The first topic is the temple personnel. God opens with a rebuke: It was an abominable thing that the Israelites did when they allowed uncircumcised aliens into the temple area during the performance of sacrifices, in the capacity of temple servants.[28] In future, these will be replaced by Levites—erstwhile Levite-priests who served the Israelites when they apostatized and worshiped idols. Those faithless priests will serve as gatekeepers[29] and general helpers of the laity. They will, for example, slaughter the people's sacrifices (and cook them in the kitchens located in the four corners of the outer court; see 46:21–24). Only descendants of Zadok, the hereditary priesthood of the Solomonic temple, were to continue in the privilege of altar service—for example, to have access to the inner court where the great altar stood—for the Zadokites alone guarded God's sacred things when the rest of Israel (and the non-Zadokites who served them) went astray. What can this refer to? The old critical explanation, still largely followed today, identifies the disgraced priests with those who, before the Josianic reform, served at local shrines. "Whatever the faults of these Zadokites had been—and

---

28. Reference is usually made to the Carian royal bodyguards who accompanied the king into the temple grounds (2 Kings 11) and to the Gibeonite hierodules (Josh. 9:27), but neither serves in the role spoken of by Ezekiel. We cannot verify Ezekiel's charge.

29. A priestly task in the Solomonic temple (2 Kings 12:10). Compare the responsibility of the Aaronide priests for "keeping guard over the sanctuary . . . and any outsider who encroached is to be put to death" (Num. 3:38). This only complicates understanding Ezekiel's polemic. See Haran, *Temples*, p. 96.

Ezekiel certainly does not judge them leniently (cf. 22:26)—they had at least steadfastly maintained the ideal of a central sanctuary, and in comparison with the rural clergy they were doubtless a purer and better disciplined body.[30] Doubts persist; for the desecration of the Solomonic temple is vividly described in Ezekiel 8, 11, and the dereliction of its priesthood is denounced in 22:26. The background of the desecration scenes must be the paganization of Judah under the reign of Manasseh, and the only way to dissociate the Zadokites from the cultic crimes of that age is to assume they were out of office during Manasseh's reign.[31] But if they were out of office, how could they have "kept guard over my sanctuary when the Israelites strayed from me" (44:15)? The problems of harmonizing this passage with the meager bits of history we know from other biblical sources have not been persuasively solved.[32] Ezekiel's meaning is clear: he distinguishes between Levite-priests, sons of Zadok, who serve at the altar and Levites who serve only in the outer court; this distinction is also reflected in the land allotment (see division [3]).

Rules governing the apparel, appearance, and personal status of the Zadokite priests follow immediately; compliance with them is a condition of entering the inner court to perform their office (44:17–27). They may not wear woolen clothing lest they sweat; they must deposit their sacred linen vestments in the holy chambers on leaving the inner court lest they sanctify the laity in the outer one (42:14); their head hair must be trim; they must not have drunk wine. They may marry only Israelite virgins or the widows of other priests;[33] the implication is that to marry otherwise disqualifies a priest from performing his office. The priestly duties of instructing about the sacred and the profane, the pure and the impure, and their roles as judges and guardians of the holy days come next, attracted from more general summaries of priestly conduct. Finally, they are permitted to incur corpse impurity only when the dead are closest relatives. Then they must wait two weeks before returning to serve at the altar, at which time they must purge themselves by a *ḥaṭṭā't*.[34]

---

30. Skinner, *The Book of Ezekiel*, p. 433. Also see Roland deVaux, *Ancient Israel* (New York: McGraw-Hill, 1961), p. 364; and Aelred Cody, *A History of Old Testament Priesthood*, AnBib 35 (Rome: Pontifical Biblical Institute, 1969), p. 136.

31. See J. M. Grintz, "Aspects of the History of the High Priesthood" (in Hebrew), *Zion* 23/4 (1958–59) 124ff.

32. Recent attempts include Cody, *History of Old Testament Priesthood*, pp. 166ff.; and Haran, *Temples*, pp. 103ff. For Y. Kaufmann, *The Religion of Israel* (Chicago: University of Chicago Press, 1960), p. 444 (including n. 11), Ezekiel's statements about the past in 44:6–16 are "fantasies."

33. ". . . Ezekiel's regulations as to priestly marriage seem as it were to strike an average between the restrictions imposed in the [Pentateuchal] law on ordinary priests [Lev. 21:7] and those binding on the High Priest [Lev. 21:13f]" (Skinner, *The Book of Ezekiel*, p. 438). On the omission of the high priest from Ezekiel's ranks, compare what was said about omissions on pp. 225–26, and what is said on pp. 233–36.

34. The rite of Numbers 19 purges corpse impurity in seven days; is this additional week for priests an innovation of Ezekiel (of typical stringency), or does it reflect ongoing priestly practice not recorded elsewhere?

Next the maintenance of the priesthood is provided: the gifts due to them are listed (closely related to Num. 18:8–19), others are covered by the generality "all contributions of all [kinds], of all of your contributions." To this is linked a feature of Ezekiel's land allotment, "the Contribution [of land]" in which priests and Levites have a major share. Which of the two accounts in 45:1–7 and 48:12–22 has priority exercises critics; it is clear that each version suits its context. As a detail, this account is logically subordinate to the complete scheme of chapter 48; but there is no way of knowing whether in fact the detail came to mind (and pen) first and the whole was spun out of it as a consequence, or vice versa (or another alternative). In no case is predication of a long time span between the versions or of another author justified. The "Contribution" also provides an estate for the chief, and this attracts prescriptions concerning the chief's duty to keep hands off his subjects' holdings (a rebuke) and his part in the maintenance of public worship.[35] An exhortation to keep honest weights and measures is followed by details of the taxes in kind (whose measures are specified) to be delivered to the chief as the public's "contribution"—the key word of this sequence— for the upkeep of temple sacrifices. The chief is responsible for the sacrifices on all holy days "to make purgation/expiation [lkpr] on behalf of all the house of Israel" (45:17).

The next two paragraphs, each introduced by a messenger formula ("thus said Lord YHWH" [45:18–25; 46:1–15]) list the occasions of sacrifice in two groups: annual and repeated within the year. Of major moment in the paragraph on annual occasions is, again, purgation. The cultic calendar is inaugurated on the first and seventh days of the first month with ceremonies purging the entire temple precinct.[36] The chief enters the picture with the two semiannual week-long festivals, Passover/Unleavened Bread in the spring and Booth ("the Festival," cf. 1 Kings 8:2) in the fall; he sponsors the series of festival sacrifices, of which the hattā't is always first mentioned.

The second paragraph, on the repeated holy days (new moons and sabbaths), gives equal space to the listing of sacrifices and the enterings and

---

35. Only these two aspects of the chief's role in the future community are specified, exemplifying the author's control of the principle of association. From such incidental notices it is hardly possible to draw large inferences regarding the chief's status (e.g., that he was an "apolitical Messiah"; see J. D. Levenson, *Theology of the Program of Restoration of Ezekiel 40– 48*, HSM 10 [Missoula, Mont.: Scholars Press, 1976], pp. 76–107). The less guessed about this subject the better; but if it comes to it, the best extrapolation from the scant data, even after a century of discussion, remains Skinner's, *The Book of Ezekiel*, pp. 447–61. The royal epithet *nāśī'*, favored by Ezekiel, is an archaism drawn from the priestly legislation and is typical of Ezekiel's antiquarian tendency (see Kaufmann, *Religion of Israel*, pp. 432ff., on this tendency; and Haran, "The Law Code of Ezekiel XL—XLVIII and Its Relation to the Priestly School," *HUCA* 50 [1979] 57 n. 24, on the epithet).

36. Medieval Hebrew commentators (e.g., Kimhi) identify these purgations with those of the altar consecration in 43:18–26 and both with a supposed future parallel to the week-long ceremonies inaugurating the desert tabernacle (Exodus 40; cf. 29:35f.). By thus interpreting our passage as a one-time ceremony, they obviated the contradiction that would have otherwise arisen between Ezekiel's annual temple purgation that occurs in the spring (first month) and that of Leviticus 16 (the day of atonement) that occurs in the fall.

exitings of chief and laity; the *ḥaṭṭā't* is not mentioned. The chief has the right to approach (but not enter) the inner court by way of its east gatehouse, on whose inner threshold he may worship as the sacrifices he sponsored are offered on sabbaths and new moons. Until evening on those days the gates of that gatehouse remain open, so that the laity may see the holy precinct beyond them and worship at the exterior entrance. On these occasions the chief must enter and exit by the same route, but on the annual festivals chief and laity must traverse the entire outer court, entering at the north and exiting from the south, or vice versa—perhaps (as Rashi suggests) so as to "appear before YHWH" maximally. The description of the regular daily sacrifice is attached to the foregoing, as belonging to the general topic, though neither the chief nor "enterings and exitings" are mentioned with it.

A fresh messenger formula introduces a final item about the chief (46:16–18). Endowments of crownland that he makes to his sons are their permanent holdings, but those made to his courtiers are to revert to the crown on "the year of release [the jubilee]." This (it is reiterated) is to prevent the chief from dispossessing the people from their holdings. The displaced appearance of this item (why not after 45:8f.?) may be explained thus: The matter of crownlands in 45:8f. was itself an appendage to a diversion—the matter of the chief, which entered only as an adjunct to the "contribution" theme. Once the subject of the chief was broached, however, the draftsman sought to stay close to his main interest—activity in the temple—by adducing only such prescriptions concerning the chief as related to the temple. Only after this diversion had exhausted itself did the draftsman round off the theme of the chief with this detail on crownlands which he deemed unsuitable for earlier insertion.

The division ends with the prophet being shown the temple kitchens: the priests' kitchen, behind (west of) the "holy chambers," for preparing their portions of the sacred offerings to be eaten (42:13 informed us that they eat in the "holy chambers"), lest they sanctify the laity by taking these portions into the outer court (cf. 42:14, the same apprehension respecting the priests' vestments); and, in the four corners of the outer court, the lay kitchens—these are described in detail—where the nonpriestly temple servants are to cook the portions of offerings eaten by the people (where they eat is not said; perhaps in the thirty chambers that surround the outer court, 40:17). This passage would not have been out of place after the description of the "holy chambers" (i.e., after 42:14), especially in view of the particulars given concerning the lay kitchens, in style so like division 1. Considerations of "chronology" may account for the (dis?)-placement: in the sequence of sacrifice—the central concern of division 2—the preparation of the meat and its consumption is the last stage. But if that is so, one may ask, why was the description of the "holy chambers" not placed here too? Perhaps the "holy chambers" and the kitchens did originally constitute a literary unit, in which their description and their use were combined. When it came to arranging the two divisions according to the criterion of assigning the static-descriptive material to division 1 and the dynamic-prescriptive to division 2, this unit (a misfit) was broken up in such a way that the passage on the "holy chambers," long and overwhelmingly static-descriptive, was put in division 1, while the shorter passage on the kitchens, in which the dynamic-use element was proportionally greater, was put according to its "chronology" at the end of division 2. Here one can feel something of the strain this heterogeneous material put on its arranger. There is no evidence for dissociating arranger from author (Ezekiel), but the complex associative linkage of this division especially indicates that its composition was in stages.

Transition: The Vivifying Water Issuing from the Temple (47:1–12)

A bridge connects the account of the activity in the temple with the last division, on the apportionment of the land: the description of a walk on which the prophet is taken along a miraculous stream of water issuing from the temple and fructifying the desert as it makes its way to the Dead Sea. The celestial "man," who has reappeared to lead the prophet away from the temple mount, measures the astonishing growth of the stream from a thin bubbling under the outer east gate to an unfordable river after a 4000-cubit flow through a desert! Idealism and practicality are combined in the "man's" account of how the water will de-salt the Dead Sea, turning it into a rich fishing ground, while leaving salt pans in the south. Unlike the general promises of fertility in 34:26f. and 36:8ff., this vision specifically connects temple and fertility[37] and singles out for transformation the most barren tract of land—the wilderness of Judah—and the body of water most inhospitable to life, the Dead Sea, a dramatic exhibition of God's beneficent presence in the temple.

3. The Apportionment of the Land among the People (47:13—48:35)

This third and last division of Ezekiel's program comprises three topics (formally each is introduced by the demonstrative "this" or "these"): the external boundaries of the future land of Israel (47:13–23), the internal allocation of territory among the tribes (48:1–29), and the city and its gates (48:30–35). How does this division relate to Ezekiel's main concern? For the preservation of the temple's sanctity (to be fit as an abode of the Majesty of God) it must be separated from the rest of the settled territory and guarded by a cordon of priests and Levites (recall 43:8). This entails a plan for the distribution of the population within the bounds of the future land.

The boundaries of 47:13–21 are approximately those of Num. 34:2–12, "the land of Canaan with its various boundaries." It thus excludes on the north the Aramean kingdoms conquered by David; on the east, the Transjordanian domains of the ancient tribes of Reuben, Gad, and half-Manasseh; and on the south, Edomite territory down to Ezion-Geber, once part of the

---

37. A connection richly developed in early Judaism. See Raphael Patai, *Man and Temple* (London: Thomas Nelson & Sons, 1947), pp. 85–91.

Judahite kingdom. The future land would thus leave out of account both the conquests of the monarchy and the territories actually settled in preexilic times; restoration involves adjustment to the boundaries of the ideal, original promised land. The prescription of v. 21: "You shall divide this land for you, for the tribes of Israel" is significantly qualified by v. 22, which grants hitherto landless resident aliens the right to landed property within their host tribe. As a general ordinance applying to all tribes equally, it precedes the detailed allocation that follows.

History is ignored not only with respect to boundaries but also in the disposition of the population; the basis for allocating the land is the ancient twelve-tribe system (as in the oracles of chap. 37 ignoring the dispersal and disappearance of the non-Judahite Israelites). Each tribe is to receive an equal share of land (and be, presumably, of equal population), not unequal, as in the irregular allocations of Joshua (in the case of the Joseph tribes, controversial; see Josh. 18:14ff.). God prescribes latitudinal strips across the breadth of the land, in which he settles, from north to south and in this order, the tribes of Dan (born to the concubine Bilhah), Asher (of the concubine Zilpah), Naphtali (of Bilhah), Manasseh and Ephraim (sons of Joseph, son of the matriarch Rachel), Reuben, Judah (of the matriarch Leah); then the "Contribution" (see below); then Benjamin (of Rachel), Simeon, Issachar, Zebulun (of Leah), and Gad (of Zilpah). The allocation of seven tribes north of the "Contribution" (containing the temple) and five south of it reflects the eccentric location of Jerusalem. Sons of concubines are located at the extremes, sons of matriarchs closer to the holy "Contribution." The most striking departure from preexilic order is the transposition of Judah and Benjamin, as though the royal tribe (Judah) were purposely removed to the place of the smallest (to humble it?). The scheme of latitudinal strips of equal size, while ideal, does not leave geographical considerations out of account, as modern commentators aver; on the contrary, given the four longitudinal zones of Cisjordan (coast, foothills, mountains, Jordan valley) the only way of parceling it equally is by latitudinal strips.[38]

The "Contribution" is so called because each tribe must surrender something so as to leave a strip of land 25,000 cubits wide for national sacred and administrative purposes. Its middle (not necessarily central!) segment is a square of 25,000 cubits divided into three east-west strips: two strips each 10,000 cubits wide, the northernmost for priests (amidst which the temple lies) and, bordering it on the south, one for Levites, both of them "holy of holies" and inalienable. The remaining strip to the south of these, 5000 cubits wide, contains a centrally located city, 4500 cubits square surrounded by a border of 500 cubits of grazing land and flanked on the east and west by strips 10,000 cubits long of farmland. The city's workers would be drawn from all the tribes of Israel. On either side of this square of 25,000 cubits, the remaining land flanking it to the Jordan on the east and to the sea on the west

---

38. As I pointed out in "Idealism and Practicality in Numbers 35:4–5 and Ezekiel 48," *JAOS* 88 (1968) 59–66.

are to be crownlands. This description of the "Contribution" expands that of 45:1–8; since its interest is in possession and occupation, it prescribes the inalienability of the sacred territories and goes into the size of the city and the provisions for maintaining and populating it.[39]

The last topic enlarges on the pan-Israelite character of the city. Each of the four sides of the city will have gates bearing the names of three tribes. The names differ from those of the tribal allotments, and for a reason: since all twelve must be represented, Ephraim and Manasseh are combined as Joseph, to enable the inclusion of Levi. Finally we learn the new name of the future city, YHWH *šamma*, "YHWH is there"; the infamous *yᵉrušalayim*, so excoriated in Ezekiel's prophecy—"polluted of name" he calls it (22:5)—will cease to be mentioned. God will be present in the temple but also among the lay cross-section of all Israel who reside in the city. Holy place and holy people will be realized in the future restoration.

EZEKIEL'S PROGRAM AND THE PRIESTLY
WRITINGS OF THE PENTATEUCH

When we pursue the analogy of Ezekiel to Moses (pp. 215–17) and compare the program of the former to the legislation ascribed to the latter great differences emerge. The nonpriestly Mosaic legislation in Exodus and Deuteronomy regulates private, civil, criminal, and public administrative realms that lie outside Ezekiel's scope. His concerns, concepts, and terminology resemble those of the priestly legislation that comprises the central parts of the Pentateuch (end of Exodus, Leviticus, Numbers). The arrangement of his program also is like that of the priestly corpus: first a description of the sanctuary, then regulation of its personnel and ritual, and finally disposition of the tribes around the sanctuary and the land allotment. The major omissions in Ezekiel, when compared with the priestly legislation, are the whole system of purity and impurity, ethics and morality (e.g., sexual conduct), idolatry, and private life (e.g., vows)—in sum, all the prescriptions of lay conduct making Israel a holy nation! Since such omissions cannot imply annulment, we must suppose Ezekiel to be highly selective, treating only of those topics in which he sought to effect revisions.[40] The system of impurity

---

39. The above summary assumes, with medievals and against moderns, that the north-to-south order of the whole chapter is not reversed in the description of the "Contributions"; hence the priests' portion (which includes the temple), mentioned first, lies to the north of that of the Levites. Ezekiel evidently intended to remove the city as far as possible from the temple, so he interposed the Levites between them. True, the temple is said repeatedly to be "amidst" *(btwk)* the priests' portion or the "Contribution," but that does not mean it was at the geometric center (Zimmerli). The admonition of 45:9 that Israel's chiefs not confiscate the people's landholdings would fit nicely here. Yet its present position, between the prescription of crownlands and the regulation of taxes to be delivered to the chief for the sacrifices has its own logic of contrast: the first and the last are legitimate means of support; the middle is not.

40. Kaufmann, *Religion of Israel*, pp. 443–45. Haran, "Law Code," argues that the priestly laws of the Pentateuch and Ezekiel's program are not directly related, but that the latter is an "epigonic outgrowth" of the same school as produced the former. His argument rests on far-reaching inferences from divergences and omissions whose ambiguity he minimizes.

is presupposed: the purgations; the heightened requirement of priestly purification after corpse-contact (44:26); religio-moral demands of the Torah are surely included in those "rules and laws" the prophet predicted would become natural for the people to observe (11:19f.; 36:26f.; 37:24); and the omission of the harlot (Lev. 21:7, 14) from Ezekiel's list of women (a priest may not marry [44:22] is perhaps connected with this). After these major subtractions, only regulations concerning the public realm of worship, "keeping guard over the sanctuary and God's sacred things" so as to ensure his continuing presence in Israel, are left.

1. Ezekiel introduces rigor into the separation and gradation of areas in the sanctuary precincts; moreover, his requirements are more stringent than those of the Pentateuch: His future temple will have two courts guarded by an imposing array of gatehouses, the inner one barred to nonpriests, instead of the one tabernacle court to no part of which was the laity barred. (Preexilic texts, including Psalms, speak of the "courts [plural] of YHWH"; whether the outer of these was not the same as "the great court" [1 Kings 7:12] that enclosed the Solomonic temple and palace is arguable; what is not is the accessibility of the inner one even to laity, since Ps. 26:6 speaks of circumambulating the altar in connection with visiting the temple.)

2. In his concern to restrict access to the holy, Ezekiel forbids priests tainted with idolatry to serve at the altar, a measure recalling Josiah's treatment of the priests of the local shrines *(bāmôt)* after he centralized worship (2 Kings 23:9). But while in Josiah's time the disqualified priests were provided for, we can only guess what provision Ezekiel intended for his "Levites"; he does not mention the tithe, in Num. 18:21–23 the Mosaic provision of their due.[41] The king's access too is restricted. In monarchic times the king might even officiate at the altar (2 Kings 16:12–13). In the future temple the chief (king) is excluded, like all laymen, from the inner court. However, he is distinguished from commoners by privileged access to the threshold of sacred spots such as the inner court or the vestibule of the permanently closed outer east gatehouse. His responsibility for the sacrificial ritual on sacred occasions is a continuation of his preexilic duty of maintaining the public worship. Finally, Ezekiel excludes the laity from any part in the sacrificial ritual: the right to slaughter, granted them in the Pentateuch (e.g., Lev. 1:5), is transferred by Ezekiel to his "Levites" (44:11). All these concerns and adjustments to later institutions are beyond the horizon of the priestly legislation of the Pentateuch.

3. All the sacrifices mentioned in Ezekiel's program are connected with public worship. The private sacrifice of the chief is the lone exception, and that is alluded to adjunct to his privilege of access to the usually closed inner east gate (46:12). There are major divergencies between Ezekiel and the priestly laws. Ezekiel's schematization of festal offerings, making more extensive use of quantities of seven and its multiples, is one. More characteristic

---

41. Haran, *Temples*, p. 127, surmises that Ezekiel meant the Levites to subsist from farming their strip of the "Contribution."

are his special purgations of the altar on the first, seventh and fourteenth of the first month. These exhibit his concern over keeping the (inevitable) contamination of the sanctuary by the impurities of the people from accumulating dangerously.

4. The land legislation also expresses the idea of separation and gradation, here in topographic form combining what is separated in Numbers 2—3 (the protective encampment of the tribes around the sanctuary) and Numbers 34 (the boundaries of the promised land) in a wholly original conception. Ezekiel seizes the occasion to set aright socioeconomic disadvantages arising from the old system of land tenure. All the tribes are equalized as to their holdings and the resident alien is for the first time given rights in real property (pursuant to Ezekiel's concern over the wronging of this class in former times [22:7, 29]). Violations of justice, no less than idolatry, are a cause of God's forsaking Israel (8:17; 9:9).

Ezekiel's program is a revision—an up-dating and a rectification—of selected topics of existent priestly legislation and practice very similar to, if not identical with, that of the Pentateuch. Obvious omissions (such as the ancient Festival of Reaping) make it hard to decide whether other omissions imply absence/annulment (no high priest in the future temple?) or are simply accidental. Our ignorance of the state and extent of preexilic priestly writings makes it impossible to decide whether divergencies in overlapping material (quantities of sacrificial materials, annual temple purgation in first/seventh month) are deliberate changes or reflections of ancient practices not recorded in the Pentateuch. Enough evidence is at hand, however, for asserting that Ezekiel felt himself called to institute basic changes in traditional practices. His program does give the impression of composition in stages, with duplication, cross-reference, and separation of related matter all indicating editorial arrangement and several returns to a given subject. Such phenomena do not imply plural authorship so long as there is no incompatibility among them.[42] We may therefore allow ourselves to be persuaded that the priest-prophet Ezekiel did not rest with mere announcements of restoration but composted an ideal revision of the institutions of the new Israel that would ensure the permanence of that restoration.

Wherever Ezekiel's program can be checked against subsequent events it proves to have had no effect. The return and resettlement of postexilic times had nothing in common with Ezekiel's vision; hence his disposition of the tribes and the "Contribution" remained a dead letter. The second temple had one or two features that recall Ezekiel's, but too little is known of the differences between Ezekiel's temple and the last stage of Solomon's to assert that it was owing to Ezekiel's influence that such features occur. In everything relating to the temple personnel and rituals the laws of Moses super-

---

42. Gese, *Verfassungsentwurf*, pp. 64ff., finds the incompatibility between 40:45 (those who guard the house are priests) and 44:13f. (those who guard the house are not priests) enough to justify working up a "Zadokite-Stratum." Can a single change of nomenclature really bear such a weight of theory?

seded those of Ezekiel. His program remains of interest chiefly as a practical extension of his prophecy; as additional evidence of his graphic mentality, his love of system and detail; and above all, for his lofty conception of a prophet's responsibility in an age of ruin.

18

Is Daniel Also Among the Prophets?

KLAUS KOCH*

By its inclusion in the prophetic corpus, the Book of Daniel with its
message of God's final control over human destiny sheds a significant
new light on the whole prophetic tradition.

In the Greek, the Latin, and all succeeding translations of the Bible, the
Book of Daniel has been positioned as one of the four major prophets. That
means that for fifteen hundred years there was no doubt among Christian
theologians about the prophetic authority of the book and its author. Since
the printing of the first Rabbinic Bible in the early sixteenth century A.D.,
however, scholars have become aware that in the Hebrew-Aramaic Bible
Daniel was placed not among the prophets but among the Writings (*Ketuvim*). It was not until the growth of historical criticism in the eighteenth
century and its applications to Daniel, however, that this issue was given
serious consideration. The English deist Anthony Collins in his *Scheme of
Literal Prophecy Considered*[1] took up the issue. He quoted Maimonides
with great pleasure: *Unanimi consensu gens nostra retulit librum Danielis
inter libros Hagiographos, non vero propheticos!*[2] Regarding the Rabbinic
Bible and its order as older and more reliable than that of the Septuagint and
its followers, Collins denied the prophetic character of the content of
Daniel's book. As did the anti-Christian Neoplatonist Porphyry (who died

---

*I would like to thank Dwight R. Daniels for improving my English. After completing this
essay, I received a copy of Robert D. Wilson's "The Book of Daniel and the Canon," *Princeton
Theological Review* 13 (1915) 352-408. Wilson reached nearly the same conclusions seventy
years ago. After checking the testimonies he remarks, "Only one witness puts the book of
Daniel under any other heading than that of the prophets. This witness is the Baba
Bathra. . . .Even Origin and Jerome, who studied with the Jewish Rabbis of their time, place
Daniel among the Prophets" (p. 384). Cf. also the notice of a prophetical "pentateuch" (Minor
Prophets, Isaiah, Jeremiah, Ezekiel, Daniel) with Epiphanius (p. 368).

1. *The Scheme of Literal Prophecy Considered* (London, 1727), pp. 153–54.
2. Moses Maimonides, *The Guide of the Perplexed*, trans. Shlomo Pines (Chicago: University
of Chicago Press, 1963), p. 400. The English translation softens the opposition: "For this reason
the nation has reached a consensus to put the Book of Daniel among the Writings, and not
among the Prophets."

about A.D. 304), Collins declared that all the Danielic predictions were *vaticinia ex eventu* (prophecies after the event), that they were written in the Maccabean era, and that they represented intentional forgeries.

Although this verdict was not accepted by all critical exegetes of the nineteenth and twentieth centuries, the strange position of the book in the Hebrew canon was debated again and again. It was, indeed, explained with reference to the historical circumstances of the formation of that canon rather than with regard to the contents of the book. By presupposing a relatively early closing of the canon of the prophetic books (about 200 A.D.), scholars made the incorporation of Daniel among the Writings a cornerstone of the so-called Maccabean Theory[3] (i.e., the theory that Daniel was written late, sometime in the first half of the second century B.C.). Subsequently, however, the question often arose whether such a pseudepigraphical book could really be called prophetic, and whether the Rabbinic doctrinal tradition that the spirit of prophecy ceased with the early postexilic century was perhaps the correct one after all. Corresponding judgments may be found in many modern introductions to the Old Testament and in commentaries on Daniel. Thus Otto Eissfeldt writes in his sophisticated *Introduction*, "The fact that the book was not included in the canon of the prophets shows already that it can only have been composed very late."[4]

In the latest important commentary Hartman and DiLella offer a similar view:

> It is possible that the rabbis did not consider the Book of Daniel as a prophetic writing. More probable, however, is the theory that because the book appeared so late (second quarter of the second century B.C.) it could not be included in the prophetic corpus which the rabbis held to be closed with the death of the fifth century B.C. prophet Malachi.[5]

As the result of regarding the incorporation of Daniel among the Writings in the Masoretic Bible as the original position, two difficult questions arose. The first concerned the date of origin. Against its own claims, Daniel was not regarded as having been written in exilic times but in late postexilic times after the close of the prophetic corpus. The second question concerned the nature of Daniel's content. If the author belonged to the Maccabean era, then his predictions are for the most part *vaticinia ex eventu*. Could he under these circumstances have been anything more than an imitator of classical prophecy? Does this not exclude the possibility that he could have been a genius of the same caliber as Isaiah? On the other hand, is it really certain that he wanted to be a prophet in the first place and that the intended circle of his readers did indeed view him as such a figure? All these issues must be

---

3. Cf. Klaus Koch, *Das Buch Daniel* (Darmstadt: Wissenschaftliche Buchgesellschaft, 1980).

4. *The Old Testament: An Introduction*, trans. Peter R. Ackroyd (New York: Harper & Row, 1965), p. 521.

5. Louis F. Hartman and Alexander A. DiLella, *The Book of Daniel*, AB 23 (Garden City, N.Y.: Doubleday & Co., 1978), p. 25. Cf. Matthias Delcor, *Le Livre de Daniel*, SB 35 (Paris: J. Gabalda, 1971), pp. 9–10; and many others.

considered if one takes seriously the location of the Book of Daniel among the *Ketuvim* in the Masoretic collection.

Must that location of Daniel be taken all that seriously, however? To be sure, the order of the Hebrew-Aramaic Bible is attested by the oldest available manuscripts, but they belong to the ninth and tenth centuries (Codex Leningradensis and Aleppo-Codex).[6] That is a rather late date. Is there any other evidence which may strengthen the case?

DANIEL—A NONPROPHETIC BOOK

1. In addition to the transmission of the order of Bible manuscripts, there are two explicit passages in the Gemara of the Babylonian Talmud which thematise the incorporation of Daniel among the *Ketuvim* and not the prophets. The first one is bBB 14b where the sequence of the Hagiographa is listed and Daniel appears before Esther and Ezra.[7] The other one is bMeg 3a where Haggai, Zechariah, and Malachi as prophets were distinguished from Daniel, who is important but not prophetic. The Babylonian Talmud was written in the fifth—eighth centuries A.D., somewhat earlier than the above mentioned Bible manuscripts.

2. A very early witness is provided by the list of the Worthies in Wisdom of Sirach (Ecclesiasticus) 44—50, about 180 B.C. The author Ben Sira names the three major prophets and Job as the fourth (49:9) together with the Book of the Twelve (i.e., the Minor Prophets) but not Daniel. Daniel's name is also absent from among the heroes of the exile and the time thereafter who are drawn from the *Ketuvim*, such as Zerubbabel, Joshua the high priest, and Nehemiah. That absence, however, reduces the value of this passage as evidence of the nonprophetic view of Daniel, because it points to a later origin for our book. Ben Sira knows no Daniel at all, neither among the prophets nor among the *Ketuvim*.

3. In the period shortly after the discovery of the Qumran texts, doubts about an originally prophetic understanding of the Book of Daniel were strengthened. Cave 6 revealed some Daniel fragments written on papyrus and not on leather; they thus appeared in a less prestigious format than the other canonical books. As a result the opinion seemed justified that the Qumran community, in spite of its high respect for the prophets, did not include Daniel in the Holy Scriptures and therefore did not accord his book prophetic rank.[8] More recently, however, that opinion has been abandoned, as we shall see below.

---

6. Most recently *Theologische Realenzyklopädie*, ed. Gerhard Krause and Gerhard Müller (Berlin: Walter de Gruyter, 1980), 6:112.

7. German translation: *Der babylonische Talmud*, trans. Lazarus Goldschmidt, 2d ed. (Berlin: Jüdischer Verlag, 1964), 8:55. English translation: *The Babylonian Talmud*, ed. Isadore Epstein, part 4.3 (London: Soncino Press, 1935), p. 71.

8. Dominique Barthelmy and Jósef T. Milik, *Qumran Cave 1*, DJD (Oxford: Clarendon Press, 1955), p. 150. See also Eissfeldt, *Introduction*, p. 565; Ernst Sellin and Georg Fohrer, *Introduction to the Old Testament*, trans. David E. Green (Nashville: Abingdon Press, 1968), p. 473.

4. Until 1965 the discussion of the prophetic claim of the book was based on evidence drawn from outside the book itself (see 1–3) or from literary critical hypotheses (the Maccabean theory). In that year Gerhard von Rad in his second volume of *Old Testament Theology*[9] turned his view to the internal contextual evidence, following some suggestions of Hoelscher[10] which had been neglected up until then. Von Rad points first to the title of the alleged author. He is named a wise man (Dan. 1:3–5; 2:48–49) and not a *nabi* ("prophet"). From a form-critical perspective Daniel does not belong to the prophetic genre, and there are no clear indications of such a genre at all. To be sure, Daniel utters predictions, but that is not due to any prophetic impulse; rather, it flows out of the interpretation of dreams, something which belonged to the task of the sages in the ancient Near East. Moreover the intention of the book is not to take part in actual social and political conflicts, something which the prophets Amos and Isaiah did. The book presents history from a spectator's point of view in a deterministic fashion and results in a positively hybrid-seeming universal gnosis. To regard the author as a successor of the prophets is completely out of the question.[11] Von Rad concluded that the only possible root from which the Book of Daniel can have grown was Wisdom.

Although von Rad is completely correct in his first observation—Daniel's title—and partially correct in the second one—the question of the genre— his conclusions about the intention of the author are rather speculative. The attribution of Daniel to Wisdom literature has to meet the severe objection that Wisdom literature shows no real form-critical parallels to Daniel. In addition, there is no sign in Wisdom literature of a special interest in eschatology in the beginning of the second century B.C. (e.g., Ben Sira), whereas this interest is dominant at least in the second part of the Book of Daniel.[12] As a result, only a few scholars accepted von Rad's views in this matter. We shall return to some of his arguments later on, but first we must consider the tradition which places Daniel among the prophetic books.

DANIEL AMONG THE PROPHETIC BOOKS

There are some early witnesses in which Daniel is called a prophet and in which his writing is placed among the prophetic books.

1. The most famous source is Matt. 24:15. Jesus is admonishing his disciples: "When you see the desolating sacrilege spoken of by the prophet Daniel *(to rhēthen dia Danièl tou prophètou)*, standing in the holy place. . . ." That is, of course, a clear reference to Dan. 9:27 (11:31; 12:11). Although explicit reference to Daniel and his prophetic utterance is missing

---

9. *Old Testament Theology*, vol. 2, trans. D.M.G. Stalker (Edinburgh: Oliver & Boyd, 1967); 1st German ed., 1965.

10. Georg Hoelscher, "Die Entstehung des Buches Daniel," *TSK* 92 (1919) 113–38.

11. Gerhard von Rad, *Old Testament Theology* 2:303–5.

12. For details see Klaus Koch, *The Rediscovery of Apocalyptic*, SBT 2, 22 (London: SCM Press, 1972), pp. 42–47.

in the parallel passage in Mark 13:14, it is nevertheless apparent that the church of Saint Matthew in the second half of the first century A.D. did reckon Daniel among the prophets. Was that solely a Christian perspective?

2. The order of the books in the Septuagint places Daniel in the second division of Scripture, namely the prophetic writings, and this is the case in all manuscripts as well as in the lists of the early church fathers.[13] Although Daniel could either precede Ezekiel (Origen, third century; Melito, second century, etc.) or follow Ezekiel (LXX^{BA}, fourth–fifth centuries; pap. 967, second or early third century), the association of Daniel with the prophetic group is consistent. At one time the Septuagint was regarded as the Alexandrinian canon.[14] Sundberg has raised some doubts about this place of origin, however. Perhaps the Diaspora in Alexandria used only the Pentateuch as normative Scripture; they are, after all, the only books quoted in the Letter of Aristeas and in the writings of Philo, both of which originated in Alexandria. In my opinion, however (against Sundberg), the firm order which already appears in the earliest papyri of the Septuagint presupposes an old Jewish Diaspora canon, whether from Egypt outside Alexandria (e.g., Leontopolis) or from Syria (perhaps Antiochis). Wherever Daniel is preserved in the Greek Bible, it is placed among the prophetic books. (In the current LXX, the original Septuagint version of the book is replaced by another pre-Christian version which was [wrongly] ascribed to Theodotion.[15] This problem does not touch the order of the Scriptures, so it may remain outside our present consideration.)

3. The next witness is Josephus, the historian. In his *Against Apion* I.38–41 (about 100 A.D.) he writes concerning books given by divine inspiration:

> ... five are the books of Moses. ... This period falls only a little short of three thousand years. From the death of Moses until Artaxerxes ... the prophets subsequent to Moses wrote the history of the events of their own times in thirteen books. The remaining four books contain hymns to God and precepts for the conduct of human life.[16]

There is no doubt that Josephus included Daniel, who plays an important role in his Judean history, among these normative Scriptures. It is also clear that the book does not belong to the above-mentioned third category, the hymns and precepts (probably Psalms, Song of Songs or Job, Proverbs, and Ecclesiastes)[17] but to the prophetic group. Josephus also writes of Daniel as one of the greatest prophets in *Jewish Antiquities* X.xi (4). Because he

---

13. Albert C. Sundberg, *The Old Testament of the Early Church*, HTS 20 (Cambridge: Harvard University Press; London: Oxford University Press, 1964), table 2, pp. 58–59.

14. Ibid., chap. 5.

15. Armin Schmitt, "Stammt der sogenannte "δ"—Text bei Daniel wirklich von Theodotion?" *NAWG* (1966) 8; Klaus Koch, "Die Herkunft der Proto-Theodotion-Übersetzung des Danielbuches," *VT* 23 (1973) 362–65.

16. *Josephus*, vol. 1, *The Life—Against Apion*, trans. Henry St. John Thackeray, Loeb Classical Library (Cambridge: Harvard University Press; London: William Heinemann, 1966), p. 179.

17. Ibid., n. *c*.

belonged to the Pharisees, Josephus certainly refers to a canon of that group, perhaps the canon of the school of Hillel.[18] For these people Daniel was one of the prophetic voices within the Scriptures.

4. There is still a good deal of dispute about which books belonged to the Holy Scriptures in the community of Qumram. Yet there is no longer any question among the experts nowadays that Daniel was regarded by them as belonging among the prophets. Since the first discoveries of papyri fragments of the book, other fragments of Daniel have been found written on leather,[19] whereas papyrus was also used for other biblical books (e.g., Kings). The type of manuscript material was therefore not an indication of the value of the Scripture written on it. Especially important, however, is a passage in 4Q Florilegium II.3[20] where a time of affliction is predicted "as it is written in the book of Daniel, the prophet." Thus we have a clear indication of the prophetic character of the book according to the Qumranic view.

5. The Jewish tradition is not unanimous. The Codex Cairensis, the oldest known manuscript of the Hebrew Bible (A.D. 895), contains the so-called former and latter prophets without Daniel. The writer Moshe B. Aser added a list of prophets: "And these are the prophets who prophesied in Babylon when they left Jerusalem: Haggai, Malachi and Daniel. All the prophets from Moses . . . to Daniel and Malachi number 117."[21]

For this Qaraean scholar the status of Daniel as a prophet was undoubted in spite of any order of the canon. Another example may be found in a Hebrew-Aramaic-Greek canon list, perhaps from the second century A.D., to which Audet has drawn attention.[22] In that list Daniel appears after the three other major prophets.

If one looks for the conclusions to be drawn from this survey of the sources, one is forced to note that there is not a single witness for the exclusion of Daniel from the prophetic corpus in the first half of the first millenium A.D. In all the sources of the first century A.D.—Matthew, Josephus, Qumran—Daniel is reckoned among the prophets. In fact the earliest literary evidence of Daniel's inclusion among the *Ketuvim* is to be placed somewhere between the fifth and eighth centuries A.D. This leads to the conclusion that at some point the rabbis transferred the book from the prophetic corpus to the last third of their collection of Holy Scripture. That probably happened long before the fifth century. Audet may be right in looking to the second century as an appropriate date. There is no clear proof

---

18. Rudolf Meyer, "Bemerkungen zum literargeschichtlichen Hintergrund der Kanontheorie des Josephus," in Otto Betz, Klaus Haacker, et al., eds., *Festschrift Otto Uschel* (Göttingen: Vandenhoeck und Ruprecht, 1974), pp. 285–99. Cf. Albrecht Oepke and Rudolf Meyer, Κρυπτο, in *ThWNT* 3:982.

19. Hartman and DiLella, *The Book of Daniel*, p. 72.

20. John M. Allegro, *Qumran Cave 4.1*, DJD 5 (1968), pp. 53–57; Alfred Merten, *Das Buch Daniel im Lichte der Texte vom Toten Meer*, SBM 12 (1971), p. 29.

21. Paul Kahle, *Der hebräische Bibeltext seit Franz Delitzsch* (Stuttgart: Kohlhammer, 1961), pp. 72–73.

22. Jean Paul Audet, "A Hebrew-Aramaic List of Books of the Old Testament in Greek Transcription," *JTS*, NS 1 (1950).

for that, but it may be conjectured that the important role played by some Danielic predictions during the first (and second?) revolt against Rome was the decisive cause. Josephus refers to one of them in *The Jewish War* VI:

> But what more than all else incited them to the war was an ambiguous oracle, likewise found in their sacred scriptures, to the effect that at that time one from their country would become ruler of the world. This they understood to mean someone of their own race, and many of their wise men went astray in their interpretation of it. The oracle, however, in reality signified the sovereignty of Vespasian, who was proclaimed Emperor on Jewish soil.[23]

Josephus was thinking of Dan. 7:13–14 or 9:26.[24] The importance of oracles taken from the Holy Scriptures is also stressed by the Roman historian Tacitus (*Historiae* V.13) and Suetonius (*Divus Vespasianus* 4.9). The confidence in the fulfillment of such prophecy connected to a reckoning of an apocalyptic timetable had led Israel into decline. Such disappointed confidence may have been the reason why the influential rabbis displaced this dangerous book, separating it from classical prophecy and placing it among the narratives of the time of the exile like Esther and Ezra. Though such an observation is pure conjecture, it would offer an understandable rationale for such a severe handling of material which was included within a sacral tradition.

MORE THAN A PROPHET

We have now seen that the search for the history of canonization and the changing place of Daniel in it leads to an ambiguous result. On the one side there is for the early centuries a rather unanimous consensus among the copyists and readers that Daniel was to be placed in the prophetic corpus. On the other side there are some indications, noted especially by von Rad, which speak against a prophetic claim raised by the author himself. How can this discrepancy between the author and his early recipients be explained? To answer that question, it is necessary to examine more fully the self-understanding of the Book of Daniel and to carry that examination beyond the observations von Rad has made.

There is more that needs to be said about the title of the hero. Indeed, it is related in Dan. 2:48 that Nebuchadnezzar appointed Daniel as chief prefect over all the wise men of Babylon. Thus his importance in the realm of wisdom was acknowledged. Yet, he is not explicitly named a wise man, and the appointment is related to the viewpoints of a non-Jewish milieu (cf. 2:18, 21; 4:3–5). The correct title, however, appears in the address of the angel in

---

23. *Josephus*, vol. 3, *The Jewish War, Books IV—VII*, trans. Henry St. John Thackeray, Loeb Classical Library (Cambridge: Harvard University Press; London: William Heinemann, 1968), p. 467.

24. Frederick Bruce, "Josephus and Daniel," *ASTI* 4 (1965) 148–62. Cf. Hermann L. Strack and Paul Billerbeck, *Kommentar zum Neuen Testament aus Talmud und Midrasch* (Munich: Beck, 1922–61), 4: 1002.

10:11, 19 (9:23): Daniel is "the man greatly beloved" (by God). Certainly this peculiar title does not mean a lesser position than a prophetic one. In reality, it designates a higher one. We are aided in understanding the meaning of that title by the interpretation accorded to it by the Babylonian kings, according to whom the spirit of the holy god(s) dwelt in him (Dan. 4:5–6, 14; 5:11, 14; cf. 6:4). The possession of that spirit elevates Daniel above the abilities of all other wise men and makes him an outstanding seer announcing the mysteries of the end of days (2:2–3) or the time of the end (11:35, 40; 12:4, 9, 13).

Daniel's strict eschatological perspective also separates this book from the ancient prophets. According to Daniel 9, what Jeremiah had written remained as dark and enigmatic as the dreams and visions of the Babylonian kings (chaps. 2, 4, 5). Only with Daniel was the true understanding of the prophetic writings revealed (9:22–23). We may suppose the same for the interpretation of the four horns of Zech. 2:1–4 by means of the conception of the four world-wide monarchies (Dan. 2:36–38; 7:1–3), of the disclosure of the real content of the decreed end announced in Isaiah 10:23 (Dan. 9:27), as well as many other interpretations of earlier prophetic utterances contained in Daniel. In this book the prophetic word always is taken as a riddle, the solution of which is given by the angel to Daniel and by Daniel to his readers.

A form-critical investigation underlines this result. Contrary to von Rad's view, there is a clear connection between the reports of the prophetic visions, especially in their last stage with Zechariah, and the genre of Daniel 7—12 (2:28–30; 4:1–3), as I have shown elsewhere.[25] There is always a two-fold sequence in Daniel: first, a vision, dream, or old prophecy is reported (thus chap. 9); and then a succeeding *peshar* (interpretation) is revealed by an angel to Daniel (or by Daniel if the vision or dream was that of a king). Daniel brings his readers the divine key for both the heathen king—ideology (chaps. 2 and 4) and for Israelite prophecy. The heavenly mysteries (2:18–19, 27–30) are finally disclosed with his message, and thus revelation has reached its last stage within this age. Clearly there is an underlying and determinative conception of a two-stage revelation: The prophets like Isaiah, Jeremiah, and Ezekiel are indispensable but preliminary spokesmen of the Word of God; it is only with Daniel that the final stage begins. So he is more than a prophet; he is "a man greatly beloved" (Dan. 10:11, 19) and not a prophet. Today some exegetes like to designate the use of Scripture in Daniel as "midrashic."[26] That is, however, a rather misleading term. Besides the form-critical differences of the genres (Daniel's use of Scripture and a midrash), there is an important theological gap: The rabbis pronouncing a midrash never claim to announce a new revelation, a hitherto unknown Word

---

25. Klaus Koch, "Vom prophetischen zum apokalyptischen Visionsbericht," in David Hellholm, ed., *Apocalypticism in the Mediterranean World and the Near East* (Tübingen: J. C. B. Mohr, 1983).

26. Brevard S. Childs, *Introduction to the Old Testament as Scripture*, 2d ed. (Philadelphia: Fortress Press, 1980), p. 617.

of God, whereas Daniel does so in nearly every chapter of the book. Thus Daniel makes quite a different claim for his interpretations of Scripture than do the rabbinic sages.

A further question arises: What are we to make of Daniel's omission of the normal prophetic identification of the prophet's message with the Word of God himself? Daniel does not present his revelations as the very utterance of God. He never uses the so-called messenger formula, "Thus saith the Lord," or similar phrases, as Isaiah or Jeremiah did. How does this modesty fit with his claim to be more than a prophet? The lack of any directly divine "I" in the book was an important element for von Rad when he argued for its non-prophetic character. We do need to take into account, however, that in the last pre-Christian centuries the immediate identity of God's words with human utterances had come under suspicion. The growing element of transcendence in the understanding of God led to the conviction that even in the prophetic books it was the Memra (Word) of the Lord (or the Holy Spirit) which was speaking, that is, an intermediary being and not God directly (cf. the frequent use of *memra'* in the Targums or the alteration of the "Word of God" [*dibre yhwh*] superscriptions, Hos. 1:1, etc.). The most instructive example in this regard, however, is none other than Jesus of Nazareth. He also abstained from any equation of his logia with the "I" of God and never used formulas like "Thus saith the Lord." According to the Synoptic Tradition there was a voice from heaven (*bat qol*) speaking to him at his baptism and heavenly being(s) speaking to him at the transfiguration and in the garden of Gethsemane, but no direct voice of God himself. Jesus in fact used more wisdom genres in his sayings than did Daniel.[27] People addressed him as "teacher" (*didaskale*). Nonetheless they did not regard him as a sage but rather as a prophet (Mark 8:28). The ancient preexilic difference between wise men and prophets (and priests) as separate institutions (Jer. 18:18) had disappeared long ago and with it the corresponding gap in the genres of language.

CONSEQUENCES OF THE CANONIZATION

The Book of Daniel was incorporated into the prophetic part of Scriptures in pre-Christian times. That was probably more than merely a pragmatic decision arising out of the necessity of giving it a place in an already threefold canon, and it had far-reaching consequences. Now Daniel spread his light over all the prophets. If we look at the Targum Jonathan on the prophets, a targum which originated in the last half century B.C.[28] and which may well represent an understanding rather contemporary to the final fixation of the prophetic corpus, we can see that all the prophets were interpreted along the lines set out in Daniel. The king of Assyria, for example, mentioned so often

27. Cf. Rudolf Bultmann, *Die Geschichte der synoptischen Tradition*, FRLANT 29 (Göttingen: Vandenhoeck und Ruprecht, 1932), I B.

28. Klaus Koch, "Messias und Sündenvergebung in Jesaja 53—Targum," *JSJ* 3 (1972) 119–20.

with Isaiah, has become a typical example of the heathen rule over Israel. Again, the expectation of the coming age ('*alam*) is found in many places in addition to Daniel.[29] A hint of a coming kingdom of God was also found in many prophetic passages.[30] In that way the apocalyptic book, once it was included among the prophets, shed light on the whole corpus and offered a concept of prophecy which is thoroughly related to the end time. Conversely, its incorporation in this part of the canon allows a new view of Daniel. The contemporary allusions meant literally by the Maccabean author also found renewed application in a typological understanding. To cite but one example: Antiochus Epiphanes did not remain as the last enemy of the people of God but became that enemy's prefiguration. By the inclusion and the resulting typological understanding of Daniel, the book lost its claim to be the final revelation.

It is against this background that the relocation of the book from the Prophets to the Writings within the canon, which occurred in the early Rabbinic period, should be seen. Removing Daniel from the prophetic corpus and placing it among the narratives of late exilic and early postexilic times like Esther and Ezra shifted the accent from eschatology to pedagogics. Now the behavior of the hero (e.g., his obedience to the Torah) appeared as the decisive point. Perhaps the exclusion of Daniel was accompanied by an altered conception of the prophetic books as well. More and more the prophets came to be understood as preachers of repentance and of the Torah and less and less as proclaimers of the coming kingdom of God.

Why did the rabbis who disapproved of a revolutionary use of the prophet Daniel not reject the book altogether? They did not hesitate to exclude other writings which at various times and places had been counted among the Holy Scriptures, for example, 1 *Enoch* or the Wisdom of Sirach (Ecclesiasticus). Daniel, on the other hand, they merely degraded by a transposition (thus preventing a possible use of it as Haphtarot in the synagogues). There is no explanation available in the extant Rabbinic text as to why they did not simply reject it, so we are forced to make assumptions. Presumably it was the generally accepted interpretation of the fourth monarchy in Daniel 2 and 7 as the Roman Empire which stayed the rabbis' hand. This Roman option, as we may call it, was current among Jews and Christians at least since the first century A.D., and it lasted until the eighteenth and nineteenth centuries. It was not intended as a reinterpretation. Given the Roman occupation of Palestine and most of its surroundings, it appeared obvious that it was the empire of the Caesars and no other which had to be the kingdom made of iron and clay (Dan. 2:33) or the monster, terrible and dreadful and exceedingly strong, which devoured all other nations (7:7). Thus for the oppressed or even persecuted Jewish and Christian communities, Daniel received an actualization beyond all other prophets. This unique significance

---

29. Cf. J. B. van Zijl, *A Concordance to the Targum of Isaiah*, SBL Aramaic Studies 3 (Missoula, Mont: Scholars Press, 1979), pp. 142–43.

30. Klaus Koch, "Offenbaren wird sich das Reich Gottes," *NTS* 25 (1978) 158–65.

offers a possible explanation for the strange fact that out of the rich religious literature of the late Israelite period (since 200 B.C.) only Daniel was commonly accepted as a part of the Holy Scripture. The perception that Daniel's prophecies were being fulfilled was strengthened after the fall of Jerusalem in A.D. 70, because along with many Christians nearly all the rabbis saw that terrible catastrophe as the fulfillment of the timetable of Daniel 9:24–27.[31] This book was therefore the only one within the Holy Scriptures which offered a key for the second destruction of the holy city and the existence of Israel in a further exile.

A STUMBLING BLOCK FOR THE MODERN CANONICAL PERSPECTIVE

In recent years several attempts have been made to stress the canonical form of a biblical book as the decisive basis for a theological understanding of it, in contrast to the historical-critical quest for the intention of the original author. Brevard Childs has provided some interesting points with regard to Daniel.[32] According to Childs, the meaning of the writing "has been sharply altered" by the canonical editors. The "description of the 'period of indignation' was now understood typologically" and the end of the age was transferred to a distant future.[33] A second change was the diminution of the significance of the apocalyptic numbers, which are especially prevalent in the last chapter. "From a canonical perspective these calculations in ch. 12 do not play a significant role for understanding the book as a whole."[34] Its aim is "to admonish the people of God in the crisis of faith. The manner in which the book was shaped in the canonical process provides a critical check against the perennial danger of politicizing and trivializing its message." Lastly, as it stands now, it "calls into question all human endeavours of 'bringing in the kingdom' or of 'humanizing the structures of society.' Rather, this biblical witness challenges the faithful to be awake and ready for the unexpected intervention of God in wrapping up all of human history."[35]

To what extent are these conclusions convincing? There can be no doubt that the process of canonization must be taken into account in exegesis, since the establishing of a corpus of Holy Scriptures makes a decisive point in late Israelite history and became the indispensable condition for the formation of both Christianity and Judaism. Years ago, writing from a form-critical perspective, I stressed the fact that "canonisation makes a deep divide in the transmission history of a biblical book."[36] A given book became finally fixed and received new accents by its incorporation into a larger composite unit.

---

31. Cf. Strack-Billerbeck, *Kommentar* 4:100–101.
32. *Introduction to the Old Testament as Scripture*, pp. 613–22.
33. Ibid., p. 619.
34. Ibid., p. 621.
35. Ibid., p. 622.
36. Klaus Koch, *The Growth of the Biblical Tradition*, trans. S. M. Cupitt (New York: Charles Scribner's Sons, 1969), p. 106.

At the same time, another way of dealing with the text arose. Instead of interpretation through internal textual additions, a practice common in pre-canonical times, new modes of interpretation exterior to the text and clearly subordinated to it became necessary for its correct understanding.

This raises a crucial difficulty. How can we identify the exact meanings intended by the canonizers? There is no evidence for any addition or gloss originating precisely at the time of canonization, so it is dangerous to speak of the canonical shape of a writing. How is one to grasp it? Perhaps one should speak in a more careful way of a canonical intention. The only way to comprehend this intention, it seems to me, is to look at the surroundings, the context, in which a certain book is incorporated. Therefore, the order of the Old Testament books and the three-fold division of the canon offer the only useful key for responsible observations. Strangely enough, Childs explicitly refrains from taking into account "whether or not the book is assigned a position in the canon among the Prophets or the Writings" ("The sequence of the books . . . had little significance.").[37] Nonetheless he maintains that the author of Daniel 8—12 only intended to interpret the (older) prophets. "He had no new prophetic word directly from God,"[38] a statement which is clearly contradicted in Dan. 9:23 (cf. 11:2).

What Childs offers as canonical perspectives is therefore a colorful bouquet of issues which belong, in part at least, to the first stage of canonization, the incorporation of Daniel into the Prophets, or else to the second stage, namely the relocation of the book from the prophetic corpus to the devotional narratives at the end of the *Ketuvim*. Perhaps most of all, the issues are related to some modern Protestant desires concerning the canon.

To the first stage of canonization belong the typological view and the extended expectation of the coming kingdom of God. To the second stage we may ascribe the admonition to the faithful for the time of crisis. Such issues, however, as the playing down of the relevance of the apocalyptic numbers or the stressing of the unexpected intervention of God which will wrap up all human history, are clearly the products of Christian theological thought. One wonders whether they can be verified by any investigation into the canon (or the extant text of the book).

The process of canonization is a historical one. As important as it is, it must be reconstructed on the basis of an elaborate analysis of the contemporary circumstances. There has never been one canon of the Old Testament but always several, and each is accompanied by a different theory about its significance for life and faith. The Book of Daniel is an outstanding example of how such theories affect the way a biblical book is understood.

37. Childs, *Introduction to the Old Testament as Scripture*, p. 622; cf. p. 503.
38. Ibid., p. 618.

19
Daniel and
His Social World

JOHN J. COLLINS

> What Daniel offers is not a practical strategy for revolution but an act
> of the imagination which affirms the freedom of the human spirit in
> defiance of any force of oppression.

Historical-critical study of the Bible has been enriched in recent years by
increased attention to social factors. The fundamental insight here is that
texts do not give us simple objective accounts of reality but are constructs
which reflect the interests of their particular authors and the groups to which
they belonged.[1] A book like Daniel cannot be understood as a timeless
handbook, either of eschatological information or of theological principles,
but must be seen in its historical and social context. This insight is not a new
one; it has long been implicit in the form-critical insistence on the *Sitz-im-
Leben*. To be sure, biblical texts do not always yield adequate information
about their setting, and the attempt to infer social data from literary evidence
has its pitfalls. Social and historical studies can only proceed from an accurate
appreciation of the genre and literary character of a text. Yet, where the data
are available, an awareness of social and ideological factors will not only
deepen our understanding of a text but also clarify its relevance for our own
modern situation.

I

We are relatively well-informed about the situation in which Daniel was
composed. Despite the persistent objections of conservatives, the composition of the visions (chaps. 7—12) between the years 167 and 164 B.C. is
established beyond reasonable doubt.[2] The tales in chapters 1—6 are older,

---

1. See the basic discussion in P. L. Berger and T. Luckmann, *The Social Construction of
Reality: A Treatise in the Sociology of Knowledge* (Garden City, N.Y.: Doubleday & Co., 1966).
2. J. J. Collins, *Daniel, with an Introduction to Apocalyptic Literature*, FOTL 20 (Grand
Rapids: Wm. B. Eerdmans, 1984), p. 36 and passim; L. F. Hartman and A. A. DiLella, *The
Book of Daniel*, AB 23 (Garden City, N.Y.: Doubleday & Co., 1978), pp. 46–54. For a recent
conservative objection: A. J. Ferch, "The Book of Daniel and the 'Maccabean Thesis,'" *AUSS* 21
(1983) 129–41.

but it is unlikely that any part of Daniel attained its present form before the Hellenistic age. Moreover, we are given a clear indication of the group for which the book speaks. In Daniel 11 we are told that the wise "teachers of the people" (maśkîlê 'am) will instruct the masses in the time of persecution. Some of them will be killed, but at the time of the resurrection they will shine like the glory of the firmament and be like the stars forever. There can be little doubt that the Book of Daniel was composed in the circles of these maśkîlîm.

Difficulties arise when we try to specify more exactly who these people were. Many commentators assume that they were identical with the Hasidim who are mentioned in the Books of Maccabees,[3] although the assumption has been severely criticized.[4] Our knowledge of the Hasidim as a party in the Maccabean era is derived from three passages. In 1 Macc. 2:42 we are told that Mattathias and his followers were joined by "a company of Hasideans [synagōgē Asidaiōn], mighty warriors of Israel, every one who offered himself willingly for the law." This follows directly on the report that a thousand persons were martyred when they refused to defend themselves on the Sabbath, but the martyrs are not explicitly identified as Hasidim. In 1 Macc. 7:12–13 it is said that a company of scribes (synagōgē grammateōn) came to the high priest Alcimus and the general Bacchides to seek peace. The passage continues "and the Hasidaeans were first among the sons of Israel and they sought peace from them." It is not clear whether the Hasidaeans here are identical with the company of scribes, or whether they were first in rank or simply took the initiative in seeking peace. Finally in 2 Macc. 14:6 Alcimus complains to the Seleucid king that "those of the Jews who are called Hasidaeans, whose leader is Judas Maccabeus, are keeping up war and stirring up sedition and will not let the kingdom attain tranquility." These three passages are the only direct references to Hasidim in the Maccabean period. When the term occurs in Psalm 149 or in the Psalms scroll from Qumran, we cannot assume that it refers to the same group.

From the statements in the Books of Maccabees we can infer very little about the Hasidim, and some common assumptions are quite ungrounded. Both Books of Maccabees present them as an active fighting force in the rebellion. They may already have been militarily active before they joined the Maccabees. In no case were they pacifists. (Even the martyrs in 1 Maccabees 2 would presumably have defended themselves on any day but the Sabbath.) Their willingness to make peace with Alcimus must be seen in perspective. According to 2 Maccabees 14, Judas Maccabee himself made a

3. E.g., Hartman and DiLella, *The Book of Daniel*, p. 43; A. Lacocque, *The Book of Daniel* (Atlanta: John Knox Press, 1979), p. 11; *Daniel et son Temps* (Geneva: Labor et Fides, 1983), pp. 131–39; W. S. Towner, *Daniel*, Interpretation (Atlanta: John Knox Press, 1984), p. 7. The "Hasidic hypothesis" has been developed esp. by M. Hengel, *Judaism and Hellenism* (Philadelphia: Fortress Press, 1974), 1:175–80; and O. Plöger, *Theocracy and Eschatology* (Richmond: John Knox Press, 1968), pp. 22–25.

4. P. R. Davies, "Hasidim in the Maccabean Period," *JJS* 28 (1977) 127–40; J. J. Collins, *The Apocalyptic Vision of the Book of Daniel*, HSM 16 (Missoula, Mont.: Scholars Press, 1977), pp. 201–5.

brief truce with Nicanor when Alcimus arrived on the scene. It is quite possible that the Hasidim resumed the fight thereafter. They may have been prominent scribes (if one so interprets 1 Macc. 7:12–13), but this is not certain; and it is questionable whether the leading scribes would have constituted such a significant fighting force. Finally there is room for doubt as to whether these pietists were an organized party at all. The term *synagōgē* is used loosely in 1 Maccabees not only for a group of scribes (7:12) but also for priests (14:28) and even fighting men (3:44). It may denote an *ad hoc* gathering. The term *Asidaioi* may be translated as pietists and may refer to a rather broad class, as we might use the terms "conservatives" or "liberals."

It is striking that the best attested feature of these pietists, their military activity, does not accord with the *maśkīlîm* of Daniel. These are said to take action in face of persecution, but their action consists of instructing the masses and enduring to the point of death. They can scarcely be identical with the "mighty warriors of Israel" who joined forces with the Maccabees. Moreover, Daniel is not the only document which attests the rise of a movement in the Maccabbean era. The Animal Apocalypse in 1 *Enoch* tells how "small lambs" were born who began to open their eyes. One of them was killed (possibly the murdered high priest Onias III); but horns grew on the others and eventually they found a leader in a horned ram, who is almost certainly to be identified with Judas Maccabee. This development is paralleled by the emergence of the "chosen righteous" in the Apocalypse of Weeks (1 *Enoch* 93:10), who are also given a sword to punish the sinners (1 *Enoch* 91:12). This Enochic evidence fits the pietists of 1 Maccabees far better than does Daniel, although the Maccabean books do not hint at the range of apocalyptic concerns which we find in 1 *Enoch*. The "lambs" of Enoch cannot be simply identified with the *maśkīlîm* of Daniel. Even apart from their differing relationships to the armed rebellion of the Maccabees, the two books derive from different traditions, with different interests. To be sure Daniel and 1 *Enoch* have important affinities too, in their literary form and overall world view; and we must assume some measure of contact between their respective tradents.[5] Yet Daniel lacks the strong speculative and cosmological interests of the Enoch books, and we must assume that it comes from a distinct group.[6] Other documents which speak of emerging groups at this time are Jubilees (which emphasizes study of the law) and the Damascus Document (which speaks of a penitential movement). All these groups may be related, and may fit under a broad umbrella of "pietism," but each has its own distinctive nuances, too.[7] The circle which produced Daniel was, indeed, pietistic, but this description is not adequate to identify its social location in Seleucid Jerusalem.

Descriptions of the Danielic group which rest on reconstructions of the

---

5. Compare, e.g., the visions of the divine throne in 1 *Enoch* 14 and Daniel 7.

6. See M. Stone, *Scriptures, Sects, and Visions* (Philadelphia: Fortress Press, 1980), p. 42.

7. See further my discussion in *The Apocalyptic Imagination in Ancient Judaism* (New York: Crossroad, 1984), chap. 2.

Hasidim must be seen to rest on a very shaky foundation. These include Tcherikover's view that the Hasidim were leading scribes whose livelihood was placed in jeopardy by the Hellenistic reform,[8] and Plöger's view that they were "eschatological conventicles" whose earlier history can be glimpsed in the eschatological prophecies of the postexilic era, such as the Isaianic apocalypse (Isaiah 24—27) and Zechariah 12—14.[9] While Daniel is surely indebted to eschatological prophecy in some way, it does not necessarily derive from the same continuous social movement.[10] Daniel may have known the prophetic material from other sources.

The most natural place to look for the prehistory of the *maśkîlîm* of Daniel 11 is in the tales which make up the first half of the book.[11] These legends provide an extended introduction to the visions and establish the fictive identity of Daniel himself. The assumption that they can also tell us something about the identity of the *maśkîlîm* is strengthened by the fact that Daniel and his friends are characterized in 1:4 as *maśkîlîm bᵉkol ḥokmāh*, skilled in all wisdom. These legends may not quite give us "a composite portrait of the ideal hasidic sage,"[12] but they reasonably may be taken as a portrait of the ideal *maśkîl* of Daniel's tradition.

Daniel and his friends are characterized in the tales by strict observance of the laws (e.g., the food laws in Daniel 1)[13] and rejection of idolatry, even at the risk of death (chap. 3). Daniel is given to prayer (6:10) and enjoys God-given wisdom. In the visions of chapters 7—12 Daniel is also a man of prayer who does penance for the sins of his people and also ponders the writings of the prophets (Daniel 9). It is interesting to compare this portrait with Sirach's sketch of the scribe as one who devotes himself to study the law of the Most High, is concerned with prophecies as well as proverbs, prays, and makes supplication for his sins. Sirach's wise man also "will serve among great men and appear before rulers and travel through foreign nations," but his primary profession is that of scholar and teacher (Sir. 39:1–11). This comparison not only shows the common elements of scribal piety but also allows the distinctive features of Daniel to emerge. In the court tales, at least, Daniel and his friends are not primarily teachers who study the Torah. They are courtiers, or royal advisors, trained in the language and literature of the Chaldeans. Daniel's primary skill is in the interpretation of dreams and mysterious revelations. For Sirach, "divinations and omens and dreams are folly."

8. V. Tcherikover, *Hellenistic Civilization and the Jews* (New York: Atheneum, 1970), pp. 125–26, 196–97.

9. Plöger, *Theocracy and Eschatology*.

10. See J. Blenkinsopp, "Interpretation and the Tendency to Sectarianism: An Aspect of Second Temple History," in E. P. Sanders et al., eds., *Jewish and Christian Self-Definition* (Philadelphia: Fortress Press, 1981), 2:3.

11. J. J. Collins, "The Court-Tales in Daniel and the Development of Apocalyptic," *JBL* 94 (1975) 218–34; R. R. Wilson, "From Prophecy to Apocalyptic: Reflections on the Shape of Israelite Religion," *Semeia* 21 (1981) 79–95.

12. Blenkinsopp, "Interpretation," p. 19.

13. There can be little doubt that the issue here is observance of dietary laws, *pace* Towner, *Daniel*, pp. 24–26.

He allows that they may be sent from God as a visitation but insists that the law can be fulfilled without them (Sir. 34:1–8). There is a marked difference in emphasis between Sirach and Daniel, and the latter's wisdom stands closer to the mantic wisdom of the Chaldeans, who were supposedly his professional colleagues.

The legends in Daniel 1—6 cannot be taken as a direct account of the predecessors of the *maśkîlîm*, but they must be held to reflect their ideology. Three aspects of the tales concern us here: the geographical setting, the fact that Daniel and his companions are in the service of the pagan king, and the fact that they show a very positive attitude to gentile rule. The last point has occasioned some surprise[14] and would be difficult to reconcile with the supposed "eschatological conventicles" of the Hasidim. Only in Daniel 2 do we find an eschatological prophecy, and even then the emphasis is on the astonishing wisdom of Daniel and his god rather than on the future expectation. There is no urgency in the tales. It is sufficient that the God of Israel is ultimately in control. When Daniel pronounces the demise of the Babylonian kingdom, the pronouncement is given to other Gentiles.[15]

The ideology of Daniel 1—6 has been explained in various ways. O. H. Steck notes its affinity to the ideology of the Jerusalem theocratic establishment, which existed in the framework of the world empires.[16] "Wisdom" circles in Jerusalem might be expected to be familiar with international lore and aspire to surpass the Chaldean wise men. Steck draws support for this thesis from the hymnic passages, the interest in temple vessels in chapters 1 and 5, and the fact that Daniel opens his windows towards Jerusalem in chapter 6. Yet it is not apparent why stories reflecting the ideology of the Jerusalem establishment should be set in the Diaspora. The contrast between Daniel and Ben Sira, the one known representative of Jerusalem wisdom with ties to the theocracy, tells against Steck's view. Allusions to Jerusalem are remarkably sparse in these chapters and the temple vessels figure prominently only in chapter 5. The treatment of Jeremiah's prophecy in chapter 9 denies that the sixth-century restoration brought an end to the "desolations of Jerusalem," in marked contrast to such theocratic compositions as Zechariah and Chronicles (see Zech. 1:12; Chron. 36:20–21). In view of this it is unlikely that Daniel's circle was closely affiliated with the Jerusalem establishment.

A more plausible view holds that the tales were written to outline "a lifestyle for the Diaspora."[17] To be sure, few Jews could hope to be as successful as Daniel, and not all who entered the royal service were necessarily so scrupulous about dietary observance. Yet we know from the case of Nehe-

---

14. Hengel, *Judaism and Hellenism* 1:179.

15. See further my discussion in *The Apocalyptic Vision,* pp. 27–59, and in *Daniel, 1 and 2 Maccabees* (Wilmington: Glazier, 1980), pp. 20–68.

16. O. H. Steck, "Weltgeschehen und Gottesvolk im Buche Daniel," in D. Lührmann and G. Strecker, eds., *Kirche* (Tübingen: J. C. B. Mohr, 1980), pp. 53–78.

17. W. L. Humphreys, "A Life-Style for the Diaspora: A Study of the Tales of Esther and Daniel," *JBL* 92 (1973) 211–23.

miah that a devout Jew could rise at court. The tales presuppose a Diaspora
setting not only in terms of the places mentioned but especially in the kinds
of problems addressed—rivalry with pagan courtiers, the dangers of refusing
to participate in the local cults. These were problems which confronted Jews
of the Diaspora rather than residents of Jerusalem. In view of this setting, it
seems reasonable to "accept the narrative's own description of the group
involved,"[18] while bearing in mind that the description is an idealized one
and is developed through narrative fictions. We may infer tentatively that the
authors and tradents of the tales were, like Daniel, upper-class, well-edu-
cated Jews, who found careers in government service in the eastern Diaspora. They were successful in the gentile world and stood to gain by
maintaining the status quo. While their historical knowledge was erratic,
they were familiar with a wide range of traditions, some of which, like the
famous four-kingdom schema, were of gentile origin. They did not adopt all
the forms of divination practised by their Chaldean colleagues, but they
developed an interest in dreams and omens which remained utterly alien to
the Jerusalem-centered wisdom of Ben Sira. At the same time, they maintained unwavering piety. The goal of the tales is ultimately not the advance-
ment of the wise men but the glorification of their God. The interest in
dreams and revelations already contained the seed of a mystical tendency
which becomes more evident in chapters 7—12.

The tales in Daniel 1—6 suggest that the social prehistory of the groups
which developed apocalypticism in the Hellenistic era must be sought in
circles very different from Plöger's eschatological conventicles. We may note
here that the other main branch of Jewish apocalypticism, which is attested
in 1 Enoch, also has roots in Mesopotamia and strong affinities with Chaldean wisdom.[19] The figure of Enoch himself was probably developed as the
Jewish counterpart to the Mesopotamian seventh king, Enmeduranki, legendary founder of a guild of diviners. There too the eschatological interest
was not originally the focal point of the group, but it emerged as a response to
new circumstances in the Hellenistic period.

II

The setting of the visions in Daniel 7—12 is very different from that of the
tales. While Daniel is supposedly still in exile (8:2 gives his location as Susa),
the visions focus on events in Jerusalem; and that is where the wise maśkîlîm
are active. We can only guess as to when, or why, the tradents of the Daniel
tradition returned from the Diaspora. Perhaps the transition of Judea to
Seleucid rule in 198 B.C. provided an occasion. The visions give little
indication of the professional occupation of the authors. From the title
maśkîlîm and from their activity in the time of persecution we may infer that
they were teachers. Their attitude to gentile rulers had changed drastically

18. Wilson, "From Prophecy to Apocalyptic," p. 88.
19. See esp. J. VanderKam, *Enoch and the Growth of an Apocalyptic Tradition*, CBQMS 16
(Washington, D.C.: Catholic Biblical Association, 1984).

from that of the tales. The change, of course, can be most directly attributed to the persecution of the Jewish religion by Antiochus Epiphanes.

Daniel views the persecution as a direct rebellion by the king against God. Other views were possible. Some Jewish authors saw the events of these years as a punishment for sin (*Jubilees, Testament of Moses*). Second Maccabees presents the persecution as an outgrowth of a long and complex struggle within the Jewish community. Even Maccabees, which attributes the suppression of Judaism to the king's desire to unify his kingdom, notes the initiative of the "lawless men" who proposed a covenant with the Gentiles. Many modern scholars have held that the primary responsibility lay with the Jewish Hellenizers.[20] Daniel, however, lays the blame almost exclusively on the king. The most detailed discussion, in chapter 11, notes that a role was played by "those who forsake the holy covenant" but claims that the king's heart was already set against the holy covenant. In chapters 7, 8, and 11 Daniel uses ancient mythic imagery which likens the king to the chaos-monster of the sea (chap. 7) or to Lucifer the son of Dawn (chaps. 8— 11).[21] Daniel's prayer in chapter 9 confesses the sin of the people and presupposes the Deuteronomic view that oppression by Gentiles is a form of divine punishment, but the angel's reply makes clear that "the desolations of Jerusalem" are decreed for a fixed duration "until the decreed end is poured out on the desolator" (9:27). It is the gentile rulers, not the Jews, who have aroused the wrath of God.[22]

The divine wrath is aroused by the measures taken by Antiochus against the Jewish religion. Daniel 7 mentions his attempt "to change the times and the law" but does not mention the desecration of the temple, which may not yet have occurred when this chapter was written. Chapter 8 focuses on the disruption of the temple cult, and this is highlighted again in chapters 9 and 11. In each case, however, the treatment of the temple is placed in the broader context of the persecution and the king's rebellion against God.[23]

We should note that Daniel does not view the issue as a conflict between Judaism and Hellenism. His problem is with the conduct of a Hellenistic king, and consequently with gentile rule over Israel, but not with Hellenistic culture as such. He refers to the Hellenizers as "violators of the covenant" but otherwise ignores the so-called Hellenistic reform. The visions draw on

20. So esp. E. Bickerman, *The God of the Maccabees* (Leiden: E. J. Brill, 1979), and Hengel, *Judaism and Hellenism* 1:277–309. For an alternative reconstruction see J. A. Goldstein, *II Maccabees*, AB 41A (Garden City, N.Y.: Doubleday & Co., 1983), pp. 84–123.

21. Collins, *The Apocalyptic Vision*, pp. 95–118. The attempt of A. J. Ferch, *The Son of Man in Daniel Seven* (Berrien Springs, Mich.: Andrews University, 1983), pp. 40–107, to deny the mythic allusions in Daniel 7 rests on a misunderstanding of the nature of a literary allusion. See my comments in "Apocalyptic Genre and Mythic Allusions in Daniel," *JSOT* 21 (1981) 83–100.

22. Steck, "Weltgeschehen und Gottesvolk," pp. 65–75, argues that Daniel 9 marks a shift in the theology of the book, due to the influence of a Deuteronomic strand of tradition. See my criticism of this viewpoint in *Daniel*, FOTL, pp. 94–95.

23. J. C. H. Lebram, "Apokalyptik und Hellenismus im Buche Daniel," *VT* 20 (1970) 503– 24, argues that Daniel is written from a priestly point of view. This is scarcely necessary. All pious Jews were distraught over the desecration of the temple.

motifs and literary forms from gentile as well as Jewish sources. The conduct of Jason and Menelaus, while it may have been sinful, is not seen as the root of the problem. Further, the complaints against the king are religious rather than social in character. The primary grievance is not the alteration of the traditional constitution by the reformers but the religious decrees of the king.

It is quite clear that the *maśkîlîm* of the Maccabean era have no stake whatever in preserving the status quo. The vehemence with which Antiochus is denounced may bespeak disillusionment with the gentile monarchs, which then is retrojected on the whole period of gentile rule. The visions do, however, retain the broad political horizon of the tales, and the historical detail of chapter 11 in particular suggests that the author was well-informed on international events. Despite his hostility to the Seleucids, Daniel does not show any sympathy for their rivals, the Ptolemies of Egypt. Rather, all the gentile kingdoms who have ruled over Israel are viewed as hostile to God.

While the visions retain the political horizon of the tales, the goals of the authors appear different. In chapters 1—6 the heroes sought promotion and acclaim within the gentile kingdom and thereby the recognition and praise of their God. Only once does Daniel decline the honors of a pagan king, and that is when he is about to prophesy the fall of Babylon to Darius the Mede. The goals of the *maśkîlîm* in chapters 7—12 are more elusive. Chapters 8 and 9 look only for the demise of the king and the restoration of the cult. Chapter 7 speaks of a kingdom which is given to "the holy ones of the Most High" or to "the people of the holy ones." Finally chapter 12 speaks of the resurrection of the dead.

The nature of the kingdom given to the "holy ones" has been the subject of much dispute. Since it follows on the series of world kingdoms, it presumably involves an era of Jewish supremacy. Yet the terminology is significant. Elsewhere in Daniel "holy ones" are angels or heavenly beings (in Nebuchadnezzar's dream in chap. 4 and again in 8:13), and this is the most usual meaning of the term in its substantive sense. The use of the term here suggests that the "people of the holy ones" has some special relationship with the angelic host. This suggestion is corroborated in chapters 10—12, where the history of the postexilic period is set against the backdrop of a heavenly battle between Michael, the angelic prince of Israel, and the "princes" of Persia and Greece.[24]

Daniel 7 does not further specify the nature of this kingdom or indicate how it will be structured. The main passage in Daniel which sheds light on the internal social and political situation is found in chapter 11. There Daniel distinguishes three parties: the wicked who violate the covenant, the people who know their God and whose leaders are apparently the *maśkîlîm*, and the *rabbîm* or masses, whose position remains to be decided. (The Maccabees are not explicitly acknowledged, unless they are included in the "little help"

---

24. For the arguments see Collins, *The Apocalyptic Vision*, pp. 123–47.

which the *maśkîlîm* will receive.) We might expect from this that the eschatological kingdom would be ruled by the *maśkîlîm* and exclude the violators of the covenant, but this is never asserted. Daniel 11—12 does not pick up the notion of the kingdom. Instead the prediction focuses on the resurrection, when the righteous will enjoy eternal life and the *maśkîlîm* will shine with the brightness of the firmament and be like the stars. The comparison with the stars is paralleled in 1 *Enoch* 104 where its meaning is clarified: "You will shine like the lights of heaven and the gate of heaven will be opened to you . . . you will have great joy like the angels of heaven" and "you shall be associates of the host of heaven."

While the hope for an earthly kingdom remains part of Daniel's expectation, the primary goals of the *maśkîlîm* are not in the political realm. Rather they concern purity and communion with the angels. Daniel himself remains the model. He is a man of prayer who fasts and repents for the sin of his people and is in constant communication with angels through his visions. The *maśkîlîm* see the persecution as an occasion for purification and are prepared to lose their lives in the process. They do not participate in the militant resistance but act as teachers to enlighten the masses. The teaching they impart is not primarily the Torah, which they surely assume, but the apocalyptic world view of the Book of Daniel itself. The mystical tendencies are paralleled in the *Enoch* literature, which was roughly contemporary in origin; but the righteous in Enoch grasp the sword and hope to "acquire houses because of their righteousness" (1 *Enoch* 91:13).[25] Daniel betrays no such temporal ambitions.

III

The symbolic world of Daniel has both temporal and spatial dimensions. On the one hand, there is the sense that the world order is falling apart, expressed most vividly in the vision of the beasts from the sea in chapter 7. This is accompanied however by a strong conviction that God is in control and that history follows a predetermined course. On the other hand there is a lively belief throughout in the activity of supernatural powers.[26] This is most directly evident in chapter 10 where we read of the angelic "princes" of Persia, Greece, and Israel. The prominence of angels has troubled some recent commentators, but it cannot be dismissed as incidental. Daniel's angelology is less developed than that of 1 *Enoch*, but this does not mean that the author keeps it "at a minimum."[27] Other second-century authors (e.g., 1 and 2 Maccabees) interpreted the Maccabean crisis with far less appeal to angels. Their role in Daniel's visions is crucial since they are the mediators and guarantors of his revelation throughout the visions. The

---

25. S. B. Reid, "1 Enoch: The Rising Elite of the Apocalyptic Movement," in *SBL Seminar Papers* (1983), pp. 147–56.

26. On the importance of angels in apocalyptic literature see C. Rowland, *The Open Heaven* (New York: Crossroad, 1982), pp. 78–123.

27. Towner, *Daniel*, p. 173.

throne of God is surrounded by "ten thousand times ten thousand" in Daniel 7 just as in 1 *Enoch,* where they are explicitly called "holy ones." In Daniel 10—12 the outcome of human history is decided by a struggle between heavenly "princes," and the archangel Michael emerges as the savior of Israel.

Modern embarrassment with this vividly mythical world view has been acknowledged most frankly by W. S. Towner. According to Towner, "God has no need of angels,"[28] and besides they are irrelevant to human actions.[29] Underlying these objections is a serious theological concern that belief in angelic activity will detract from the sovereignty of God and from the significance of human action in the present.

We need not dwell here on the difficulties of pronouncing on what God does or does not need. The more fundamental point is that the Book of Daniel was not written to express the needs of God but those of a group of Jews in face of persecution. The question is not whether angels exist but whether they are meaningful symbols within Daniel's world view.

The very abundance of angels in apocalyptic literature should caution against too hasty a conclusion that they had no meaning for the persecuted Jews. Their meaning is quite clear in Daniel 10—12. Faced with a situation where those who were faithful to their religion were subject to death, Daniel's *maśkîlîm* found consolation and strength by imagining another level of reality where things were different. The righteous were powerless on earth, but on the hidden level they were championed by Michael, who would surely prevail. The "knowledge" of this future course of events, which constitutes the understanding of the wise, is in turn guaranteed by the revealing angels. The angelic world was so meaningful and important for the *maśkîlîm* that they staked their lives on it. The reward they hoped for was part of this mythical universe.

We must emphasize that neither determinism nor belief in supernatural powers detracts in any way from the seriousness of human action. While the course of events is predetermined, the fate of individuals is not. The certainty with which the crisis comes to a head sharpens the context for a human decision. The *rabbîm* are called on to take their stand on one side or another. While the battle is in the hands of Michael, his victory will not benefit all Jews indiscriminately. The judgment is still based on the actions of human individuals.

If we look on the angels as part of Daniel's construction of reality, the issue is not whether this belief was correct but whether it was fruitful. It was precisely their faith in the angelic world, and in the possibility of future participation in it, which enabled these *maśkîlîm* to withstand the persecution without compromising their integrity.[30] Not only did they reject the

---

28. Ibid., p. 118.

29. On this point Towner follows Hartman and DiLella, *The Book of Daniel,* p. 91.

30. See my essay, "Apocalyptic Eschatology as the Transcendence of Death," in P. D. Hanson, ed., *Visionaries and Their Apocalypses* (Philadelphia: Fortress Press, 1983), pp. 61–84. See also the fine discussion of the theology of Daniel by Lacocque, *Daniel et Son Temps,* pp. 169–223.

demands of the king, but they also avoided the violence of the Maccabees and the compromises which it involved. One cannot fail to be impressed when integrity is maintained at the cost of life itself. Ultimately what the angelic world symbolizes is the transcendence of values, the conviction that there is more to reality than the physical world and that some commitments are even more important than the prolongation of one's individual life.

IV

The contrast with the Maccabees highlights the problem of appropriating the Book of Daniel in a modern situation. The difficulty is not ultimately in the imagery of Daniel, if we take the time to understand it. Neither does it lie in the peculiarity of Daniel's historical and social situation. There are sufficient analogies between the religious persecution of Maccabean times and any modern situation of oppression, however different the specifics may be. Rather, the problem lies in Daniel's ethic of quietism. To the best of our knowledge it was Judas Maccabee, rather than the archangel Michael, who brought about the end of the persecution. While Daniel was certainly concerned with the welfare of the whole people, his effect was primarily in the realm of personal integrity. In his view, the dynamics of history and the structures of society were not of human making and not subject to change by human forces. Accordingly, the pragmatic Maccabees appear to have had a more direct effect on the good of Jewish society as a whole. The question arises whether the visions of Daniel were not illusions which distracted the "wise" from coming to grips with the problem at hand.

The apocalyptic belief in supernatural powers and in a future judgment beyond present verification is a prime example of the kind of religion criticized by Karl Marx. "Man," wrote Marx, "looked for a superman in the fantastic reality of heaven and found nothing there but the reflection of himself. . . . The abolition of religion as the illusory happiness of the people is required for their real happiness. The demand to give up the illusions about its condition is the demand to give up a condition which needs illusions."[31] Modern liberationists, who take their cue from Marx, will find the Maccabees more congenial than Daniel.

Yet Marx surely dispensed too hastily with what he called "illusions." A wiser T. S. Eliot said that "humankind cannot bear very much reality,"[32] and that is especially true in times of persecution and oppression. Moreover, myths and symbols have their own reality and play no small part in shaping human lives. Daniel's vehement denunciation of the king and the belief in supernatural help surely contributed to the morale of the entire Jewish resistance. We know that some apocalyptic visions—for example, those in *1 Enoch*—were used more directly to support the Maccabean cause. Besides,

---

31. K. Marx, "Toward the Critique of Hegel's Philosophy of Right," in *Basic Writings on Politics and Philosophy: Karl Marx and Friedrich Engels* (Garden City, N.Y.: Doubleday & Co., 1959), pp. 262–63.

32. T. S. Eliot, *Murder in the Cathedral* (London: Faber & Faber, 1965), p. 75.

the legacy of the Maccabees had its own ambiguities. While the armed rebellion against Antiochus Epiphanes was successful, similar struggles against Rome later would prove catastrophic. It is not always given to humanity to change the conditions which need illusions. What Daniel offers is not a practical strategy for revolution but an act of the imagination which affirms the freedom of the human spirit in defiance of any force of oppression. The symbolic world which it conjures up may be an "illusion" in positivistic terms, but it can be inspiring and life-giving nonetheless. It does not necessarily give us an ethic for all seasons, but it has its proper place among the resources for living bequeathed to us by the Hebrew Scriptures.

20

A Journey Through
Danielic Spaces: The Book
of Daniel in the Theology and Piety of the
Christian Community

John G. Gammie

Seeing the way Daniel has been interpreted in other times calls
attention to the impoverishment critical studies have imposed upon
the contemporary preacher who seeks in Daniel a word for our time.

Parts I–III of this work constitute a selective investigation of the ways the
Book of Daniel has affected the theology and world view of Christians from
the time of Irenaeus up to the Protestant Reformation.

I

Irenaeus (ca. 130–200), bishop of Lyons, utilized the Book of Daniel
extensively in his treatise *Against Heresies* to expound his doctrine of Christ,
the Bible, and the millennium. The stone not hewn with hands of Daniel 2
which smashes the great statues is a figure of Christ in that Jesus was not
conceived through any human agent (3.21.7).[1] Jesus, indeed, will be the one
who will destroy temporal kingdoms and will himself fill the earth as foretold
in Daniel 2 (4.20.11) and thus establish an eternal kingdom to be introduced
at the resurrection of the just (5.26.2). As the body has many members, so
Jesus is prefigured in many ways in the prophets (4.23.10)—as Son of Man
who will come in the clouds even as he previously appeared as the Son of
God in the burning furnace with the three young faithful Israelites (4.23.10;
Daniel 3 and 7).

According to the divine dispensation, Christ is the treasure hidden in the

---

1. The citation here, as hereafter in section I, is to divisions within the tractate under review.
For access to the thought of the early church fathers I have relied chiefly on Alexander Roberts
and James Donaldson, eds., *The Ante-Nicene Fathers*, 5 vols. (1885; Grand Rapids: Wm. B.
Eerdmans, 1950).

field of the first Testament until the time of the consummation when knowledge will be enriched. Under the old dispensation God was forming his kingdom beforehand and also proclaiming beforehand "that the one who loves God shall arrive at such excellency as even to see God" (4.26.1). This doctrine of Scripture Irenaeus grounds in the text from Dan. 12:4 where the prophet is instructed to "shut up the words and seal the book, until the time of the end" when "knowledge shall increase." The moment of disclosure transpired at the cross of Christ (4.26.1). At the first Advent Christ was the stone rejected by the builders (Ps. 118:22), but at the second he will come upon the clouds (4.33.1; Dan. 7:13). What is interesting about Irenaeus' doctrine of the Scripture is that already in the second century A.D. we see expressed the doctrine for which St. Augustine is better known two centuries later: ". . . *et in Vetere Novum lateat, et in Novo Vetus pateat*" ("Both the New [Testament] is concealed in the Old, and the Old revealed in the New").[2]

As for the millennium, Irenaeus reasoned that inasmuch as God took six days to create the world, so it would be six divine days before its consummation and the Sabbath rest. Because of this correspondence, he reckoned there would be six thousand years before the millennium, the seventh divine day of a thousand years (5.28.3). At the time of the consummation the antichrist would reign for three-and-a-half years (5.28.2; Dan. 9:27); he would sit in the temple and desolate the holy place (5:25:4; cf. Dan. 7:13). This antichrist would come from the tribe of Daniel (5.30.s; cf. Jer. 8:16). At the consummation the kingdom and dominion would be given to the saints of the Most High (5.34.2; Dan. 7:27). Thus the Book of Daniel, supplemented especially by the Book of Revelation and 2 Thessalonians, furnished the elements for a full-blown millenarian eschatology. Irenaeus himself did not posit the date of creation, and hence the date of the consummation, but his successors were soon to become explicit where he remained indefinite (see below on Africanus and Hippolytus). Irenaeus, however, did exert a formative influence on the Western millenarian outlook.[3]

The Latin father and attorney Tertullian (ca. 160–200) from Carthage is similar to Irenaeus in his millenarian expectations. The common bond appears to be Montanists who originated in Asia Minor, home of Irenaeus, and whom Irenaeus defended in Rome. Scholars are divided, however, on the extent to which Irenaeus embraced Montanism. Irenaeus did not go so far as the Montanists who felt the consummation was so imminent that they set a specific date for its arrival and went to Phrygia to await it.[4] There is no such disagreement with respect to Tertullian's sympathy with Montanist doctrine and millenarianism. Even though the expected end did not arrive, the

2. Cited in Jack B. Rogers and Donald M. McKim, *The Authority and Interpretation of the Bible: An Historical Approach* (San Francisco: Harper & Row, 1979), pp. 33, 66 n. 155.

3. See the excellent historical survey by Norman Cohn, *The Pursuit of the Millennium: Revolutionary Millenarians and Mystical Anarchists of the Middle Ages*, rev. ed. (London: Oxford University Press, 1970), p. 27.

4. Ibid., p. 25.

movement spread. Tertullian joined it around 207 and reports how a wondrous portent had been seen in the sky in Judaea early every morning for forty days, only fading away as the day advanced. This sign was taken to be, as Norman Cohn put it, "a sure sign that the Heavenly Jerusalem was about to descend."[5] Tertullian later left the Montanists but retained many of their beliefs as we see from the following summary of his use of Daniel. (1) His tractate *On Fasting* (ca. 208) opens with a sally against the extremes to which the Montanists wished to press the importance of fasting—to the point of eschewing marriage. He goes on, however, to encourage fasting and xerophagy (the eating of dried foods), using the example of Daniel in the court of Nebuchadnezzar to bolster his case. From this course of strict diet there came to Daniel wisdom which he interprets as "recognition of the mysteries to be obtained from God" (chap. 9). (2) Similarly to Irenaeus, Tertullian taught there would be two advents of Christ, except that the stone of Dan. 2:34 which would crush the image of the secular kingdom is now understood to be Christ's church (*Against Marcion* 3.7). (3) In the same tractate, Tertullian described at length the glory of Christ's millennial kingdom, drawing upon many scriptural passages, including Daniel 7 (3.25). (4) To the prophet Daniel, God revealed how Jesus would come as Son of Man in the clouds (4.10; Dan. 7:13) even as he was seen before with the three men in the furnace (4.21); his second coming would be accompanied by terrible signs (4.40; cf. Luke 21:31). In the everlasting kingdom which will not be destroyed, "men shall not die, neither shall they marry, but be like the angels" (4.40; cf. Dan. 7:14). Thus Tertullian interpreted Daniel to uphold the ideal of an angel-like celibacy at the millennium (cf. Mark 12:25).

An interesting diagram might be drawn to show the correlation between a church father's fervor of millenarian expectation on the one hand and his attitude toward culture and pagan philosophy on the other. At one side of the diagram one would clearly place Tertullian, whose millenarian expectations were as keen as his anticultural sentiments were fervent. On the opposite side of the diagram would be found Clement of Alexandria (ca. 150–216) whose millenarian expectations were weak and who, contrary to Tertullian, saw in pagan philosophy, not an enemy to Christianity, but a preparation and training ground.[6] Clement's "attempt to combine appreciation of culture with loyalty to Christ"[7]—which in many ways foreshadowed the stance of mainline denominations today—did not lead him in his reading of Daniel to reflect upon the eschaton beyond history but rather upon how its prophecies had been fulfilled within historical time. Thus, Clement reasoned, since there were sixty-two weeks till the cutting off of the anointed one (Dan. 9:26), the subsequent seven weeks must have related to the period of time immediately following the crucifixion of Jesus (*Miscellanies* 1.21). Indeed, Dan. 9:26b, "the people of the prince who is to come shall destroy the city

---

5. Ibid., p. 26.
6. See H. Richard Niebuhr, *Christ and Culture* (New York: Harper & Row, 1951), pp. 64–69, 130–35.
7. Ibid., p. 134.

and the sanctuary," referred to the destruction of Jerusalem in A.D. 70. Not all Clement's interests in Daniel were historical. He also drew practical lessons from the book. Because the Ancient of Days is vested in white (Dan. 7:9), he taught one should neither dye one's hair (*Miscellanies* 3.3) nor wear dyed clothing (*Miscellanies* 2.11). On the other hand, Clement took Daniel's wearing of the purple (Dan. 5:7, 29) as illustrative of how believers may make concessions on minor points so long as they do not compromise in essentials (*Miscellanies* 6.15).

Clement's most famous pupil, Origen (ca. 185–254), carried forward his teacher's application of the Scripture to historical events and persons, but he also displayed considerable independence. Like his teacher, Clement, Origen espoused a realized eschatology, differing only in a slight historical nuance. The cutting off of the anointed one (the crucifixion of Christ the ruler) was not something that occurred after sixty-two weeks, but "after the seventy weeks were fulfilled" (*On First Principles* 4.5). Further, as prophesied in Job, Christ subdued the Great Fish (Leviathan, a figure for the enemy, the devil, cf. Job 41:1) and gave his true disciples power to tread upon serpents and scorpions without sustaining any injury from them (cf. Luke 10:19). The battle against the antichrist was thus a present battle for which the Scripture of both Testaments, properly understood, prepared the initiant (*Against Celsus* 2.49; 6.45). Thus the words of Dan. 8:23–25 about the "king of bold countenance" who would "destroy . . . the holy people," Origen understood in a general, but unmistakably prophetic, fashion. Elsewhere Origen is more explicit. In his exposition of the Book of Job, for example, he identifies the "flaming torch" going forth from the mouth of Leviathan (Job 41:19) as the heretical Gnostics, archenemies of the church: Marcion, Valentinius, and Basilides; "but," he said, "their flames will not touch us."[8] In a line of theological deduction which is carried much further into the high Middle Ages by St. Thomas, Origen draws upon Dan. 7:10 ("ten thousand times ten thousand stood before him") as the basis upon which to conclude there exists "a multitude" of "beings friendly to us" (*Against Celsus* 8:34). The superiority of Daniel the prophet to pagan prophetic figures, such as the Phythian priestess to Apollo at Delphi or those who delivered oracles at Dodona, Origen saw demonstrated precisely in Daniel's abstinence and in his simple diet of water and grain (*Against Celsus* 7.7). Proof of the existence of the heavenly city of God, Origen argued, is to be found also in the Book of Daniel wherein it is asserted, "His works are truth" (*Against Celsus* 7.31; Dan. 4:37). A distinction must be drawn, he said, between "the works of God" and "the works of God's hands"—"the latter of which are of an inferior sort." Even though Sextus Julius Africanus (ca. 160–240) questioned on linguistic grounds whether the tale of Susanna and the Elders (Daniel 13) could possibly have been written originally in Hebrew or Aramaic, Origen staunchly defended the authenticity of this chapter and the providential

---

8. J. P. Migne, ed., *Patrologiae Graecae* 12, *Origenes* 2 (Paris: Migne, 1862), pp. 1048–49.

intent to minister to the edification of all the churches of Christ through the Sacred Scriptures which were used in the churches (*Letter to Africanus* 4).

It is not surprising that the first Christian commentator on the Book of Daniel was a disciple of Irenaeus. Fragments from the Commentary (ca. 202) by Hippolytus (ca. 170–236) are relatively accessible in English translation.[9] Hippolytus, like his teacher, posited that six thousand years would pass from the creation to consummation of the times. In agreement with his contemporary, Sextus Julius Africanus,[10] he also taught that Christ had been born in the year 5550 after creation. With this teaching, an editor of Hippolytus has rightly asserted, Hippolytus "cut the nerve of expectation of the end in that the Second Coming would come only in the distant future."[11] The date, however, was to become increasingly important—curiously, not so much around the year A.D. 500 (for the consummation of 6000 years since creation) but just prior to the year A.D. 1500 (the putative date of the completion of the millennium of the Sabbath rest).

Like the other church fathers, Hippolytus drew on the Book of Daniel to make certain homiletic exhortation: Thus Daniel teaches "that it is not earthly meats that give to men their beauty and strength, but the grace of God bestowed by the Word" (comment on Dan. 1:12). Similarly, Hippolytus proposed an allegoric interpretation of Daniel 13:

> Susannah prefigured the Church; and Joachim, her husband, Christ; and the garden, the calling of the saints who are planted like fruitful trees in the Church. And Babylon is the world, and the two elders are set forth as a figure of the two people that plot against the Church—they are, namely, of the circumcision, and the other of the Gentiles. ("Fragments from Commentaries" 6, on Dan. 13:7)

As for the antichrist, Hippolytus taught there was not simply one, but at least three: Antiochus Epiphanes, Augustus, and one more whom he defined in rather vague terms (*Treatise on Christ and the Antichrist*, 49–50; cf. 61). A contemporary of Hippolytus, Cyprian, the converted rhetorician (ca. A.D. 246) and martyred bishop of Carthage (A.D. 250), often referred prophetically to the faithful refusal of the three young men to engage in idolatry (*Epistle 55* 5; *Exhortation to Martyrdom* 11; Daniel 3). Cyprian carried forward the christological and ecclesiological interpretation of the "stone" of Daniel 2 by positing that after smashing the image, Christ (the stone) would fill the earth through the spiritual children born to him and his bride the church (*Testimonies* 17–19). In his *Treatise* 8, Cyprian used Daniel's exhortation to Nebuchadnezzar to "practice righteousness" (Dan. 4:27, RSV) as grounds for the practice of almsgiving (*Works and Alms* 5). This understanding of the original Aramaic *ṣidqah* as "almsgiving" reached the Latin by way of the Greek. As early as the Greek translation of the Pentateuch (ca. 250 B.C.), the

---

9. Roberts and Donaldson, eds., *The Ante-Nicene Fathers* 5:177–93.

10. In his *History of the World* (*Chronographiai*) to A.D. 217; so *Oxford Dictionary of the Christian Church*, ed. F. L. Cross (London: Oxford University Press, 1957), p. 755.

11. G. Nathanael Bonwetsch, *Studien zu den Kommentaren Hippolyts zum Buche Daniel und Hohen Liede* (Leipzig: J. C. Hinrichs, 1897), p. 53.

Hebrew *ṣedaqah,* "righteousness," had come to be understood as "almsgiving" (see the LXX of Deut. 6:25; 24:13).

II

Even before the acceptance of Christianity by the Roman emperor Constantine, the main lines of the interpretation of Daniel had been established. Christians drew upon the tales as exemplifications of worthy acts of faith and practice; they understood the book to contain a wondrous prediction of the crucifixion of their savior (Dan. 9:26) and of his triumph over worldly kingdoms (Dan. 2:34). Hippolytus and Africanus had predicted that that moment of triumph remained in the future, to come in the year A.D. 500. Following the sack of Rome in A.D. 410 by the Visigoths, however, Christians were forced to rethink whether or not the Almighty had not already established with the coming of Christ a city which would not perish. Thus, Augustine contrasted the *civitas dei,* the church, with the *civitas terrena,* the Roman Empire.[12] He did not remove altogether a sense of expectancy, however. Thus referring to Dan. 7:15–28 and Jerome's commentary on it he wrote: ". . . He who reads this passage even half-asleep, cannot fail to see that the kingdom of the Antichrist shall fiercely, though for a short time, assail the church before the last judgement of God shall introduce the eternal reign of the saints."[13]

Next to the commentary by Hippolytus, Jerome's is the fullest remaining to us from the early centuries of the church. Of special interest for our purposes are the following: (1) his earnest attempt to seek out Jewish interpretation;[14] (2) his understanding that Daniel and his three friends were eunuchs; and (3) despite his disagreements with them, his preservation of many of the arguments used by the pagan Porphyry in favor of a Maccabean dating of the book.

Thus far in this survey attention has focused on the theological writings. During the same centuries Christian writers edited and wrote in a more popular vein a series of Oracles under the name of the ancient prophetess Sibyl. These Sibylline Oracles combined, like the Book of Daniel, historical surveys with predictions of the end time. The tremendous impact of these writings not only in the early centuries but throughout the Middle Ages is dramatically illustrated in the Sistine Chapel wherein Michelangelo interspersed portrayals of five Sibyls (the Persian, Erythrean, Delphic, Cumean, and Libyan) among his portrayals of the prophets (Isaiah, Jeremiah, Ezekiel, Daniel, Zechariah). The Sibylline Oracles[15] draw occasionally on the Book of

---

12. See *The City of God by St. Augustine,* 2 vols., ed. Marcus Dods (1872; New York: Hafner Pub. Co., 1948), 1:436; 2:356–60 (11.1; 20.7).

13. Ibid. 2:394 (20.23).

14. Fully documented in Jay Braverman's recent study, *Jerome's Commentary on Daniel,* CBQMS 7 (Washington, D.C.: Catholic Biblical Association, 1978).

15. This originally Jewish work continued to be expanded. The full range of oracles, recently translated by John J. Collins, now can be conveniently found in *Apocalyptic Literature and Testaments,* vol. 1 of James H. Charlesworth, ed., *The Old Testament Pseudepigrapha* (Garden City, N.Y.: Doubleday & Co., 1983), pp. 317–472.

Daniel: in its description of combat in the heavens and the starry hosts (1.314; cf. Dan. 8:10–11); in its woe pronounced against Libya for its having "destroyed the great house of the Immortal" and having "chewed it terribly with iron teeth" (3.329; cf. Dan. 7:7). One of the most popular and widely spread of works classified as belonging to the Sibylline texts is the so-called Pseudo-Methodius.[16] This apocalyptic prophecy, written in Syria sometime in the eighth century A.D. after the stunning Islamic conquests, bears in common with the Sibylline texts, among other things, an expectation of a righteous worldly ruler prior to the return of Christ. Contrary to most of the Sibylline texts which thought in terms of ten (or nine) stages in world history, the vision of pseudo-Methodius also incorporates the timetable of Hippolytus and Africanus, which, it will be recalled, placed the end of the six millennia from creation at the year A.D. 500 and thus the end of the world at A.D. 1500. The author explicitly refers to the prophetic allusion to the *australem brachium* ("southern forces") of *Danihel* (Dan. 11:15) and interprets them to be the sons of Ishmael, the Cushites. This work taught: "*adpropinquavit consumatio saeculi et non erit longitudo temporum amplius*" ("the consummation of the ages has drawn near and the length of time will not be much longer," chap. 10). In 1474 a Dominican monk showed how it had predicted the defeat of the Turks (Ishmaelites).[17] The next year the Latin translation was published in Cologne. In 1496 a commentary on the work was published in Augsburg and republished in 1498 with woodcuts. Even though the fated year 1500 passed, copies of the Latin and of vernacular translations continued to be made until the seventeenth century.[18]

Albeit in transmuted form, the prophecies of Daniel burned brightly in the apocalyptic vision attributed to Bishop Methodius of Patara who lived four hundred years before the probable date of composition.[19] Other fascinating examples of the vitality of the apocalyptic tradition, and therefore of the Book of Daniel in yet other forms of transmutation, may be found in the recent works of Bernard McGinn of Chicago[20] and in the previously noted historical survey by Norman Cohn.[21]

---

16. For the Latin text see Ernst Sackur, *Sibyllinische Texte und Forschungen* (Halle, 1898; Torino: Bottega d'Erasmo, 1963), pp. 59–113.

17. Later versions of the Latin translation made the reference to the Turks increasingly explicit.

18. Ibid., p. 3.

19. According to the *Oxford Dictionary of the Christian Church*, it is doubtful whether Methodius, the martyred bishop of Olympus in Lycia (d. ca. A.D. 311), ever was bishop of Patara (p. 895).

20. See esp. Bernard McGinn, *Apocalyptic Spirituality: Treatises and Letters of Lactantius, Adso of Montier-en-Der, Joachim of Fiore, the Fransiscan Spirituals, Savonarola*, Classics of Western Spirituality (New York: Paulist Press, 1979), and idem, *Visions of the End: Apocalyptic Traditions in the Middle Ages* (New York: Columbia University Press, 1979). For an entertaining fictional account of how heightened apocalyptic expectations were in the late Middle Ages, see Umberto Eco, *The Name of the Rose*, trans. William Weaver (New York: Harcourt Brace Jovanovich, 1983).

21. See n. 3 above. Cohn is especially helpful in pointing to the common sociological setting of the apocalyptic movements from the second to the sixteenth centuries. Curiously both McGinn and Cohn fail to point to the virtually certain contribution that pseudo-Methodius made to heightened eschatological expectations for the year 1500.

III

Down through the ages Christian theology has been enriched through Jewish theological formulations.[22] The early church fathers built upon the model for blending Platonism and monotheism which had been fashioned by Philo Judaeus (ca. 40 B.C.–A.D. 30). Similarly, in the Middle Ages Albertus Magnus (ca. 1200–1250) and his more famous pupil Thomas Aquinas (1225–1274) built upon the model for blending Aristotelianism and monotheism which had been fashioned by Maimonides (1135–1204) in his justly famous *Guide of the Perplexed*.[23] It is instructive to see how Aquinas used the Book of Daniel in the course of his more than four dozen citations in the *Summa Theologica*. Like Maimonides, the great doctor of the church both differentiated degrees of prophetic vision and utilized the prophet Daniel in so doing. The "intellective vision" such as Daniel had (Dan. 10:1) Aquinas considered superior to "imaginative vision" (Part II–II, Q. 173, Art. 2); and the lowest of the three levels of vision, "a supra mundane, bodily vision," he understood to be illustrated by the handwriting on the wall (Dan. 5:24–27; Part II–II, Q. 175, Art. 3).[24] In his understanding of angels as "immaterial substances," Aquinas explicitly cited Maimonides (Part I, Q. 50, Art. 3).

Following the pattern of the church fathers' drawing on the Book of Daniel for homiletic purposes, Aquinas often refers to Daniel's abstinence (Daniel 1) as instructive; "abstinence and chastity dispose man very much to the perfection of the intellectual operation" (Part II–II, Q. 15, Art. 3); "Daniel abstained from pleasures to adapt himself to the heights of contemplation" (Part II–II, Q. 142, Art. 1). To illustrate the perverting power of lust, Aquinas cited the two elders and accusers of Susanna (Dan. 13:56; Part II–II, Q. 153, Art. 5). In addition, Aquinas found support in Daniel for the following doctrines: (1) limbo (Dan. 12:2; that "many," but not all, "shall awake," implies some did not; Supplement Q.75, Art. 2); (2) that almsgiving is a work of justice and not of charity (Dan. 4:24; Part II–II, Q. 32, Art. 1); (3) that the prayers of sinners, though not meritorious, may be "impetrative" (successful in moving the deity; Dan. 9:17–18; Part II–II, Q. 83, Art. 17; Q. 114, Art. 6); (4) that there is a universal hierarchy: "[T]he order of divine providence has disposed not only among the angels, but also in the whole universe, that inferior things are administered by the superior" (Dan. 7:10; Part I, Q. 112, Art. 2; cf. Maimonides, *Guide of the Perplexed* 2.3–11; 12a–24a); (5) that through entering religion people may obtain remission for all their sins: "For if by giving alms a man may forthwith satisfy for his sins,

---

22. In our day Christian thinkers have similarly been awakened to the depths of biblical personalism and of the divine *pathos* for justice through the writings of respectively Martin Buber and Abraham Joshua Heschel.

23. For a recent translation and helpful introductory essay by Leo Strauss, see Moses Maimonides, *The Guide of the Perplexed*, trans. Schlomo Pines (Chicago: University of Chicago Press, 1963).

24. Translations used here and below have been taken from St. Thomas Aquinas, *Summa Theologica*, 3 vols., trans. Fathers of the English Dominican Province (New York: Benzinger Brothers, 1947).

according to Dan. 4:24, much more does it suffice to satisfy for all his sins that a man devote himself wholly to the divine service by entering into religion" (Part II–II, Q. 189, Art. 4).

It is somewhat disconcerting to realize that Christian theologians who have appealed to the same biblical authority have not infrequently drawn opposite, or nearly opposite, doctrinal conclusions. Such in any event is the case when the uses of the Book of Daniel by the reformer Martin Luther are compared with those of Thomas Aquinas. In his treatise "The Babylonian Captivity of the Church" (1520) Luther challenges the validity of the last cited position of Aquinas. God was able, he said, to sanctify Daniel, Hananiah, Azariah, and Mishael "in their perilous mode of living" without desiring it to be an example to others: "Besides, it is certain that none of them was saved through his vows and his 'religious' life" (2.240).[25] Instead of underlining how abstinence and chastity are conducive to intellectual perfection and contemplation, Luther, drawing on the Vulgate text of Dan. 11:37–38, taunts the pope, whom he considers to be the antichrist,[26] for fulfilling the prophesy of disregarding the God of his fathers, having no woman to wife but instead honoring his God Moazim, the God of the Mass ("Answer to the Leipzig Goat" [1521], 3.36a; cf. "On the Councils and the Churches" [1539], Part 3, 5.284). In the succeeding verses of Daniel (11:39–40) Luther had seen earlier a prophecy fulfilled which spoke of the antichrist's filling its coffers ("An Open Letter to the Christian Nobility of the German Nation Concerning the Reform of the Christian Estate" [1520], 2.82). Furthermore, it was God's will that the Babylonian empire should be ruled by the holy princes Daniel, Hananiah, Azariah, and Mishael "much more than is it His will that this empire be ruled by the Christian princes of Germany" ("An Open Letter to the Christian Nobility," 2:156). In his letter to Pope Leo X, written also in 1520 before the break with Rome had become complete, Luther likened the pontiff to "a lamb in the midst of wolves, like Daniel in the midst of the lions" (2.304). The lions for Luther were the Roman curia. On occasion Luther was less polemical and more pastoral in his use of Daniel. Thus he commended the preaching office and the care of souls on the basis of Dan. 12:3: "They that teach others shall shine as the heavens" ("A Sermon on Keeping Children in School" [1530], 4.146). In the same work he defended, on the basis of Daniel's example, the importance of the work of chancellors, secretaries, and jurists (4.166).

Millenarian expectations were running high in the year 1530,[27] the year

---

25. *Works of Martin Luther*, 6 vols., ed. C. M. Jacobs et al., Philadelphia edition (Philadelphia: Muhlenberg Press, 1930–43). References in parentheses here and hereafter are to this series.

26. The identification of the bishop of Rome as the antichrist was not unique to Luther. For a full documentation of Luther's teaching on this subject and its antecedents, see Hans Preuss, *Die Vorstellungen vom Antichrist im späteren Mittelalter bei Luther* (Leipzig: J. C. Hinrichs, 1906).

27. "According to [Melchior] Hoffmann the Millennium was to begin after a period of 'messianic woes' and many signs and wonders, in the year 1533, which was supposed to be the fifteenth centenary of the death of Christ" (Cohn, *The Pursuit of the Millennium*, p. 258).

that Luther published separately his translation of Daniel and a fairly long preface to it. In that preface, as C.M. Jacobs puts it, "Luther expressed his conviction that the end of the world was near at hand" (6.438). Such an expectation is not so surprising when it is recalled: "In 1529 an outbreak of Black Death devastated Westphalia and at the same time the crops failed; between 1529 and 1530 the price of rye almost trebled. Finally in 1530 an extraordinary tax was levied to finance resistance to the Turkish invasion of the eastern territories of the Empire."[28]

Interpretation of the Book of Daniel by John Calvin (1509–64) differs from that of Luther's in two primary ways: (1) Calvin remained unconvinced that the millennium was imminent, and (2) he displayed greater hesitancy in concluding that the book clearly referred to the Roman pontiff as the antichrist. On (1) Calvin did, however, believe that 2 Thessalonians 2:4 clearly applied to the pope and that the Book of Daniel threw some light on the nature of the antichrist (*Institutes of the Christian Religion* 4.7.25; 2.1444).[29] On (2) the prophecies concerning the foes of the people of God referred primarily, he thought, to imperial Rome (Daniel 2 and 7) and to Antiochus Epiphanes (Daniel 8) rather than to the pope or Mahomet (Muhammed), the way some other interpreters had posited (Daniel 11).[30] This reformer, who fled religious persecution in his native France in 1535, liberally drew pastoral and doctrinal lessons from the book as the following citations from the *Institutes* will illustrate. (1) Though the church is persecuted, God will prevent it from being consumed by the persecutor's flames even as he protected the three children in the furnace ("Prefatory Address," 6.1.25). (2) Even though the Book of Daniel has been used by others as the basis on which to conclude there exists a hierarchy of angels, Calvin saw no justification whatsoever in Scripture so to conclude (1.14.8; 1.168).[31] (3) Daniel's exhortation to Nebuchadnezzar to give alms (Dan. 4:27) furnishes no basis for concluding that righteousness and money would propitiate God. Rather he was saying to the king: "You have treated your people harshly and unjustly; now replace with mercy and righteousness your unjust exactions, your violence and oppression" (3.4.36; 1.666). (4) Daniel's prayer in chapter 9 furnishes a model which encourages people to pray confidently, without terror, but with reverential fear (3.20.14; 1.869). (5) Because righteousness belongs to God (Dan. 9:7), when savage, impious, greedy, or slothful princes wreak havoc on the faithful, "it is not for us to remedy such evils; that only this remains, to implore the Lord's help, in whose hands are the hearts of

28. Ibid., p. 257.

29. The second reference here and in the citations hereafter is to John Calvin, *Institutes of the Christian Religion*, 2 vols., Library of Christian Classics 20–21, trans. Ford Lewis Battles (Philadelphia: Westminster Press, 1960).

30. See *Calvin's Commentaries, Daniel*, 2 vols. (Grand Rapids: Wm. B. Eerdmans, 1948). These sixty-six lectures were first published in Latin in 1561 and in French in 1562.

31. Of modern theologians it is Karl Barth who makes this same point and emphatically asserts that Michael is called an archangel in the New Testament (Jude 9) only because he represents God's election of Israel. See *Kirchliche Dogmatik* 3/3: *Die Lehre von der Schöpfung* (Zurich: A. G. Zollikon, 1950), pp. 532–34.

kings, and the changing of kingdoms" (4.20.29; 2.1516–17). (6) However, obedience to human beings must not become disobedience to God as the example of Daniel shows (Daniel 6) for "the king had exceeded his limits" and "Daniel denies that he has committed any offense against the king when he has not obeyed his impious edict" (4.20.32; 2.1520). Thus in the last two items Calvin opposes violent civil disobedience yet leaves room for a peaceful form should such obedience to magistrates or kings "lead us away from obedience to him, to whose will the desires of all kings ought to be subject" (4.20.32; 2.1520).

IV

Of all the features observed thus far in the above journey, perhaps the most surprising to this mainliner was the extent to which the millenarian tradition has constituted so integral a part of Christian thought and piety. Mainline Protestants and Catholics have generally not wanted to tarry long at millenarian halting places. Indeed the tendency has been to erase them from the landscape. Thus Norman Cohn notes that the millenarian chapters in Irenaeus' *Against Heresies* were suppressed for a long time.[32] Similarly, Luther's strongest millenarian views in his "Preface to Daniel" were simply omitted from the Philadelphia edition. The present seems an appropriate time to wrestle more earnestly with the fact that dispensationalism and millennialism have been a more integral part of Christian thought down through the centuries than many of us have cared to acknowledge.[33]

A second conclusion to be drawn from our journey through Danielic space is more intuitive and not immediately obvious. Those of us who accept the essential correctness of historical and literary criticism have so tended to stress the original historical matrix of the Scripture that we have, as a rule, played down the way in which the New Testament itself and centuries of Christian theology have seen in the prophet Daniel[34] a number of wondrous predictions of the first and second coming of Jesus the Christ. I advocate a retreat neither from historical and literary criticism nor from a staunch Christian theism. Contemporary apologetics and defense of the faith must simply seek other grounds than a simplistic paradigm of prophecy fulfillment. If in comparison to previous centuries the Book of Daniel today seems more peripheral, less central to the faith, one of the obvious reasons for this

---

32. *Pursuit of the Millennium*, pp. 29–30.

33. For a fine study which demonstrates the extent to which dispensational and millennial thinking has been a part of American Protestantism, see George M. Marsden, *Fundamentalism and American Culture: The Shaping of Twentieth Century Evangelicalism 1870–1925* (New York and London: Oxford University Press, 1980). For an excellent analysis of the goals of millenarian movements, see Kenelm Burridge, *New Heaven, New Earth* (Oxford: Basil Blackwell, 1969). Relevant to understanding millenarianism also is its close affinity with ecstatic phenomena; see Joseph Blenkinsopp, *A History of Prophecy in Israel* (Philadelphia: Westminster Press, 1983), p. 45; and I. M. Lewis, *Ecstatic Religion* (Harmondsworth: Penguin Books, 1971).

34. On Daniel as a prophetic book see Klaus Koch, chap. 19 of this book.

decline in mainline Christian circles is the retreat of christological interpretations. The issue before us then is: How shall the churches appropriate
the message of the Old Testament which is being shorn of passages previously treasured as prophetic of the Christ?[35]

---

35. I have attempted to identify and address this issue in my book *Daniel*, Knox Preaching
Guides (Atlanta: John Knox Press, 1983), pp. 72, 88–92. For a thorough discussion of yet another
issue raised by the history of the interpretation of Daniel, namely, the applications of its allusions to the interpreter's own day, see W. Sibley Towner, "Were the English Puritans 'the Saints
of the Most High'?—Issues in the 'Pre-critical' Interpretation of Daniel 7," *Int* 37 (1983) 46–63.

21

The Preacher in the Lions' Den

W. Sibley Towner

The claims of Daniel upon our world will be kept freshest if we see in the text paradigms of a consistently renewed experience of the triumph of God's redeeming power over death and corruption.

Settle back in your chair now and let me mix you a metaphor. As a preacher or theologian confronted with the Book of Daniel, you find yourself in a veritable lions' den of difficulties. Frankly, the book is a bear!

The problem is not with the first six chapters, those delightful narratives about Daniel and his heroic Judean friends who carry the fight for true faith in God right to the heart of the courts of Babylon and Persia. Those stories, while fraught with wondrous elements, are properly told as edifying tales. As such, they need pose for the twentieth-century interpreter no overwhelming problems but, in fact, endless delight.

No, the bear is lurking in the second half of Daniel, chapters 7—12. Very simply put, there we have a series of failed apocalypses on our hands.

The problem is familiar, but perhaps it can be freshly illustrated by recourse to a parable of a filmmaker. Let history itself be the scene spread out before the lens, and let the Book of Daniel be the camera. Suppose the filmmaker were to set up the tripod exactly in the space between v. 8 and v. 9 of chapter 7 of Daniel. Pivoting the camera around in one direction, the filmmaker could zoom in effectively on the series of four great beasts as they came up out of the sea (Dan. 7:1–8). Although they would give the film all the bizarre quality of a horror movie—just imagine a lion with eagle's wings which was given a man's mind, a bear with three ribs sticking out of its mouth, a leopard with four wings of a bird and four heads, and a terrible beast with iron teeth and ten horns!—the focus nonetheless would be clear. The viewers would know what the cameraman knew, that these beasts represented four great world empires (Dan. 7:17) that had actually arisen within the historical memory of the *hasisdim* or observant Jews who gave us the Book of Daniel. We would detect that we were looking at Babylon, Media, Persia, and the Hellenistic empire founded in the east by Alexander the Great. Even as the eleventh horn came up on the fourth beast, uprooted three horns, looked around with its spooky eyes, and spoke enormities with its loud mouth (7:8), we would still be in focus, knowing that we were looking at a symbol of the tyrant of the Hellenistic-Syrian kingdom of Antioch, Antiochus IV Epiphanes (175–163 B.C.). We could speak of the success of this vision, not its failure, because we know that all of these things had come to pass. History would correspond to the images on the film. This clarity of focus and accuracy of characterization would prevail because the seer had the advantage that comes to anyone who prophesies after the fact.

Should the camera operator pivot on the tripod in the other direction, however, and shoot forward, an uneasiness would begin to afflict the viewer. Oh, the focus would remain clear enough on the film which the camera Daniel produces, but the picture would no longer correspond to the pictures of history made through other lenses. There is the Ancient of Days seated on the throne; a thousand thousands serve him and ten thousand times ten thousand stand before him; the fourth beast is slain and its body burned with fire; and to "one like a son of man" who arrives "with the clouds of heaven" is presented an everlasting dominion (Dan. 7:13–14). We can see the picture all right, but we would not be able to make out exactly what this means. Things never happened this way in the second century B.C. nor at any other time. The hindsight sequences of the film would be beautifully clear, but the foresight, brilliantly depicted as it may be and powerfully effective in its rendition of the judging power of God, nevertheless would remain disconcertingly irrelevant to the actual course of events.

The filmmaker is, of course, the seer himself, and the tiny space between Dan. 7:8 and 9 is exactly where he had set up his own picturing apparatus; it was the spot in which he had positioned himself to live through the trials that certainly lay ahead at the hands of the tyrant of Antioch, the first commissioner of a genocide against Jews (1 Macc. 1:54–61).

We can apply the same metaphor of the filmmaker to the last panel of the Book of Daniel, the great historical résumé which begins with the announcement of angelic revelation in chapter 10 and concludes with the final remark of the angelic interpreter to Daniel in 12:4. The tripod is set up in the space between 11:39 and 11:40. As the operator faces the camera backward in time, a rich and accurate retrospective picture of Middle Eastern history is recorded, beginning with the Persian conquest of Babylon (Dan. 11:2–3). Alexander the Great appears on the scene in 11:3, and his empire is divided among his four generals, the *Diadochi*, in 11:4. In the following passages, the fortunes of the Ptolemies of Egypt and the Seleucids of Antioch are elaborately traced, culminating in the conquest of Palestine by Antiochus III in 198 B.C. and the marriage of his daughter Cleopatra to Ptolemy V. After a brief glimpse of his successor in verses 18–19, the rest of the film will be devoted to the rise of the tyrant Antiochus IV Epiphanes in 175 B.C., his military conquests, his political machinations in Israel, and his ultimate outrage of seizing the temple for the use of the Syrian garrison and erecting upon the altar there the "abomination that makes desolate" (11:31). Indeed, we see him moving ever closer to the assumption of divine kingship in verses 36–39. All this remains in sharp, clear relationship to the real reel of history that unwound itself at the end of the Old Testament era. Then at v. 40, as the filmmaker whirls around to point the camera toward the future, the film seems to pop right off the reel. The sequence is clear enough, all right, and it is very interesting. We make out a picture of an attack upon Antiochus by Ptolemy, the outlines of a conquest of Libya and Ethiopia by Antiochus, and his return to pitch his camp and to meet his fate on the coastal plain near Jerusalem (11:45). Suddenly surreal, the scene switches to the terrible visage of the archangel Michael, the patron angel of Israel, who introduces a tribulation such as never has been. The picture ends with the opening of graves, some of the dead being raised to everlasting life and some to shame and everlasting contempt (12:1–3).

The seer pictured this history as if it were all of a piece, and he succeeded as long as he had the benefit of hindsight, but as soon as he tried to make a portrait of the future, he failed. Antiochus in fact made no attack on Libya or Ethiopia, nor did he meet his end between the sea and Jerusalem. Chances are that he died in bed, either in Ecbatana of a disease of the bowels (2 Macc. 9:3) or possibly in Babylon of grief and remorse (1 Macc. 6:1–16). As far as the resurrection of the dead to shine "like the stars for ever and ever" (12:3), it has not, to our knowledge, occurred. The stars remain the stars, thank God, and we who must die will be gathered into the dust to await whatever destiny will be ours at the hour of God's victory over death and decay.

The failure of these apocalypses is made all the sharper for us by the fact that the writer had resorted to the well-known ancient Near Eastern literary device of prophecy-after-the-fact in order to give credibility to his future predictions. Such prophecies were not unknown in the earlier biblical tradition (see, e.g., 1 Kings 13:2; Isa. 7:8b; Ezek. 26, 29:17–20), but they reached the status of a literary art in apocalyptic texts. The credibility which they sought to ensure had soon, and has yet, to endure the challenge of disconfirmation. Furthermore, as if the failure of prophecy and the literary conceit of prophecy-after-the-fact were not difficult enough problems amid which to drop the interpreter, the entire sense of the predetermination of history which permeates Daniel 7—12 really misfires if the end of it all does not come off. History is presented through these chapters as if it were a film made in advance, and the seer is presented as if he were a person who had seen the whole show before. Because each scene appears exactly on schedule in the film just as the seer predicted it would, the confidence of the readers is aroused that the culminating scene will also appear in its proper sequence. In fact if that does not take place, a dissonance surely arises in the readers' minds which might even lead them to question whether the alleged predetermination of history was in fact correct at all. Could it then not be the case that history just bashes along quite out of the control of God or anyone else, and the end of it cannot be predicted in any meaningful way?

With all of these problems, one would assume that the generations of Israel who survived the pogrom by Antiochus against the Jews, and instead

of an eschaton saw the happy recovery and cleansing of the temple by the
Maccabean freedom fighters, would have conspired to get rid of the failed
prophecy of the Book of Daniel. Why didn't they just junk it?

OPENING UP THE CLOSURE

Yet they didn't junk it. On the contrary, they treasured it as Sacred
Scripture and continued to regard it as a meaningful clue regarding the
significance of history and the outcome of the future. They were able to do
this because they found ways of keeping the end of it open.

In case it strikes you that to keep open a prophecy of ultimate closure is a
contradiction in terms, let me remind you that open-endedness was often, if
not always, the mode in which those texts of the Old Testament which turned
toward the future expressed themselves. The culminating sermon of the
Book of Deuteronomy, which ought to have reported Israel's final definitive
oath of allegiance to the covenant stipulations of a treaty between Israel and
Yahweh (cf. Josh. 24:21–22), constitutes instead a kind of open-ended invitation: "I call heaven and earth to witness against you this day, that I have set
before you life and death, blessing and curse; therefore choose life, that you
and your descendants may live..." (Deut. 30:19). Rather than achieving
closure, the culminating thrust of the great evangelical document we call
Deuteronomy leaves the option of obedience open, always available, always
efficacious. Even if all of the old securities should be lost forever, including
the temple, Jerusalem, the very land itself, the possibility of choosing life by
loving the Lord can never be alienated.

A similar open-endedness characterizes the end of the deuteronomistic
history. Beginning with the dynastic oracle of the prophet Nathan to David
in 2 Sam. 7:16, "And your house and your kingdom shall be made sure
forever before me; your throne shall be established forever," the scarlet
thread of the Davidic dynasty runs through the history of the apostate kings
of Israel and Judah until it reaches the end of that history. Its conclusion is
curiously inconclusive. The last Davidide, Jehoiachin, closes out the account, enjoying his regular daily dinner at the table of the king of Babylon (2
Kings 25:27–30). What happened after that we are never told, but at least the
scarlet thread of the Davidic monarchy is left hanging out of the end of the
history of the kings of Israel. Even though subsequent generations knew full
well that no descendant of David was left still clinging to that thread, the
open-endedness of the deuteronomistic history encouraged them to think
that in some way the promise of an anointed one might yet be realized.

In a similar way, the prophetic juxtaposition of threat and promise, exemplified above all in the combination of Isaiah 1—39 with Isaiah 40—55,
keeps open-ended the irrevocable judgment pronounced against an apostate
nation. Of course, the prophecies of judgment enjoyed the verification of
actual history. The books were closed on the judgment. The promises of
salvation, on the other hand, not only did not enjoy such verification but in a
broad sense were falsified by the Babylonian exile and the subsequent

meager recovery of Jewish life in a much attenuated Persian province of Judea. Yet the combination of verified threat coupled with hoped-for promise kept the prophetic message open and available to the imagination and the faith of future generations. Every age could trust that the other side of the coin of judgment is renovation!

Yet the question will not down: How was the ancient community able to keep open to the future the apparently ironclad prophecies of doom found in the apocalypses of Daniel once the "time, two times, and half a time" (= three and one-half years) of Dan. 7:25; 9:27; and 12:7 had come and gone? That question can be answered in several different ways from within the scriptural tradition itself. At a very simple mechanical level, the end of the Book of Daniel adjusts the timetable by a few months, perhaps with a sense of desperation as the promised date of disaster was disconfirmed by actual events. Whether done by the seer himself or an editor, Dan. 12:11 lengthens the time before the end to three years, seven months (dividing 1,290 days by 43 lunar months of 30 days each). Yet another adjustment is made in verse 12 with the benediction, "Blessed is he who waits and comes to the 1,335 days" (now the time is three years, eight and a half months).[1]

Obviously such trivial and mechanical means of adjusting the promised end to the realities of history could not survive the threat of disconfirmation very long. Yet the Book of Daniel did survive that threat. In fact, it was accepted as canonical by persons who knew full well both that the little horn on the fourth beast (Dan. 7:8) was intended to be Antiochus IV Epiphanes, that Antiochus had not met his fate in the predicted way, nor had history reached its ultimate climax at the time of his demise. This suggests that these canonizers had already made a move essential to the survival of the message, namely, a severing of the tie of the Book of Daniel to the particular history of the era in which it was written. Following a principle of the canonizing process which he describes as the detaching of "a collection of material . . . from its original historical mooring and [providing it] with a secondary theological context,"[2] Brevard Childs suggests that the canonizers already had transferred the identity of the fourth kingdom from the Seleucid kingdom of Antiochus to Rome. He remarks that "there is strong evidence to suggest that the interpretation of the Book of Daniel has been sharply altered by those who edited it. Although the original author of the vision appeared to have identified the fourth kingdom with the tyranny of Antiochus, this interpretation was no longer held."[3] As support for this contention that the editors/canonizers already had made the move that would keep the apocalyptic scenario open-ended, Childs cites 2 Esdr. 12:10–29 as an early midrash on Daniel 7 that clearly identifies the fourth beast with Rome. He also shows that Mark 13 and Matthew 24, by their allusions to Daniel, are

---

1. See W. Sibley Towner, *Daniel*, Interpretation (Atlanta: John Knox Press, 1984), pp. 170–71.

2. B. S. Childs, "The Exegetical Significance of Canon," VTSup 29 (1977) 70.

3. B. S. Childs, *Introduction to the Old Testament as Scripture* (Philadelphia: Fortress Press, 1978), p. 619.

using the book to interpret the meaning of their own persecuted and tragic circumstances in the period of the Roman Empire.

Within the Jewish apocalyptic tradition (particularly 1 *Enoch* and 2 Esdras 3—14) and those New Testament texts which are heavily influenced by it (the "little apocalypses" in Matthew 24—25; Mark 13; Luke 17:20–37; and of course the Book of Revelation), the failed eschaton of Daniel is simply transformed into an as yet unfulfilled future event of cosmic proportions which no longer has anything to do with Antiochus or history of the second century B.C. Elements in the "little apocalypses" suggest that the writers of these texts (which many scholars attribute to the early church rather than to Jesus himself) thought that the culmination would be within their own near futures: "truly I say to you, this generation will not pass away before all these things take place" (Mark 13:30). Lest the vision of God's triumph in the overcoming of evil and the renovation of the cosmos be prematurely closed off and wasted, however, the traditioners immediately moved to open the end of the prophecy up again: "But of that day or that hour no one knows, not even the angels in heaven, nor the son, but only the Father" (Mark 13:32; see also the famed eschatological reservation in Mark 13:10: "And the gospel must first be preached to all nations"—similar end-opening reservations are inserted in Matt. 24:14, 36). The transformation of the originally time-specific predictions of Daniel to the relatively more open-ended vision of the future in the Gospels and in Revelation 20 (which is itself in part a transformation of Daniel 7) raises, of course, a new set of problems which are commonly discussed under the rubric "the delay of the Parousia." This problem of the failure of the Son of Man to return on clouds of glory to judge sinners and to usher in the kingdom of heaven was as vexing for the New Testament community as the failure of Daniel's apocalypse to materialize must have been to the circle of *hasidim* which gave rise to that work. It lies outside the scope of this essay to discuss that matter further; suffice it to say that like the late Old Testament community, the early Christians also found mechanisms with which to deal with the disconfirmation of their expectation of the imminent eschaton.[4]

CONTEMPORARY MILLENNIALISM: SLOUCHING TOWARD ARMAGEDDON

Before making certain hermeneutical endorsements of the device of severing the tie of history from apocalyptic prediction in our own use of the material, note should be taken that the way in which the first editor of Daniel handled the failure of the eschaton to materialize on schedule still enjoys a vogue among us. Literalistic readers of biblical apocalyptic, particularly those who are associated with the heretical doctrine (from a Reformed point

---

4. See esp. John G. Gager, *Kingdom and Community: The Social World of Early Christianity* (Englewood Cliffs, N.J.: Prentice-Hall, 1975), chap. 2.

of view) of the premillennial dispensationalism, have found it possible to keep Old Testament apocalyptic open by merely deferring the last scene of the end-time scenario. They argue that the judgment pictured in Dan. 7:9–14 simply has not yet occurred. The tiny little gap of white paper which sits between vv. 8 and 9 is actually millennia in its extent, for the prophet Daniel was writing of a specific moment in history. Because that moment has not yet occurred, the culminating judgment upon the latter-day descendants of the Roman Empire and the reception of an everlasting kingdom by one like a Son of Man must lie yet in the future; but, of course, that future is our future. All around us literalists see signs that things which were described more than two millennia ago are now for the first time achieving their fulfillment. This proves that the historical referents of these prophecies never were to be found in the writers' own time but actually were spoken for our age and our age alone. The threats against Israel by the king of the north (Dan. 11:15) and the apparent participation in the end-time scenario of the king of the south (Dan. 11:40) bespeak nothing other than Russia and Egypt, or perhaps some African confederacy, battling it out with nuclear bombs in the twentieth century.[5] In keeping the end of the failed apocalyptic scenario open in this mechanical and simplistic way, this approach forfeits the possibility which Scripture itself gives to the interpreter (particularly in the manner in which the New Testament reutilized Old Testament apocalyptic vision), namely to sever the ties of these prophecies from a specific period of history altogether. The contemporary literalists prefer to reattach the failed apocalyptic scenario of Daniel to events of our own time, thus ensuring yet another failure of this scenario to materialize.

THE DYNAMICS OF DELAY

That we should be confronted in the twentieth century with sectarian attempts to rescue the literal terms of the Danielic end-time scenario from their failure to come to pass should come to us as no surprise. The impulse is as old as the Old Testament itself. In fact, biblical apocalyptic literature itself is the product of an attempt to deal with the nonfulfillment of earlier prophetic visions of a renewed Jewish commonwealth centered around an exalted and glorified Jerusalem. Paul Hanson has shown that the postexilic Judean circles which first drew the cosmic and mythically influenced apocalyptic drama out of the soil of earlier prophetic eschatology were disillusioned with the direction being taken by the ruling priestly theocracy in those years.[6] Faced with the evident disconfirmation of the glorious promises of Deutero-Isaiah—promises of universal salvation (Isa. 49:8–13), of universal acknowledgement of the sovereignty of God and of the centrality of Israel (49:22–26), and of peace and reconciliation (55:12–13)—these visionaries were able to project them onto a much broader cosmic scale, which was incidentally much less subject to disconfirmation by historical experience.

---

5. Hal Lindsey, *The Late Great Planet Earth* (Grand Rapids: Zondervan, 1972), p. 68.
6. Paul Hanson, *The Dawn of Apocalyptic* (Philadelphia: Fortress Press, 1975), esp. chap. 1.

Building upon the seminal work on the theory of "cognitive dissonance" done by Leon Festinger and his followers (and particularly upon Festinger's fascinating book *When Prophecy Fails*,[7] which describes the reactions of a contemporary sect to the failure of the prediction by their founder and leader that the world would end by flood and that they would be rescued by flying saucers), Robert P. Carroll argues that the fundamental inner biblical hermeneutic for dealing with the phenomenon of prophetism in the Old Testament arose as a response to the failure of prophetic expectations to materialize. The dissonance or unhappiness experienced by the believer when confronting facts which disconfirmed earlier hopes and beliefs drove that believer to make serious adjustments. Carroll is able to show that the "wrong" predictions of the prophets "were treated by the later communities as ongoing possibilities for their future."[8] Language itself played a significant role in this process. At the lowest level, prophetic language was thought to have magical qualities, which is to say that its predictions might yet come to pass because the very utterance of them unleashed divine power adequate to bring about that of which they spoke. Prophetic language also is cultic in character and holds out the promise of salvation which cult promotes and never permits to be closed down. It is symbolic language in that much of the excessive optimism of oracles of salvation can be reduced to the simple and historically verifiable fact that the Judean exiles were finally free to go home. It is conditional language, intent on effecting change and repentance more than it is determined accurately to name the terms of the future. Above all it is performative language. Prophecy does not just say things, but in saying them achieves things, persuading the community to follow. Social phenomena played a role as important as language phenomena in enabling followers of the prophets to adjust the failed promises to a new age. They could engage in avoidance techniques by grouping together in exclusive conventicles, thereby escaping contact with other ideas and facts which challenged the belief system. They could seek social validation by the support of a group to which they belonged and, interestingly, to which they eagerly sought converts even after the disconfirmation of the prophecy. Finally they could engage in explanatory schemes or rationalizations which is the process that we call hermeneutic.[9]

Biblical and postbiblical writers alike became so adept at these ways of handling the unfulfilled prophecies of the past that each community or generation would develop an entire system—what James Barr calls a "resultant system," "the system which interpretation runs out"[10]—by means of which the failed prophecies of the past could be revitalized. It was such a system that enabled the Qumran community to rescue the Book of Habakkuk from the oblivion of unfulfilled prophecy by applying it to their own time

7. Leon Festinger et al., *When Prophecy Fails* (Minneapolis: University of Minnesota Press, 1956).

8. Robert P. Carroll, *When Prophecy Failed* (New York: Seabury Press, 1979), p. 58.

9. Ibid., p. 118.

10. James Barr, *Old and New in Interpretation* (London: SCM Press, 1966), p. 108.

and leaving it to others to see how the failure of their application was to be handled. It was such a resultant system that enabled Philip to make sense of the prophecies of the past to the Ethiopian eunuch who failed to understand the meaning of Isa. 53:7–8 (see Acts 8:26–39).

The work of Festinger and Carroll makes clear that all believers have to deal with cognitive dissonance; and that this is by no means all bad, for it is the fuel that fires the hermeneutic of biblical texts. It is also clear that the most viable way of handling this cognitive dissonance is neither to deny it nor to explain away the failure of past predictions; instead, it is to affirm the essentially performative nature of these utterances. In that case, one can also affirm that Daniel and the apocalyptic texts were written in order to effect change and to enable more hopeful and energetic human attitudes toward the destiny of the community and of the world, and then it becomes possible powerfully to restate their hopes without needing to connect them to specific moments of history, past or future. It becomes possible to regard them as paradigms for the way in which God and God's people can deal with the issues of the future.

PROPHECY AS PARADIGM

In my opinion, it is utterly essential that the theological truth claims of biblical apocalyptic in general and the Book of Daniel in particular be kept alive in our midst. It is also my opinion that those claims will be kept freshest if we insist on viewing the text as paradigms of a constantly renewed experience of the triumph of God's redeeming power over death and corruption, evil and decay. The alternative to regarding these brilliant stories about the future as paradigms is to regard them as timetables or as historical dramas filmed in advance, but surely that option must be rejected. To contend that biblical writers living at the end of the first millennium B.C. could accurately predict events that would close out the era of human history some two millennia hence, I am persuaded, would be to deny one of the most cardinal tenets of Christian belief, namely, that the Word of God comes to us in incarnate form. If the Word of God about the future is mediated to us in an incarnate form, that is to say, in the words of human beings transmitted through human brains and uttered by human lips, then I do not see how it can give us an accurate delineation of the history of our time. Human beings, even inspired biblical writers, simply cannot predict the future two thousand years in advance, and to say that they can is in my view to deny this fundamental tenet of our faith. No, we have no timetables, no histories written in advance; instead, we have paradigms, models, types that can make our present experience meaningful and shape our attitude toward our own future. To say that Dan. 7:9–14 can function paradigmatically is to say that it need not be closed out simply because the writer erred in expecting the last judgment to take place during the reign of Antiochus IV Epiphanes. Daniel 7:9–14 and 11:40—12:4, when read paradigmatically, are open-ended narratives about God's certain triumph over tyranny. They are deep affirmations of the conviction of their ancient writers that God keeps faith with all who are just and faithful and that God has a rendezvous with our destinies at the end of the age.

What would it mean to pay no further attention to the timetable which the author of the Book of Daniel may well have intended, to make a clean break from the failed history of the end which that writer puts forth, but to give all serious attention to the theological truth claims of the text taken as a paradigm for continued obedient existence in this world? First of all, the stories of Daniel 1—6 would emerge as renditions of "interim ethics" at work. The Daniel who can survive in the exile and beat the wise men of Babylon at their own game, the Daniel who does not merely passively await God's final intervention but issues forth into the fray, is the Daniel who illustrates how one should live in the time before God's great day. The saint is more than one who simply hangs on, observes all the blue laws of her sect, and survives. She is one whose courage encourages those around her, the one who gives hope to those who are losing their hope. He is the one who in his own way helps bring about a world in which God is honored, idolatry is ended, the needs of the needy are met, the oppressed are liberated.

Notice how similar that portrait is to the picture of the ministry of Jesus. That ministry is to the "little apocalypses" of the Gospels what the stories of Daniel 1—6 are to the apocalypses of Daniel 7—12. The new age of the kingdom is surely coming, and God is surely victor. That is the apocalyptic paradigm from which one can conjugate a style of living. For Jesus, the kingdom provides a stimulus for the future, not simply a timetable for it, just as the pearl of great price was stimulus, not a timetable, to the merchant who sold everything to buy it (Matt. 13:45–46). Set in their proper contexts, the messages of the apocalyptic texts are not calls to quietism but calls to action. They are invitations to people to give in their own lives foretastes of the flavor of the coming kingdom.

Hear now what the voice of the biblical apocalyptic tradition is calling out to believers in the twentieth century: "Come on into the future with trust, because the future belongs to God." That is a paradigmatic statement, not purporting to be historical in character but intending to make a claim profound enough to draw people toward it from east and west and north and south.

> Although God alone can introduce the polity of the new age, and only God can build the new Jerusalem, you who have the vision can imitate that new order in your individual and communal lives, so that, as it were, where you are a dominion which shall endure forever is already underway, and resurrection to new life is already taking place.

That is a paradigmatic statement made on the basis of Dan. 7:14 and 12:1–3 which accepts the fact that these texts are significant not as maps of future history but as affirmations about the meaning of that history and the name and power of the sovereign of that history.

The biblical vision of the future says:

> The world and its human community are worth protecting at all costs because

they are destined by God for full redemption from their present bondage to sin and decay (Rom. 8:18–25). Do not listen to the siren song of those who say it is hopeless and that the world must surely end with the bang of nuclear exchange or the whimper of overpopulation and famine. The world surely must not, and you who call yourselves "saints" can make common cause with other persons of good will to seek the safety of the world and its creatures.

That is a paradigmatic reading of biblical apocalyptic, one which allows us to be drawn into the future with a lifestyle appropriate to the exigencies that lie ahead. It is a reading of the future that calls us into active evangelical proclamation, not of impending doom but of ultimate victory.

Taken as a whole, the biblical eschatological vision of a reconciled community of shalom in the future may be the single most profound source of hope available today among all of our contemporary ideologies and religions. Only Marxism and Islam offer rival eschatologies, and both of them radically foreshorten the vision by requiring the elimination of capitalists and infidels as a prerequisite of the emancipated human community of the future. Taken as a whole, our vision is absolutely encompassing. On that great day "*every* knee shall bow and *every* tongue confess" (Phil. 2:10–11, emphasis added).

The confidence in the future which springs out of the eschatological texts of the Bible read as paradigms is given an utter seriousness for the Christian believer by the conviction that the first outbreak of the coming kingdom has already taken place among us. The events envisioned in Daniel 7 are paradigms for understanding the person, ministry, death, and resurrection of Jesus of Nazareth as well. In his own life of advocacy of the poor and of the sick, that Son of Man has already given us a foretaste of life in the everlasting kingdom that has no end. That Son of Man has already unmasked and challenged evil, and God has already awarded him the kingdom by vindicating him from the death which ought to have defeated him. Where he and his people are, the kingdom beyond the day of Yahweh is already anticipated. "The people who know their God . . . stand firm and take action" (Dan. 11:32); and all of this is but the first blush of what is yet to come.

The Old and New Testament apocalyptic texts were written at definable moments along the indefinable timetable that links promise to fulfillment. They were treasured in tiny embattled communities that looked back upon a long and honorable struggle to make sense of disconfirmed prophecies and that looked forward to contemplate full redemption of the groaning cosmos. Eschatological hope, based upon paradigmatic readings of the prophecies of the past, gave energy to their evangelical calling. In every ensuing age, the saints have carried on their mission suspended in that same dynamic tension between promise and fulfillment, never certain of their place on the timetable of history, but always sustained by hope. Now that the task of proclaiming God's sovereignty over all of history, even its end, and God's love for every creature in the cosmos has fallen to us, we find that we too are pointing backward and forward. Pivoting around to look behind us, we behold the makers of the paradigm, the people of faithful obedience and eager anticipation, and above all the Son of David who is also called the Son of Man. Pivoting forward again, we discern the contours of the kingdom. Yes, they match the paradigm which we have received; and though we have no real history of that future age, no timetable by which to check our progress, we know the direction in which we will go now. We even feel welling up within us the courage to be, the courage which flows toward us from the Lord of the future.

Resources for
Studying the Prophets

James Limburg

The following is a listing of works recommended to pastors, teachers, and students as particularly helpful for understanding the prophetic literature. For an instructive survey of study of the prophets since about 1945, see Gene M. Tucker, "Prophecy and the Prophetic Literature," in *The Hebrew Bible and Its Modern Interpreters*, ed. Douglas A. Knight and Gene M. Tucker. The Bible and Its Modern Interpreters (Philadelphia: Fortress Press, 1985). My own piece, "The Prophets in Recent Study: 1967–77" (in *Interpretation* 32 [1978]: 56–68), surveys the years indicated. For comprehensive bibliographical listing, see the work by Blenkinsopp cited below.

1. GENERAL ORIENTATION TO PROPHECY

Blenkinsopp, Joseph. *A History of Prophecy in Israel*. Philadelphia: Westminster Press, 1983.

Bright, John. "The Prophets of Israel: Some Preliminary Remarks." In *Jeremiah*. AB. Garden City, N.Y.: Doubleday & Co., 1965.

Heschel, Abraham. *The Prophets*. New York: Harper & Row, 1962.

Newsome, James D., Jr. *The Hebrew Prophets*. Atlanta: John Knox Press, 1984.

Peterson, David L., ed. *Prophecy in Israel: Search for an Identity.* Issues in Religion and Theology. Philadelphia: Fortress Press; London: SPCK, 1987.

"Prophecy in Ancient Israel" and articles on individual prophets in *The Interpreter's Dictionary of the Bible: Supplementary Volume*. Edited by Keith R. Crim. Nashville: Abingdon Press, 1976.

"Prophetēs" in Kittel's *Theological Dictionary of the New Testament*, vol. 6. Grand Rapids: Wm. B. Eerdmans, 1968.

von Rad, Gerhard. *Old Testament Theology, Vol. II: The Theology of Israel's Prophetic Traditions*. Translated by D. M. G. Stalker. New York: Harper & Row, 1965.

Westermann, Claus. *Elements of Old Testament Theology.* Translated by Douglas W. Stott. Atlanta: John Knox Press, 1982.

————. *A Thousand Years and a Day.* Translated by Stanley Rudman. Philadelphia: Fortress Press, 1962.

2. PROPHECY IN ITS HISTORICAL
SETTING

Bright, John. *A History of Israel*. 3d ed. Philadelphia: Westminster Press, 1981.

Wilson, Robert R. *Prophecy and Society in Ancient Israel.* Philadelphia: Fortress Press, 1980.

3. THE PROPHETIC LITERATURE

Childs, Brevard S. *Introduction to the Old Testament as Scripture.* Philadelphia: Fortress Press, 1979.
Gottwald, Norman K. *The Hebrew Bible—A Socio-Literary Introduction.* Philadelphia: Fortress Press, 1985.
Rendtorff, Rolf. *The Old Testament: An Introduction.* Translated by John Bowden. Philadelphia: Fortress Press, 1985.
March, W. Eugene. "Prophecy." In *Old Testament Form Criticism.* Edited by John H. Hayes. San Antonio: Trinity University Press, 1974.
Westermann, Claus. *Basic Forms of Prophetic Speech.* Translated by H. C. White. Philadelphia: Westminster Press, 1967.

4. PREACHING FROM THE PROPHETS

Achtemeier, Elizabeth. *Deuteronomy, Jeremiah.* Proclamation Commentaries. Philadelphia: Fortress Press, 1978.
Anderson, Bernhard. *The Eighth-Century Prophets.* Proclamation Commentaries. Philadelphia: Fortress Press, 1978.
Mays, James Luther. *Ezekiel, Second Isaiah.* Proclamation Commentaries. Philadelphia: Fortress Press, 1978.
Ward, James M. *Amos and Hosea.* Knox Preaching Guides. Atlanta: John Knox Press, 1981.
Wolff, Hans Walter. *Confrontations with Prophets.* Translated by Margaret Kohl. Philadelphia: Fortress Press, 1983.
————. ed. *Old Testament and Christian Preaching.* Translated by Margaret Kohl. Philadelphia: Fortress Press, 1986.
————. *Micah the Prophet.* Translated by Ralph D. Gehrke. Philadelphia: Fortress Press, 1981.
————, *Jonah: Church in Revolt.* St. Louis: Clayton Publishing House, 1978.

5. SPECIAL TOPICS

Brueggemann, Walter. *The Prophetic Imagination.* Philadelphia: Fortress Press, 1978.
Hanson, Paul D. *The Dawn of Apocalyptic.* Philadelphia: Fortress Press, 1975.
Limburg, James. *The Prophets and the Powerless.* Atlanta: John Knox Press, 1977.
Miller, Patrick D., Jr. *Sin and Judgment in the Prophets.* Chico, Calif.: Scholars Press, 1982.

6. COMMENTARIES ON ISAIAH

Achtemeier, Elizabeth. *The Community and Message of Isaiah 56—66.* Minneapolis: Augsburg Publishing House, 1982.
Bright, J. "Isaiah—I." In *Peakes Commentary on the Bible.* Edited by Matthew Black and H. H. Rowley. London and New York: Thomas Nelson & Sons, 1962.
Clements, R. E. *Isaiah 1—39.* Grand Rapids: Wm. B. Eerdmans, 1980.

Watts, John D. W. *Isaiah 1—33*. Waco, Tex.: Word Books, 1985.
Westermann, Claus. *Isaiah 40—66*. Translated by D. M. G. Stalker. Philadelphia: Westminster Press, 1969.

7. COMMENTARIES ON JEREMIAH

Bright, John. *Jeremiah*. AB. Garden City, N.Y.: Doubleday & Co., 1965.
Holladay, William L. *Jeremiah 1* (Chapters 1—25). Hermeneia. Philadelphia: Fortress Press, 1986.
McKane, William. *A Critical and Exegetical Commentary on Jeremiah*. Vol. 1, Jeremiah 1—25. Edinburgh: T & T Clark, 1986.

8. COMMENTARIES ON EZEKIEL

Eichrodt, Walther. *Ezekiel*. Translated by C. Quin. OTL. Philadelphia: Westminster Press, 1970.
Greenberg, Moshe. *Ezekiel 1—20*. AB. Garden City, N.Y.: Doubleday & Co., 1983.
Zimmerli, Walther. *Ezekiel 1*. Translated by R. E. Clements; and *Ezekiel 2* translated by James D. Martin. Hermeneia. Philadelphia: Fortress Press, 1979, 1983.

9. COMMENTARIES ON THE MINOR PROPHETS

Achtemeier, Elizabeth. *Nahum—Malachi*. Atlanta: John Knox Press, 1986.
Allen, Leslie C. *Joel, Obadiah, Jonah and Micah*. Grand Rapids: Wm. B. Eerdmans, 1976.
Fretheim, Terence E. *The Message of Jonah*. Minneapolis: Augsburg Publishing House, 1977.
Hillers, Delbert R. *Micah*. Hermeneia. Philadelphia: Fortress Press, 1984.
Mays, James Luther. *Amos*. OTL. Philadelphia: Westminster Press, 1969.
_____. *Hosea*. OTL. Philadelphia: Westminster Press, 1969.
_____. *Micah*. OTL. Philadelphia: Westminster Press, 1976.
Petersen, David L. *Haggai and Zechariah 1—8*. OTL. Philadelphia: Westminster Press, 1978.
Smith, Ralph D. *Micah—Malachi*. Waco, Tex.: Word Books, 1984.
Wolff, Hans Walter. *Hosea*. Translated by Gary Stansell. Hermeneia. Philadelphia: Fortress Press, 1974.
_____. *Joel and Amos*. Translated by W. Janzen et al. Hermeneia. Philadelphia: Fortress Press, 1977.
_____. *Micah*. Translated by Gary Stansell. Minneapolis: Augsburg Publishing House, 1987.
_____. *Obadiah and Jonah*. Translated by Margaret Kohl. Minneapolis: Augsburg Publishing House, 1986.